Religion and Ecology in the Public Sphere

Religion and Ecology in the Public Sphere

Edited by

Celia Deane-Drummond
and
Heinrich Bedford-Strohm

t&t clark

Published by T&T Clark International
A Continuum Imprint
The Tower Building, 11 York Road, London SE1 7NX
80 Maiden Lane, Suite 704, New York, NY 10038

www.continuumbooks.com

All rights reserved. No part of this publication may be reproduced or transmitted in any form or by any means, electronic or mechanical, including photocopying, recording or any information storage or retrieval system, without permission in writing from the publishers.

© Celia Deane-Drummond, Heinrich Bedford-Strohm and contributors, 2011

Celia Deane-Drummond, Heinrich Bedford-Strohm and contributors have asserted their right under the Copyright, Designs and Patents Act, 1988, to be identified as the Author of this work.

British Library Cataloguing-in-Publication Data
A catalogue record for this book is available from the British Library

ISBN: 978-0-567-32520-4 (Hardback)
        978-0-567-03508-0 (Paperback)

Typeset by Fakenham Photosetting Ltd, Fakenham, Norfolk
Printed and bound in India

Contents

Acknowledgments   vii

List of Contributors   viii

    Introduction   1
    Celia Deane-Drummond and Heinrich Bedford Strohm

    The Baltic Sea as a Case Study: The Ecological and Political
    Challenges of the Baltic Sea   15
    Erik Bonsdorff

PART I: Concepts of Religion in the Public Sphere   19

1. Who Shall Speak for the Environment? Translating Religious,
    Scientific, Economic, and Political Regimes of Power and Knowledge
    in a Globalized Society   21
    Peter Beyer

2. Public Theology of Ecology and Civil Society   39
    Heinrich Bedford-Strohm

3. Right Out of Time? Politics and Nature in a Postnatural Condition   57
    Peter Manley Scott

4. Climate Change and the (Economic) Value of Nature – The Role of
    Economic Thinking in the Public Sphere   77
    Hans Diefenbacher

PART II: Contextual Approaches

5. Latin American Liberation Theologians' Turn to Eco(theo)logy –
    Critical Remarks   91
    Elina Vuola

| 6 | Geology vs. Theology? Uranium Prospecting and Theological Arguments in Northern Carelia 2006-2009
Pauliina Kainulainen | 111 |
| 7 | Towards an African Inculturated Sophiology: The Case of African Wisdom Tradition from Myths for Ecological Concerns
Loreen Maseno | 125 |

PART III: Towards Public Theologies of Nature 139

8	Environmental Amnesia or the Memory of Place? The Need for Local Ethics of Memory in a Philosophical Theology of Place *Forrest Clingerman*	141
9	Public Theology as a Substantial Contribution to an Ecumenical and Ecological Culture *Daniel Munteanu*	161
10	Public Theology as Contested Ground: Arguments for Climate Justice *Celia Deane-Drummond*	189

Bibliography 211

Index of Subjects 233

Index of Names 239

Acknowledgments

The occasion for the publication of this volume was the 2nd international conference of the European Forum for the Study of Religion and Environment that met in Åbo/Turku, Finland from 14–17th May 2009. We are grateful to Sigurd Bergmann, chair of EFSRE, and for all those on the organizing committee, especially Björn Vikstöm (Åbo Akademi University) for arranging the stimulating conference. We are also particularly grateful to The Foundation of Åbo Academi University, who provided some financial assistance for the publication of this volume that was used to support the English expression for non-native speakers contributing to this volume and other editorial assistance. In this regard we are particularly grateful for the patient and meticulous contribution of Becky Artinian-Kaiser.

Celia Deane-Drummond would like to acknowledge the benefits of being a friend to St Deiniol's library, renamed Gladstone's Library in October 2010, where much of the task of editing this volume took place uninterrupted by other demands. The example of Sir William Ewart Gladstone (1809–1898), twice UK Prime Minister, who set up this library explicitly for the 'pursuit of divine learning' is surely a tribute to the quest set out in this book, namely, marking out the field of religion and ecology in the public sphere.

Celia Deane-Drummond was on secondment from the University of Chester from 1 July 2009 to 1 July 2010 to the Catholic Fund for Overseas Development (CAFOD). This provided her with the opportunity to attend the United Nations Summit on Climate Change in Copenhagen in December 2009, and in June 2010 to visit development projects in Kenya that were struggling to adapt to the impact of climate change. Thus the chapter that she contributed to this volume emerged directly from this experience, rather than from a paper given at the conference in Finland. Celia Deane-Drummond would therefore like to acknowledge the support of CAFOD and also the University of Chester for supporting her absence from the theology and religious studies department.

Finally, we would both like to acknowledge the support and vision of Thomas Kraft, commissioning editor for T&T Clark at Continuum, for supporting the publication of this volume and offering helpful suggestions to enable its timely fruition.

List of Contributors

Heinrich Bedford-Strohm holds the Chair of Systematic Theology and Contemporary Theological Issues in the Faculty for Human Sciences at the Otto-Friedrich University of Bamberg, Germany. He was Dean of the Faculty from 2006–2009. He is also, from 2009, Extraordinary Professor at the Theological Faculty in Stellenbosch, South Africa. Bedford-Strohm is Director of the Dietrich Bonhoeffer Research Centre for Public Theology in Bamberg, which is a member of the Global Network for Public Theology. He is President of the Society of Protestant Theology in Germany and deputy Chairman of the Chamber for Social Responsibility of the German Protestant Churches. He has been the main editor of the journal 'Evangelische Theologie' since 2009. His books focus on themes of social justice – *Vorrang für die Armen. Auf dem Weg zu einer theologischen Theorie der Gerechtigkeit* (Gütersloher Verlagshaus, 1993), social cohesion in modern society – *Gemeinschaft aus kommunikativer Freiheit. Sozialer Zusammenhalt in der modernen Gesellschaft. Ein theologischer Beitrag* (Gütersloher Verlagshaus, 1999) and the ecumenical discussion on creation – *Schöpfung* (Vandenhoeck und Ruprecht, 2001). In 2009 he edited three volumes: (a) on globalization – *Globalisierung* (Gütersloher Verlaghaus, 2009), (b) on climate change – *Und Gott sah, dass es gut war. Schöpfung und Endlichkeit im Zeitalter der Klimakatastrophe* (Neukirchener Verlag, 2009) and (c) on religion and nature – *Nature, Space and the Sacred: Transdisciplinary Perspectives* (Ashgate, 2009).

Peter Beyer is Professor of Religious Studies at the University of Ottawa, Canada. His specializations include religion and globalization, sociological theory of religion, religion and migration, and religion in Canada. His publications include *Religion and Globalization* (Sage, 1994), *Religion in the Process of Globalization* (Ergon, 2001), *Religions in Global Society* (Routledge, 2006), *Religion, Globalization, and Culture*, edited with Lori Beaman (Brill, 2007) and *Religious Diversity in Canada*, edited with Lori Beaman (Brill, 2008). He is currently completing a series of research projects on the religious expression of second-generation immigrant young adults in Canada. He works on religion and ecology in the context of his work on religion and globalization.

Erik Bonsdorff is Professor of Marine Biology and Head of the Department of Biosciences at Åbo Akademi University in Finland. His research interests include the ecology and environment of the Baltic Sea and the interdisciplinary aspects of environmental governance in marine systems, aiming at decision-support tools for the benefit of the environment and the sustainable use of the goods and services provided by marine ecosystems. He is a member of the ScanBalt Academy and Societas Scientarum Fennica (The Finnish Society of Sciences and Letters) and serves on several national, Nordic, and international expert advisory panels on science and the environment. He is also active in Nordic graduate schools in marine ecology. He has published about 100 international research papers within marine ecology and environmental issues in journals such as *Ambio, Australian Journal of Ecology, Environmental Science and Technology, Estuarine Coastal and Shelf Science, Journal of Aquatic Animal Health, Journal of Experimental Marine Ecology and Biology, Journal of Sea Research, Marine Biology, Marine Ecology – Progress Series, Marine Pollution Bulletin*, and edited two books on the Baltic Sea environment.

Forrest Clingerman is Assistant Professor of Philosophy and Religion at Ohio Northern University, where he teaches courses in theology, ethics, and the history of religious thought. Much of his work resides at the intersection of philosophy and religious thought. Beginning with his doctoral work in modern religious thought at the University of Iowa, his research has investigated how philosophical hermeneutics intersects with the aims of environmental theology. More recently, he has started work on the intersection between aesthetics, the theology of culture, and environmental thought. In all of his research, the concept of place is an important motif, especially as an object of interpretation. His work has been published by the journals *Ethics, Place and Environment, Worldviews, Environmental Values* and *Literature and Theology*, as well as in edited collections on religion and ecology. Along with Mark H. Dixon, he is co-editing the forthcoming collection, *Placing Nature on the Borders of Religion, Philosophy and Ethics*. He is also working with several philosophers in the US and Europe on a project seeking to advance philosophical interest in environmental hermeneutics.

Celia Deane-Drummond holds the Chair in Theology and the Biological Sciences in the Department of Theology and Religious Studies at the University of Chester. She is Director of the Centre for Religion and the Biosciences, established in 2002 and was elected Vice Chair of the European Forum for the Study of Religion and Environment (EFSRE) in May 2009. She was editor of the international journal *Ecotheology* for six years from 2000 to 2006. From July 2009 to July 2010 she was seconded to the spirituality team at the Catholic Fund for Overseas Development (CAFOD), working explicitly in the area of environmental justice and climate change. She holds honours degrees in both Natural Science and Theology, and doctoral degrees in both Plant Physiology and Systematic Theology. Her more recent books relevant to the theme of this volume include *Creation through Wisdom* (T & T Clark, 2000), *ReOrdering Nature* (Continuum, 2003), *The Ethics of Nature* (Blackwells, 2004), *Wonder and Wisdom: Conversations in Science, Spirituality and Theology* (DLT, 2006), *Ecotheology* (DLT/Novalis/St Mary's Press, 2008), *Christ and Evolution: Wonder and Wisdom* (Fortress/ SCM Press, 2009), *Creaturely Theology: On God, Humans and Other Animals*, edited with David Clough (SCM Press, 2009) and *Seeds of Hope: Facing the Challenge of Climate Justice* (CAFOD, 2010).

Hans Diefenbacher is Extraordinary Professor for Economics in the Alfred-Weber Institute at the University of Heidelberg. He is also Deputy Director of the Protestant Institute for Interdisciplinary Research (FEST) at Heidelberg. He studied economics at the universities of Heidelberg, Freiburg and Kassel. His main areas of research include: the relation between economy and ecology, sustainable development, and applied statistics. His publications include: 'Measuring Welfare in Germany – a suggestion for a new welfare index' (FEST/FFU, 2009) http://www.umweltbundesamt.de/uba-info-medien-e/mysql_medien.php?anfrage=Kennummer&Suchwort=3903, 'Environmental Justice: Some Starting Points for Discussion from a Perspective of Ecological Economics' in *Ecotheology* (2006) and *Gerechtigkeit und Nachhaltigkeit* (Wiss. Buchgesellschaft, 2001).

Pauliina Kainulainen is a researcher at the University of Eastern Finland, Joensuu, and a pastor of the Evangelical Lutheran Church of Finland. Her research interests are in Latin American liberation theology, feminist theology, and ecotheology and spirituality, including pre-Christian Finnish spirituality. She has published, edited and co-edited books, and written numerous articles on these topics, mostly in Finnish. Her dissertation (2005) is on the ecofeminist theology and epistemology of the Brazilian theologian Ivone Gebara. The dissertation is in Finnish, with the English abstract 'The Wisdom of the Earth: Ivone Gebara's Ecofeminist Concept of Knowing and Theology'.

Daniel Munteanu is Privatdozent (Dr. habil.) in the Faculty of Human Science at Otto-Friedrich University of Bamberg; Dietrich Bonhoeffer Visiting Teaching Scholar at Union Theological Seminary in New York (Fall 2010). He is the editor-in-chief of the bilingual online *International Journal of Orthodox Theology – Internationale Zeitschrift für Orthodoxe Theologie* (www.orthodox-theology.com). His books include *Der tröstende Geist der Liebe. Zu einer ökumenischen Lehre vom Heiligen Geist über die trinitarischen Theologien von J. Moltmann und D. Staniloae* (Neukirchen-Vluyn, 2003), for which he earned the John Templeton Award for Theological Promise in 2007, and *Was ist der Mensch? Grundzüge und gesellschaftliche Relevanz einer ökumenischen Anthropologie anhand der Theologien von K. Rahner, W. Pannenberg und J. Zizioulas* (Neukirchen-Vluyn, 2010). His main research areas are pneumatology, trinitarian and ecumenical theology, anthropology, ecotheology, and public theology.

Loreen Maseno is Lecturer in the Department of Religion, Theology and Philosophy at Maseno University, Kenya. She has a BA (Hons) in Religious Studies and Sociology from the University of Nairobi, Kenya; an MPhil in Contextual Theology, an MPhil in Higher Education and a PhD in Systematic Theology, all from the University of Oslo, Norway. Her research interests include Christology, widows' Christologies, feminist theology, ecotheology, anthropology, and gender approaches to contemporary issues. She has a BA Hons in Religious Studies and Sociology (University of Nairobi, Kenya), a MPhil in Contextual Theology (University of Oslo, Norway), a MPhil in Higher Education (University of Oslo, Norway), and a PhD in Systematic

Theology (University of Oslo, Norway). Her key publications include *Widows' Christologies: A Preliminary Feminist Analysis of Abanyole Widows' Christologies Considering Kinship, Gender and the Power of Naming* (2008) and 'Gendering Inculturation in Africa: A discussion of three African women theologians' entry into the inculturation scene', *Norwegian Journal for Missions* (2004). She has served as a member of the World Council of Churches Drafting Group for the Ecumenical Declaration on Just Peace. She was a grant recipient of the Centre for Gender Research to take a course, Transnational Feminism and Local Perspectives, at the European University of St Petersburg, Russia (2006). She also received the Nordic Students Grants Scholarship awarded for studies at the Nordic Africa Institute in Uppsala, Sweden (2005) and the Quota Programme Scholarship awarded for PhD studies at the University of Oslo, Norway (2005).

Peter Manley Scott is Senior Lecturer in Christian Social Thought and Director of the Lincoln Theological Institute at the University of Manchester, UK. He is the author of *Theology, Ideology and Liberation* (CUP, 1994; paperback edition 2009), *A Political Theology of Nature* (CUP, 2003) and *Anti-human Theology: Nature, Technology and the Postnatural* (SCM, 2010); and is co-editor of *The Blackwell Companion to Political Theology* (Blackwell, 2004; paperback edition 2006), *Future Perfect* (Continuum, 2006), *Re-moralising Britain?* (Continuum, 2008), *Nature Space and the Sacred* (Ashgate 2009), *Ecotheology* 11:2 – special issue on theology and technology (Equinox, 2006) and the *International Journal of Public Theology* 2:1 – special issue on urban theology (Brill, 2008). His research is to be found at the intersection between theology and studies of nature, technology and society, politics and salvation and he is widely published on these topics. His current research is towards a monograph, *A Theology of Postnatural Right*.

Elina Vuola is currently Professor of Latin American Studies in the Department of World Cultures at the University of Helsinki, Finland. She holds a PhD in Theology, focusing on the philosophy of religion and theological ethics. Between 2002–03 she was a Research Fellow at the Womens' Studies Programme at Harvard Divinity School. She was a visiting researcher at the Departamento Ecuménico de Investigaciones (DEI) in San José, Costa Rica in 1991–93 and in 1999–2000. Her publications include *Limits of Liberation: Feminist Theology and the Ethics of Poverty and Reproduction* (Sheffield Academic Press and Continuum, 2002), 'Seriously Harmful for Your Health? Religion, Feminism and Sexuality in Latin America' in *Liberation Theology and Sexuality: New Radicalism from Latin America*, edited by Marcella Althaus-Reid (Ashgate, 2006), 'Radical Eurocentrism. The Death, Crisis, and Recipes of Improvement of Latin American Liberation Theology' in *Interpreting the Postmodern: Responses to Radical Orthodoxy*, edited by Marion Grau and Rosemary Radford Ruether (T & T Clark and Continuum 2006), and 'Patriarchal Ecumenism, Feminism and Women's Religious Experiences in Latin America' in *Gendering Religion and Politics: Untangling Modernities*, edited by Hanna Herzog and Ann Braude (Palgrave MacMillan, 2009).

Introduction

Celia Deane-Drummond
Director of the Centre for Religion and the
Biosciences, Department of Theology and
Religious Studies, University of Chester, UK

and

Heinrich Bedford-Strohm
Director of the Dietrich Bonhoeffer Research
Centre for Public Theology, University of Bamberg,
Germany

If we look at our intellectual history and focus our attention on our generation and the ideas it has generated and developed, the theme of ecology might well be considered one of the shooting stars. Ideas need a long time to develop. Worldviews are deeply embedded in existing cultures and often seem to be set in stone. Changing such worldviews, and the habits which accompany them, takes a long time. Given this persistence in the 'habits of the heart'[1], with which we grow up and which become part of our personalities and identities, the rise of the idea of ecology in intellectual history and increasingly in the daily lives of ordinary people over the past three decades is remarkable.[2] This remains true despite the sober

---

[1] R. N. Bellah, R. Madsen, W. Sullivan, A. Swidler, and S. Tipton, *Habits of the Heart: Individualism and Commitment in American Life* (Berkeley, Los Angeles and London: University of California Press, 1985).

[2] South African theologian Ernst Conradie speaks of 'three or four decades of environmental conscientising', in *Christianity and Ecological Theology: Resources for Further Research* (Stellenbosch: Sun Press, 2006), p. 19. This process has now spread to biblical studies encouraging a developing ecological hermeneutics. See, for example, D. Horrell, C. Hunt, C. Southgate, and F. Stavrakopoulou (eds), *Ecological Hermeneutics: Biblical, Historical and Theological Perspectives* (London: T & T Clark/Continuum, 2010). Ecological theology in the

acknowledgment that the rise of the idea of ecology is not only a consequence of the creativity and inventiveness of the human mind, but is more and more a pure necessity for survival.

It was only 40 years ago that ecological ideas, which were previously only in the minds of some unheard prophets, reached the wider public. Conferences given by institutions such as the World Council of Churches (WCC) reflected ecological challenges much earlier than others.[3] In 1970 the WCC dealt with these questions at a conference in Geneva between 28 June–4 July, initiating a study process under the title 'The Future of Humanity and Society in a World of Science-Based Technology',[4] having already reflected on ecological challenges. The first widely publicized document of ecological awareness was the Report to the Club of Rome on the 'Limits of Growth' in 1973. The oil crisis and then later the public debate on the use of nuclear energy, especially after the Chernobyl incident, led to social movements that voiced their ecological concerns in public. However, such movements understood themselves as antithetical to a political class that – with good reasons – was perceived to conserve the societal and economic framework of an ecologically damaging lifestyle.

The rise of Green parties in various countries, first in Europe and then elsewhere in the world, represented an effort to bridge the divide between the visions of a social movement and the daily political business. The fact that this phenomenon developed with particular force in Germany can be read as the consequence of the deep historical impact which the experience of seduction by National Socialism made on the German cultural memory. Post-war Germany developed a political culture that was explicitly attentive to societal developments which might lead to destructive consequences. The will never again to be silent in the face of destructive societal developments was ingrained in the soul of German political discourse culture. The ecology movement in Germany saw ecological destruction as something to struggle against on all levels, including the political one.

This process was the beginning of what can be called the 'Greening of Politics'. Ecological ideas have entered the programmes of many political parties with otherwise differing agendas. And yet, this process has not led to the radical change of political and cultural patterns that is needed in times of ever-greater limitation of the earth's natural resources and carrying capacity, of massive reductions in global

public sphere was not, however, discussed in this volume. The possible relationship between environmental disasters and American dispensationalism received a mention (p. 253), as did world trade issues associated with sustainable countryside in the UK (p. 288). However, this was situated within a focused discussion of the contribution of an ecological reading of biblical texts.

[3] D. Gosling, *A New Earth, Covenanting for Justice, Peace and the Integrity of Creation* (London: CCBI, 1992).
[4] H. Bedford-Strohm, 'Die Entdeckung der Ökologie in der ökumenischen Bewegung', *Hoffnungswege: Wegweisende Impulse des Ökumenischen Rates der Kirchen aus sechs Jahrzehnten* (H. G. Link and G. Müller-Fahrenholz (eds); Frankfurt: Otto Lembeck, 2008), pp. 321–347; I. Breitmaier, *Das Thema der Schöpfung in der Ökumenischen Bewegung 1948 bis 1988* (Frankfurt et al.: Peter Lang, 1995), p. 68.

biodiversity, and climate change. While there may be considerable theoretical awareness of the need for change, the actual change of attitudes and lifestyles does not match the theoretical readiness for change – a gap that has been recently shown clearly by empirical research.[5]

In addition to these general political and social trends, there is a tendency to delegate all hope for change to the realm of politics, resulting in considerable disappointment at its failure. Among the populations in different countries of the world, there is great dissatisfaction with the incapacity of politicians globally to negotiate binding rules for the sustainable use of the world's natural resources. Internet-based organizations like 'Avaaz.org' or '350.org' mobilize millions of protest mails to politicians expressing this dissatisfaction. The poor result from the Copenhagen negotiations has become a symbol for global political failure. So far there is little evidence in civil society of a readiness to act without the backing of global political frameworks – the task seems almost too large to energize committed action.

There is good reason to believe that in this situation there is a special need for intensified action and reflection along the theme of this volume. The large majority of people across the world understand religion to be an important part of their lives, even if they reject institutionalized religious frameworks. Given continuous change, exact numbers are hard to determine, however, the immense importance of religion cannot be disputed. In 2007 Britannica Online listed 2,199,817,400 Christians, 1,387,454,500 Muslims and 875,726,000 Hindus in addition to many other religious affiliations with lower numbers. Only 776,826,000 of the world's population are listed as non-religious.[6] According to new calculations, in Sub-Saharan Africa alone there are 371 million Muslims, which comprise 45 per cent of the population, 304 million Christians, and 137 million adherents of traditional religions.[7] The recent Bertelsmann Religion Monitor has clearly shown that tight secularized societal contexts like East Germany or Tschechia are the exception. In the USA the monitor has found that 62 per cent of the population is highly religious (Germany: only 18 per cent), while only 8 per cent are non-religious (Germany: 28 per cent).[8]

Religion reaches both minds and hearts. In a time when carefully reflected political action has to be taken and fundamental habits have to be changed, we need an increasing awareness of the interchange between these two dimensions in developing ecologically sustainable structures and environments for continued

---

[5] U. Kuckartz, 'Leben im Einklang mit der Natur. Einsichten aus der Sozialwissenschaft', *Und Gott sah, dass es gut war: Schöpfung und Endlichkeit im Zeitalter der Klimakatastrophe* (H. Bedford-Strohm (ed.); Neukirchen-Vluyn: Neukirchener Verlag 2009), pp. 59–69.
[6] 'Religion', http://de.wikipedia.org/wiki/Religion (accessed 15 July 2010).
[7] Le Monde Diplomatique, *Atlas der Globalisierung* (Berlin: Le Monde Diplomatique/taz Verlag, 2009), p. 144.
[8] H. Joas, 'Die religiöse Situation in den USA', *Woran glaubt die Welt?. Analysen und Kommentare zum Religionsmonitor 2008* (Bertelsmann Stiftung (ed.); Gütersloh: Verlag Bertelsmann-Stiftung, 2009), pp. 329–347 (331).

life on this planet. As Mary Evelyn Tucker and John Grim have stated, 'religious traditions may indeed be critical in helping to re-imagine the viable conditions and long-range strategies for fostering mutually enhancing human-earth relations.'[9] Some cutting edge works are appearing that recognize the importance of religion in philosophical and ethical debates around topics such as climate change. *Future Ethics*, for example, offers an important innovative contribution in mapping out the philosophical and ethical issues behind the rhetoric of climate change.[10] Yet the religious voice in *Future Ethics*, such as it is present at all, was not intended to be a public theology, but rather somewhat muted and adapted to the needs of its primary audience, namely, policy makers, activists and social theorists.

The task of developing a public theology of ecology thus remains. The contributions in this volume give good reason to suppose that renewed attention to religious traditions and their capacities to reach minds and hearts will be very helpful in this endeavour.

We therefore need a new public theology of ecology that takes account of the richness of religious resources and relates those resources to the requirements of political praxis. Such public theology reflects critically on the contribution of religious views to cultural patterns destructive of the natural environments. But it also highlights the tremendous potential for change that lies in the idea of the giveness of human and non-human nature, implied by the concept of creation. The special profile of a public theology lies in the constant effort to translate theologically opaque concepts into a language understandable by a public that is increasingly characterized by a pluralism of worldviews, including those that may be secular rather than explicitly religious.

This translation of theology into concepts meaningful in public discourse applies to the explicitly political and policy realm, as well as to public debate as such. Ecological ideas generated by religious traditions must be shown to be a valuable resource for the daily political business of policy and governance as well as for a fundamental change of culture. It is not enough to describe alternative ways of thinking, or even to highlight the witness of alternative ecological communities in order to show that a different life is possible. Theology and religion must also give an account of how to reorient political and economic life. The ethical dilemmas that such effort reveals cannot be a reason to shy away from this task; instead, it must lead theology to deepen its ethical reflection and, in this process, maybe even develop a certain humbleness toward those who take responsibility in politics.

This volume offers a modest beginning for this enterprise in translation by showing the contexts of political debate and religiously inspired models for reorientation towards a new ecological culture alongside the political, economic and legal structures that support it. Public theology must develop a language that

---

[9] M. E. Tucker, and J. Grim, 'Series Foreword', *Christianity and Ecology* (D.T. Hessel, and R. Radford-Ruether (eds); Cambridge: Harvard University Press 2000), pp. xv–xxxii (xvii–xviii).
[10] S. Skrimshire (ed.), *Future Ethics: Climate Change and Political Action* (London: Continuum, 2010).

enables religious communities – in the Christian case, the churches – to become vital agents of civil society by giving substantial and plausible contributions to the public discourse on ecology. This will remain a fundamentally important task that deserves to be taken up in different contexts that are not represented here. It is our hope, however, that this volume will contribute to energising this process in Europe and beyond.

The collection of essays in this volume brings to the surface vital dimensions in the engagement between religion and ecology in as much as they impinge on public encounter and debates in different global regions and from different local contexts. The writers in this collection are unanimous in perceiving the public sphere not as a neutral place in diverse civic societies, separated from the state; instead, the public sphere denotes a determination to engage in the work of theo-political imagination, re-envisioning the sphere as inclusive of the religious dimension within which political decision-making takes place around ecological issues. Although these essays show a diversity of perspectives on both what public theology means and what public theology might contribute to this issue, the consistent argument is that we need to take seriously the theological and religious contribution to the public debates on ecological issues. The focus of this collection of essays is on Christian theology, while taking into account broader social and political issues associated with religion and ecology. The editors of this volume believe that while this imposes some limitation, the focus is necessary in order to tease out different aspects of the discussion from the perspective of this tradition. It is not intended, however, to suggest or to imply that other religious traditions are marginal or insignificant as contributors to public theology, but that given the dominance of Christianity in the history of Western democracies, it is legitimate, at least initially, to focus on this tradition. It is intended, therefore, to be a first step in a mapping exercise, laying out different aspects of religion and ecology in the public sphere from the perspective of different voices within Christian theology. We hope for and welcome the appearance of other religious voices as the public debate widens in different global and social contexts.

Ecology is, as perhaps never before, at the forefront of global public concern. This was epitomized by the intense debates in the lead up to the United Nations Summit meeting on climate change in Copenhagen in December 2009. But the debate on climate change can still seem elitist in as much as the groundswell of public support for change has not yet taken root across a sufficient range of societies in order to make a viable difference. Sociologist Ulrich Beck asks the question, 'How can a kind of cosmopolitan solidarity across boundaries become real, a *greening of societies*, which is a prerequisite for the necessarily transnational politics of climate change?'[11] Such problems as the lack of profound public response to this question are now becoming so acute that atheist scientists, such as the President of the British Science Association, Lord May, are calling for even greater attention to these issues by religious groups. The

---

[11] Ulrich Beck, 'Climate for Change, or How to Create a Green Modernity', *Theory, Culture and Society* 27 (2010), pp. 254–266 (255). Italics added.

secular scientific mind has, it seems, reached its limit in facing such problems.[12] This applies not only to climate change, but also to environmental problems more generally. We seem to have reached an impasse. Sociologist Ulrich Beck analyses the problem in this way. He believes that if the environment 'only includes everything that is not human, not social, then the concept is sociologically empty'.[13] But, one might ask, is this ever the case when there are discussions about environmental issues? One of us (Deane-Drummond) has worked for a development agency where, at least for the uninitiated, a common attitude by its supporters was that ecology had relatively little to do with human development. This was in spite of publicity around climate change where connections between human activity and global environmental impacts might seem more obvious. But Beck seems to imply more than this here. He means that if we focus on environmental issues and questions, then we might not notice what is happening to modern society itself. Hence, 'It is not the 'environment', but modern society itself which is being transformed by the unseen consequences of the insatiable appetite for natural resources'.[14] The process of modernization is, therefore, highly ambivalent. The post-war modernization narrative pre-supposed the separation between 'natural' and 'social' forces. Climate change upsets such a separation and 'demonstrates and enforces exactly the opposite, namely an ongoing extension and deepening of combinations, confusions, and "mixtures" of nature and society'.[15] More controversial, perhaps, is another of his theses that 'if the concept includes human action and society, then, it is scientifically mistaken and politically suicidal'.[16] By this he seems to mean that if we simply add climate to politics, for example, then this '*castrates* climate politics. It ignores the fact that climate politics is precisely not about climate, but about transforming the basic constitutions and institutions of a first, industrial nation-state modernity'.[17] There is a need, then, to explore the social reach of inequalities associated with environmental impacts, and not just the impacts themselves.

---

[12] As reported by Robert Alleyne in *Daily Telegraph* on Monday, 7 September on the eve of the annual conference of the British Science Association. He is particularly concerned with the lack of real public concern about climate change. He is reported to have said that a supernatural punisher may be part of the solution and that religion may have helped protect human society from itself in the past and it may be needed again. Further, he said, 'Given that punishment is a useful mechanism, how much more effective it would be if you invested that power not in an individual you don't like, but an all-seeing, all powerful deity that controls the world'. This article demonstrates clearly the need for theologians to get involved in public debate. God conceived as divine punisher is not recognisable by mature Christian theology, and while Alleyne's call for religious involvement is commendable, his attempt at providing a theological argument is misguided. See R. Alleyne, 'Maybe Religion is the Answer Claims Atheist Scientist', *Daily Telegraph* (7 September 2009), http://www.telegraph.co.uk/journalists/richard-alleyne/6146656/Maybe-religion-is-the-answer-claims-atheist-scientist.html (accessed 20 July 2010).
[13] This is a core part of his argument, U. Beck, 'Climate for Change', e.g., p. 254.
[14] Ibid., p. 256.
[15] Ibid.
[16] Ibid., p. 255.
[17] Ibid., p. 256.

Beck argues that the focus has to shift towards a 'greening of modernity'. This seems a reasonable proposal rather than the more radical and somewhat unrealistic suggestion of a total rejection of modernity. But then we have to ask, where does resistance to such change come from? And where might we find the inspiration for widespread change that is socially and environmentally responsible? Social inequality and globalized political domination become exacerbated through climate change and environmental impacts detrimental to human flourishing. Religion has traditionally been concerned about inequalities and issues of social justice. The difference that climate change and environmental limits more generally make is that a conversation within and across national boundaries becomes all the more urgent. Indeed, from a sociological perspective 'The sense of emancipation and power that arise from overcoming national barriers is what could potentially awaken enthusiasm for a greening of modernity'.[18] The authors in this collection are aware of not only the political urgency, but also the need to delve into a variety of diverse cultural traditions in order to resource such a task; namely, what might religious traditions contribute to such debates? Those contributing to this collection gathered together to refine their ideas at the second international European Forum for the Study of Religion and Environment that met at Åbo Akademi University on the coast of Finland in May 2009.

The particular geographical context of the meeting was that of the Baltic Sea, and the case study following this introduction by Professor Erik Bonsdorff provides a striking example of what is happening to ecological systems and some of the practical problems that ensue. Such an initial reflection illustrates for the reader an example of the environmental and policy issues under discussion. There is no attempt in this book to give a full survey of the breadth of possible ecological problems and the pressures of climate change even in this limited region. Instead, this first short case study gives the reader one example of what specific problems look like according to ecological science, while at the same time bringing to the surface the complex nature of political and policy decision-making around these issues.

But the purpose of this collection of essays is to go much further than this, even though it provides an excellent starting point. We recognize the importance of situating such a discussion of ecological and environmental problems in a wider secular discourse about the way economics, religion and theology relate to environmental issues, and the first section of this collection on concepts of religion in the public sphere reflects this awareness. Peter Beyer takes a systematic sociological perspective on environmental issues, arguing that different sociological, political and religious regimes translate environmental questions into their own particular systems of knowledge and power. Through such an analysis the public dimensions of such debate may surface in chaotic ways, since the capacity to speak specifically for the environment is filtered through other powerful societal systems.

The possibility of speaking for the system as a whole is therefore hampered by the way in which such discourse is adapted to the particular social systems in place in different geographical locations. Beyer challenges us to be more aware

[18] Ibid., p. 264.

and conscious of the social pressures in place that lead to tendencies to categorize according to the particular knowledge structures dominant in a given society. It is therefore a useful starting point for this collection of essays, since, without a clear idea of at least some of the presuppositions that embed different contemporary societies, public discussion is more likely to be superficial in analysis. Of course, not all readers will agree with the case Beyer makes for a system's theory approach to such an analysis. This systems approach certainly brings clarity, but perhaps this is at the cost of appreciating the sheer diversity and complexity of political and religious traditions and their impact on society. Nonetheless, his essay encourages us to think through both the sources of authority and the structures of religious and cultural knowledge and their impact on how the environment is perceived.

Heinrich Bedford-Strohm offers the second essay in this section of the book on framing the relevant dimensions of what a public theology looks like in an ecological setting. He concentrates not so much on the limits of the place of environmental issues in religious systems of knowledge, as in Beyer's essay, but on the meaning and significance of public theology and its role in a public discussion of environmental issues. His essay is grounded in a view of public theology as theological encounter that responds to the search for ethical orientation in questions of public relevance. It does this by drawing from resources in the Judaeo–Christian tradition and then voicing its findings in the public square. He argues that since the public sphere of modern civil societies is pluralistic, public theology must be bilingual, speaking a theological language as well as a language that can be understood by all people of good will.

Public theology therefore tries to develop answers that can be relevant for the public political debate in civil society. Such public theology can be understood as a form of enabling liberation theology for a democratic society. But his essay also raises a range of other important questions. In the first place, how can public theology raise ecological concerns voiced by ecotheology in a way that can be helpful and relevant to the public political debate? Second, should fundamental critical concerns in ecological questions be transformed into concepts that work within the political system? Third, what might be the role of the churches as agents of ecological transformation in civil society? These steps set the scene for the subsequent theological reflections in ecology and theology in the public sphere that are developed by other authors of this volume.

Peter Manley Scott begins with the recognition that in Western democracies in particular our urban lifestyles have taken us away from the consciousness of ecological dependencies, and therefore recognition of the political importance of ecological thinking is more difficult. He illustrates this concept by a suggestive analogy: that we are living in a *camera obscura* world, one that views our world upside down. This is also true of public discussion that tends to prioritize economic questions rather than ecological ones. This presupposes that religions have something to contribute to the public domain, and, like Bedford-Strohm, Scott believes that we need to clear the intellectual ground in order that religious perspectives can begin to take root. Drawing on a distinction between programmatic and procedural secularism, Scott favours the latter, since the former in effect excludes the possibility that religion may be able to make a contribution to public debate. A programmatic approach also resists substantive notions of flourishing and the common good. For procedural secularism, on the other hand, the sources of different religious traditions are tolerated in the name of wider representation from a diversity of perspectives. Moreover, he argues, these diverse positions are constitutive of the public realm.

Scott also develops in this essay an original notion of the postnatural condition in which the public sphere is unsettled still further by reference to what might be termed ecological knowledge – it needs therefore to be re-naturalized and de-secularized. In public discourse this means exposing the historical basis for the place of nature and its gradual occlusion in the political realm.

Hans Diefenbacher's final essay in this section on concepts of religion in the public sphere enlarges an aspect that is crucial in almost all political discussions of the issue, namely, economics. He is particularly concerned with how economic thinking is shaping current understanding of both the value of the natural world and ecological change. He argues that economic thinking is influencing our perception of different ecological problems and their possible solutions. Yet this also poses, in turn, a significant shift in the way in which economic thinking might be understood, since ecology is one of the challenges of the twenty-first century that disturbs mainstream economic theory. Climate change has also become one of the focus points for the need to transform economics into an integral part of the public sphere.

The second section of this book, contextual approaches, moves from essays that concern themselves with broad trends in sociological, theological, political, and economic discourse to those that are more narrowly circumscribed to particular contexts and localities. They therefore serve to ground the more theoretical discussions in the first section by examining particular case studies and contexts from different regions of the world. Of course, such an account can only ever be illustrative rather than exhaustive.

Elina Vuola begins this section by taking a critical look at Latin American liberation theologian's absorption of ecology into their discourse. Traditional Latin American theology viewed the natural world as in need of liberation and humanity as the source of that agency. While some theologians are now critical of this position, she also argues that the turn to ecology has in some cases cut deeper still, and unsettled the focus on human subjectivity and agency. Her particular dialogue partners in this discussion are through the works of Ivone Gebara and Leonardo Boff. Yet her own knowledge of new social movements comes into play here, in that she is critical of the work of these theologians in as much as they do not take sufficient account of the newer grass-root protest movements that challenge the traditional view of human flourishing as presented in liberation theology. Even in such cases she argues that there is a weakness in the way they have failed to keep up with what might be termed the 'signs of the times' in Latin America. This kind of liberation theology is still, therefore, feeding off the political structures of oppression that are now no longer intact. For once these oppressive regimes are removed, this opens up new possibilities for more radically orientated social protest movements. For Vuola, liberation theology will be left behind unless it does what it promises to do, namely, engage in context and therefore take more seriously what is evident from the ground, such as the social and religious importance of indigenous traditions.

Pauliina Kainulainen draws on her experience of working alongside a religious community in Eastern Finland, where there are heated public debates about uranium mining coming to the region. She looks specifically at the role of the Lutheran community in this debate and the way that this one issue has raised environmental awareness more generally in this community. There are difficulties, however, mostly associated with the possible economic advantages of such prospecting, leading to situations of public conflict and dispute. The exposure of the place of the Church in this debate comes to the fore, and serves as a salutary tale of how the presence of ecclesial figures in the midst of such arguments can be a cause of celebration or dismissal. Those who object to the Church's role are more likely to view the secular sphere in a programmatic way, with religions seeming to come from outside the source of legitimacy (cf. Scott, above). Those who welcome the interventions of the Church are more likely to view the secular sphere as being a procedural space in which different voices can be heard.

Yet the hostility towards the religious interventions in the public debate seems to go further than this categorization implies. For Kainulainen notes that a geologist accuses religious leaders of becoming embroiled in matters where they are ignorant and of using scientific information that is 'pseudo-science'. The religious community is therefore challenged when it comes to speaking on any matter that seems to require expert knowledge; while at the same time the public trustworthiness of that science may be called into question. Such a claim is not convincing to the author of this essay, and she believes it reflects an arrogance born of modernity that assumes scientific language and logic are the only relevant ways of understanding the world. We can also add that this presupposes not just relevance, but also public authority; that science has the final authority in matters of public concern.

Loreen Maseno moves the discussion from the colder climes of Finland to African mythology. Her focus also turns from theology more generally to a core element in Christian belief, namely, how to think about the person and work of Christ. She suggests that in an African contextual environment, the dominance of anthropocentrism within Christian theology comes to the fore in a highly visible way. This dominance marginalizes the value and contribution of other life forms in a way that is challenged as much by African mythology as by ecological thinking. She presents the case for African mythology as rooted and grounded in earth images, stories and reflections on the natural world, where human beings are an integral part of the web of life. Drawing on the image of Christ as the Wisdom of God, Maseno finds resonance with wisdom traditions in African myths and traditions. She also seeks to push this further, however, by arguing that Christology itself be transformed through this engagement. In this way her understanding of an African-inculturated sophiology both draws on the cultural mythology of African traditions and is also connected with imagery that is embedded in the natural world. The religious voice from an African context is therefore one that is thick with religious imagery of the earth in a way that recognizes the interconnectedness of human beings with the natural world.

The final section of this book seeks to develop *public theologies of nature* in relation to particular issues of concern. Forrest Clingerman begins this discussion by probing the particular role of memory of place in public discourse about the natural world. He teases out different aspects of the meaning of memory in order to arrive at a rich understanding of why there is, he argues, a widespread environmental amnesia. While this memory still seems to be there in some parts of the world, as Maseno's essay suggests, the context in which Clingerman writes is one that resonates with Scott's analysis, namely, that human beings in Western liberal democracies have largely forgotten what it means to connect deeply with the natural world. He suggests that one of the core elements of environmental theology is an attempt to recapture the memories of human experiences of nature, and thereby reignite concern for the natural world and its goods. Indeed, it behoves a public theology of the environment to take account of this place of memory if it is to have lasting impact in the public sphere.

Daniel Munteanu addresses more explicitly the ecumenical dimensions of public discourse on ecology from an Eastern Orthodox perspective. He argues that ecology can provide the basis for a public platform through which Christians from different traditions can come together in order to develop an ecumenical perspective. Such an ecumenical perspective envisages theology as a cultural force, helping to create a transformative vision of the future. Further, ecology may serve to challenge previous paradigms in ecumenism and therefore contribute to an ongoing discussion about the meaning and purpose of ecumenical theology. Using an analysis of culture as a sign system of society, he argues that an ecumenical public theology puts such signification into practice by expressing inter-confessional and intercultural communication. Further, Christian theology may enhance involvement in such practices and encourage participation.

The final essay by Celia Deane-Drummond raises a specific issue for public debate, namely, the meaning of social justice in the context of hotly debated and contested claims for climate justice. She attempts to map out a specific instance of what public theology might look like where the economic and social stakes are high. Drawing on her particular experience of attending part of the UN global summit on climate change in 2009, she argues that purely economic or technocratic solutions to complex global problems are bound to fail. We need, therefore, to go further than just clearing the ground for theology to have a say in public discourse, important though this is in secularized societies. Rather, from a global perspective, religious issues come to the fore in a way that strengthens the case for a richer version of human flourishing that moves away from considerations of development in terms of GDP.

A core issue addressed in this book is how contemporary theology might become public theology, one that is deeply relevant to the particular problems and issues of today. But this then raises important theoretical questions about how theology might engage with politics, given the history of how political thinking has incorporated the concept of nature into its discussion. The diverse methodological approaches possible within Christian theology are represented in this collection, including those drawing on particular traditions such as Eastern Orthodox,

Roman Catholic, and Reformed and Lutheran theology, through to self-consciously contextual approaches in liberation, African and feminist discourse. Although the European Forum for the Study of Religion and Environment, from which this book takes its root, encourages an ecumenism that is inclusive of other religious traditions, the particular focus of this edited collection is on the contribution of Christian theology to the debate. It therefore includes a section that explicitly addresses the issue of how a public theology of nature might be formulated in a way that takes into account public discussion on ecology and climate change. However, it is situated within a discussion of more general sociological analysis of religious traditions and their possible contribution to public debates on ecology. In this sense it provides a case study that is relevant for any religious tradition as it approaches contested issues over its representation in the public sphere. We recognize the shortcomings of this volume in as much as it makes no attempt to represent the full range of religious traditions, including those even within the diverse Christian traditions and their varied cultural and global expression.

This already marks the *first of the three most important tasks* for research in the future. So far, research on public theology has been done particularly in Christian theology. Ecological issues, however, maybe more than any others, demand global solutions and require global public discourse. Public theologies need to be developed which can be the basis for increased theological communication between different religious traditions. Existing efforts like the book series 'Religions of the World and Ecology', initiated by the Center for the Study of World Religions at Harvard and edited by Mary Evelyn Tucker and John Grim, need to move into the centre of public debate and develop explicit public theologies of the different religious traditions, thus providing ethical guidance for public policy. In their foreword to this series Tucker and Grim already describe various activities that provide a basis for interreligious dialogue on ecology.[19] Most recently a report to the World Future Council by the Sri Lankan public intellectual and former International Court of Justice Vice-President, C. G. Weeramantry, has analysed the teachings of different religions on ecology and outlined wide grounds for common public activities.[20]

The *second task* for future research is the relationship between contextuality and inter-contextuality in public theology. Many of the contributions that have been given to the development of public theology are strongly contextual. Long-standing pluralistic democracies, like the United States or various countries of Europe, provide different contexts from those of societies like Brazil and South Africa that

---

[19] M. E. Tucker, and J. Grim, 'Series Foreword', pp. xv–xxxii.
[20] C. G. Weeramantry, *Tread Lightly on the Earth. Religion, the Environment and the Human Future* (Pannipitiya: Stamford Lake Ltd., 2009). A conference of world religion representatives by the World Future Council and the Bertelsmann Foundation on 7–9 March 2010 in Berlin, in which Weermantry's report was discussed, ended with a call for new efforts to develop public theologies of ecology by different religious traditions. See 'Wanted: A Public Theology Dedicated to Sustainable Development, http://www.bertelsmann-stiftung.de/cps/rde/xchg/SID-0968CF92-55BE9599/bst_engl/hs.xsl/nachrichten_100592.htm (accessed 20 July 2010).

are transforming from dictatorial or authoritarian regimes into democracies and only gradually developing a civil society. What is needed are efforts to analyse and honour this contextuality and at the same time investigate where the common features of all contextual public theologies can be found. There is good reason to suppose that the challenges of ecological reorientation of global societies are a major field in which strong inter-contextual overlaps will be found.

The *third task* of future efforts for developing a new public theology of ecology is the interplay between pragmatic 'real politics', which is strictly orientated towards short-term solutions, and longer term visions that express seemingly unreachable goals. Theologically this can be expressed as the tension between public discourse and prophetic speech. One of the characteristics of public theology is its inter-disciplinary orientation. As such, this provides one basis for affirming the validity for such theology for those in positions of power who are looking for ethical guidance. There is a gap between solutions to ecological problems that seem possible now and those that require fundamental reorientation. Public theology will have to reflect on this gap and take it into account.

We hope that this collection will inspire readers to think more seriously about these questions and the contribution that religious traditions and their academic counterparts can make to that debate. There is urgency in this task that continues to ferment in different public contexts. Amidst the media frenzy and public concern, which can lead to fear or anxiety in discussions over the uncertainties of climate change science or the environmental pressures leading to biodiversity loss, the reflective capacity of theological traditions offer a genuine gift in the public sphere.

Bibliography

Beck, U., 'Climate for Change, or How to Create a Green Modernity', *Theory, Culture and Society* 27 (2010), pp. 254–266.

Bedford-Strohm, H., 'Die Entdeckung der Ökologie in der ökumenischen Bewegung', *Hoffnungswege. Wegweisende Impulse des Ökumenischen Rates der Kirchen aus sechs Jahrzehnten* (H. G. Link and G. Müller-Fahrenholz (eds); Frankfurt: Otto Lembeck, 2008), pp. 321–347.

Bellah, R. N., R. Madsen, W. Sullivan, A. Swidler, and S. Tipton, *Habits of the Heart: Individualism and Commitment in American Life* (Berkeley, Los Angeles and London: University of California Press, 1985).

Breitmaier, I., *Das Thema der Schöpfung in der Ökumenischen Bewegung 1948 bis 1988* (Frankfurt et al.: Peter Lang, 1995).

Conradie, E., *Christianity and Ecological Theology. Resources for Further Research* (Stellenbosch: Sun Press, 2006).

Gosling, D., *A New Earth, Covenanting for Justice: Peace and the Integrity of Creation* (London: CCBI, 1992).

Horrell, D., C. Hunt, C. Southgate, and F. Stavrakopoulou (eds), *Ecological Hermeneutics: Biblical, Historical and Theological Perspectives* (London: T & T Clark/Continuum, 2010).

Joas, H., 'Die religiöse Situation in den USA', *Woran glaubt die Welt? Analysen und Kommentare zum Religionsmonitor 2008* (Bertelsmann Stiftung (ed.); Gütersloh: Verlag Bertelsmann-Stiftung, 2009), pp. 329–347.

Kuckartz, U., 'Leben im Einklang mit der Natur. Einsichten aus der Sozialwissenschaft', *Und Gott sah, dass es gut war: Schöpfung und Endlichkeit im Zeitalter der Klimakatastrophe* (H. Bedford-Strohm (ed.); Neukirchen-Vluyn: Neukirchener Verlag 2009), pp. 59–69.

'Le Monde Diplomatique', *Atlas der Globalisierung*, (Berlin: Le Monde Diplomatique/ taz Verlag, 2009)

Skrimshire, S. (ed.), *Future Ethics: Climate Change and Political Action* (London: Continuum, 2010).

Tucker, M. E., and J. Grim, 'Series Foreword', *Christianity and Ecology:Seeking the Well-Being of Earth and Humans* (D. T. Hessel, and R. Radford-Ruether (eds); Cambridge: Harvard University Press 2000), pp. xv–xxxii.

'Wanted: A Public Theology Dedicated to Sustainable Development, http://www.bertelsmann-stiftung.de/cps/rde/xchg/SID-0968CF92-55BE9599/bst_engl/hs.xsl/nachrichten_100592.htm (accessed 20 July 2010).

Weeramantry, C. G., *Tread Lightly on the Earth: Religion, the Environment and the Human Future* (Pannipitiya: Stamford Lake Ltd., 2009).

The Baltic Sea as a Case Study: The Ecological and Political Challenges of the Baltic Sea

Erik Bonsdorff
Department of Biosciences, Environmental and Marine Biology, Åbo Akademi University, Finland

Why should one worry about the state of the sea? Water is abundant everywhere and 71 per cent of the surface of the earth is covered by oceans (and oceans stand for about 97 per cent of all water on earth). With an average depth of 3,800 m, there is actually about 300 times more space for life in the seas than on land! Over 50 per cent of global primary production and 75 per cent of global consumer production is found in the oceans, so regardless of how we look at the seas, their importance for us all is very large. Biodiversity is also very high in the oceans, and new phyla, taxa and species are recorded continuously! Just like in the rainforests on land, we are currently threatening the wellbeing of the entire global marine environment, while we do not even know what we are destroying. Hence, there is a strong need for coupling the ecological challenges with political and economic demands.

May 2010: Imagine the 'ginormous' oil spill in the northern parts of the Gulf of Mexico. Hundreds of thousands of litres of crude oil have been pouring out from an oil-well some 80 km off the coasts of Louisiana, Mississippi, and Alabama. Their vulnerable marine and coastal ecosystems and rich fisheries (over 25 per cent of the total USA coastal fisheries annually; even higher for specific target-organisms) fish, shrimp and oyster-beds are threatened in what is now called 'the largest environmental accident in the USA'. Added to this, the northern parts of the Gulf of Mexico for several years have been suffering from massive and repeated hypoxia/anoxia in the bottom-near waters, influencing marine life over large areas. In the case of hypoxia (lack of oxygen), the roots of the problem lie inland, within the vast watershed of the mighty Mississippi River (roughly one-third of the US drains into the Gulf of Mexico through a network of rivers draining water from parts of 31 states) running through rich and fertile agricultural land, industrial regions and major cities. The water is loaded with nutrients that over-enrich the coastal parts of the Gulf of Mexico causing algal blooms and a subsequent lack of oxygen. This is a very complex and complicated chain of events that has been known for decades, and yet it has not been properly taken care of, as the short-term interests of people seem more important than the state of the sea. 'As long as commercial fisheries can be sustained, why worry?', seems to have been the policy. The oil spill is a 'simple matter' in this respect: an oil-drilling platform exploded, and the spill is a tragic fact. The consequences are dire, with thousands of barrels of oil entering the water phase of the Gulf for a prolonged period of time (roughly 800,000 litres each day). Most of the effects could and should have been avoided by using safety vaults that are mandatory in other parts of the world. The first response of the USA government was not really to do something about the spill, but rather to blame the oil company that owned the rig: 'you will pay for this', says the sheriff. Then came suggestions as to what to do: burn oil (adding air pollution to the environmental problem) and spread chemicals by airplane (adding toxic effects for the biota to the problem). In other words, society was not ready for yet another ecological disaster.

Finally, the oil reached the shallow coastal waters and land, and not much could be done to prevent the harmful ecological effects that followed: dead birds, fish, turtles, and invertebrates floated ashore. The impact of this chain of environmental political ignorance may be present in the ecosystem for decades to come, directly affecting local human society where the economic consequences may be severe for a long time.

One may ask why is the Gulf of Mexico of interest in an introduction to a chapter on the Baltic Sea? The reason is that in the case of the Gulf of Mexico, described above, we deal with one country with one set of common rules, where an unfortunate mix of ignorance of environmental issues has been prevailing (it could be described as 'amoral collective behaviour'). The ecological and political challenges for the marine ecosystem should be relatively easy to meet, even in relation to the economic interests of the local and regional communities (e.g. at state level). For some reason, the state of the marine environment and the human welfare on land have been decoupled far too long; we are gradually beginning to pay the price in the form of declining catches of fish on a global scale, reduced recreational and other coastal benefits in both rich and developing countries, and in hazardous influences on human health (harmful algal blooms, mass-occurrences of poisonous jellyfish, etc.).

Moving on to the Baltic Sea, we are faced with an entirely different picture: instead of an open marine coast with good water mixing, we have a land-locked body of water that is surrounded by a watershed roughly four times the area of the sea surface, draining water from no less than 14 independent countries, nine of which have coasts on the Baltic Sea. Different political systems, languages, cultures, currencies and different problems and relations to the environment all contribute to the vast problems of joint management, which would form the basic rules for sustainable use of natural resources. Differing opinions on what the sea really is as an ecosystem in its own right and on what it is in terms of producing ecosystem goods and services, such as fisheries, transport routes, recreational areas, etc., further complicate the picture. We know that the current environmental state of the

Baltic Sea is a product of an unfortunate cocktail of multiple stressors (natural and anthropogenic), with added and unforeseeable effects that have been dramatically escalating since the mid-twentieth century.

The Baltic Sea drainage area is inhabited by almost 90 million people, which produce many of the same stressors on the marine ecosystem that were mentioned for the Gulf of Mexico. The Baltic Sea suffers from large-scale hypoxia/anoxia (annually an area roughly of the size of Denmark, or anything from 40–60,000 km^2 is devoid of higher life due to oxygen concentrations below 2 ml/l), the system has been a dumping ground for toxic wastes for well over a century, and, for the last 50–60 years, gross nutrient over-enrichment (eutrophication) has become a major problem. Harmful algal and bacterial blooms have become annual phenomena affecting the livelihood of millions of people. Filamentous algal mats suffocate shallow water coastal and archipelago areas, and the nutrient pool is now so large that even if effluents from land have been greatly reduced, positive effects still remain to be seen in the marine ecosystem. This 'internal loading' will maintain a very high level of primary production and pronounced cyanobacterial blooms for decades to come. Added to all of this, over-fishing is a serious threat, not just to the individual fish stocks (cod and salmon being the prime examples), but indeed to the entire ecosystem through a phenomenon known as 'trophic cascades' where effects on one end of the spectrum (in this case, both reducing the presence of top predators – the so called top-down effect; seals and large fish – and increasing the amounts and availability of the limiting nutrients, namely phosphorus and nitrogen, i.e. bottom-up effects) will influence the entire trophic network ('food chain') of the ecosystem. These regime shifts in the marine ecosystem have opened the floodgates for invasive non-native species to enter the Baltic Sea; currently some 120 species of non-Baltic origin have viable populations in this low-diversity system. Thus, the marine ecosystem of the Baltic Sea today is very far from what it once was and, in our efforts for a better Baltic Sea, we must bear this fact in mind when we set the targets we want to achieve! To complicate matters even further, there is the issue of climate change to consider: warmer water, less sea ice in winter and reduced salinity due to higher runoff from land in combination with ocean acidification may alter the entire ecosystem structure in that many species will have to adjust their ranges of distribution. Simultaneously, the expected physical changes of the water mass may enhance the effects of eutrophication by strengthening stratification of the water column, increasing hypoxia and anoxia even further, giving rise to even higher leakage of phosphorus from the sediments. In other words, the ecological, political and ethical challenges for maintaining a balanced and diverse marine ecosystem in the Baltic Sea are enormous.

One major difference between the Gulf of Mexico-scenario and the one pictured for the Baltic Sea lies in the complicated political and economical challenges to the ecosystem. In the case of the Gulf of Mexico, a seemingly 'simple' matter has been more or less neglected (efforts have been made to reduce eutrophication in order to combat hypoxia), whereas in the Baltic Sea region serious efforts to counteract the negative consequences of human behaviour have been initiated, and strong measures are currently being implemented. Thanks to the Baltic

Marine Environment Protection Commission (HELCOM) (www.helcom.fi) and independent research, we now have specific targets agreed upon by all coastal states surrounding the sea. Since November 2007 the Baltic Sea Action Plan (BSAP) lists specific goals for each country on the minimum amounts of nutrient reductions (phosphorus and nitrogen) that should be made. The overall goal is to achieve better water quality with less algal blooms and clear surface waters. For the coastal waters, the European Union has agreed upon specific targets as well, concerning specific biological criteria (EU WFD 2000), and currently the European Marine Strategy is underway, further strengthening the ecosystem-approach of how to manage an entire sea, even including fisheries in the same management-tool. It is vital to keep the management of all components of the ecosystem within the same toolkit; previous experience shows that when, for example, fisheries have been dealt with independently, the cascading effects have largely been neglected.

Thus, for the Baltic Sea, it is generally agreed that eutrophication, the effects of over-fishing, harmful substances, traffic, loss of habitats, and general threats to biodiversity are some of the main problems, which are further enhanced by ongoing climate change, likely to dramatically affect the Baltic Sea within the next 100 years. Alterations in the structure of the entire ecosystem have already caused major functional changes (often referred to as regime shifts). Such drastic change puts limits on what to save and protect and raises important questions about how we define and agree upon what might be acceptable change. It also raises questions about how to define the aims and goals of what the Baltic Sea might be like 100 years from today, and how to achieve this goal. Decision makers in the countries bordering on the Baltic Sea agree that strong measures are needed in order to counteract the negative trends. Hence, irrespective of the strategies and frameworks proposed, we need to combine knowledge and expertise from several disciplines and tackle the problems from multiple perspectives simultaneously in order to achieve truly integrated management options for sustainable solutions both for the entire Baltic Sea and its specific regional problems. We must ask ourselves if the concept of sustainable use of the marine resources is possible at all, given the growing demand, and we must identify the gaps in our knowledge where science can provide some answers. While science can only show the potential outcome of different environmental scenarios, the final responsibility lies with society at large, i.e. the informed citizen, the areas with specific local or regional interests, the decision-makers, politicians and managers. To engage the environmental challenges of the Baltic Sea that inevitably lie ahead of us, we need strong interdisciplinary research, definitions of common and acceptable environmental targets, socio-economic agreement of costs, new technologies (accepting that there is no silver bullet) and long-term commitment. Only then can science, management and politics interact for the benefit of the marine environment!

Part I

Concepts of Religion in the Public Sphere

1 Who Shall Speak for the Environment? Translating Religious, Scientific, Economic, and Political Regimes of Power and Knowledge in a Globalized Society

Peter Beyer
University of Ottawa, Canada

I. Introduction: Distinguishing the Environment

As much as, and perhaps more than, most concepts, the ideas of environment and ecology are fundamentally relational ones. Environment is that which surrounds, but it thereby implies whatever it is that is surrounded. Ecology refers to the relationship of things, generally life-forms to their surroundings, and usually including other things or life-forms. It also refers to the study or understanding of such relationships: the knowledge or *logos* of the *eikos* or household. Both concepts have a totalizing quality: an environment, without further qualification, is everything not included in whatever is surrounded; ecology includes all relationships and therefore extends to the point where there are no more relationships or, more often, where and at what point in time one stops looking for them. When looking at the most important connotations of these words in contemporary discourse, however, this totalizing or holistic quality of the concepts is maintained, but in a highly particular form. Even though ecological and environmental questions do not need to refer to human beings, today they are predominantly those having to do with the very specific relationship between human beings and the world that surrounds them; or, perhaps more precisely, between what human beings do and the world in which they do it. What is more, that relationship is necessarily an artefact of what humans do, since ecology and environment along with the ideas of world and human beings are all concepts whose existence is limited to appearing as elements in human thought and communication. They are not part of that to which they refer except in this sense. It is in light of this conceptual predication that the analysis which follows asks, 'who shall *speak* for the environment', and not directly what *are* the relationships to which the ideas of environment and ecology refer. Thus the focus in this chapter is on the *communication* about environmental issues and only indirectly about the issues as such.

II. Communication, Systems of Communication, and Religion in Contemporary Society

Communication is the stuff of social realities. Without these processes in which we human beings participate but which go beyond any particular person and emerge from the interactions among us, there would be nothing that could properly be called social.[1] So much is this the case that even to speak this sentence is already to demonstrate this assertion. If we call the encompassing network of such communication 'society', then the question of who speaks for the environment becomes the following: 'Where and how in the network of communication that constitutes our society is communication about the environment situated?' And what does this tell us about that society and that communication? The answer to these questions must depend to a significant extent on how communication in our society is structured, and what patterns that it exhibits might have an influence on the character and consequences of communication about the environment.

In any society, communication will concentrate in various ways so that, as it were, not everyone is talking to everyone else about everything at the same time. Social contexts do not have to become very broad before this sort of structuring becomes a practical necessity. Historically and today, the two most common strategies for effecting such concentration or structuring are according to location and socially defined group of people. We communicate with those whom we encounter most often physically, the local people, and with those whom social norms define as appropriate interlocutors. Very often locality helps to define group and group locality. The physicality of the human body and the limited spatial range of that body become relatively easy constraints and therefore symbolic elements for helping to define social boundaries. Beyond these basic commonalities, however, different societies have differentiated communicative situations in quite diverse ways, and these structures of differentiation have been the constant topic of the modern social sciences which, be it noted, are themselves such structures of communication. That observation, in turn, points to how the society which we inhabit structures itself in an historically rather peculiar way.

---

[1] This perspective on what constitutes the social adapts key elements of the sociological theory of Niklas Luhmann, a theory that informs the entire analysis. See N. Luhmann, 'Die Ausdifferenzierung der Religion,' *Gesellschaftsstruktur und Semantik: Studien zur Wissenssoziologie der modernen Gesellschaft* (Vol. 3; Frankfurt: Suhrkamp, 1989); N. Luhmann, *Social Systems* (trans. J. Bednarz, Jr. and D. Baecker; Stanford, CA: Stanford University Press, 1995).

The original version of this chapter was presented as a paper at an academic conference. That conference was not just a gathering of social scientists, but it did largely consist of a group of academics from different disciplines who amassed in a particular locality, to some extent from different parts of the world, but almost entirely as academics and therefore as communicators who are specialized in a particular type of communication that we can call modern science.[2] Conferences of this kind are themselves differentiated social structures that certain people reproduce and inhabit on a regular basis to communicate the scientific communication which they consider themselves responsible for generating. Such conferences are, moreover, on the one hand physical and local; they require bodily presence by the participants and therefore gathering in a specific locality. On the other hand, they acquire their larger meaning only in the context of a wider network of communication which is translocal and indeed global; and which depends for its transmission on media other than physical presence and talking directly with one another, print and electronic media especially. This wider network has all sorts of other structures which carry it, including journals, books, universities, associations, disciplines, subdisciplines, websites, personal collegial networks and so forth. What unites and defines this peculiar kind of communication, however, are not just these structures, but more critically the characteristic and self-referential type of communication that we call science. And helping to differentiate this communication as science is the fact that there exists a lot of other communication, in which the conference participants also participate every day, which does not count as science. The boundaries between scientific and non-scientific communication may in various ways be somewhat fluid and even ambiguous, but by and large that boundary is maintained, in among other ways, by a difference in the sort of language that people use – language that is oftentimes difficult for 'outsiders' even to understand because of its specialized nature built up over a long period of time. One could go on from here to note how different disciplines are analogously structured, reproduced and differentiated, the disciplines themselves having their own networks, history of discussion, literatures, associations, university structures and so forth.

The example of the conference and the science which it helps to reproduce points to a wider structural feature of the society in which we live, and that is that there have risen to prominence within it, over the past few hundred years, more than a few such more or less well defined domains of communication. These I would call systems of communication, and here, as noted earlier, I am using a very Luhmannian sense of the idea of system – each of which has its typical structures and types of communication. These systems of communication have become so pervasive, so powerful and so ineluctable that they are, I suggest, at the structural

---

[2] The word science is used here more with the broader meaning that it has in French, as *sciences*; or in German, as *Wissenschaft*. In English, it would include what are called the natural sciences, the social sciences *and* the humanities. At this stage of the analysis, this includes theologians; but I shall have to distinguish theological observation from other sorts of scientific observation below.

heart of the fact that almost all of us in the contemporary world inhabit a single global society, at the same time as we live in more local societies. The most obvious – because so often observed as having this effect – are the (global) capitalist economy and the (global) political system of sovereign states. Indeed, when the now much overused word, globalization, appears in contemporary discourse – both within and outside the disciplines of economics and political science – the most common reference is to the power, structure and effects of the capitalist economic and state political systems.[3] Yet the system for science is just as globally pervasive,[4] especially in the form of its natural and applied science disciplines with their powerful (and, by the way, marketable!) technological products ranging from drugs, fertilizers and cell phones to aircraft, power plants and (increasingly) nuclear weapons. To these systems one could add others, notably systems for academic education (schools), biomedical health, law, sport, mass media and art. Most importantly, in the context of this conference, I would also add to this list a parallel system for religion.

The limited context of this chapter does not permit me to defend with any kind of thoroughness the idea that there exists such a global system for religion. I have tried to do that elsewhere.[5] The features that I think are constitutive of it are, nonetheless, reasonably clear and important for the current discussion. First and foremost, perhaps, the religious system has, parallel to and like the others, arisen historically and therefore contingently. It did not have to happen. It is not simply the form that some transhistorical phenomenon called religion takes in today's society. At its core is a type of communication that one can style in various ways, for instance, religious practices or religious ritual, but which in generalized form could be called communication with supra- and super-empirical entities that are deemed to be the agents for the imparting of information and the understanding of human efforts to communicate with them. Related to this feature and aiding instrumentally in the differentiation of religious communication is the idea, explicit in the way it is structured, that its purpose is to render access to a level of reality more fundamental than any other, and indeed a level that is the condition for the possibility of all of reality, including human and social reality. Communication with these features has probably existed in most societies at most times; but it has not previously been structured and incorporated into one societal system beside others such as we have today. Moreover, and as a consequence of the selectivity of all these systems, in today's society there is a good amount of such communication that escapes being incorporated into the religious system, just as there is a good amount of knowledge that is not incorporated into the system of science. The system for religion is like the system for economy, in terms of which, in spite of laments to the contrary, not everything exchanged in our society is commodified; that is, exchanged through price and purchase with money. This religious system is

---

[3] See J. A. Scholte, *Globalization: A Critical Introduction* (London: Palgrave Macmillan, 2nd edn, 2005), for an excellent overview.

[4] R. Stichweh, 'Science in the System of World Society', *Social Science Information* 35 (1996), pp. 327–340.

[5] P. Beyer, *Religions in Global Society* (London: Routledge, 2006).

highly selective in what it includes; which is to say that not everything that could count as religion does count as religion. This is no clearer than in contemporary scientific debates (outside the system for religion) about religion, which are notoriously inconclusive about what exactly should and should not be considered as religion.[6] For the most part, what does constitute part of the religious system are those communications that reproduce what we call the religions, albeit even here what precisely is Christian or Jewish or Hindu is not nearly as structurally clear as, say, what exchange activity reproduces the capitalist economy or even what constitutes a valid scientific statement within science. In this respect religion is a lot more like art than economy, science or state.

The historical arising of this religious system has occurred very explicitly with reference to, and in parallel with, the arising of the other systems. It makes social and historical sense only in that context, such that the rise of religion as system has been conditional on the rise of the other systems, and vice versa. Reflective of this mutuality, the single most widespread religious concept for the environment of the religious system, for that which is not-religion from the perspective of religion, is the *secular*, and most particularly the 'secular' systems for economy, state, science and others. It is in this context that many observers both within and outside the system have come to understand religion in terms of distinctions like religious/secular, sacred/profane and transcendent/immanent, where religion is located in the first term of each pair; even though so doing runs into all sorts of difficulties as one observes religion constantly crossing the boundaries that these dichotomies imply. The work that these distinctions help to accomplish is to differentiate religion from that which is not religion, even though the purview of this religion is not at all limited to one term rather than the other. This feature is critical for understanding how religion can and does speak for the ecological environment. By implication, it is also critical for understanding that, and how the other systems also speak for this environment, but with their own peculiar systemic rationales and logics, not that which we have structured as religion. In other words, while religious speaking for the environment is both possible and inevitable, such speaking will have no automatic priority over parallel speaking for the environment in other systems, nor will it have a direct effect on such parallel speaking without first being translated into the peculiar idioms of those systems. That, of course, still leaves open the possibility of indirect effects and that religious speaking will be thus translated.

III. Religious Speaking for the Environment

The peculiar selectivity and *sectionality* of religion in our society has some very particular implications for how this religion can speak about and for the ecological

---

[6] See, from a large literature A. L. Greil and D. G. Bromley (eds), *Defining Religion: Investigating the Boundaries between Sacred and Secular, Religion and the Social Order* (Vol. 10; London: Elsevier Scientific, 2003).

environment. On the one hand, the holistic quality of the idea of environment – the whole natural world – appears to resonate with religion's typical claims to holistic and foundational perspectives, as represented, for instance in its 'god' and 'ultimate reality' concepts. These typically ground the possibility of anything and are understood as indeterminable in their determinacy, including within themselves both what is or can be and what is not. They are so holistic that they really cannot be 'said' at all because to do so would be to draw a distinction. Furthermore, and this I have argued elsewhere, the relatively greater development of the sort of power and knowledge characteristic of some of the non-religious systems – particularly science, state, and economy – has, at least until recently, been accompanied by the widespread perception, concern, or expectation (a) that we are living in a relatively 'secularized' society; (b) that the 'secular' systems or spheres are more primarily sectional in their rationales and perspectives; (c) that their power and their sectionality has rendered the relationship between society and the larger whole, the environment, in various ways problematic; and (d) that religion, being both holistic and somewhat marginalized, therefore resonates in a fundamental way with the ecological environment, the whole that is neglected and even contradicted by the powerful sectionalities of the secular systems.[7] On the other hand, religion has itself been structured in a highly sectional way, its differentiated forms of power and rationality standing, as I have argued, structurally and discursively parallel to those of the other systems. Consequently, one should expect that religious speaking about and for the ecological environment will show certain strains reflective of this religious 'sectional holism'.

Two well-known examples of speech about the ecological environment and about religion's role with relation to it can serve to illustrate my point. These are J. E. Lovelock's Gaia hypothesis and Lynn White's analysis of the roots of the ecological crisis.[8] What is especially notable about the former is that it frames the environmental question through visibly religious symbols and relationships among those symbols, yet it does so outside the reflexive discourse of any of the commonly recognized religions. The latter, by contrast, locates the source of ecological problems squarely in the religions that constitute the religious system, in particular the religion of Christianity.

Lovelock first translates the abstract concepts of ecology and environment into the concrete form of the planet, Earth; he then transposes this Earth into the formally religious idiom of the ancient Greek goddess of the Earth, Gaia; and finally recasts her as an anthropomorphic and female gendered being whose organic self is threatened by the destructive attitudes and behaviour of her own offspring, us. In form and content, this is mytho-religious talk. It finds parallels in various other religious perspectives, for instance, in the upsurge over recent decades among aboriginal peoples in the Americas of reference to 'Mother Earth' as the core

---

[7] P. Beyer, 'The Global Environment as a Religious Issue: A Sociological Analysis', *Religion* 22 (1992), pp. 1–21; P. Beyer, *Religion and Globalization* (London: Sage, 1994), pp. 206–224.
[8] J. E. Lovelock, *Gaia: A New Look at Life on Earth* (Oxford: Oxford University Press, 1987); L. White, 'The Historical Roots of Our Ecological Crisis', *Science* 155 (1967), pp. 1203–1207.

goddess of aboriginal spirituality, for whom aboriginal people have always known profound respect and which others around the world have neglected at their peril.[9] Notably, most of those representing this aboriginal spirituality also resist the casting of these religious ways as a religion, as one of the sectional religions.[10] Lynn White's thesis complements the logic contained in both Mother Earth and Gaia speech by seeking to show how the purportedly problematic relation between humans and the environment has its roots precisely in sectional religion. Here the Christian religion is particularly recognized as the historical carrier of a problematic orientation in this regard, namely, the idea that God created man (the gendered reference is explicit) and told him to have dominion over the Earth, which is to say exploit it for his own purposes and as something different or sectional that is over against him. This orientation, in a logical turn reminiscent of Max Weber's Protestant ethic thesis, has been taken up and amplified by the secular analogues of this religion, especially in the form of modern scientific technology and capitalist economy.

Not surprisingly, given the ways religion and religions have come to be structured in our society, the responses of the religions, particularly through some of their activist and theological representatives, have been not just to deny accusations such as those of White, but to insist on the holistic perspective that religion offers and to include critique of what I am here calling sectionality in their proffered solutions to environmental problems. For example, Hindu, Buddhist, Jain, Jewish and Islamic representatives have insisted that their religious traditions, far from being a source or contributor to the 'ecological crisis', have at their core insights, orientations, injunctions and knowledge that, if followed, could have avoided the crisis and can now be at the basis of real solutions to it.[11] The religions, it turns out, are and have always been environmentally friendly and provide ways of life that, if followed faithfully, can address the mess which we humans in our hubris have created. Christian responses in this regard are particularly interesting since that religion has been singled out as a prime source of the problem, and because of its dominant place among the world's differentiated religions. Indeed, for at least some observers, when we talk of sectional religion, we are really talking about Christianity.[12]

---

[9] Cf. S. Gill, *Mother Earth: An American Story* (Chicago: University of Chicago Press, 1987).
[10] P. Beyer, *Religions in Global Society*, p. 274.
[11] See, as examples, A. H. Badiner (ed.), *Dharma Gaia: A Harvest of Essays in Buddhism and Ecology* (Berkeley, CA: Parallax, 1990); C. K. Chapple (ed.), *Jainism and Ecology: Nonviolence in the Web of Life* (Cambridge, MA: Center for the Study of World Religions and Harvard University Press, 2002); O. P. Dwiwedi and B. N. Tiwari, *Environmental Crisis and the Hindu Religion* (New Delhi: Gitanjali, 1987); R. C. Foltz, F. M. Denny, and A. Baharuddin (eds), *Islam and Ecology: A Bestowed Trust* (Cambridge, MA: Center for the Study of World Religions and Harvard University Press, 2003); H. Tirosh-Samuelson (ed.), *Judaism and Ecology: Created World and Revealed Word* (Cambridge, MA: Center for the Study of World Religions and Harvard University Press, 2002).
[12] S. N. Balagangadhara, *The Heathen in His Blindness...: Asia, the West, and the Dynamic of Religion* (Leiden: E. J. Brill, 1994); T. Fitzgerald, 'A Critique of "Religion" as a Cross-Cultural Category', *Method & Theory in the Study of Religion* 9 (1997), pp. 91–110.

The kinds of Christian responses to the situation, and therefore the kind of Christian speech about the environment, has been quite varied, but for the sake of presentation they can be divided into two sorts, each with a great deal of internal variety.[13] On the one hand, and parallel with discourse emanating from other religions, different perspectives insist that at the heart of the Christian message and worldview, there exists the injunction to care for the environment as God's *creation*, that for instance, from a Christian perspective, humans are the stewards of the environment, that they are co-responsible for the integrity of creation, or that a Christian orientation can ground a creation spirituality.[14] One notes the translation of the idea of ecology or environment into specifically theological or properly religious terms through these ideas, especially that of creation. Creation becomes in effect the religious marker for the immanent, the profane and the secular, thereby sacralizing the entire world and rendering it actionable in specifically religious terms. The other sort of response has been broadly called the eco-justice orientation. These responses assert a close relation between ecological problems and specifically social and economic justice issues. In particular, they link Christian notions of justice – such as in the liberationist 'option for the poor' with ecological problems by asserting that the two sorts of 'injustices' (toward the poor and the planet) are different manifestations of the same problem, and that therefore the solution to the one contains the solution to the other. Even more clearly than the response centred on the theological notion of creation, this justice-centred approach locates both problems in the sectionality of global systems, in their selective – and in this sense, heretical – vision. The global capitalist economic system is the particular target of such critique, but not to the exclusion of the others.[15]

One could look in greater detail at the environmental responses emanating from the other religions to gain an appreciation for just how widespread and varied these are. I cannot do that here, but the conclusion that I would draw from them would be the same. As in the Christian case, religious speaking for the environment is substantial in world society, whether this comes from within the constructed religions that largely compose the globalized religious system or from outside of it. It is varied and significant, yet one of its defining characteristics is that it invariably translates environmental questions into specifically religious idioms and symbolic clusters. Environment becomes 'creation', 'Gaia' or 'Mother Earth'; ecological problems become religio-moral justice issues. These translations allow one to express ecological matters in religious terms and thereby permit a connectivity

---

[13] See L. Kearns, 'Religion and Ecology in the Context of Globalization', *Religion, Globalization and Culture* (P. Beyer and L. Beaman (eds); Leiden: Brill Academic Publishers, 2007), pp. 305–344; Laurel Kearns, 'Saving the Creation: Christian Environmentalism in the United States', *Sociology of Religion* 57 (1996), pp. 55–70.
[14] See, as a by now classic example, M. Fox, *The Coming of the Cosmic Christ: The Healing of Mother Earth and the Birth of a Global Renaissance* (San Francisco: Harper & Row, 1988).
[15] See P. Beyer, *Religion and Globalization*, p. 206ff, and L. Kearns, 'Saving the Creation: Christian Environmentalism in the United States.' for further references and examples.

with religious remedies. I insist on the religious translation of environmental issues into religious speech because, unsurprisingly given the character of the differentiated structures, the 'secular' systems do something analogous: they also 'translate the environment' into their own idioms to render them communicable in terms of their own rationales.

IV. 'Secular' Systems Speaking for the Environment

The parallel translation of the environment into the terms of the other systems is not difficult to document. Let us begin with the economic system. The fundamental rationale of the capitalist economic system, parallel to the religious rationale of enabling access to the indeterminable condition for all possibility (enlightenment, salvation, harmony etc.), is to generate capital. Environment therefore has to be translated ultimately into terms of profit and loss, revenue and cost. The capitalist system will therefore be able to incorporate – read: understand in its own terms – ecological questions to the extent that one can make a profit thereby, perhaps by producing and marketing more energy efficient products or environmentally 'friendly' consumer goods like biodegradable computers. It can also incorporate them in terms of cost, such as is done through cap and trade systems, through the potential for negative corporate images that hurt profitability, and so forth. Moving on to the political state system, here the basic rationale is getting and using the regulatory and collectively binding decision-making power of the state, namely, government. For the political system, environmental issues have to be translated into the terms of political truth, which is to say political expediency. If ecological issues can become election or re-election issues; if they can become matters of geopolitical relations such that failure to address them results in pressure and even interference from other countries or international agencies; then environmental problems will become political problems and be dealt with as such. Science, in parallel but also by contrast, has to translate the environment into terms of theory and data. Scientifically, for instance, climate change has to be measured and demonstrated, alternative interpretations of the data discussed in terms of different theories, thereupon to arrive at a general, but provisional, consensus as to what is the scientific truth in this regard. Research on environmental questions has to be published and be subject to scrutiny, conferences focussing on them have to be organized and held, and research has to be reproduced. This is the case not only for the natural sciences, such as biology or climatology, but also for the social sciences and the humanities disciplines. As already noted, the conference for which an earlier version of this chapter was written was first and foremost a scientific affair, and what I am attempting to do here is in effect offer some theoretical analysis of data observed, mainly in other scientific literature, but also, in an admittedly impressionistic way, in the field.

I could continue this observation of parallel translations in other systems with more examples, for instance, the way that legal systems have to translate ecological questions into environmental law and rulings in terms of that law; the way that educational systems have to translate such issues into curricula, evaluation, and accreditation structures before they can be taught; or the way that mass media would have to translate and 'broadcast' them into news and information about the environment and the questions surrounding it. The one other sectional domain or system that I do want to focus on briefly, however, is the realm of art. Here the translation issue is rather direct: environmental issues have to be translated into works of art, whether that be a song, a painting, a play, a novel, a building or some other artistic form of expression. Art is a path for creating iconic images and stories, for crystallizing environment into memorable concrete and plastic representations that 'stand in' for the overall issue. Works of art are translations quite as much as scientific theories, political platforms or business strategies for 'going green'. Their power – and we are always dealing with forms of power in this discussion, in addition to forms of knowledge – is illustrated, for instance, in photographs of wide-eyed baby harp seal pups (perhaps with the hunter's weapon poised to strike above their heads), in futuristic novels like John Christopher's *No Blade of Grass*, in speculative essays like Rachel Carson's *Silent Spring* or in movies and videos like Al Gore's *An Inconvenient Truth*.[16] What is particularly intriguing about artistic productions in this context is that they show with such clarity how a sectional idiom is irreducible to any of the others. Gore's and Carson's productions are not science, although they can use scientific styles as thematic resources to get their message across. Nor are they religion, except again as an artistic resource that can be plastically formed to render the artistic production coherent and effective in its own terms. Art thereby also demonstrates, and this is my next theme, how sectionality always also implies and involves intersectionality: the systems are interdependent in that their differentiated functioning assumes, and even perhaps requires, the others to operate in their respective environments.

V. Interdependence and Lack of Hierarchy in Speaking for the Environment

The differentiated systemic idioms that I have just adumbrated do not operate in isolation, from the rest of society, from other systems, and indeed from the biological and physical environment that is at issue here. Rather the opposite is the case. Differentiation does not mean autarchy but rather independence within interdependence. The examples of the different translations of the ecological environment illustrate this, not only in the case of art, but also for economy, politics, science and religion. Business firms can be and are subject to political regulation and legal rulings and, as contract law or the recent credit crisis show, depend on them. They use scientifically developed technology to, for instance, extract oil from the tar sands of Alberta or produce LED lightbulbs; they depend

---

[16] R. Carson, *Silent Spring* (Boston: Houghton Mifflin, 1962); J. Christopher, *No Blade of Grass* (New York: Avon, 1956); A. Gore, *An Inconvenient Truth* (Hollywood, CA: Paramount, 2006).

on these scientific endeavours. States do not run without money, revenue that is ultimately generated by the economy. Science often takes its cue as to what it is important to research from government, from business, from the biomedical health field and so forth. Religion operates in environments of political regulation, requires at least some money to operate, and has a long history of using art to concretize and structure its communication. One could go on, but I think the point is not that difficult to understand or to illustrate. What is in fact new to the modern era is the independence of these spheres of endeavour in the form of these systems, not the interdependence among them.

While this interdependence exists, and is critical to the operation of these sectional systems, their mutual relations do not amount to either a clear or a consistent hierarchy among them. To be sure, some of these systems, notably the economic, political and scientific, generate significantly more power than others, and this relative imbalance in development has undoubtedly been a main factor in having given us the impression that we are living in secularizing societies. In addition, there are from time to time attempts to establish such a hierarchy, especially by seeking to set up one system as the part that represents and controls the whole. State socialism of the twentieth century in countries ranging from the Soviet Union and Cuba to China and North Korea is an example of such prioritization of the political state system. The neo-liberal ideology that has held such sway in most of the world since the early 1980s can be seen as an attempt, once again, to insist that economy is the fundamental system that, if left unfettered, will take care of the rest. And perhaps we can add the experiment of the Islamic Republic of Iran in the 1980s as an example of seeking to give the religious system such priority, although this attempt rather quickly transformed into a state-centred system run by formally religious clerics, and attempts to reproduce it elsewhere have not been particularly successful. In all these cases, however, whether economic, political or religious, the arrangements have been difficult to maintain, even to put properly into practice, and where they seem to have been maintained, as in the case of North Korea thus far, so many social power resources have to be used just to keep the rest of the world out, that there does not seem to be enough left to do anything else, like feed one's population instead of developing nuclear weaponry. The 2007–2008 economic crisis, in this regard, may turn out to be a strong indicator of the demise of the neo-liberal vision. Invariably, it seems, such attempts at establishing single system priority eventually succumb to the power of the more 'chaotic' and 'invasive' arrangements around them. Indeed, the non-hierarchical operation of the main systems has had as one of its effects precisely the sort of globalization and globalized society that has received so much attention over the past few decades. It is arguable that the imperial and colonial success of the European powers over the past centuries in projecting their power and influence to all corners of the world rested in large part on this relatively uncoordinated development of these sectional systems of which they were for a long time the dominant carriers.

The combination of sectionality and lack of structural hierarchy among the systems means that, although all of them, as it were, can and do 'speak for the environment', none of them can do so either directly (that is, without translation) or primarily. To the extent that the environment can be or is a religious, an economic or a scientific issue, for instance, this is always the case only in particular and mediated form, such that the particular idiom of one system cannot be universalized to the others or to the society more generally except as that particular form, or in that it is first translated or re-particularized in another. None of them speaks for the whole and yet all of them do, each in a particular way from their particular perspectives. One could say that the whole is necessarily a partial question with respect to these systems. And that includes religion: if it speaks from the perspective of the whole, then that is still a partial or sectional speaking. Among the questions that emerge from this analysis are these two: first, are there ways of speaking for the environment in our society that escape these systems and their peculiar rationales and which therefore might address this incommensurability? Second, given that the very power of many of these systems is a critical part of how the environment has become a problematic issue in our society; or, to put it another way, given that the most powerful systems that can speak for the environment are precisely those that, through their impetus toward constant growth, have been instrumental in bringing about the environment as a critical problem in our society; how can this system-based speaking for the environment possibly address the problem if it is the source of the problem? The first question can be addressed through a discussion of the important function of social movements; the second points to a fundamental conundrum that will bring us back to the issue of religious speaking for the environment.

VI. Social Movements and Environmental Issues

In introducing the idea of these systems or sectionalities earlier, I noted that, while they represent the dominant power and knowledge structures of our global society, they are also highly selective, excluding in large measure not only each other and communication that might otherwise well be included under them, but also a great deal of social process that is neither. These systems are dominant but not encompassing. The strong role that social movements play in this society is one manifestation of that selectivity. Social movements are somewhat fluid and even amorphous social forms that construct themselves around specific discourses that define problems and goals which identify the movement, and reproduce themselves both through these discourses and through characteristic events, which is to say through movement-specific mobilization. They can form in the context of the dominant systems or outside of them; they can centre around any number of themes and questions. In contemporary society, they often come to be identified in terms of social movement organizations, but they are more than these organizations. As much of the sociological literature about them makes clear, socio-structurally, their reproduction depends on resource mobilization.[17]

---

[17] Cf. B. Klandermans, H. Kriesi, and S. Tarrow (eds), *From Structure to Action: Comparing Social Movement Research Across Cultures, International Social Movement Research: A Research Annual* (Vol. 10; Greenwich, CT: JAI Press, 1988).

Given their flexibility and their ability to operate across other social boundaries, notably those that the dominant systems define, it is perhaps not surprising – and socio-structurally even to be expected – that one of the more notable social movements globally over the past half century has been what is often called the environmental movement. This particular movement – or perhaps better, set of movements – began solidly in the 1960s, and has had a complex and variable set of manifestations ever since. Its central discourse defines a specific problem: the 'natural environment' – and the movement discourse has been critical in giving this concept its contemporary form or meaning – is being threatened or destroyed by human activity and failure to address this issue will result in disaster for life on Earth, including human life. The solution to this core problem flows from the definition of the problem: humans must alter their activity in such a way as to reduce or reverse the detrimental effect that they are having. On the basis of this fundamental definition of the problem and the solution, the movement has concretized itself in a complex array of events or mobilizations that include efforts to reproduce and increase the presence of its central discourse, the founding and perpetuation of a plethora of movements specific organizations, protest campaigns, campaigns to change individual activity, and, most importantly in the context of this analysis, efforts to have the discourse incorporated (translated) into the characteristic communication of the dominant systems. The movement has 'infiltrated' the economic system, making it, for instance, economically viable for companies to 'go green' (or at least appear to do so), or translating itself into 'fair trade' and 'organic' enterprises. It has mobilized to bring about a vast array of regulation and legislation and to have that legislation enforced. It has led to an enormous amount of scientific research specifically on ecological issues. It has become a prominent theme in art and mass information media. It has become to some extent a part of school curricula. And, not least, it has expressed itself and come to be taken up as theological discourse in various religions – and here theological discourse is not scientific discourse. I put particular stress on these systemic 'infiltrations' because they demonstrate the degree to which 'changing people's behaviour and consciousness' and 'spreading the word' are not enough; that the dominance of the sectional systems is such that any movement that hopes to 'succeed' is almost structurally forced to seek such infiltration. The systems represent the dominant forms of power in our society and therefore to eschew them simply as the 'source of the problem' would be to doom the movement to marginal presence and certainly marginal effect. One cannot, it seems, simply 'change one heart at a time' and achieve movement-defined success, unless that effort is a means to exerting systemic influence, which is to say, having the movement-specific speaking about and for the environment translated into the sectional idioms and sectional power of the systems.

The upshot of this consideration of social movements is that they can and do provide a mode of action that to a significant degree escapes the idioms of the sectional systems. Social movements can therefore make the environment their focussed issue. They can crystallize environment as a specific issue. Yet because the prime locations of forms of power in our society are located in the sectional systems, environmental movements will at some point have to seek translation of their impulse into sectional systemic form. This then brings us to the question of religion's possibilities in this scenario. As a sectional system that operates from foundationally holistic perspectives, does it have properties that are sufficiently different from the other systems that it might play a special role when it comes to addressing the issue of the environment?

VII. Religious Sectional Communication and Environmental Issues

From what I have said thus far, it should not be surprising that I am not terribly sanguine about the possibilities of a *special*, as opposed to a distinct, role for religion. To be sure, religion and religions have come to be constructed as ways of communicating, as orientations and as a system that is different from the others in relatively clear ways. For one, it is perhaps not the only system – I am thinking of art as another one – but it is certainly one system whose relative strength around the world does not follow the same core-peripheral patterns as do the others. Economic, political, media, scientific, sport, health and legal power seem to vary together, meaning that those regions which are powerful in one respect will tend to be powerful in the others as well, and those that are peripheral are so in terms of all these systemic power modalities at the same time. Religion, by contrast, does not follow this pattern, and if we were to divide the world into the religiously more and religiously less powerful (or developed!) regions, we would likely arrive at a very different view of where the periphery of the global religious system is and where is the core.[18] This difference may give religion a certain advantage as a perspective that appears to be less directly implicated in the reproduction of those power structures that are deemed to be responsible for the 'ecological crisis'. That, combined with its foundationally holistic perspectives, would seem to be an advantage. And here is perhaps why environmental speaking so often takes on at least a kind of quasi-religious flavour, even when it eschews being and is not considered to be reproductive of a particular religion. Nonetheless, if we then ask how such thus advantaged religious communication or speaking about and for the environment can then be brought to bear on the problem that it helps to concretize and make salient, then the answer will not flow directly from these advantages. Speaking 'from the outside' or 'from the perspective of the whole' is not an advantage in a society where the most powerful forms of communication are sectional, even if that sectionality is convincingly communicated as a key aspect of the problem.

In this light, religion as sectional system is likely to continue to play two important roles. On the one hand, it can and to some extent will translate environmental questions and concerns into religious communication, here religious

---

[18] See P. Beyer, *Religions in Global Society*, pp. 95–106.

practice and religious ritual that includes moral exhortation on the basis of the diverse religions, theological reflection, as well as such peformances as prayer, meditation, sacrifice, and so forth. This kind of communication is parallel to what gets done in other systems, such as scientific research focused on ecological questions, teaching about such issues in school curricula, or producing art with an ecological message. On the other hand, religions can act as an important resource from which environmental social movements draw meanings with which to formulate discourse and inform mobilization. That also is parallel to other systems. All the other sectional systems are, formally speaking, in an analogous situation. A key question, however, is whether the relatively greater social power of some of the other systems, especially the economic, political and scientific, will make it appear that these roles for religion will be perceived to be comparatively marginal. That is likely to be a question to which the answer will be different depending on which systemic perspective one takes. Those 'inside' the religions may very well be more likely to see and communicate religion's role to be greater than those whose perspective is from the 'outside'.

The central irony remains: in contemporary global society, the more we focus in on the sectional sources of environmental problems, the closer we get to the realization that the solutions to those problems have to be constructed also in the partial yet powerful idioms of those 'sectional interests'. They cannot be constructed in opposition to them, from the perspective and in the interests of the whole because the whole is itself at best only a sectional or partial interest. The alternative, given the situation we have constructed for ourselves, is to undo the dominant sectionality sufficiently rapidly so as to prevent 'further damage'; but that would have the effect of bringing about the destruction of the majority of human life on this planet since it would undo the society on which these humans depend for their existence. Even if we posit, for the sake of argument, this as an acceptable or even a necessary outcome, it is extremely unlikely that it is a 'solution' that we can expect us humans to take, at least not deliberately and in terms of our speaking about the environment. Much more likely is the development of orientations and values that, as it were, perpetuate the sectional systems, ones which translate the problem, for instance, into problems of 'sustainability', and even more peculiar, into problems of 'sustainable development'. This last term, perhaps more than most, shows graphically what sort of almost oxymoronic position we find ourselves in: the solution to the problem appears to be the source of the problem itself.

Bibliography

Badiner, A. H. (ed.), *Dharma Gaia: A Harvest of Essays in Buddhism and Ecology* (Berkeley, CA: Parallax, 1990).

Balagangadhara, S.N., *'The Heathen in His Blindness ...': Asia, the West, and the Dynamic of Religion* (Leiden: E.J. Brill, 1994).

Beyer, P., 'The Global Environment as a Religious Issue: A Sociological Analysis', *Religion* 22 (1992), pp. 1–21.
—*Religion and Globalization* (London: Sage, 1994).
—*Religions in Global Society* (London: Routledge, 2006).
Carson, R., *Silent Spring* (Boston: Houghton Mifflin, 1962).
Chapple, C. K. (ed.), *Jainism and Ecology: Nonviolence in the Web of Life* (Cambridge, MA: Center for the Study of World Religions and Harvard University Press, 2002).
Christopher, J., *No Blade of Grass* (New York: Avon, 1956).
Dwiwedi, O. P., and B. N. Tiwari, *Environmental Crisis and the Hindu Religion* (New Delhi: Gitanjali, 1987).
Fitzgerald, T., 'A Critique of 'Religion' as a Cross-Cultural Category', *Method & Theory in the Study of Religion* 9 (1997), pp. 91–110.
Foltz, R C., F. M. Denny, and A. Baharuddin (eds), *Islam and Ecology: A Bestowed Trust* (Cambridge, MA: Center for the Study of World Religions and Harvard University Press, 2003).
Fox, M., *The Coming of the Cosmic Christ: The Healing of Mother Earth and the Birth of a Global Renaissance* (San Francisco: Harper & Row, 1988).
Gill, S., *Mother Earth: An American Story* (Chicago: University of Chicago Press, 1987).
Gore, A., *An Inconvenient Truth* (Hollywood, CA: Parmount, 2006).
Greil, A. L., and D. G. Bromley (eds), *Defining Religion: Investigating the Boundaries between Sacred and Secular, Religion and the Social Order* (vol. 3; London: Elsevier Scientific, 2003).
Kearns, L., 'Religion and Ecology in the Context of Globalization', *Religion, Globalization and Culture* (P. Beyer and L. Beaman (eds); Leiden: Brill Academic Publishers, 2007), pp. 305–344.
—'Saving the Creation: Christian Environmentalism in the United States', *Sociology of Religion* 57 (1996), pp. 55–70.
Klandermans, B., H. Kriesi, and S. Tarrow (eds), *From Structure to Action: Comparing Social Movement Research Across Cultures, International Social Movement Research: A Research Annual* (vol. 3; Greenwich, CT: JAI Press, 1988).
Lovelock, J. E., *Gaia: A New Look at Life on Earth* (Oxford: Oxford University Press, 1987).
Luhmann, N., 'Die Ausdifferenzierung der Religion', *Gesellschaftsstruktur und Semantik: Studien zur Wissenssoziologie der modernen Gesellschaft* (Vol. 3; Frankfurt: Suhrkamp, 1989), pp. 259–357.
—*Social Systems* (J. Bednarz, Jr. and D. Baecker (trans.); Stanford, CA: Stanford University Press, 1995).
Scholte, J. A., *Globalization: A Critical Introduction* (London: Palgrave Macmillan, 2nd edn, 2005).
Stichweh, R., 'Science in the System of World Society', *Social Science Information* 35 (1996), pp. 327–340.

Tirosh-Samuelson, H. (ed.), *Judaism and Ecology: Created World and Revealed Word* (Cambridge, MA: Center for the Study of World Religions and Harvard University Press, 2002).

White, L., 'The Historical Roots of Our Ecological Crisis', *Science* 155 (1967), pp. 1203–1207.

2 Public Theology of Ecology and Civil Society

Heinrich Bedford-Ströhm
University of Bamberg, Germany and University of Stellenbosch, South Africa

I. Introduction: The Dynamics of the Political Debate. Three Experiences

Speaking of 'Public Theology' and 'Civil Society' means using two phrases which each represent a whole programmatic cosmos. Reflecting upon them theologically, and reading them from ecological discourse, means grounding them in the social and political contexts in which they play a role. 'Whatever is an *important matter* in ecological discourse', Norwegian theologian Sigurd Bergmann has stated, '... is also an important matter for theology. It is *not* theologians, however, who determine which matters are to be viewed as 'important', but rather the partners in the various public spheres that theology enters into dialogue with, as well as, within the paradigm of liberation theology, the victims and those affected by ecological problems.'[1]

Before giving insight into the debates surrounding the terms 'public theology' and 'civil society', and relating them to ecological questions, I want to illustrate the social and political context in which these debates are situated by highlighting three experiences in April 2009 from my home country, Germany. These will guide us directly into the topic.

Experience 1: The synod of my home church, the Lutheran church of Bavaria, chose the topic of creation and climate change as its convention theme. One of the guest speakers was Markus Söder, now Bavarian cabinet minister for environmental affairs, formerly General Secretary of the Christian Social Union, the conservative party which has ruled Bavaria for half a century and which, for a long time, fought the

---

[1] S. Bergmann, *Creation Set Free: The Spirit as Liberator of Nature* (D. Stott (trans.); Grand Rapids and Cambridge: William B. Eerdmans Publishing Company, 2005), p. 46.

environmentalist ideas of the Green Party. In his speech, Söder presented himself as a champion of the fight for the integrity of creation. He publicly supported the fight against the artificial enlargement of the Danube River in Lower Bavaria which has long been on the agenda of church supported environmental activists.

Why has Markus Söder turned into an environmentalist?

Experience 2: On 14 April, the German cabinet minister for agriculture and consumer protection, Ilse Aigner, a member of the same Bavarian conservative party, gave a long-awaited press conference in which she announced her decision on the legal status of Monsanto's genetically modified corn crop Mon810 in Germany. The European Union's decision had been positive and since EU legislation has considerable bearing on national laws, many observers expected her to keep the present legal status of this crop in Germany, especially since her party formerly advocated the promotion of genetically modified crops. Claiming its potential dangers, many farmers in the Bavarian villages fought this food crop, and protested against the power of transnational corporations who would gain control over the farmers' seeds. The Bavarian Lutheran synod had also just affirmed a decision to not rent any land to farmers who intended to grow genetically modified crops. All German newspapers announced Aigner's decision in their front-page headlines. She said 'No' to Monsanto's Mon810.

Why did she make this decision, even though she was not an opponent of GM crops?

Experience 3: On 15 April, only one day after the GMO decision, Bavaria was again the focus of national news. Reports were broadcast from a big demonstration in downtown Munich which included a whole herd of pigs. The protest included many traditional farmers and was organized by a large coalition of organizations ranging from Greenpeace and the Green Party to the Catholic aid agency Misereor and the German milk cow farmers' association. Some of the demonstrators held up signs saying 'Gruß an Frau Merkel! Kein Patent auf Ferkel!' ('Greeting to Mrs. Merkel, no patent for pigs!'). The crowd had assembled close to the European patent office in Munich which in 2008 had given a patent on pig genes. The patent with the number EP 1651777 had belonged to Monsanto but was meanwhile sold to the American company Newsham Choice Genetics. The demonstrators demanded outlawing the possibility of patenting human, animal or plant life. Among the demonstrators the Bavarian environmental minister Markus Söder was spotted giving TV and radio interviews. 'The integrity of creation', he spoke into the microphones, 'is a task of the whole society which must be more important than the profit interests of some gene grasshoppers.'

Did Söder only react to popular opinion? Or did he really turn into an authentic defender of creation? And why did we see a crowd of people from various political backgrounds protesting against economic powers in a way so far only known of leftist grassroots activists?

These three experiences are closely related to the theme of 'Public Theology and Civil Society'. However one interprets the change of opinion by political leaders responsible for environmental decision-making, it cannot be understood apart from the practice of civil engagement, which this article wants to reflect upon in theory. It is difficult to empirically determine the effects of the civil engagement of the churches, or of other religious or secular groups. And it is equally hard to determine whether politicians only react to popular opinion or whether they have really changed because of new insights gained in public discourse. But even if they only follow public opinion, it is a success. It is remarkable how public sensitivity towards threats to the environment has increased in the last decades. The Conciliar Process of the Churches for Justice, Peace and the Integrity of Creation in the 1980s is one vivid example of how the church played a role in generating change.[2]

With this positive experience in the background, we now need to look at the concepts addressed in the title of my lecture. What do we mean by 'civil society'? And how can the concept of 'public theology' help us to understand the general role of the churches and religious communities in the public discourse of a pluralistic society? I will now address these two questions and then conclude by describing consequences for the role of religious communities in the public discourse on ecological questions.

II. What is 'Civil Society'?

The term 'civil society' has had an impressive career in the social sciences and beyond in the last decades.[3] At the same time, it has been increasingly used as a weapon in the political debate and thus, we face two dangers. First, emphasizing the role of civil society can be a rather empty theoretical claim: the claim is so general that it does not really say anything interesting anymore. Second, it can also be introduced into the political debate to support an agenda that arises from other motives. In this case the strategy is simply to use a key word from the debate in the social sciences or philosophy that carries the promise of a wide consensus as a way of persuading others to adopt a certain agenda. Therefore, it is important to be more specific in what one means if one uses this term.

Even though it has been reintroduced into the political debate only recently, the term has a long history dating back to ancient political theory. Its roots lie

---

[2] For an expanded treatment of the theme of creation in the Conciliar Process, see H. Bedford-Strohm, *Schöpfung* (Göttingen: Vandenhoeck & Ruprecht, 2001), pp. 122–54. See also Bedford-Strohm, 'Tilling and Caring for the Earth: Public Theology and Ecology', *International Journal of Public Theology* 1 (2007), pp. 230–248; Bedford-Strohm, 'Die Entdeckung der Ökologie in der ökumenischen Bewegung', *Hoffnungswege: Wegweisende Impulse des Ökumenischen Rates der Kirchen aus sechs Jahrzehnten* (H. G. Link and G. Müller-Fahrenholz (eds); Frankfurt: Otto Lembeck, 2008), pp. 321–347.

[3] See J. von Soosten, 'Civil Society: Zum Auftakt der neueren demokratietheoretischen Debatte mit einem Seitenblick auf Religion, Kirche und Öffentlichkeit (Literaturbericht)', *ZEE* 37 (1993), pp. 139–157.

in the Aristotelian 'politike koinonia', a communal sphere of politics which then was translated into the Latin term 'societas civilis', later becoming 'société civile' or 'civil society'. Until the eighteenth century the term basically meant the sphere of the state. Its modern profile developed only in the revolutionary changes that led to what we now call modernity; these included the differentiation of different societal spheres and the development of a public sphere which increasingly filled the space between the individual on one side and the state on the other. As early as 1767 the Scottish moral philosopher Adam Ferguson, in his 'Essay on the History of Civil Society', placed the civil societal discourse between market and state. A society which is more and more oriented towards the market, says Ferguson, needs civil taming to prevent the pursuit of personal interest from being the only capital increased in society.[4] This early warning against the totalitarian tendency of the market could not be more timely today. It signifies a use of the term 'civil society' which is a corrective to the market rather than its servant.

This leads us directly into the politics of the use of the term 'civil society' today. I will show what I mean by describing two different understandings of the term which we can find in present political debates. I call the first one the 'economically liberal understanding' and the other one the 'communitarian liberal understanding'. The economically liberal understanding primarily addresses the activity of the state in economics and social policy. Its theoretical roots lie in the liberalistic theories of the eighteenth century (e.g. Adam Smith) which argue against the intrusion of the state in the sphere of a market driven economy. This type of 'civil society' argument was revitalized in the 1980s by the Eastern European reform movement fighting against a state that not only dominated the political but also the economic sphere. Liberation from communism also meant the revival of the activity of the free entrepreneur in the economic sphere, making use of his economic freedom rights and thereby helping to develop a free market economy that would lead to prosperity for everybody in the long run.[5] This anti-etatistic use of the term 'civil society' was warmly received by those political forces in Western societies which had for a long time argued against the strong role of the state in modern welfare states; they found new arguments for the responsibility of each individual to take care of his or her own life and arguments for poverty assistance based on private initiative rather than on legal entitlements guaranteed by the state. Thus, the term 'civil society' gained special prominence in the party programme of the German Free Democratic Party, which is the driving force of free market economics in Germany. Individual rights and personal initiative are the main characteristics of this interpretation of civil society.

The liberal communitarian interpretation takes a very different path. In this interpretation, 'civil society' is a programmatic term for the renewal of democracy along the lines of solidarity and participation. Its historic roots are manifold. One

---

[4] A. Ferguson, *Versuch über die Geschichte der bürgerlichen Gesellschaft* (Frankfurt: Suhrkamp, 1988), p. 289.

[5] For more on this understanding, see E. Gellner, *Bedingungen der Freiheit. Die Zivilgesellschaft und ihre Rivalen* (Stuttgart: Klett-Cotta, 1995).

of the most quoted witnesses is Alexis de Tocqueville whose theory of free associations between state and individual arose out of his study of American political and communal life in the nineteenth century. The most well-known advocate of this interpretation is the German philosopher Jürgen Habermas. The point of this interpretation of civil society is not the critique of state activity in the social welfare system. On the contrary, civil society can even criticize a reduction of state activity, for example, by cutting down support programmes for the poor, and call for an intensified engagement of the state. Civil society includes voluntary associations, networks, initiatives and social movements which can be sensors for deficient political developments. According to Habermas, they sense the effects of societal problems in peoples' private lives; they then take up such problems, amplify them, and carry them into the sphere of public debate.[6] Their function is not to protect market actors from outside intrusion, but to be a voice for those who do not have the political or economic power to make sure their concerns are considered in the political process. Civil society, in the liberal communitarian sense, therefore especially protects the vulnerable and marginalized; however, we can also say, it potentially protects the interests of nature that are so often ignored in the dominant paradigm of economics, now with a global horizon.

It is interesting how the place of religious communities has shifted in Habermas' thinking in the last decade. Formerly in his theory of civil society, the churches as institutional voices of religion were listed with other associations like sports clubs, interest groups or leisure activity groups – a diagnosis which has led Michael Welker to see serious deficiencies in the analysis of reality and grave theoretical deficits in Habermas' theory.[7] More recently, however, Habermas has started to appreciate the special value of religious communities as public agents in a democracy.

Habermas now goes beyond the argument normally connected with secularization theory, according to which, a modern liberal state has to base its political decisions purely on reason instead of faith. He speaks of a 'post-secular society' which is in danger of losing a scarce but very important resource: a sense for the meaning of life ('Sinn').[8] Therefore, the civil public will need to develop a new sensitivity to the potential of religious traditions to contribute to this sense for the meaning of life. Habermas describes a kind of 'osmosis' of reason and faith.[9] Both have to be open to each other. Each has to try to understand the language of the other.[10]

Habermas' new interest in the public role of religion is motivated by more than just respect for people who integrate faith and reason. There are *philosophical* reasons for learning from religious traditions: holy scriptures and religious traditions have kept alive intuitions of mistaken life and redemption from such

---

[6] J. Habermas, *Faktizität und Geltung. Beiträge zur Diskurstheorie des Rechts und des demokratischen Rechtsstaates* (Frankfurt: Suhrkamp, 1992), p. 443

[7] M. Welker, *Kirche im Pluralismus* (Gütersloh: Gütersloher Verlagshaus, 1995), p. 23f. Other sources of a similar critique can be found there.

[8] J. Habermas, *Glauben und Wissen* (Frankfurt: Suhrkamp, 2001), p. 29.

[9] J. Habermas, *Glauben und Wissen*, p. 15.

[10] J. Habermas, *Glauben und Wissen*, p. 22.

mistaken life. Thus, they have a hermeneutical function for society as a whole. Religious communities, as long as they avoid dogmatism, can help society develop sensitivity for misdirected life, for societal pathologies, and for deformed societal relationships.[11] Habermas speaks of a 'complementary learning process',[12] in which secular citizens learn from the unique potential of religious traditions and religious people show readiness to engage in a critical dialogue with the secular public on the basis of reason.

Of course, this presupposes overcoming a secularist exclusive understanding of modernity, according to which religious convictions are a relic from archaic times.[13] Freedom of religion – in such a mindset – is not much more than a legal expression of something like a World Wild Life Fund activity for endangered species.[14] Habermas affirms that it is unreasonable to reject apriori the idea that world religions have a place in modernity because their cognitive value has not been fully redeemed. It cannot be excluded that they harbour a semantic potential that can inspire society as a whole.[15]

These cautious phrases show that we cannot attribute to Habermas a conversion to personal piety resulting from the wisdom of the old age. He remains an Enlightenment philosopher sceptical of all but rational arguments. But he takes the Enlightenment one step further by leaving open the possibility that religious contributions to the public debate can be a source of new insights for all people of good will, rather than only for those who share their specific religious views.

What I have shown in the work of Jürgen Habermas can also be shown in the development of the work of the American philosopher John Rawls. Rawls, at least in his later writings, does not relegate strong religious or philosophical convictions to the private realm, as many interpreters have supposed. On the contrary, as long as they are compatible with the overlapping consensus that is expressed in the constitution, they can bring life to pluralism in a democratic society.[16] For Rawls, such comprehensive doctrines, whether they are religious or non-religious, are the 'vital social basis' of reasonable political conceptions, 'giving them enduring strength and vigor'.[17]

---

[11] J. Habermas, *Zwischen Naturalismus und Religion. Philosophische Aufsätze* (Frankfurt: Suhrkamp, 2005), p. 115. Also in J. Habermas and J. Ratzinger, *Dialektik der Säkularisierung. Über Vernunft und Religion* (Freiburg, Basel, and Wien: Herder, 2005), p. 31.

[12] J. Habermas, *Zwischen Naturalismus und Religion. Philosophische Aufsätze* (Frankfurt: Suhrkamp, 2005).

[13] I have described Habermas' own development in that respect in H. Bedford-Strohm, 'Nurturing Reason: The Public Role of Religion in the Liberal State', *Ned Geref Theologiese Tydskrif* 48 (2007), pp. 25-41.

[14] J. Habermas speaks of cultural protection of the environment ('kultureller Naturschutz für aussterbende Arten'), *Zwischen Naturalismus und Religion*, p. 145.

[15] J. Habermas, *Zwischen Naturalismus und Religion*, p. 149.

[16] As Celia Deane-Drummond has shown in this volume, the public that Rawls reflects upon is constricted to the form of democracy characteristic of a nation state, rather than that between nation states.

[17] J. Rawls, *Collected Papers* (S. Freeman (ed.); Cambridge: Harvard University Press, 1999), p. 592.

These contributions normally should be presented in a language that is understandable to other traditions as well. But Rawls goes even further and sees contributions to the public debate by religious traditions *in their own language* as sometimes crucial for the development of a pluralistic society; he cites as examples the nineteenth century Christian anti-slavery movement and Martin Luther King's involvement in the civil rights movement as examples. It is, however, decisive for such contributions that good political reasons confirm what is expressed on the basis of a comprehensive moral doctrine. In the case of the Abolitionists and those in the civil rights movement this proviso was fulfilled, 'however much they emphasized the religious roots of their doctrines, because these doctrines supported basic constitutional values – as they themselves asserted – and so supported reasonable conceptions of political justice'.[18]

Rawls also sees a place for biblical language in public. He explicitly stresses the value of the public use of the biblical parable of the Good Samaritan, and adds: '... citizens who cite the Gospel parable of the Good Samaritan do not stop there, but go on to give a public justification for this parable's conclusions in terms of political values.'[19] In a footnote, especially of interest for theological ethicists, Rawls explicitly confirms and acknowledges the parallel between his difference principle and the Catholic option for the poor.[20] These examples make very clear that Rawls is far from relegating religion to a private realm; on the contrary, he sees reasonable comprehensive doctrines of religion as viable and precious agents in the public culture of a democratic society.[21]

What we have now seen is something that can hardly be overestimated in the development of recent intellectual history. The two most influential philosophers of our time have developed to a point in their thought where they now clearly acknowledge the public role of religion as a vital source for democratic civil society. At the same time, they also make clear that fulfilling this role requires the development of a theology that is compatible with the idea of public reason as a reference point for all agents of civil society.

The theology which I think best fills these plausible requirements, is 'public theology'.

---

[18] J. Rawls, *Collected Papers*, p. 593. Rawls adds in a footnote: 'I do not know whether the Abolitionists and King thought of themselves as fulfilling the purpose of the proviso. But whether they did or not, they could have. And had they known and accepted the idea of public reason, they would have' (footnote 54).

[19] J. Rawls, *Collected Papers*, p. 594.

[20] J. Rawls, *Collected Papers*, p. 594, footnote 55. This parallel was one of the central reasons for my own account of the convergence between Rawls' theory and theological ethics (*Vorrang für die Armen, Auf dem Weg zu einer theologischen Theorie der Gerechtigkeit* (Gütersloh: Gütersloher Verlagshaus, 1993), p. 306.

[21] As far as I can see, the only theologian who has really honoured this endorsement of the public role of religion by Rawls is Ronald Thiemann in his brilliant book *Religion in Public Life: A Dilemma for Democracy* (Washington D.C.: Georgetown University Press, 1996), esp. pp. 80–90, where he gives a thorough and sharp account of Rawls' development in this respect.

III. Public Theology as Liberation Theology for a Global Civil Society

In May 2007, a group of about 40 theologians from all over the world founded the Global Network for Public Theology at a conference in Princeton. It unites institutions from various contexts which are dedicated to the task of reflecting on ethical questions debated in the public discourse, investigating the response of the Christian tradition to these questions of public interest, and voicing the fruits of this research in the debates of civil society. At the same conference the new *International Journal of Public Theology* was launched which has since become the primary location for scholarly debates on public theology. As a consequence of the Princeton conference, I myself founded the 'Dietrich Bonhoeffer Research Centre for Public Theology' at the University of Bamberg in January 2008.[22]

This new momentum reflects a development in theology which takes seriously the growing importance of a global civil society and tries to root this concern in the centre of theology. One could probably say: public theology is the theological response to global civil society. I want to specify this definition by enriching it with theological content: *public theology is liberation theology for a global civil society*.

Liberation theology has generated an explosion of new thinking in theology in the last third of the twentieth century. It developed out of a context in which liberation movements were struggling against dictatorial regimes that suppressed any form of civil societal engagement. The impulse was to find liberation from the oppression of such regimes. Liberation theology, originally developing in this context in Latin America in the 1970s, was later expanded and enriched by theological reflection on the oppression of women by a patriarchal system and on the human-made destruction of nature by the dynamic of a capitalist system driven by the logic of growth. Such concerns were increasingly articulated in civil society debates. The rhetoric and basic paradigms of liberation theology, however, were

---

[22] For information in English on the Center see: http://www.uni-bamberg.de/ev-syst/leistungen/forschung/dietrich_bonhoeffer_research_center_for_public_theology_english_website/ (assessed 21 June 2010). For the paradigm of public theology see: W. F. Storrar and A. R. Morton (eds), *Public Theology for the 21st Century: Essays in Honour of Duncan Forrester* (London and New York: T&T Clark, 2004); from a South African context D. Smit, *Essays in Public Theology: Collected Essays 1* (E. Conradie (ed.); Publications of the Western Cape, Stellenbosch: Sun Academic Press, 2007). See also the programmatic first issue of the *International Journal of Public Theology*, 1 (2007). The opening article by William Storrar, 'A Kairos Moment for Public Theology', pp. 5–25, gives an insight into the development of this paradigm in the last decades. An important contribution in the earlier development is: R. Thiemann, *Constructing a Public Theology: The Church in a Pluralistic Culture* (Louisville: Westminster/John Knox Press, 1991). For a more thorough discussion of the concept and its terminological roots in the USA, France, and Germany, see also W. Vögele, *Zivilreligion in der Bundesrepublik Deutschland* (Gütersloh: Gütersloher Verlagshaus, 1994), pp. 418–425. This book is part of a German book series with the programmatic title *Öffentliche Theologie* ('public theology'), edited by W. Huber and H. Bedford-Strohm. The role of public theology in the transformation of societies has been recently explored in: C. Lienemann-Perrin and W. Lienemann (eds), *Kirche und Öffentlichkeit in Transformationsgesellschaften* (Stuttgart: Kohlhammer-Verlag, 2006).

originally shaped by a situation of suppression of democratic rights, which made open civil debate impossible, and therefore, required fundamental opposition. Theology must react to the changes that have happened since then. The African National Congress in South Africa, once a liberation movement fighting a racist regime, has now governed the country for 15 years but is still struggling with the challenge of being in the position of power with all the dilemmas involved in it. Brazil – which can be called one of the mother countries of liberation theology – has become one of the most dynamic countries in the South. Brazil's president, Lula da Silva, has been one of the icons of the liberation movements in the South and now jets between the World Economic Summit in Davos and the World Social Forum in Belem (2009). Many leaders of Latin America come from a similar background. They all share a history of fundamental criticism of oppressive regimes; however, seeking liberation from a current regime can no longer be the basis of their political involvement. Now that they are governing themselves, they need a new orientation not for resistance but for governing. They need guidance in their efforts to implement policies that are rooted in the ideals they fought for in their liberation struggle. They need to be critiqued when they are in danger of betraying their old ideals.

Ethical guidance in concrete political decisions and the critical accompaniment of governments is the task of public theology. Public theology goes beyond a fundamental critical position that is suspicious of every power and shies away from the task of giving advice to those in power. Public theology, however, also goes beyond a position that tends to adapt to the values of modern secular society. It develops a theological profile that challenges society and leads toward political structures and societal values that are inspired by the perspective of the kingdom of God and nurtured by the insights of practical reason.

A public theology that fits this design needs to be *bilingual*.[23] As its first language, it needs to speak the language of the Bible and of theological tradition, taking seriously the witness of the prophets in speaking the truth and using the parables of Jesus to inspire new insights.

As Ronald Thiemann has stated, the task is 'to show that a theology shaped by the biblical narratives and grounded in the practices of Christian community can provide resources to enable people of faith to regain a public voice in our pluralistic culture. Our challenge is to develop a public theology that remains grounded in the particularities of the Christian faith while genuinely addressing issues of public significance.'[24]

If public theology wants to fulfil this task, it needs a second language. It also needs to speak the language of reason. It needs to give explanations and insights that make its points plausible to all people of good will. It needs to be in dialogue with other disciplines like philosophy and science in order to introduce theology's

---

[23] For the historical basis of the notion of bilinguality, see E. Harasta, 'Karl Barth, A Public Theologian? The One Word and Theological "Bilinguality"', *International Journal of Public Theology* 3 (2009), pp. 188–203.

[24] R. Thiemann, *Constructing a Public Theology: The Church in a Pluralistic Culture*, p. 19.

critical voice into their debates; it also needs to learn from their insights and avoid a dogmatic approach. Such immunization against the dynamics of public debate in democratic societies would be irreconcilable with the idea of public reason as described by philosophers like John Rawls and Jürgen Habermas.[25]

If public theology is designed in this way, it can join other religious communities in giving an answer to what in the German debate has become well known as the 'Böckenförde-Dilemma'. In 1967, the German Supreme Court justice Ernst Wolfgang Böckenförde described this dilemma in words that have made a quote career in the German speaking academic world as well as in the political world, which is rather unique: *'The liberal secular state lives from sources it cannot guarantee itself'*.[26] The dilemma behind this phrase consists of the following two alternatives: either the liberal state ignores religion and runs the risk of losing its cohesive forces, or it promotes religion at the risk of losing its neutrality in religious affairs. The answer to this dilemma is the vibrant involvement of religious traditions in civil society. Public theology tries to take this task seriously. Through inter-religious dialogue it joins with other religious traditions to regenerate social cohesion in society based on an overlapping consensus of certain fundamental values.[27]

What are those fundamental values? Certainly one of those values would be social justice. Public theology introduces the powerful witness of the biblical preferential option for the poor into civil societal debate to give life to the overlapping consensus in this respect.[28] But another value, especially interesting for our theme,

---

[25] See J. Rawls, 'The Idea of Public Reason Revisited', *Collected Papers*, pp. 573–615.

[26] 'Der freiheitliche, säkularisierte Staat lebt von Voraussetzungen, die er selbst nicht garantieren kann.' E. W. Böckenförde, *Säkularisation und Utopie. Ebracher Studien. Ernst Forsthoff zum 65. Geburtstag* (Stuttgart: Kohlhammer, 1967), p. 93; and E. W. Böckenförde, *Recht, Staat, Freiheit. Studien zur Rechtsphilosophie, Staatstheorie und Verfassungsgeschichte* (Frankfurt: Suhrkamp, 2nd edn, 1992), p. 112. See W. Vögele, *Zivilreligion in der Bundesrepublik Deutschland* (Gütersloh: Gütersloher Verlagshaus, 1994), p. 183, 309. Recently Böckenförde explicitly referred to his phrase from almost 30 years ago and reaffirmed it: 'Meine nahezu vor 30 Jahren formulierte These: "Der freiheitliche säkulare Staat lebt von Voraussetzungen, die er selbst nicht garantieren kann, ohne seine Freiheitlichkeit in Frage zu stellen" halte ich nach wie vor für richtig' ('Fundamente der Freiheit', *Was hält die moderne Gesellschaft zusammen?* (E. Teufel (ed.); Frankfurt: Suhrkamp 1996), pp. 89–99 (89)).

[27] I have dealt with the public role of religion in a democratic society more thoroughly elsewhere; see H. Bedford-Strohm, 'Nurturing Reason: The Public Role of Religion in the Liberal State', pp. 25–41. See also H. Bedford-Strohm, 'Theological Ethics and the Church: Reconsidering the Boundaries Between Practical Theology and Theological Ethics in Light of the Debate on Liberalism and Communitarianism', *Reconsidering the Boundaries Between Theological Disciplines. Zur Neubestimmung der Grenzen zwischen den theologischen Disziplinen* (M. Welker and F. Schweitzer (eds); Münster: Lit, 2005), pp. 175–186.

[28] See for a more thorough treatment: H. Bedford-Strohm, 'Poverty and Public Theology: Advocacy of the Church in Pluralistic Society', *International Journal of Public Theology* 2 (2008), pp. 144–162.

IV. Public Theology and the Minimization of Violence against Nature

I do not have to describe here the developments that have led to the situation in which human domination of nature threatens to destroy the very basis of human and non-human life, which has developed for billions of years. Larry Rasmussen, in his book *Earth Ethics, Earth Community*, has used the metaphor of a ten-volume encyclopaedia in which the history of the cosmos is written down. Even if we skip the first two-thirds of the development of the universe, we still have five billion years in the ten volumes. If each volume is 500 pages thick, every page tells the story of one million years. The most amazing insight of this metaphor concerns the place of humankind and its activities in the development of the universe. Humankind shows up on page 499 of the last volume. The last two words of the last page tell the story of human civilization; the story of the human destruction of nature begins with the last syllable of the last word of the last volume.[29]

This metaphor shows with impressive clarity how humankind has only recently captured the earth, subjecting it to human interests. The immense time spans, which climate researchers introduce into the public debate to show how climate change is human-made, currently give an especially clear idea of this insight. The role of Christian tradition in this development has been the subject of intense debate. Lynn White[30] and Carl Amery[31] both have tried to argue that it is the biblical idea of the dominion of the earth ('dominium terrae', Gen. 1.28) that is mainly to blame for nature's destruction.

This accusation underlines all the more the task of public theology in the public debate on ecological questions. I want to respond to this task by giving five guidelines for theology and for churches in their activity in the public debate. The first directly reacts to the debate concerning Christianity's role in generating the ecological crisis.

a. A Public Theology of Ecology must Reclaim its own Traditions
If it is true that biblical texts like Genesis 1.28 have played a role in the cultural history of the occident with its seizure of nature, the very first task of a public theology is to reclaim its own traditions. It has to critically question the use of its traditions to legitimate political and economic developments that arise from very different motives. The relevance of this theological enterprise can therefore not be

---

[29] L. L. Rasmussen, *Earth Community, Earth Ethics* (Geneva: WCC Publications, 1996), pp. 27–28.
[30] L. White, 'The Historical Roots of Our Ecological Crisis', *Science* 155 (1967), pp.1203–1207.
[31] C. Amery, *Das Ende der Vorsehung. Die gnadenlosen folgen des Christentums* (Reinbek: Rowohlt, 1972).

limited to the academic discipline of theology. Since these biblical texts are part of the cultural memory of the occident, and have deeply influenced Western culture, this task is clearly of public relevance.

Biblical scholarship in the last several decades[32] and the ecological theology based on it and developed by scholars such as Günther Altner,[33] Gerhard Liedke[34] and Jürgen Moltmann,[35] has shown that the subjugation of nature was generated by a human self-centeredness that stands in sharp contrast to biblical intentions. These theologians have emphasized that the modern destruction of nature is a perversion of the call to dominion in the Bible. The call for human dominion over the earth in Genesis 1.28, they argue, has to be seen in the context of God's creation of human beings in the image of God, whereby being in the image of God is irreconcilable with any destructive use of the earth. In his famous Genesis commentary, Claus Westermann shows that in the Hebrew Bible the 'dominium' of a king, in which the king uses his subjects purely as instruments for his own egoistic purposes, is unthinkable.[36] For a king, there is always a moment of care for his subjects, an acknowledgment which can be made despite well argued feminist concerns against the use of monarchical language here. The task of a king, given to him by God, is to protect the rights of his people, especially its weakest members. Likewise, the concept of dominion over the earth can be adequately understood only if the element of care for the earth is included. Robert Murray suggests that the background of Genesis 1.26–28 'makes it clear that the verbs commonly translated 'subdue' (*kbs*) and 'have dominion' (*rdh*) have been understood too crudely by those who say that they both connote violent subjection without implying limits on how humans may treat other creatures.'[37] Thus, Genesis 1.28 must be interpreted in light of Genesis 2.15, which gives human beings the task of 'tilling and keeping' the earth.

From this perspective it becomes evident that biblical texts cannot function as legitimizers of an anthropocentrism of interests, which views non-human nature, primarily or even exclusively, not as a means to satisfy human needs but as something with dignity independent of humanity. Nature is created not by humanity but by God. If human beings see themselves as created by God, they must acknowledge the independent dignity of a non-human creation equally created by God. Simply making nature the object of human interests is therefore theologically excluded, an insight which, once acknowledged, would be of enormous public significance.

---

[32] See especially C. Westermann, *Genesis 1–11* (Minneapolis: Augsburg Fortress Press, 1994).
[33] G. Altner, *Schöpfung am Abgrund. Die Theologie vor der Umweltfrage* (Neukirchen-Vluyn: Neukirchener Verlag, 1974).
[34] G. Liedke, *Im Bauch des Fisches: Ökologische Theologie* (Stuttgart: Kreuz, 1979).
[35] J. Moltmann, *Gott in der Schöpfung: Ökologische Schöpfungslehre* (München: Kaiser, 1985).
[36] C. Westermann, *Genesis 1–11*, p. 227.
[37] R. Murray, *The Cosmic Covenant: Biblical Themes of Justice, Peace and the Integrity of Creation* (Piscataway, N. J.: Gorgias Press, 2007), p. 99.

b. A Public Theology of Ecology must Acknowledge the Conflict between Human Beings and Non-Human Nature

A theological view of nature, understood as God's creation, must be distinguished from a romantic perspective on nature. Such a romantic perspective is nurtured by the awe we feel when we look at how beautiful our natural environment is. Each one of us probably knows this feeling of awe which leads to a deeper understanding of the wonders of nature and which points towards something beyond human understanding. This awe is indeed very biblical. 'O God, how manifold are your works! In wisdom you have made them all; the earth is full of your creatures', exclaims Psalm 104.24. Nature is seen as a wonder of God that glorifies God's name. The potential of such awe to fuel the desire to protect the environment should not be underestimated.

And yet, the Bible knows very well that there is also a conflict between human beings and nature. Nature is also seen as a destructive power against which God has to protect human beings. 'I placed the sand as a boundary for the sea, a perpetual barrier that it cannot pass; though the waves toss, they cannot prevail, though they roar, they cannot pass over it' (Jer. 5.22). God's continuing creation is an effort to overcome chaos, or, to put it differently, to minimize violence. The vision of animal peace in Isaiah 65.25 describes a new heaven and a new earth in which 'the wolf and the lamb shall feed together, the lion shall eat straw like the ox; but the serpent – its food shall be dust! They shall not hurt or destroy on all my holy mountain, says the LORD.' There is violence in nature and the eschatological vision of overcoming it all the more underlines its existence in the present world.

While the biblical texts reflect a situation in which human beings have to be defended against the violent power, the situation is now reversed. Human beings have developed such enormous power over nature that nature has to be defended against human beings. Nevertheless, it is very clear that the conflict between humans and nature and within nature has to be accounted for. A romantic view of nature is therefore neither accurate nor biblical.

This insight is part of our everyday experience. Let me give an example. We all know that academic conferences – including those discussing the ecological reorientation of global society – result in massive violence against nature. Most of us have flown to Finland to participate, despite the well-known consequences for the environment. We are here anyway because we think personal exchange and a widening of our horizons is even more important than what we do with it to nature. And it leads us to a much more fundamental insight: human civilization, as such, necessarily means violence against nature. The promise to live in harmony with nature – let me say this clearly – is a false promise if we think we can achieve it in the here and now. What we can achieve is the minimization of violence against nature. Images of harmony with nature have their place as an eschatological inspiration for the minimization of violence in the here and now. If they obscure our view of the conflictive dimension of life in nature, they become counterproductive.

Why this is so will be more evident when we look at the third guideline.

c. A Public Theology of Ecology must Acknowledge Political Dilemma Situations

If civil societal engagement by religious communities uses harmonistic images of nature, it speaks over the heads of those responsible for political decisions. Political life – and this is especially evident in ecological questions – is permanently confronted with dilemma situations. A theology that does not acknowledge such dilemma situations, or does not even have a language for those situations, cannot be a *public* theology. In neglecting such dilemma situations, theology not only fails to do justice to the situation, it also fails to do justice to the parties involved. Here is an example. The reorientation of the energy production of a country towards regenerative forms of energy is one of the most burning issues of our time. There is no doubt that it is an important part of a political strategy to minimize violence against nature. And there is good evidence that in the long run it also will be good for jobs in a national economy. It is equally clear that there is a need for a massive reconstruction of the economy that may result in real people losing their jobs. If we ignore the negative consequences of certain ecological strategies for certain people, we not only fail to do justice to them but we also lose credibility in political debates. Only if we acknowledge the dilemmas connected with them, can we develop strategies – like social support measures for those affected – to deal with them. The danger of ignoring the negative consequences of ecological reforms for real people far away from the contexts of those who envision the reforms should not be underestimated.

However, the acceptance of ecological inputs in the global civil societal debate is not only dependant on the realism with which it is being presented, it also depends on an assessment of the value ecology of our societies.

d. A Public Theology of Ecology must Critically Reflect Fundamental Socio-Cultural Values

The best political proposals will not succeed if their socio-cultural undertones are ignored. Religious contributions to civil society are especially sensitive to the deep value dimension of our daily priority decisions. It is evident that the question of how we define wealth in our societies depends on how we assess the value of human brotherhood and sisterhood or the relationship between our own wellbeing and the wellbeing of our literal neighbours. It also depends on whether we have a utilitarian individualist view of nature, in which nature is an instrument for furthering our anthropocentric interests, or whether we believe that nature has dignity in itself and, therefore, advocate for an anthropocentrism of responsibility which leads to an ethic of human self-limitation towards nature.[38] Thus, alongside the continuing work of political reform and the structural reorientation of society, the crucial task is the reorientation of societal values to minimize violence toward nature. Public theology is in the forefront of such endeavour.

With all this in mind, public theology needs to become very concrete.

---

[38] For this distinction, see W. Huber, *Konflikt und Konsens* (München: Kaiser, 1990), pp. 231f.

e. A Public Theology of Ecology must Induce Guidance for Concrete Political Decisions

Public theologians profit from being rooted in social and political practices. If they are familiar with political discussions and are in some way close to the political process, for example, by being involved in political parties, by working in political initiatives, or even by getting regularly engaged in political discussions in their own circles, they acquire an intuition for the validity of political proposals which goes beyond the knowledge of books. This is an important ingredient for the substance of ethical guidance that public theology tries to give to the political process. If the consequence of a public theology of ecology is a concrete proposal for an ecological tax reform, it is important to know the places from which critical responses are to be expected. Entrepreneurs in energy-intensive production might not be the only ones to oppose this proposal; family lobbyists could also complain that another tax on consumer products would burden large families dependent on such products and increase their already high mobility costs.

The more these often hidden consequences are considered in the concrete proposals presented, the more credible such proposals are as expressions of a theological ethical view. It is obvious that public theology cannot be equally competent in all concrete political issues. Public theology needs to be engaged in interdisciplinary research and rooted enough in concrete political contexts that it exemplarily shows its proposals can be realized and are able to promote the ethical goals they contain. Even if working out such proposals can rarely be done by public theology itself, it must be principally possible on its basis.

V. Conclusion

We have now seen how public theology potentially can make an impact on public opinion in a civil society. Whether this programmatic claim also has an empirical basis is difficult to say. However, what can be said on the basis of new empirical scholarship is that there is a clear positive correlation between religious beliefs and increased engagement in ecological issues. Recently, empirical data, generated biannually by the ministry of environmental affairs on environmental awareness in Germany, was, for the first time, analyzed in light of the levels of religious belief. As Udo Kuckartz, the director of the research programme discovered, religious people are more aware of global climate change and its consequences, are more engaged in protecting the integrity of their environments, less often hold the view that environmental problems are exaggerated, and exhibit higher levels of voluntary engagement in the environment.[39]

Such religiously-based attitudes and preferences provide the background for the public theological activities which already can be identified in some of the

---

[39] U. Kuckartz, 'Leben im Einklang mit der Natur. Einsichten aus der Sozialwissenschaft', *Und Gott sah, dass es gut war: Schöpfung und Endlichkeit im Zeitalter der Klimakatastrophe* (H. Bedford-Strohm (ed.); Neukirchen-Vluyn: Neukirchener Verlag, 2009), pp. 59–69 (68).

involvement of Bavarian church groups or institutions in civil society. This involvement has a clear theological profile; for example, in Bavaria regular public prayers are held by the river Danube as part of the activities to protect its natural shape. However, it also includes engagement in discussions beyond religious language at various levels. It does not shy away from building alliances with concrete political forces; for example, the 'Bavarian climate alliance', formed by the Bavarian government and various civil society associations as well as the churches, promotes ecological awareness and strategies against climate change.[40] Finally, public theological involvement connects respect for creation with concrete political proposals, such as the banning of genetically modified seeds from Bavarian farmland. There is good reason to suppose that the remarkable ecological turn of the Bavarian minister for environmental affairs was at least influenced by the public theology-based involvement of churches in environmental affairs.

These experiences from my home church in Bavaria are only examples of activities performed by churches all over the world; these activities are often much too timid and cautious, sometimes courageous and clear. These activities, however, indicate a potential for change that should not be underestimated. Churches are connected in a unique worldwide network and can be a strong force in the move towards a global ecological reorientation of civilization and the political changes which are involved in it. The new heaven and the new earth that Christians are expecting can certainly not be reduced to earthly ecological healing, but such earthly ecological healing is equally a clear sign of the very visible consequences of this great vision.

Bibliography

Altner G., *Schöpfung am Abgrund. Die Theologie vor der Umweltfrage* (Neukirchen-Vluyn: Neukirchener Verlag, 1974).

Amery C., *Das Ende der Vorsehung. Die gnadenlosen folgen des Christentums* (Reinbek: Rowohlt, 1972).

Bayerisches Staatsministerium für Umwelt und Gesundheit, http://www.stmug. bayern.de/umwelt/klimaschutz/allianz/ (assessed 15 March 2010).

Bedford-Strohm, H., 'Die Entdeckung der Ökologie in der ökumenischen Bewegung', *Hoffnungswege. Wegweisende Impulse des Ökumenischen Rates der Kirchen aus sechs Jahrzehnten* (H. G. Link and G. Müller-Fahrenholz (eds); Frankfurt: Otto Lembeck, 2008), pp. 321–347.

—'Nurturing Reason: The Public Role of Religion in the Liberal State', *Ned Geref Theologiese Tydskrif* 48 (2007), pp. 25–41.

—'Poverty and Public Theology: Advocacy of the Church in Pluralistic Society', *International Journal of Public Theology* 2 (2008), pp. 144–162.

—*Schöpfung* (Göttingen: Vandenhoeck & Ruprecht, 2001).

—'Theological Ethics and the Church: Reconsidering the Boundaries Between

---

[40] See Bayerisches Staatsministerium für Umwelt und Gesundheit, http://www.stmug.bayern. de/umwelt/klimaschutz/allianz/ (assessed 15 March 2010).

Practical Theology and Theological Ethics in Light of the Debate on Liberalism and Communitarianism', *Reconsidering the Boundaries Between Theological Disciplines. Zur Neubestimmung der Grenzen zwischen den theologischen Disziplinen* (M. Welker and F. Schweitzer (eds); Münster: Lit, 2005), pp. 175–186.

— 'Tilling and Caring for the Earth: Public Theology and Ecology', *International Journal of Public Theology* 1 (2007), pp. 230–248.

— *Vorrang für die Armen, Auf dem Weg zu einer theologischen Theorie der Gerechtigkeit* (Gütersloh: Gütersloher Verlagshaus, 1993).

Bergmann, S., *Creation Set Free: The Spirit as Liberator of Nature* (D. Stott (trans.); Grand Rapids and Cambridge: William B. Eerdmans Publishing Company, 2005).

Böckenförde, E. W, 'Fundamente der Freiheit', *Was hält die moderne Gesellschaft zusammen?* (E. Teufel (ed.); Frankfurt: Suhrkamp, 1996), pp. 89–99.

— *Recht, Staat, Freiheit. Studien zur Rechtsphilosophie, Staatstheorie und Verfassungsgeschichte* (Frankfurt: Suhrkamp, 2nd edn, 1992).

— *Säkularisation und Utopie. Ebracher Studien. Ernst Forsthoff zum 65. Geburtstag* (Stuttgart: Kohlhammer, 1967).

Ferguson, A., *Versuch über die Geschichte der bürgerlichen Gesellschaft* (Frankfurt: Suhrkamp, 1988).

Gellner, E., *Bedingungen der Freiheit. Die Zivilgesellschaft und ihre Rivalen* (Stuttgart: Klett-Cotta, 1995).

Habermas, J., *Faktizität und Geltung. Beiträge zur Diskurstheorie des Rechts und des demokratischen Rechtsstaates* (Frankfurt: Suhrkamp, 1992).

— *Glauben und Wissen* (Frankfurt: Suhrkamp, 2001).

— *Zwischen Naturalismus und Religion. Philosophische Aufsätze* (Frankfurt: Suhrkamp, 2005).

Habermas, J., and J. Ratzinger, *Dialektik der Säkularisierung. Über Vernunft und Religion* (Freiburg, Basel, and Wien: Herder, 2005).

Harasta, E., 'Karl Barth, A Public Theologian? The One Word and Theological "Bilinguality"', *International Journal of Public Theology* 3 (2009), pp. 188–203.

Huber, W., *Konflikt und Konsens: Studien zur Ethik der Verantwortung* (München: Kaiser, 1990).

Kuckartz, U., 'Leben im Einklang mit der Natur. Einsichten aus der Sozialwissenschaft', *Und Gott sah, dass es gut war: Schöpfung und Endlichkeit im Zeitalter der Klimakatastrophe* (H. Bedford-Strohm (ed.); Neukirchen-Vluyn: Neukirchener Verlag, 2009), pp. 59–69.

Liedke G., *Im Bauch des Fisches: Ökologische Theologie* (Stuttgart: Kreuz, 1979).

Lienemann-Perrin, C., and W. Lienemann (eds), *Kirche und Öffentlichkeit in Transformationsgesellschaften* (Stuttgart: Kohlhammer-Verlag, 2006).

Moltmann J., *Gott in der Schöpfung: Ökologische Schöpfungslehre* (München: Kaiser, 1985).

Murray, R., *The Cosmic Covenant: Biblical Themes of Justice, Peace and the Integrity of Creation* (Piscataway, N.J.: Gorgias Press, 2007).

Rasmussen L., *Earth Community, Earth Ethics* (Geneva: WCC Publications, 1996).

Rawls, J., *Collected Papers* (S. Freeman (ed.); Cambridge: Harvard University Press, 1999).
Smit, D., *Essays in Public Theology: Collected Essays 1* (E. Conradie (ed.); Publications of the Western Cape, Stellenbosch: Sun Academic Press, 2007).
Soosten, J. v., 'Civil Society: Zum Auftakt der neueren demokratietheoretischen Debatte mit einem Seitenblick auf Religion, Kirche und Öffentlichkeit (Literaturbericht)', *ZEE* 37 (1993), pp. 139-157.
Storrar, W. F., 'A Kairos Moment for Public Theology', *International Journal of Public Theology* 1 (2007), pp. 5-25.
Storrar W. F., and A. R. Morton, *Public Theology for the 21st Century: Essays in Honour of Duncan Forrester* (London and New York: T&T Clark, 2004).
Thiemann, R., *Constructing a Public Theology: The Church in a Pluralistic Culture* (Louisville: Westminster/John Knox Press, 1991).
—*Religion in Public Life: A Dilemma for Democracy* (Washington D.C.: Georgetown University Press, 1996).
Vögele, W., *Zivilreligion in der Bundesrepublik Deutschland* (Gütersloh: Gütersloher Verlagshaus, 1994).
Welker, M., *Kirche im Pluralismus* (Gütersloh: Gütersloher Verlagshaus, 1995).
Westermann C., *Genesis 1-11* (Minneapolis: Augsburg Fortress Press, 1994).
White, L., 'The Historical Roots of Our Ecological Crisis', *Science* 155 (1967), pp.1203-1207.

3 Right Out of Time? Politics and Nature in a Postnatural Condition

Peter Manley Scott
Lincoln Theological Institute, University of Manchester, UK

I. Introduction

We live in a *camera obscura* world, in which everything is upside down. A *camera obscura* is a type of basic projector in which a camera can be rotated 360° and the image is projected onto a concave screen. Crucially, the image is upside down; the view is comprehensive but the image is reversed.[1] The camera provides a full but topsy-turvy view. The appearance is one of an all-round view; the reality...

What do I mean by using this image of a *camera obscura*? It is my contention that city-dwelling northerners experience everyday living in a way that fundamentally mis-recognizes the ecological dependencies of our situation. For us, our experience of ecological matters is upside down: we fail to appreciate the range and quality of our dependencies on our environment. And precisely because they are upside down, these matters are ignorable.[2] As a result, we may come to see ourselves as a force of occupation in a built environment. We live in 'a zone of hard surfaces, engineered to get the world to conform to our expectations of it'.[3]

Perhaps the switch goes something like this: humanity appears to be standing on a platform and the world is then understood to be that which bends to our purposes. That, indeed, is how we northerners live our lives. Ecologically, the matter is different: human life is more precarious and more dependent than we urban dwellers tend to appreciate. Is this an accurate characterization of part of the Northern circumstance: we live in a *camera obscura* world in which ecological matters can be ignored?

Politics also struggles to acknowledge ecological matters. Here is an example of how we find these ecological matters ignorable at the level of politics. At its October

---

[1] Famously, Marx and Engels use this image in *The German Ideology* (London: Lawrence & Wishart, 2nd edn, 1974), p. 47.
[2] P. M. Scott, 'The City's Grace? Recycling the Urban Ecology', *International Journal of Public Theology* 2 (2008), pp. 123–25.
[3] Ibid., p. 123.

2008 meeting, the leaders of the European Union were confronted by two matters: making a response to turbulence in the financial markets and setting targets for carbon emissions. While there was some agreement on actions to fix the first, there was little agreement on the second. This presents us with a question: Why is it so difficult for ecological issues such as climate change to be matters of public concern? Why is it so difficult for long-term ecological constraints to emerge fully in public discourse?[4] We oftentimes sense urgency here: that we might be right out of time is perhaps beginning to dawn us. Phrases such as 'runaway climate change', 'tipping points' and 'points of no return' – with their apocalyptic overtones – are becoming more common.[5] Yet, the debate on ecological constraints has little public impact in terms of political commitments to binding targets on emissions. The curious outcome of the UN meeting, COP15, on climate change, held in Copenhagen in December 2009, points to the same conclusion.

The comparison with the present finance/banking crisis is instructive, in my view: the British government, for example, declares that it will 'stand behind the banks' and 'do whatever it takes' to maintain the (security of the?) banking system. According to the UK Budget 2009 report, *Building Britain's Future*, the Special Liquidity Scheme involves the loan of £185 billion from the HM Treasury to the Bank of England and a loan of £123 billion in the Direct Support to Banks scheme.[6] The cost of this remains unknown, depending on how much of the loan is paid back, and over what time period. Yet, we do not hear this kind of rhetoric about the environment. As we negotiate the in-betweeness of nature, our interweaving or entanglement with other creatures, it may be wise to acknowledge our ecological interdependencies in the sense of developing a rhetorical position that says we stand with or in our environment, and acknowledge that the state stands behind our environment in a metaphorical and secondary sense, that is, of conserving or preserving natural resources. (It is metaphorical because human political activity is always ecological activity; and it is secondary because the resources to which the state seeks to control access are not renewable by the state.)

In this essay, I argue that if we are to address our *camera obscura* circumstances, then two conditions must be fulfilled. The first condition is political and the second condition is metaphysical.[7] The political condition requires that there is some sort of

---

[4] News report dated 3 April 2009: 'The US must balance science with what is politically and technologically achievable on climate change, America's lead negotiator has said. Speaking at UN talks in Bonn, Jonathan Pershing said the US must not offer more than it could deliver by 2020. Poor countries said the latest science showed rich states should cut emissions by 40 per cent on 1990 levels by 2020. President Barack Obama's plan merely to stabilize greenhouse gases at 1990 levels by 2020 is much less ambitious.' http://news.bbc.co.uk/1/hi/sci/tech/7980441.stm (accessed 1 May 2009).

[5] See C. Russell and Z. Nyssa, 'The Tipping Point Trend in Climate Change Communication', *Global Environmental Change* 19 (2009), pp. 336–344. I thank Stefan Skrimshire for drawing my attention to this reference.

[6] HM Treasury, UK Budget 2009 report, *Building Britain's Future*, available online at www.hm-treasury.gov.uk/bud_bud09_index.htm *(accessed 2 May 2009).*

[7] R. W. Jenson, 'Is There an Ordering Principle?', *Essays in the Theology of Culture* (Grand Rapids, MI: Eerdmans, 1995), pp. 67–75 (70–75).

public space or sphere to which the religions might make a contribution. In the first part of the paper, I explore this condition through a brief discussion of the 'secular'. The metaphysical condition I consider by attempting to develop an account of a postnatural condition in which what is common to human creatures includes nature or includes the ecological. To think and act in a postnatural condition is to affirm that the human of course exceeds the natural – this is a *post*natural condition – and yet as post*natural*, the human can never be separated from its entanglements with nature. Of course, metaphysics and politics can never be separated. So, in the final section I explore the intersection of these two by indicating some implications of what I call postnatural right – a new concept that I explicate in the fifth section and following – for the public sphere.

II. The Political Condition: Public Sphere and Religion, and Ecology

In order to address the matter of a political condition, we need to consider the nature of the public realm of Western democracies. For example, Hent De Vries has helpfully argued that we should be suspicious of a public realm understood in terms of 'autonomy, neutrality and homogeneity'[8] – this understanding of the state as autonomous, neutral, and homogeneous is a recent development, he argues, and is central to the state's self-presentation as 'secular'.

What is meant by secular in this context? As analysed by Rowan Williams, in a strong form of the secular, a secular society conducts its debates by way of a public reason on which all are agreed. For this strong form, religions are troubling because religious arguments are, it is claimed, based on revelation rather than reason. Such religious arguments are sourced in an epistemological 'elsewhere', and so are not challengeable by those who do not accept the existence of this 'elsewhere'.[9] And with this suspicion of revelation often comes the suspicion that the religions wish to promote an agenda for society, whereas a liberal polity operates rather to maximize the life choices of individuals. Religions always wish to propose an agenda – a normative agenda – for society, so the criticism goes. (The word, theocracy, gets shouted out at this point.) The religious contribution is thereby under-determined epistemologically and over-determined morally; the religious contribution is not public but proposes what is good for all.

Of course, we do not need to understand the secular in this strong way. Nor do we need to understand religions and the secular as externally related or as opposed. One helpful way is to propose a difference between 'programmatic' and 'procedural' secularism, as argued by Rowan Williams.[10] Programmatic secularism

---

[8] H. De Vries, 'Introduction: Before, Around and Beyond the Theologico-Political', *Political Theologies: Public Religions in a Post-Secular World* (H. De Vries, and L. E. Sullivan (eds); Fordham: Fordham University Press, 2006), p. 75.

[9] I set aside the matter of whether this is a convincing objection.

[10] R. Williams, 'Secularism, Faith and Freedom', *The New Visibility of Religion* (G. Ward and M. Hoelzl (eds); London: Continuum, 2008), pp. 45–56 (47–49). See also G. Ward, *The Politics of Discipleship: Becoming Postmaterial Citizens* (Grand Rapids, MI: Baker Academic, 2009), pp. 120–21.

is suspicious of transformative versions of human flourishing. It regards these as wishing to enforce a view of the good life on society. The problem with such a programmatic approach is that it appears to rule out all substantive discussion of the common good – apart from, that is, what is required for 'a minimal account of material security and relative social stability'.[11] The public sphere is empty.

Once the secular is understood *procedurally*, however, the way is open to consider the public realm in terms of its diversity. Here the public sphere is full of argument from a range of positions. Of course, no one position is permanently privileged and it remains a matter of open possibility that cherished positions maintained by religious groups will not be accepted under this procedural secularism. It is the task of the state here to operate the procedures, so to speak, to the advantage of the public conversation. All that is required of religious traditions is that their contributions be understandable to others; neither the source nor the acceptability of such contributions is here in question.

If the public realm is only procedurally secular, we may then understand the public realm by reference to a range of traditions. (In this sense, I suppose, the secular is also a tradition.) That is, the public realm is *constituted* by traditions. And included in this constitution is a variety of religious traditions. It is important to note that there is a clear link between such traditions and the law as a codified form of an overlapping consensus formed by those traditions.[12] The understanding that law is a varied concept that does not exclude traditions can be gleaned by reviewing Cicero's presentation of natural law, as offered by A. P. D'Entrèves, and noting the ways in which distinctions offered by Ulpian, Gaius and Paulus differ.[13] There is more variation in natural law than is often considered. Moreover, there is Hobbes' caustic point that we are not ruled by law but by men. That is, laws are made by men – preferably the sovereign – and so even under the law by men, men are ruled.[14] The reminder of humans as fabricators of the law is well-taken. Yet we must also remember that laws are not invented out of nothing but made out of traditions.[15]

In other words, I am proposing that the public realm is not best understood as a pre-constituted whole to which a range of traditions – including religious traditions – are externally related. Instead, I want to argue that the whole of the public sphere is internally constituted by the traditions that comprise it. In this more dialectical understanding, these traditions are not externally related to the public sphere but

---

[11] R. Williams, 'Secularism, Faith and Freedom', p. 47.
[12] See also the discussion of Habermas in H. Bedford-Strohm, 'Public Theology of Ecology and Civil Society', this volume.
[13] A. P. D'Entrèves, *Natural Law: An Historical Survey* (New York: Harper Torchbooks, 1951), pp. 21–26.
[14] A. P. Martinich, *Hobbes: A Biography* (Cambridge: Cambridge University Press, 1999), p. 50.
[15] And law is central to the western monotheisms: see R. Brague, *The Law of God: The Philosophical History of an Idea* (Chicago & London: University of Chicago Press, 2008).

are instead constitutive of it.[16] Of course, the dominant religious tradition that has played a significant role in the development of the public sphere in Europe is Christianity. This history is why the European Union struggles to work out how to recognize Turkey, with its Islamic history.

I propose, then, to understand the public sphere as secular and yet also as open: constituted by many traditions, including religious traditions. Thereby, I wish to explore, first, the place of religious traditions as the proposers of a politics, and as recommenders of the political based in the theological. In other words, I am working from the position that there is an intimate relationship between the political and the theological; there is always a conditioning and reciprocal interaction between power and salvation.[17] And, furthermore, theological traditions might have a contribution to make to the re-consideration of the politics of nature. Of course, there is more than one level from which this issue can be addressed. One common distinction differentiates between 'politics' and 'the political': politics refers to governance, and the political to the basic structures through which political power is exercised. In what I have to say, I am working almost exclusively at the level of the political. That is, space is opened for engaging theological traditions of thinking about the political and relating this to our political understandings of nature.

In order to address the matter of a political condition, we need, second, to explore the relationship between public sphere and *ecology*. When I challenge the understanding of the public sphere as autonomous, neutral and homogeneous, I mean to offer that challenge also from an ecological perspective. So we need to understand the public sphere as less autonomous, neutral and homogeneous – by reference to ecology. That is, to grasp the public sphere in three different ways: as relative/interdependent, as disputational/confessional/traditioned and as heterogeneous/diverse by reference to some concept of nature. Why is this important?

In my view, it is damage to our ecologies that raises the question most sharply about the task of the public sphere. I have already made the religious point that a secular polity does not need to deny all substantive discussion and claim that its function is the narrow one of maximising the choices of individuals. Indeed, it must no longer deny and narrow. Why so? For crises in our ecologies raise the matter of goods-in-common: that the choices of individuals have an impact on goods-in-common, and we shall need some agreement on how to use these. The decision to travel by plane is a good example: air travel makes the highest contribution to CO_2 emissions of all types of transport, and makes a contribution greater than that of domestic use. As such, a non-renewable resource is being used up, and causing a contribution to a changing climate. We shall need to make decisions as to how this sort of travelling is to be restricted; that is, how our choices are going to be restricted. If this is to be done fairly, then some agreement on what it is to access goods-in-common will, I consider, be required.

---

[16] G. Ward, *The Politics of Discipleship*, p. 133, n. 57, on the problems of conceiving civil society today.
[17] P. M. Scott, 'Politics and the New Visibility of Theology', *The New Visibility of Religion* (G. Ward, and M. Hoelzl (eds); London: Continuum, 2008), p. 170.

III. Re-considering Nature: The Role of Nature in our Politics

So far I have argued that one problem that European politics faces today is to consider the presence of nature in our politics. At the present, economy trumps ecology. And this is a strange phenomenon, given that both are constitutive of the human *oikos*. We need then to focus on the deployment of the concept of nature in our politics in its variety. And doing this will lead to a re-appraisal of what we mean by the public sphere. For this public sphere will need to be re-thought in reference both to ecology and to the religions; that in some fashion the public sphere will need to be re-naturalized and de-secularized.

Given the example above from the work of the EU, we have seen that polity and *oikos* are often held to be separate. In other words, that politics does not include the natural. In this essay, by contrast, I try to develop the notion of the postnatural in which 'the political'[18] is re-considered along with the natural. I try to develop a demand for a re-institutionalization of nature in which the question is asked: 'what form of polity best provides a rich, flourishing human life'.[19] Moreover, in our postnatural circumstance, we shall need to expand this question: What form of polity, we might say, provides for a rich, flourishing life for humans *and others*? What is required here, as John Ely suggests, is the re-thinking of a 'way of life' in more comprehensive ways than heretofore; a move in thinking towards a postnatural way of life.

Before we do that, however, we must attend to my second condition: the metaphysical. Such consideration of metaphysics is not alien to European traditions of thought. The histories of natural law and natural right, for example, may be understood as histories of the metaphysical interactions between politics and nature. Here are some examples of this metaphysical history. Sometimes the *natural* refers to that which is to be contrasted with human making, as in a distinction between natural law and positive law (Aquinas). Sometimes *natural* refers to that which unites all peoples or that which all peoples share (Roman law). On other occasions, a *natural* condition of humankind refers to a postpolitical circumstance from which the sovereignty of the monarch, agreed to by all parties as part of a social contract, rescues people (Hobbes). Or, the *natural* condition of humanity may refer to that natural state that secures human freedom and private property (Locke). As A. P. D'Entrèves writes of the history of natural law: '... the history of the law of nature is really nothing else than the history of the idea of nature in law and in politics'.[20]

Why do we make reference in our politics to nature? There are two levels to an answer to this question. First, an epistemological point is easily made: when trying to determine in what ways humanity is a political animal, it is instructive to reflect

---

[18] P. M. Scott, 'Politics and the New Visibility of Theology', p. 171.
[19] J. Ely, 'Ernst Bloch, Natural Right and the Greens', *Minding Nature: The Philosophers of Ecology* (D. Macauley (ed.); New York: Guilford, 1996), pp. 134–166 (134).
[20] A. P. D'Entrèves, *Natural Law: An Historical Survey* (New York: Harper Torchbooks, 1951), p. 11.

on what humanity might be when placed beyond such political society. Does understanding a pre-political humanity in some fashion help in thinking politically about the human? Reference to nature or the natural state of the human offers a contrast to the human as a political animal.

From the epistemological point, we may move towards a second, normative, level. Here we encounter my metaphysical condition. And this is the important point I want to make. For reference to nature in our politics is a way of indicating that in our politics nature encounters us; that humanity and nature are, so to speak, the outcome of these encounters. If we are to develop some ecological notion of the common good, then that good must be available to be known; that is, it must be intersubjective. As Robert Jenson puts this matter, 'But if there is to be a common good, then the good must be known, not only decreed but discovered, not only willed but also apprehended'.[21] Traditionally, nature has functioned in our politics to indicate what is discoverable in our politics. What is fascinating is why nature is referred to in specific ways, and the work it does in the defence of different types of politics. Indeed, we might agree with Noberto Bobbio that nature is one of the sources of legitimization in politics.[22] Appeal to a concept of nature offers a grounding of our politics in that which precedes our politics.

To pursue this issue of a metaphysical condition, we need to enquire which sort of metaphysics we are dealing with here. Indeed, we need to ask *why* we keep making the distinction between the natural and the artificial, and *why* we apply it in the ways we do in our politics. In this chapter, I offer an example from the history of political philosophy in the work of the seventeenth century English philosopher, Thomas Hobbes. His argument from the state of nature or, more accurately, the 'natural condition of mankind' has been deeply influential in English-language political philosophy.

Indeed, I hold the view that despite its high importance in English language political philosophy, the contribution of Hobbes is not adequately described as the continuation of the natural law tradition as received out of medieval Catholicism. For Hobbes, as we shall see, distinguishes the objective and subjective in the notion of right, thereby driving apart liberty and law. Indeed, from a continental European perspective, and whatever the many differences, even in the work of Kant a sense of the objective is maintained by its reference to *ius* as a 'total situation of external lawfulness'.[23] Moreover, this point may be reinforced by reporting the aim of natural law thinking as presented by John Finnis: 'A theory of natural law claims to be able to identify conditions and principles of natural right-mindedness, of good and proper order among men and in individual conduct'.[24] When we consider Hobbes, we will see that that the effort to identify a good and proper

---

[21] R. W. Jenson, 'Is There an Ordering Principle?', p. 70.
[22] N. Bobbio, *Democracy and Dictatorship* (Cambridge: Polity, 1989), p. 83
[23] See W. Kersting, 'Politics, Freedom and Order: Kant's Political Philosophy', *The Cambridge Companion to Kant* (P. Guyer (ed.); Cambridge: Cambridge University Press, 1992), p. 364, footnote 1 [by Paul Guyer].
[24] J. Finnis, *Natural Law and Natural Rights* (Oxford: Clarendon, 1980), p. 18.

order is not central to what Hobbes means by right. Moreover, for us today in our postnatural condition, a good and proper order must be also an ecological order. To anticipate my conclusion, it is doubtful that our metaphysical condition can be met this way.

IV. Hobbes: the natural condition of humanity

Hobbes' presentation of the natural condition of humanity (or state of nature) and natural right are intimately related. Indeed, they follow one another in *Leviathan*. In their natural condition, Hobbes argues, humans are broadly equal in both mental and physical capacities. In that they are equal – none is safe from the other – all are distrustful of others. And from this distrust comes the assertion of dominion, and thence the path to war (*Leviathan* XIII, 1–4). We may note immediately that the natural state emerges out of an interpretation of human nature narrowly conceived. What is natural to the human is not also shared with animals. Indeed, this state of nature seems oddly social and, to the extent that it is dominated by self-interest, also rational. To secure gain and safety, and advance their reputation, 'men' go to war, Hobbes concludes. Yet, in such a situation of war and preparation for war, civilization cannot advance.

Hobbes argues that the propensity for people to fight each other is confirmed by experience. He then offers three examples of this state of nature: 'savage people' in America, civil war, and states poised to go to war against one another. Once again, we are presented with a peculiar understanding of what is meant by natural: tribes living alongside one another may be primitive and that is certainly one meaning of natural. Yet, it does not follow that primitiveness is warlike so the example is an odd one. Civil war is a political rather than a pre-political condition. As for competing states, it is hard to see how these are in a natural condition: all such states will be governed by some authority. And why in any natural condition should states behave like individuals, unless states are somehow corporate individuals? By natural, we may conclude, Hobbes means something quite specific and perhaps idiosyncratic.

Nor is it easy to see how such a state of lawlessness comports well with a sense of the sovereignty of God. Indeed, in the Latin version of *Leviathan*, Hobbes expresses surprise that readers should doubt the existence of the war of all against all. After all, he ventures, did not Cain kill Abel, and if there had been a common power would Cain have dared such a thing? Hobbes conveniently omits to point out that, according to Genesis 4.11–12, Cain was immediately punished by the power of YHWH.

In theological terms, therefore, we may draw the conclusion that there cannot be an only natural state of humanity – if natural here means independent of God and beyond God's rule. Humanity is always governed by the rule of God and resourced by the goodness of God in creation. Humanity is never pre-political. The same point can be made in relation to the concept of *natura pura*. In theological explorations of the relationship between grace and nature, a *natura pura* can be posited as a technical exercise. Yet this is no argument for its actuality.[25] Likewise, as part of an exploration of the relationship between human right and government, a natural condition of humanity can be posited. Yet this is no argument for its actuality for the human is never beyond the governance of God. And, as we shall see, in that the human is never beyond the governance of God, so the human is never without its natural attachments.

What is interesting here is the way in which arguments from *natura pura* and the natural condition of humanity both develop independently of theological concerns. While I cannot speculate in either case why this non-theological development took place, we can at least be alert to any consequences. And the consequence is the same in each case: abstraction in the sense of the separation of the human from other creatures; the self-sufficiency of humanity, especially in terms of the value assigned to the competence of reason; and a tendency to entrench right in the human as the basis of a 'subjective' effort (eventually, the only effort?) to defend the human.[26]

It is likely then that by 'natural', Hobbes is not referring to some state of grace, some Edenic condition. And he seems not to be referring to the natural as primitive; the Americans are savage rather than primitive. Kinch Hoekstra argues – if I may generalize his point – that the natural condition of humanity is a postpolitical condition; it is the state into which humanity falls if the commonwealth fails.[27] The state of nature is thereby that which is corrupted. In that sense, the natural condition of humankind is unnatural. Of course, it emerges from Hobbes' account of human nature but it is not the *telos* of the human in anything other than a limited and circumscribed sense. To put the same point differently, because the society of the boys in William Golding's novel *The Lord of the Flies* breaks down as a corrupt human nature emerges, is not to say that this corruption is the destiny of the human.

V. Right

Some of Hobbes' contemporaries found his presentation of the natural condition of 'mankind' troubling. From a theological perspective, it is easy to see why this might be so. For his first readers disputed that the natural condition in which human beings were placed as described by Hobbes – to which they added, placed by God – could be the gift of a good God. Indeed, even if we grant that Hobbes is working with a contrast between a corrupted 'natural' state and the peace of the

---

[25] See L. Dupré, *Passage to Modernity: An Essay in the Hermeneutics of Nature and Culture* (New Haven and London: Yale University Press, 1993), pp. 174–81.
[26] See R. Geuss, *History and Illusion in Politics* (Cambridge: Cambridge University Press, 2001), pp. 138–46 (146).
[27] K. Hoekstra, 'Hobbes on the Natural Condition of Mankind', *The Cambridge Companion to Hobbes's Leviathan* (P. Springborg (ed.); Cambridge: Cambridge University Press, 2007), p. 114.

commonwealth, the case presented by Hobbes is still troubling. For the question not asked – and it is a theological question – is 'what is the relationship between the corrupted condition of mankind – the condition to which it reverts by its nature when outside the commonwealth – and the wider nature in which that humanity is placed?' It is as if the redemptive action of the commonwealth pulls 'man' out of its natural condition. Redemption cancels creation; contract negates covenant (indeed, Hobbes even associates covenant with contract, *Leviathan* XIV, 11). In this perspective, there can be no thinking back from the corrupted creature to a consideration of what has been given by God in creation.

In turn this means that it is not possible for Hobbes to affirm that redemption begins with creation. What is lost is the theological orientation on creation. This loss of the theological tends towards atomism, self-sufficiency and individualism. In other words, to see the natural condition as corrupt isolates the human: human freedom is understood as freedom from others, and I enter into the commonwealth on the entirely rational ground of trying to secure this 'freedom from'. And in order to gain this 'freedom from', I may be prepared to give up my part of my freedom as long as there is a commensurate loss of freedom by others.[28]

This conclusion informs the concept of right that Hobbes now proposes in *Leviathan*, Chapter XIV. For here Hobbes makes an influential distinction. 'The Right of Nature', he argues, 'which writers commonly call *ius naturale*, is the liberty each man hath to use his own power …' And now Hobbes makes a momentous distinction between right and law: 'For though they that speak of this subject use to confound *ius* and *lex* (*right* and *law*), yet they ought to be distinguished, because Right consisteth in liberty to do or to forbear, whereas Law determineth and bindeth to one of them; so that law and right differ as much as obligation and liberty, which in one and the same matter are inconsistent' (*Leviathan*, XIV, 1, 3).

In making this distinction between law and right we have, as John Finnis argues, crossed a watershed that is to be located somewhere between the Middle Ages and the early modern period. In this transition, *ius* loses its meaning as that which is just and becomes a kind of power. In Hobbes, this power has become liberty. Indeed, reference to that which is objective in right – the just act, event or state of affairs – falls away. Before Hobbes, the sense of that which is just or right is not lost, although it has been 'transformed by *relating it exclusively to the beneficiary* of the just relationship'.[29] With Hobbes, however, we seem to have entered a brave new world from which it should come as no surprise that we should wish to be rescued. We seem to be beyond even the distinction made between objective and subjective right in which objective functions as an adverbial qualification of a situation and subjective as identifying the agent who has a claim or entitlement.[30]

---

[28] C. B. Macpherson, *The Political Theory of Possessive Individualism* (Oxford and New York: OUP, 1964 paperback), p. 264.
[29] J. Finnis, *Natural Law and Natural Rights* (Oxford: Clarendon, 1980), p, 207.
[30] R. Geuss, *Philosophy and Real Politics* (Princeton: Princeton University Press, 2008), pp. 60–70 (62).

If the exercise of liberty is also informed by the duality of corruption/grace, then there is no justice, natural law or divine dispensation in and through which this right might be exercised. That realm of corruption dispenses with such things. The corrupting natural condition of the human corrupts; it does not guide. Moreover, the state of grace that is the commonwealth must be entered into, and in that process such liberty is circumscribed by the sovereign. Liberty is thereby without guides in the natural condition yet can be impeded by the sovereign; however, it is never conditioned. In a precise sense, therefore, it is never natural.

In case this seems like an introspective theological discussion, we can see that this matter has significance beyond theology. We can easily see that this Hobbesian position turns upon a contrast between the natural state of the human and the preferred state of the human in a social contract. Hobbes presents the natural condition as one to be escaped from; I have used the word, corruption, to describe it. There are two consequences. First, what I am calling the goodness of our natural condition is called into question. Second, the emphasis on right as liberty also de-naturalizes the human. For such liberty is an act to do or not do in which context – that which comes with the act – is not important. What is 'natural' is thereby both an unhappy condition and one upon which the natural context does not impinge.

VI. How Much of Society is Present in this Nature?

Repair work is called for. This right, and its liberty, needs to be reconstructed for a postnatural condition. In other words, human liberty occurs always in ecological situations; human liberty is always natural liberty. Furthermore, I shall be arguing that there are rich resources in theology that are helpful in making such a transition from *nature* to *postnature*.

Although only a beginning can be made here, we can start to discuss the matter by exploring how nature is functioning in our politics and thereby discern some ways in which nature has been institutionalized; thus we can ask in what ways we are presented by the reality of our postnatural condition. For some commentators, the position Hobbes argues for is an indication of the bourgeois nature of his political philosophy.[31] The confusion of the natural state of humankind and bourgeois conditions of early capitalism is not a mistake. It indicates that there is no straightforward divide between the human and the non-human. Nor should we expect to establish definitively that divide. The point is rather: Why do we keep calling for that divide? Why do we keep trying to identify the divide between the natural and the artificial, the given and the made? What matter of concern is being addressed in this distinction?

---

[31] This position is articulated by C. B. Macpherson, *The Political Theory of Possessive Individualism*; its details have been strongly criticized: see K. Thomas, 'The Social Origin of Hobbes's Political Thought', *Hobbes Studies* (K. C. Brown (ed.); Oxford: Blackwell, 1985), pp. 185–236, especially pp. 227–236.

For Hobbes, the matter of concern is social and political order in the face of our natural condition of dis-order. Yet in situating Hobbes in this way we should not congratulate ourselves too easily. At present, the concerns embedded in our perspectives on nature are impossible to satisfy. For we wish to affirm the non-artificiality of nature; that nature is that which is not to be sourced to human willing; it exists independently. And yet this alterity is being compromised by human activity. Together with this, we also note that in practice this alterity is difficult to maintain in that we are now mixing human labour with nature to such a depth of penetration that we are re-engineering the genetic basis of some organisms. We are re-designing nature, so to speak. In such change, the alterity of nature is compromised. It is by this conundrum – the otherness of nature and the manipulability of nature as actions in a public realm – that we Westerners are faced. We desire limits, but the condition from which we desire them – our manipulation of nature – is also the reason why they are not available.

Our concern is thereby to identify *limits* to that effort at mastery. Our difficulty is that in order to identify limits we must already have passed them. Our concern, then, is that in the flex of the dialectic, order is accompanied by disorder. What sort of metaphysics of nature should we be working with in order to understand better these sources of order and dis-order? [32]

VII. From Nature as Udder to Nature as Other

In such circumstance of confusion over limits, we should expect to find that our *camera obscura* un-reality takes the form of anthropocentrism. For as Terry Eagleton says, we desire that '[r]ather than being stonily indifferent to our ends, the world appears to be on familiar terms with us, conforming obediently to our desires and bending to our motions as obsequiously as one's reflection in the glass'.[33] Eagleton continues:

> Ideology reinvents the imaginary at the level of society as a whole, for those fully evolved human subjects who might otherwise realise with a *frisson* of alarm that the world does not owe them a living and is as indifferent to them as the weather. Caught in this comfortable delusion, the subject can rest assured that society lays special claim to it, singles it out as uniquely precious and addresses it, so to speak, by its name. In beckoning us from the ruck of faceless citizens around us and turning its visage benignly towards us, the super-subject of ideology fosters in us the flattering faith that reality could not get along without us and would be inconsolably distressed to see us lapse from existence ...

What is useful in this Lacanian-Althusserian position is that we have here an anti-human position of a sort: the criticism of 'bovine anthropocentrism' in which we

[32] L. Daston, 'The World in Order', *Without Nature: A New Condition for Theology* (D. Albertson, and C. King (eds); New York: Fordham University Press, 2010), pp. 15–33, stresses that our desire for nature is expressive of a desire for order.
[33] T. Eagleton, *Trouble with Strangers* (Oxford: Blackwell, 2009), pp. 10–11.

regard the world as an udder to feed ourselves – Eagleton quotes *Middlemarch* – and that the world regards us as endlessly valuable. By this anthropocentrism, we are invited to understand ourselves as infinitely valuable subjects, interpellated into precious existence. In such a view, we tend to regard that which is trustworthy as that which reinforces our view of ourselves as centred super-selves, parading centre-stage; also such a centre-stage position supports our conviction that a coherent performance is possible. And we regard as untrustworthy those messages and events that call into question such udder-oriented anthropocentrism.

Although then we wish to posit 'natural limits', we do not wish to say that the world does not owe us a living and is as indifferent to us as the weather. We are therefore caught in the dilemma of positing limits out of our anthropocentrism. How then are we to move from nature as udder to nature as other? In a refusal of *camera obscura*, we need to give institutional form to indicate that nature does not conform to our desires, that we shall never be able to control it. Nature shapes us as well as us shaping nature. Nature is a production, yet also a re-production. This nature does not owe us a living nor, as is evident from swine flu, is it always benign. Moreover, we shall need to say that a postnatural society is not a polity of coherent narratives and of the infinite recognition of the individual. Postnatural right stresses human liberty beyond state and economy. We encounter the issue of the re-institutionalization of nature as a source of anti-anthropocentric trust.

VIII. The Metaphysical Condition: Postnature as the Force of the Real

State of nature arguments have been deeply influential in Anglo-Saxon political thinking. In other words, these arguments pose a question about the relationship between the human and the natural. And one way of exploring that relationship is by way of the notion of right, and the ways in which in our contemporary politics we understand the human as in a natural state or condition. It is this appeal to a sort of naturalness, I shall be arguing, that must be refused. And yet this refusal is founded in the reality of the relationship between the human and the non-human, between the human and its natural context. What is fundamental is the coalition of animals, human and non-human, in a wider natural context: the contrast human/natural must be refused in favour of a concept of *postnature* as a way of trying to develop a way of thinking about the re-institutionalising of nature. We arrive at the issue of a metaphysics of postnature.

I have said that we continue to make the distinction between the natural and the artificial. However, we tend also to see ourselves as moving from the natural to the artificial. In other words, we move from the animal to culture or from natural law to positive law. The natural is seen as that which is pristine or simple and these precede the sophisticated. And then the pristine circumstance can be presented in the manner of nostalgia, the Garden of Eden, for example; or as inhospitable, as in Hobbes' condition of war in the state of nature.

In order to develop a metaphysics of postnature as a critique of bovine anthropocentrism and as the affirmation of the interaction between nature and the human,

I shall argue that the basic distinction is not that between the natural and the conventional, the given and the made. Instead, following C. S. Lewis, I argue that the basic distinction is better understood as that between the *real* and the *conventional*.[34] Moreover, this distinction is helpful in addressing our *camera obscura* world. This distinction relocates human creatures in a common realm shared with other creatures in which there is the hope that not everything is to be viewed as upside down. The primary distinction is thereby neither between natural/artificial nor unspoiled/sophisticated, but instead the primary contrast is between the *real* and the *conventional*. The issue here is what the content of the real is and what its relationship is to the conventional. In other words, there are not two human realities, one natural and the other historical. There is only the embeddedness or worldliness of the human, presented through a diversity of historically contingent social forms.

This is a departure from standard ways of construing this matter. Typically, we explore the conventional before the real, regarding the former – the conventional – as historical. The real is not considered to be historical or, if it is, yet it remains purposeless. We access the real via the historical. And, moreover, we try sometimes to dismiss the real by calling it nature. This is, I am arguing, a mistake: we should say instead that the conventional is derivative of the real, although the asymmetries between the two are highly complex. And although I concede that we access the real by way of the historical, this does not mean that the real is somehow supplanted by the historical nor so reduced that it cannot encounter us. The crucial point here is how to give some content to the real. What is the real condition of the human, and how does this bear upon the conventions of the public sphere?

The real is a mixture of nature and the human and not merely – posing as sophisticated – the conventions of the human. Postnatural right emerges as the effort to explore our capacities to act as human animals but also as participants in a *logos*, a pattern, a dynamic working of ecological relationships, a dis-order, an anti-rule. This real is not a pre-social animality but a social animality: the actuality of postnature. The postnatural condition is then an effort to identify this reality of the human, and postnatural right an effort to identify real human action.

Moreover, such a postnature will be a *teleological* postnature. That is, because this postnature is concerned with what is normative, with what is good, we cannot say that this postnature now is. Nor can we be confident that any creaturely agent can secure or achieve this good. Instead, as Jenson puts it, 'The good is what *ought* to be: that is to say, it is what may not be now and may never be, and is no less the good for all that'.[35] And precisely on account of its elusive quality, this good is teleological: for if this good is not yet and indeed may never be, then it can only be anticipated: this reality is a good that may or may not be achieved. It is precisely an eschatological good. We arrive at the metaphysics of postnature: nature accompanies the

---

[34] C. S. Lewis, *Studies in Words* (Cambridge: Cambridge University Press, 2nd edn, 1967), pp. 58–62.
[35] R. W. Jenson, *Essays*, p. 71.

human, both for God, for itself and for the human. And such metaphysics indicates a good: precisely, a postnatural good.

IX. Postnatural Right: Implications for the Public Sphere

Finally, what might it mean to think institutionally about this shared or common realm for the public sphere: if postnature – this coalition of the human and others – is to be our politics, what might that look like?

Nature is here re-institutionalized as postnature: as that which does not conform, as that which resists, as that which is heedless of the situation and circumstance of the human, and as that which cannot be engineered. It is re-institutionalized as teleological: as part of the goodness that is to come out of the revolution of the resurrection. In this process of re-institutionalization, the metaphysical condition rejoins the political condition. That is, postnature requires a metaphysics and a political space. The metaphysical and the political here converge.

As re-institutionalized, nature is incorporated within the moral subject of creaturely community. In other words, the political condition of the overcoming of the secular that I presented at the beginning of this paper also needs to overcome the secular prejudice against nature. We do not need to agree with John Ely that 'modernity and its disembedded conventionalism leaves us directionless', to agree that the force of the real requires a shift away from a disembedded conventionalism and the reconnection of moral thinking with worldliness that is neither conventional nor natural. That is, we need an account of the real that is the criticism of a bovine anthropocentrism.[36] Overcoming the secular prejudice against nature means that 'virtue is and must be embedded in a way of life ... in the world'. This is the basis of a postnatural 'project of emancipation'.[37]

The metaphysical condition and the political condition converge on postnatural right. In what way? 'When we have been historically creative,' Jenson argues, 'it is because we have shared some look into the future, some metaphor of freedom and goodness or purity or mutuality, that could draw us forward through time'.[38] To be historically and ecologically creative at the present time, we should explore what we share – in incomplete ways – at the present time. I propose that postnatural right, as teleological, is an *historical* phenomenon. Such postnatural right has, in other words, historical content: it assumes the ideal of production for exchange, and notes that this production makes greater wealth; and it is associated with a distributive pressure towards equality. That is, our idea of right is not a-historical but changes and has changed over time. Right now includes productive activity and we now work from the principle that what we make is available to be redistributed. This we share. Yet my position also notes a further historical development: all wealth making has an *ecological* component. Value and nature are related in this

[36] J. Ely, 'Ernst Bloch, Natural Right and the Greens', p. 139.
[37] Ibid.
[38] R. W. Jenson, *Essays*, p. 72.

historical development and change through the development. This we share also, although it remains a work in progress and not an achievement. What postnatural right identifies and secures is an *abstract* notion of the free, eco-productive individual, living co-operatively in a determinate ecological circumstance.

As teleological, moreover, postnatural right is not, *pace* Hobbes, some ability to do or not do; it is an ideal of activity that is, as postnatural, historical. That is, it has built into it a free creativity and reference to the otherness and productivity of nature. It has a political and a metaphysical condition. So it is grounded in reason in the sense that it is grounded in a postnature that is yet to come (and so in ideology critique against naturalness), and it is grounded in nature in the sense of a wider nature in which the human is placed: the sociality of animal-nature. In that it is teleological, postnatural right is *abstract* and *revolutionary*. It is abstract in the sense that it calls upon that which is not yet; it is revolutionary in the sense that it demands an equality of basic regard among creatures.

As *abstract*, a central task of the public sphere related to postnatural right will be a renewal of the debate of ends of the human and the ends of nature: to what *teloi* are these directed? Unlike the desire for unending alteration and competition for change, these ends will be the affirmation of trust/faith by way of equity in the distribution of nature's goods, the re-founding of liberty, hope in the transformation of our categories for interpreting the nature of postnature, a love of postnature, and the courage to act. Of course, none of this can be thought except by reference to 'this transcending facet of a teleological system was always firmly rooted in or concretely mediated by real political circumstances'.[39] What will be required is the reconstruction of the public sphere in which trust in wider processes and structures of a postnatural condition, a sense of belonging in a specific place of postnature and the possibility of teleological, political action are secured. The public sphere is discursive but it is not solely directed towards the building-up of communicative competence. We also need a 'theory of the institutions providing the good life' in support of a 'form and nature of a *free and equal political mode of life*'.[40] For, if I am right, there can be no free and equal political mode of life without a metaphysics of postnature that is also directed to what we can risk in not defending the human.

As *revolutionary*, postnatural right demands an equality of basic regard among creatures. What is required is what Kathryn Tanner calls 'a vision of cosmic justice in which all beings are due equal consideration at some basic level of moral concern' as the moral outworking of a teleological metaphysics of postnature.[41] This, we might say, is what needs to be real-ized in our situation. The equality of human beings among themselves, and in relation to nature, is here an important matter: social equality invokes an equality of access to nature's goods. And sharing of the wealth of nature will require forms of co-operation. One way of thinking

---

[39] J. Ely, 'Ernst Bloch, Natural Right and the Greens', p. 140–141.
[40] Ibid., p. 138.
[41] K. Tanner, 'Creation, Environmental Justice, and Ecological Justice', *Reconstructing Christian Theology* (R. Chopp, and M. L. Taylor (eds); Minneapolis: Fortress Press, 1994), pp. 99–123 (118).

about this is to think about wealth not in terms of its creation but instead in terms of its making. The good to which we aspire is the making of wealth in which nature is also a partner in this making. And this would allow the effort of working for a society in which things are priced according to their value. And what is our vision for our society? Not a community of free individuals but a co-operation of postnatural individuals that is seeking fairer and more sustainable access to nature's goods.

Epilogue – Right out of time?

We may now appreciate that a 'secular' society, and 'secular' people, have a stake in this debate. For teleologies of the human and nature ground universal claims of the project of postnatural emancipation in a normative good that extends to both the human and nature. Here is the operation of a metaphysics of postnature: as a normative good that relates to both nature and the human, the good advanced is not narrowly religious but seeks to found our thought and action in a reality beyond convention. This is the criticism of ethnocentrism. As Ely notes, it is these normative claims that have been 'central to the development of humanism as a specifically civic phenomenon as well as the notion of philosophical reason as a universal quality of the 'political animal'.[42] For my present purposes, I need only to maintain that this right is grounded in worldly realities of the common realm of nature and humanity. This, then, is a theological contribution to an argumentative public sphere: the goodness of created sociality is not a narrowly religious matter but provides a *telos* in which all might share. This *telos* is grounded theologically, but in that it is grounded in the doctrine of creation, it thereby applies to all. Of course, whether such a position is acceptable in the public sphere is another matter. What I hope to have shown is that such a position is intelligible and practical in a postnatural condition.

I have been arguing that attention should be paid to the political and metaphysical conditions that we need to attend to if there is to be a renewal of the public sphere for an ecologically distressed period. 'Right out of time?' The notion of right that I am proposing is a sort of anachronism; it is out of the present time, and rooted in a theological tradition and ecclesial life that has in Europe been marginalized. Yet these are serious times that demand the evaluation of all our cultural resources if we humans are not indeed to be right out of time.

Bibliography

Bobbio, N., *Democracy and Dictatorship* (Cambridge: Polity, 1989).
Brague, R., *The Law of God: The Philosophical History of an Idea* (Chicago & London: University of Chicago Press, 2008).

---

[42] J. Ely, 'Ernst Bloch, Natural Right and the Greens', p. 140.

Daston, L., 'The World in Order', *Without Nature: A New Condition for Theology* (D. Albertson and C. King (eds); New York: Fordham University Press, 2010), pp. 15–33.

D'Entrèves, A. P., *Natural Law: An Historical Survey* (New York: Harper Torchbooks, 1951).

de Vries, H., 'Introduction: Before, Around and Beyond the Theologico-Political', *Political Theologies: Public Religions in a Post-Secular World* (H. de Vries, and L. E. Sullivan (eds); Fordham: Fordham University Press, 2006), pp. 1–88.

Dupré, L., *Passage to Modernity: An Essay in the Hermeneutics of Nature and Culture* (New Haven and London: Yale University Press, 1993).

Eagleton, T., *Trouble with Strangers* (Oxford: Blackwell, 2009).

Ely, J., 'Ernst Bloch, Natural Right and the Greens', *Minding Nature: The Philosophers of Ecology* (D. Macauley (ed.); New York: Guilford, 1996), pp. 134–166.

Finnis, J., *Natural Law and Natural Rights* (Oxford: Clarendon, 1980).

Geuss, R., *History and Illusion in Politics* (Cambridge: Cambridge University Press, 2001).

—*Philosophy and Real Politics* (Princeton: Princeton University Press, 2008).

HM Treasury, UK Budget 2009 Report, *Building Britain's Future*, www.hm-treasury.gov.uk/bud_bud09_index.htm *(accessed 21 June 2010)*.

Hoekstra, K., 'Hobbes on the Natural Condition of Mankind', *The Cambridge Companion to Hobbes's Leviathan* (P. Springborg (ed.); Cambridge: Cambridge University Press, 2007), pp. 109–127.

Jenson, R. W., 'Is There an Ordering Principle?', *Essays in the Theology of Culture* (Grand Rapids, MI: Eerdmans, 1995), pp. 67–75.

Kersting, W., 'Politics, Freedom and Order: Kant's Political Philosophy', *The Cambridge Companion to Kant* (P. Guyer (ed.); Cambridge: Cambridge University Press, 1992), pp. 342–366.

Lewis, C. S., *Studies in Words* (Cambridge: Cambridge University Press, 2nd edn, 1967).

Macpherson, C. B., *The Political Theory of Possessive Individualism* (Oxford and New York: OUP, 1964 paperback).

Martinich, A. P., *Hobbes: A Biography* (Cambridge: Cambridge University Press, 1999).

Marx, K., and F. Engels, *The German Ideology* (London: Lawrence & Wishart, 2nd edn, 1974).

Russell, C., and Z. Nyssa, 'The Tipping Point Trend in Climate Change Communication', *Global Environmental Change* 19 (2009), pp. 336–344.

Scott, P. M., 'The City's Grace? Recycling the Urban Ecology', *International Journal of Public Theology* 2 (2008), pp. 119–135.

—'Politics and the New Visibility of Theology', *The New Visibility of Religion* (G. Ward and M. Hoelzl (eds); London: Continuum, 2008), pp. 170–186.

Tanner, K., 'Creation, Environmental Justice, and Ecological Justice', *Reconstructing Christian Theology* (R. Chopp, and M. L. Taylor (eds); Minneapolis: Fortress Press, 1994), pp. 99–123.

Thomas, K., 'The Social Origin of Hobbes's Political Thought', *Hobbes Studies* (K. C. Brown (ed.); Oxford: Blackwell, 1985), pp. 185–236.

Ward, G., *The Politics of Discipleship: Becoming Postmaterial Citizens* (Grand Rapids, MI: Baker Academic, 2009).

Williams, R., 'Secularism, Faith and Freedom', *The New Visibility of Religion* (G. Ward, and M. Hoelzl (eds); London: Continuum, 2008), pp. 45–56.

4 Climate Change and the (Economic) Value of Nature – The Role of Economic Thinking in the Public Sphere

Hans Diefenbacher
Forschungsstätte der Evangelischen Studiengemeinschaft (FEST) / Alfred-Weber Institut, Universität Heidelberg, Germany

I. Introduction

Is climate change an economic issue? Is it advisable to use economic thinking to find solutions? Is it, in a certain manner of speaking, appropriate to economize climate change? Apparently, it can be economically profitable to expand greenhouse gas emissions, but if we do so on a global scale many people will suffer from it, especially in the future. Economists adore optimal solutions, at least in theory. Is there something like an optimum of climate change?

In the following text, some attempts to find answers to these questions are presented. But before we can approach them directly, we have to make a little detour to deal with more general questions. These are: to what extent is it useful to assign economic values to nature, or to calculate economic costs of the destruction of nature? Can it be done, and if so, which scientific methods do we need to fulfil this task? Or should we, for ethical reasons, refuse to do so? We will move from these general considerations in a first step to more practical thoughts on climate change as a second step and, with concluding remarks, back to theory and policy recommendations how to both limit and use the role of economics to improve the perception of ecology in the public sphere.

II. The Price of Nature

More than twenty years ago, two interesting public debates about the relation between economy and ecology took place. The first one came from a theoretical perspective and dealt with what might be the right understanding of the relation between nature and (economic) value. The second one took a more practical viewpoint and discussed the request by a small group of scientists – among them myself – to abolish the gross domestic product (GDP) as a measure for economic welfare, and to replace it by a somewhat 'green' domestic product. These more practical discussions took the theoretical debates a step further.

The first discussion – the one starting with theoretical considerations – began with an essay written by Hans Immler who argued that the participation of nature in the production process should be more prominently accounted for in any theory of value; there would be no way out of the ecological crisis unless this was taken into account. If society refused to recognize the true value of nature in the economic process, measured as an economic value – so to speak, appreciated in the language of economy – it would always tend to underestimate the value of nature and, hence, over-use and destroy it.[1]

Iring Fetscher took a contradictory viewpoint by saying it would be wrong to blame value theory: we would misconceive its cognitive interest by challenging the way it tends to 'forget' nature. According to this opinion there are other theoretical considerations, much more plausible than arguing with a misguided theory of value, that we might use in order to explain the vast ecological destructions caused by industrial mass production. Most important: the theory of external (negative) effects which emphasizes that what is profitable for a single company might be a disaster for the economy or society as a whole. Hence, society must learn that rationality within one of its subsystems might turn out to be completely irrational for the system as a whole.[2]

Finally, to render the theoretical discussion even more confusing, Andreas Beckmann warned that we should not prematurely try to smooth the logic of ecology and the logic of economy, which are completely different in his opinion. If this is really the case we cannot hope to reconcile ecology and economy by improving the production of ecological value in a market economy. If we follow this opinion, there is only one way of integrating ecology, namely, to make economic decisions to an increasing degree according to the logic of ecology, not according to the logic of economics.[3]

The destruction of nature that human beings are responsible for has become a global problem. We know that by now. We even know that mainstream economic theory will not set off alarm bells for those who are responsible for decisions in the economic or political sphere. Such theory would indicate eventually the necessity to limit economic growth in order to prevent its negative external effects on

---

[1] H. Immler, *Frankfurter Rundschau* (7 November 1989).
[2] I. Fetscher, *Frankfurter Rundschau* (19 December 1989).
[3] A. Beckmann, *Frankfurter Rundschau* (30 January 1990).

nature, and sometimes even social coherence.[4] On the contrary: in many official statements, the idea of sustainability is perverted in that further globalization is expected to produce 'sustainable growth'.

We know by now that there are limits to growth, that there are limits to the exploitation of nature, limits to the emission of pollutants and, above all, to the emission of carbon dioxide. But the conclusions that we draw from this knowledge are trivial and abstract in a very peculiar way, so that they do not become relevant for the political day-to-day practice. Of course, we have to protect the environment. Of course, we have to preserve the integrity of creation for future generations. There is not a single nation in the world that could permanently get richer by destroying nature. What we have to do, though, is to integrate the external effects on the natural world into our economic decision-making. These are very nice sentences indeed, often heard in political speeches, and virtually nobody would contradict any of them. But again: how can we overcome this gap between a nice theory and a rather annoying political practice of just letting the economy go on?

The core of the economic problem is apparently that it is impossible to find a correct or even a just price for nature. Since the expulsion from paradise, men and women can only survive if they work. But within any economic value created by the work of men and women, there is a significant contribution of nature that came into existence without any effort of human beings. Without nature, human beings will not be able to create any economic value, and therefore any economic calculation, which attempts to look at nature as a whole using economic categories of value theory, will fail.

But if we like it or not – within our daily economic transactions we implicitly and permanently give value to different parts of nature. Natural resources, plots of land and nowadays even emissions, everything has its price (how could it be different?) given in units of money. Initially, it is completely open as to who is paying this price: those who benefit from the exploitation of nature, or those suffering from this activity. Very often, nobody is paying now, but the bill will be presented to future generations. Our economic system has managed to institutionalize a specific type of un-responsibility, because economic theory looks at nature from the viewpoint of a barter economy. This viewpoint, of course, is then transferred to any kind of economic policy that has been shaped as an offspring from this kind of theory. Whether we produce or consume, nature is always necessary. Its usage is governed and valued according to criteria that have been developed in the economic sphere of market exchange. In other words, we use nature as a whole, but we value economically only a few parts of nature, and our guidelines for the valuation of nature are an offspring of our economic system and do not reflect an understanding of the ecological sphere.[5]

If we value parts of nature in units of money, we can continue to act in our day-to-day life as if we could compare these values with immense numbers of other

---

[4] C. Leipert, 'Ist 'humaner Wohlstand' möglich?', *Universitas* 41 (1986), pp. 1109–1120 (1111).

[5] H. Immler, *Natur in der ökonomischen Theorie* (Opladen: Westdeutscher Verlag, 1985).

goods and services, because we measure these values in the same single dimension: money. But by doing so, we accept a huge loss of ecological complexity. Also, we tend to ignore all those parts of our reality that cannot be expressed in units of money.

As far back as 1983, Frederic Vester published a calculation that intended to show that private profit maximization will not lead to optimal welfare if the economic valuation of nature is not well done, and if it is not done by the appropriate institutions.[6] The calculation begins by adding the market value of the materials of a small singing bird, a whinchat: feathers, bones and meat. This led to a result of about two eurocent. But in the second part of the paper, Vester shows step by step that our whinchat is part of a very complicated system of the environment of human beings, in which it serves a lot of different functions. Some of them can be valued in units of money – more or less convincingly – others not. Our little bird is eating quite a lot of insects serving as a sort of natural pest control. It can be regarded as an early warning indicator of the quality of the ecological system where it is living: if the number of whinchats is declining, or if they even disappear, something has gone wrong. People walking through gardens and forests thoroughly enjoy the melodies of the little bird; they calm down, they recover from the stress of their daily life, and so we can credit our little bird the cost of maybe several hours of psychotherapy because it made them dispensable. Vester concluded that if we tried to value economically all these services within the average life span of our little bird the result would not be 2 eurocent, but roughly €700. But the true value of this calculation is the insight, that the economic categories of costs and benefits, expenses and yields cannot be transferred to the sphere of ecology. If we insist on doing so, we are running the severe risk of producing ridiculous results.

There is even another important obstacle that we face if we try to value parts of nature in units of money. Market prices are current prices, they reflect the current economy together with the expectations for the future that people currently have. This mixture is very hard to understand, because our forecasting abilities concerning future developments of markets and societies in general are very limited. Future generations cannot participate in markets today. But very many men and women living today are excluded from the current price finding mechanism. Very many people are not able to articulate their needs in the market because they do not have the purchasing power that is necessary to play an active role there: these are the poor in our societies, and a much larger percentage of the population in the poor countries. Imagine: this is more or less the same situation as if a painting by Picasso or Michelangelo would be auctioned in a classroom, and the only purchasing power admitted would be the money that the students accidentally would have in their pockets. Therefore, we consume the material wealth of nature much too fast, and we roll off the negative external effects to future generations. What we have to develop is a sort of wise governance of an economy in the long run. Such a long-term economy cannot operate without being consistent with the logic of ecology.

---

[6] F. Vester, *Der Wert eines Vogels* (München: Kösel-Verlag, 1983).

III. First Conclusions

Let us draw some preliminary conclusions from what has been said until now. These conclusions come as a paradox.

(1) We are not able to find the right monetary values for nature.
(2) But if we abstain from economizing, the value of nature will be vastly underestimated, and nature will be disrespected and over-exploited in the market economy.
(3) For this reason, we should try to economize as carefully as possible, but
(4) Show at the same time that there are limits to this process of economizing.

We will try to further elaborate these conclusions by looking to the problem of assessing the costs of climate change, and, from this starting point, show what could be done to avoid a wrong understanding of the 'wealth of nature' that would inevitably lead to a wrong understanding of the 'wealth of nations'.

IV. The Cost of Climate Change

If we look into the costs of climate change more in detail, we can identify four different categories of economic costs that must be accounted separately.

(1) The easiest to assess are the repair costs. Climate change can lead to an increased probability and severity of droughts, but also of floods and maybe hurricanes. This will lead to damages that might be repaired. Most insurance companies have an excellent database on repair costs after different types of calamities and catastrophes of the past. Some of them even dare to give forecasts.

(2) A second type of cost are adaptation costs. Already these are much more difficult to assess. If the seawater level is predicted to rise due to climate change, dikes and dams will be heightened. We might need different trees in the Rhine valley, for example, and we will have to grow different sorts of vine. These costs can be calculated fairly well. But how might we assess the loss of some small island states in the Pacific that might disappear? Is it just the relocation expenses for the people losing their country? Is there any economic calculus at all that could be justified? I would like to argue that we have to answer this question in the negative. Adaptation costs, therefore, cannot express the whole story; they are just a memento indicating necessary developments with negative effects that cannot be covered by economics alone.

(3) Maybe the most interesting category of costs embraces those actions that can be identified as mitigation. We can introduce new technology to improve the efficiency of using non-renewable resources like oil or gas, or we can switch to renewable energies. By doing so, we might, however, have positive external economic effects; for example, the bills for oil and gas will go down. Sometimes, these positive external effects might be the prime motive for engaging in this type of economic action; in the classical 'win-win situation' – good for the economy, and good for the ecology – we perhaps will not be able to decide what the impetus for

change had been. And in this case, it might not be justified to ascribe these costs to mitigation in the context of climate change; maybe it is just saving money or promoting technological innovation.

Another type of mitigation is again disrupting traditional economic categories of calculation. Mitigation can stand for abstaining from certain economic activities in order to reduce greenhouse gas emissions, for example by changing one's lifestyle: public transport, or at least smaller cars; no flights, or at least no short-distance flights; vegetarian food, or at least a drastic reduction of meat consumption are just a few simple ideas. Whether the net result of such changes is an increase or a reduction of costs is dependent on the alternatives that people select.

(4) The last category of costs is the most difficult to understand from an economic point of view. What happens if we just go on to increase our greenhouse gas emissions – without adaptation, without mitigation, even without repairing damages? At first sight, nothing will happen. But if we look more carefully, we will first of all recognize that certain costs will be just transferred to future generations. Other negative external effects never will be cared for, they just result in a lower quality of life that will not lead to any activity that could be directly measured in units of money.

If we try to find some intermediate conclusions, we could again summarize some of them in the form of paradox:

- Some of the economic costs of climate change will be immediately paid for, for example, the repair costs. But if we pay these costs, they will increase the Gross National Product (GNP). The more we repair, the higher the GNP.
- Other parts of economic answers to climate change will result in a decline of economic activity, for instance, some elements of the mitigation strategy: the more we mitigate via changes in lifestyle, the lower GNP will be.
- Large parts of external effects of climate change do not touch the economic sphere at all. Within economic cost calculations, they remain invisible.
- But even the elements that are visible partially neutralize each other within aggregate economic indicators like the GNP. Positive effects tend to reduce GNP, while undesirable effects can increase GNP. In other words, those who want to influence the GNP positively might just go in the completely wrong direction.

V. Sustainability and the Price of Nature

These findings lead us to another far-reaching conclusion: namely, that our economy might be misguided because the information we have on costs and benefits of economic activities is not correct. We are collecting the wrong data. Our statistical measurement system is not appropriate for converting data into relevant information. This is one important reason why our economic policy is not able to cope with the problems our societies are confronted with in the ecologic sphere today.

That the national accounting system very often turns the facts upside down is not a new insight. For more than 30 years, there is an ongoing discussion in the

Federal Republic of Germany, the United States and Japan on the value of the Gross National Product (GNP) as a measure of economic and social welfare.[7] Already in 1976, Ursula Wehner related the concept of ecological and social costs of production to the national income accounting system;[8] some years later, Utz Peter Reich and Carsten Stahmer analyzed the suitability of national welfare measures in regard to its ability to include indicators for environmental quality.[9] In 1985, Adolf Theobald suggested the GNP be replaced by an 'ecological national product' that should combine new indicators for the quality of life.[10]

One of the first publications of an empirical analysis in this field that attracted greater attention was an attempt to develop a new method of an ecologically oriented bookkeeping.[11] Criticism on the national accounting system is widespread but had been theoretically oriented for a long time. Only recently it has led to some experiments of calculating ecological and other damages that are not included in the GNP or – even worse – contribute to its growth.

In the following part of my contribution I will identify problems where we still lack adequate statistical information. I will try to show what could be done to improve this situation, such as how the national accounting system would have to be changed to reflect these problems more adequately within the statistical representation of the economy. But we should never restrict our interest to statistics only: at least questions should be raised in order to arrive at a better understanding of how to transform an improved database into a re-orientation of economic policy towards social and ecological sustainability.

The first problem we want to address here is the fact that many economic activities enter our productivity and wealth calculations like the GNP as positive factors that do not contribute to the creation of welfare:

- either because they are ecologically or socially destructive,
- or because they repair the damage from other economic activities,
- or because they are just superfluous or uncalled-for.

Of course, it might be difficult, or even controversial, whether one or the other economic activity belongs to one of these categories; certainly this cannot – or,

---

[7] A comprehensive overview of the beginning of the German discussion in this field is the paper of F. Rubik, 'Das Bruttosozialprodukt als Indikator für Lebensqualität? Kritik und Alternativen', *Arbeiten im Einklang mit der Natur* (Projektgruppe Ökologische Wirtschaft (ed.); Freiburg: Dreisam-Verlag, 1985), pp. 145–176.
[8] U. Wehner, 'Ökologische soziale Kosten und volkswirtschaftliche Gesamtrechnung' (unpublished doctoral dissertation; University of Köln, 1976).
[9] U. P. Reich and C. Stahmer (eds.), *Gesamtwirtschaftliche Wohlfahrtsmessung und Umweltqualität* (Frankfurt: Campus-Verlag, 1983).
[10] A. Theobald, *Das Ökosozialprodukt – Lebensqualität als Volkseinkommen* (Osnabrück: Verlag A. Fromm, 1985).
[11] R. Müller-Wenk, *Die ökologische Buchhaltung – ein Informations- und Steuerungsinstrument für umweltkonforme Unternehmenspolitik* (Frankfurt: Campus-Verlag, 1978).

at least, should not – be determined by a 'green dictator'. But it is possible to imagine a social discourse where these questions would be openly debated and where a consensus might be formed around certain items.[12] The fact that the GNP counts these expenditures as part of the net value added disguises one of the most important trends in the industrialized countries: namely, that more and more resources are needed to 'create' the same gain from the use of goods and services.

Other defensive expenditures are much harder to trace than those in the ecological sphere. The relationship between increased medical expenditures and the health situation in a well-nourished, if not to say over-nourished society is very difficult to assess. From a merely statistical point of view, there is no clear relationship between health expenditures and productivity that might be assumed. More money being spent for medical care should result in a healthier population, which in turn should lead to lower absenteeism at work and higher productivity. C. W. Cobb quotes a US National Center for Health statistics reporting that the number of 'restricted-activity-days' per employee increased from 16.4 in 1965 to 19.1 in 1980, a period during which real per capita expenditures on health care increased by over 70 per cent.[13] On the basis of this and other statistical data,[14] it seems to be realistic that at least half of the real growth in private and public health expenditures is purely defensive, in other words, compensating for growing health risks due to urbanization and industrialization.

Let us come back to the relation between ecology and economy. A necessary condition for a sustainable economy would be a sustainable natural capital. Natural capital includes not only fuels and minerals, but wetlands and farmlands, plants and animals, the variety of landscapes and national parks, as well as a limit to climate change to tolerable degrees. Renewable resources would have to be exploited only according to their regeneration rate, non-renewable resources only according to the degree they can be substituted by other resources. Even this would have to include a large-scale safety margin, because we have to allow future generation to use non-renewable resources for economic activities that today we cannot even imagine (and, therefore cannot invent substitutes for!). The faith in the infinite substitutability of non-renewable resources is founded on the experience of a peculiar period in history, as C. W. Cobb points out,[15] and, as one might add, a period the end of which has come into sight. It was a period in history during which energy was extremely cheap. The falling prices of natural resources during the first 80 years of the last century were a single phenomenon upon which a faulty view of our economic future had been built.

A common belief among economists, that the consumption of finite resources is compensated in value by the formation of other capital, seems to be erroneous,

---

[12] C. W. Cobb, 'The Index for Sustainable Economic Welfare', *For the Common Good. Redirecting the Economy Toward Community, the Environment and a Sustainable Future* (H. E. Daly, and J. B. Cobb, Jr (eds); Boston: Beacon Press, 1989), p. 416 (Appendix), p. 416.
[13] See Index in C. W. Cobb, *For the Common Good*, p. 403.
[14] For data on the United Kingdom see R. Douthwaite, *The Growth Illusion* (Hartland, Devon: Green Books, 1992), pp. 101–119.
[15] See Index in C. W. Cobb, *For the Common Good*, p. 406.

too.[16] The production of capital goods consumes resources without leaving the freedom for future generations to use them in another way. Capital goods and infrastructure investments deteriorate over time and require maintenance costs that would not occur if the resources were to be used only when they are really needed. The depletion of non-renewable resources is, in any case, a cost that has to be borne by future generations. Therefore, it should be subtracted from the capital account of the present generation. This capital account has to consider climate and climate change as well.

Again, we are faced with considerable problems finding the 'right' methodology. S. El Serafy developed an approach to estimate the amount of money that one would have to set aside in order to generate a permanent income stream that would be as great in the future as the portion of the income from the non-renewable assets that are consumed in the present.[17] Although this model seems very clear on the theoretical level, one is faced with a lot of problems if one actually tries to implement it into any national accounting system. For how long and from when should this income stream last? How can we figure out the income shares that are to be attributed to the depletion of the resource and not to the human effort to transform the resource into a consumer or investment good? We will not go into the technical details here,[18] but it has to be concluded that even in the best effort to account for depletion of natural capital, there is a great deal of arbitrariness. But, even if the tax or rent that is set aside according to El Serafy's rule is very moderate, as a 5, – € for 1 ton of coal equivalent, that is 0.5 eurocent for 1 kg coal or 0.7 litre of gasoline in the calculation of the Index of Sustainable Economic Welfare, the accumulated effects are tremendous.

There is one simple result common to all serious analysis of long-term economic development that becomes more obvious the more we expand the time horizon for our research. It is very easy to show that any society whose economy is growing will glide continuously into exponential growth dynamics which will lead, in the long run, to an extreme destabilization of the economy, even if the average annual growth rate is rather low. An annual growth of 1 per cent e.g., of the GNP – means doubling the starting value in 72 years, an annual growth rate of 4 per cent doubles the starting value in 18 years. Such calculations can turn into absurdity by working out that today the revenue from €1 invested in the year of the birth of Christ at an interest rate of 4 per cent should sum up to $1.04^{1990} = 7.8 \times 10^{33}$ €. The weight of the earth is 5.9×10^{27} g; that means that this revenue would buy roughly 82,000 balls made of gold of the weight of the earth, given the actual price of gold with 9 €/g. In

---

[16] E. J. Mishan, 'GNP – Measurement or Mirage', *National Westminster Bank Quarterly Review* (1984), p. 13; see also R. Solow, 'Intergenerational Equity and Exhaustible Resources', *Review of Economic Studies* 41 (1974 supplement), pp. 29–45.
[17] S. El Serafy, 'The Proper Calculation of Income from Depletable Natural Resources', *Environmental and Resource Accounting and their Relevance to the Measurement of Sustainable Income* (E. Lutz and S. El Serafy (eds); Washington, D.C.: World Bank, 1988).
[18] See Index in C. W. Cobb, *For the Common Good*, pp. 438–442.

other words: long-term economic growth based upon the current consumption of energy and resources of the industrialized countries cannot be sustainable.

This simple consideration nourishes the suspicion that traditional economic policy – and theory! – does not attempt to include considerations showing the way from a growth-oriented towards a sustainable world economic system: a way to manage a reduction of economic growth in the developed world by the combination of an efficiency 'revolution' and a positive change of lifestyles. Such a strategy would aim at a deliberate and democratically planned reduction of economic growth. Such a reduction would have to be the consequence of political influence and control, a result of changing values in our societies, and not the consequence of a bellicose world economic crisis that inevitably will occur if we keep on following the current growth strategies.

There is another point that is important to understand in order to arrive at a workable concept of sustainable economic development. I pointed out that there is no concept of sustainability possible without considering the long-term consequences of our economic activities. If we agree on this, we have to occupy ourselves again with the problem of distributional inequality. Notabene: an economic system with a considerable share of capital income that is spent as re-investment in the capital market will negatively affect the income distribution. The more unequal the distribution is, the higher the probability that the system develops into an even more unequal income distribution, and the higher the pressure for unsustainable growth rates.

VI. Economizing Climate Change

What has been said so far can be summarized in the following points:

(1) Politicians, the mass media and the public like to have figures that pretend to be easily understandable. The GNP is one of them. Therefore, the temptation is high to present similar simple figures that pretend to tell the ecological truth. But this can be done only to a certain extent.

(2) If we start to economize climate change by giving monetary values to external effects of economic activities, we have to recognize that there is no easygoing calculus. If we stay within the logic of the national accounting process, positive and negative effects tend to neutralize each other, because some of the negative effects tend to increase the GNP, and some of the positive effects tend to decrease the GNP.

(3) What we need to do, therefore, is to keep things separately, at least for a while. We have to address the different aspects one by one, and with each different problem we have to tell the public not only the results, but also the limits of our calculations. There is no meaningful economic value either for the loss of a whole country or for an increase of potential years of life lost due to climate change. The most important negative external effects are at the same time those that we cannot find economic values for.

(4) In other words, economizing climate change can be useful, but only to a very limited extent. The Stern-Report came to the conclusion that fighting climate change would not cost too much money if we would start to act quickly.[19] This message was politically extremely helpful. But we would misuse this message by calculating how much it would cost us if we continue to do nothing.

Economizing climate change completely would not reconcile economy and ecology. By its very nature, economics tend to emphasize short-term optimization. This is not the rationale of ecology. The advocates of economizing are very strong and very present in today's markets. The advocates of ecology are comparatively weak, hamsters and kingfishers are not very active at the stock exchanges. But the future generations of human beings are strongly underrepresented too. We cannot balance this mismatch by trying to find prices for every piece of nature. It helps a little if we try, but mainly by showing us the limitations of the economic calculus. Setting an economic price for any piece of nature is a political action, nothing that could be solved by economic science alone. Climate change urges us to find a new type of economy, an 'economy of enough', as Harry de Lange and Bob Goudzwaard said,[20] but above all, it urges us to recognize the limits of the economic calculus.

Bibliography

Cobb, C. W., 'The Index for Sustainable Economic Welfare', *For the Common Good. Redirecting the Economy Toward Community, the Environment and a Sustainable Future* (H. E. Daly, and J. B. Cobb, Jr (eds); Boston: Beacon Press, 1989), p. 416 (Appendix).

De Lange, H., and B. Goudzwaard, *Economie van het genoeg* (Kampen: Kok Agora, 1985).

Diefenbacher, H., 'A Different Kind of Globalization – Resistance and Opportunities', *Globalisierung. Wirtschaft im Dienst des Lebens – Stellungnahme der Evangelischen Kirche von Westfalen zum Soesterberg-Brief* (Evangelische Kirche von Westfalen (ed.); Bielefeld: EKvW, 2006), pp. 123–139.

Douthwaite, R. *The Growth Illusion* (Hartland, Devon: Green Books, 1992).

El Serafy, S., 'The Proper Calculation of Income from Depletable Natural Resources', *Environmental and Resource Accounting and their Relevance to the Measurement of Sustainable Income* (E. Lutz and S. El Serafy (eds); Washington, DC: World Bank, 1988).

HM Treasury, *Stern Review on the Economics of Climate Change* (1976), http://www.hm-treasury.gov.uk/stern_review_report.htm (accessed 14 May 2010).

Immler, H., *Natur in der ökonomischen Theorie* (Opladen: Westdeutscher Verlag, 1985).

---

[19] HM Treasury, *Stern Review on the Economics of Climate Change* (1976), http://www.hm-treasury.gov.uk/stern_review_report.htm (accessed 14 May 2010).

[20] H. de Lange and B. Goudzwaard, *Economie van het genoeg* (Kampen: Kok Agora, 1985).

Leipert, C., 'Ist 'humaner Wohlstand' möglich?', *Universitas* 41 (1986), pp. 1109–1120.

Mishan, E. J., 'GNP – Measurement or Mirage', *National Westminster Bank Quarterly Review* (1984), p. 13.

Müller-Wenk, R., *Die ökologische Buchhaltung – ein Informations- und Steuerungsinstrument für umweltkonforme Unternehmenspolitik* (Frankfurt: Campus-Verlag, 1978).

Reich, U. P., and C. Stahmer (eds), *Gesamtwirtschaftliche Wohlfahrtsmessung und Umweltqualität* (Frankfurt: Campus-Verlag, 1983).

Rubik, F., 'Das Bruttosozialprodukt als Indikator für Lebensqualität? Kritik und Alternativen', *Arbeiten im Einklang mit der Natur* (Projektgruppe Ökologische Wirtschaft (ed.); Freiburg: Dreisam-Verlag, 1985), pp. 145–176.

Solow, R. 'Intergenerational Equity and Exhaustible Resources', *Review of Economic Studies* 41 (1974 supplement), pp. 29–45.

Theobald, A., *Das Ökosozialprodukt – Lebensqualität als Volkseinkommen* (Osnabrück: Verlag A. Fromm, 1985).

Vester, F., *Der Wert eines Vogels* (München: Kösel-Verlag, 1983).

Wehner, U., 'Ökologische soziale Kosten und volkswirtschaftliche Gesamtrechnung' (unpublished doctoral dissertation; University of Köln, 1976).

Part II

Contextual Approaches

5 Latin American Liberation Theologians' Turn to Eco(theo)logy – Critical Remarks

Elina Vuola
Department of World Cultures,
University of Helsinki, Finland

In this chapter, I will look at some prominent Latin American liberation theologians' turn to eco(theo)logical issues. For some of them, it has meant a new assessment of the central liberation theological paradigm of seeing nature in need of liberation. For others, the turn has created distance from classical liberation theology and its anthropocentric understanding of subjectivity and agency. I will critically analyze some of the presuppositions and consequences of this eco(theo) logical turn.

An important part of this turn in liberation theology, also in Latin America, is the inclusion of feminist ecotheology and philosophy. I will refer mostly to the works of two Brazilian Catholic theologians, Ivone Gebara and Leonardo Boff, who among Latin American liberation theologians have written most on ecological issues and who understand themselves to be ecotheologians. They represent the first-generation of liberation theology. Both have written extensively on issues of ecology, ecotheology and liberation theology. Gebara also defines herself as a feminist theologian. Boff, a first-generation male liberation theologian, has also written on gender, women and feminism, and is an example of someone who takes feminist critique seriously and engages it with his own thinking. For Boff and Gebara, gender issues are important. Both of them – even if for somewhat different reasons – depart from or distance themselves from classical Christianity and its theology in ways traditional liberation theology did not.

In this chapter, I will limit myself to a few critical remarks and focus on specific issues which I think raise critical questions for both liberation theology and ecofeminism or feminist ecotheology, especially in the Latin American context. These issues are: (1) the addition of nature to the list of the oppressed in need of liberation; (2) the role of (eco)feminism; and (3) the role of indigenous peoples, cultures and 'popular religion'. An overarching question combining these three points is liberation theology's contemporary context in relation to social and political movements.

Liberation theology has formed since its beginning an important – and in some cases central – space in Latin America's public sphere. In the 1970s liberation theology, the *iglesia popular* (popular church) part of the Catholic Church, and some Protestant churches, were at the forefront of a new type of emerging civil society in Latin America. In many countries liberation theology offered the language, the rationale, and even the legitimization for people in Christian churches to question economic policies that left large parts of society under the poverty line, as well as for outright opposition to military regimes and their human rights violations. If early liberation theology and the church groups close to it are analyzed as democracy movements, as I think it is correct to do, it could be said that they have succeeded in their goals: democracy, even if fragile in many countries, has been attained. Latin America is no longer a continent of military dictatorships. Liberation theology was *de facto* a public theology during the military regimes.[1] My argument in this Chapter is, however, that liberation theology has by and large lost this role. It does not mean that liberation theology is dead as is often said. Many political debates in contemporary Latin America directly or indirectly touch on some important issues in the Catholic Church and Christian theology, such as constructions of gender and sexuality, racism and ethnocentrism, and anthropocentrism. Liberation theologians have been reluctant to side with those political movements that make political demands on these issues. What is interesting is that although liberation theology can be partially credited with the continent's democratization, it is no longer at the forefront of today's radical political demands for democracy.

David Lehmann analyzes the public role of early liberation theology with the help of the concept *basismo*, which could be translated as 'basism' or grassroots activity. By *basismo* he means the combination of Church groups, labour unions, non-governmental organizations and grassroots movements, intellectuals and think-tanks (including liberation theologians), and human rights groups which together mobilized 'from below'. They were the principal representatives of the civil society and its demands for democracy during the military dictatorships.

According to Lehmann, the presence of church people, base communities and liberation theology provided this broad democracy movement and the Latin American social movements of those years with a different type or *alternative* discourse and ideological framework to that of Marxism and Latin America's traditional left.[2]

Thus, Lehmann's argument is quite different from those that tend to analyze liberation theology primarily in relationship to the Soviet type of socialism. In such

---

[1] I have analyzed this in more detail in E. Vuola, 'Radical Eurocentrism. The Death, Crisis, and Recipes of Improvement of Latin American Liberation Theology', *Interpreting the Postmodern: Responses to Radical Orthodoxy* (M. Grau and R. Radford Ruether (eds); London and New York: T & T Clark and Continuum, 2006a), pp. 57–75.

[2] D. Lehmann, *Democracy and Development in Latin America: Economics, Politics and Religion in the Postwar Period* (Cambridge: Polity Press, 1990); pp. xiii, 147.

reasoning, liberation theologians' political alliances with the Latin American left are wrongly interpreted as supporting authoritarian state socialism and its rigid Marxism. Following Lehmann, it could be said that the inbuilt Christian ethos, in both theory and practice, may be one of the special features of the Latin American left. Identifying it with Eastern European or Soviet socialism is thus quite problematic. The realities of the Cold War and the hierarchical view of the Church made it impossible for the late pope, John Paul II, to understand the deeply spiritual and ethical core of liberation theology: the vision of and trust in a God who sides with the poor and oppressed, on the one hand, and the conviction based on such an image of God that human freedom and value must become reality in society, on the other hand.

I. The Poor and Other Oppressed Groups

Classical liberation theology offered critical reflection both on the roles of society and politics in maintaining poverty and violence, but also on the ways theology and the churches participated in these oppressive structures. These liberationists claimed the poor as their starting point for their critique of theology and the role of Christian churches vis-à-vis massive poverty in areas colonized by Christian Europe. Since the classical period of liberation theology (1970s–1980s), this starting point has been further developed. The poor as a central category has been expanded and specified, especially due to the critique that poverty and the poor cannot be conceived merely in economic or material terms. Women, indigenous people, and descendants of African slaves on the continent have all criticized liberation theology for having a too narrow view of poverty and the poor. Issues of racism and sexism have not been central in liberation theology, nor have they been elaborated into a deeper and more nuanced understanding of how poverty affects different people differently, even when the poorest in Latin America are to be found in racially and ethnically disadvantaged groups, as well as among women. In other words, the poverty of indigenous people, Afro Latin Americans and women (especially women among those groups) is aggravated because of their ethnic, racial, and gender status.

Because of this critique, many – if not all – first-generation liberation theologians have modified their thinking concerning the poor. For example, in later editions of his classic *Teología de la liberación*, Gustavo Gutierréz was careful to mention that the poorest of the poor are women, children and indigenous people. Nevertheless, this inclusion of other forms of oppression has been minor and to some extent superficial: no substantial change has occurred theoretically or practically. The list of the oppressed is expanded and new forms of oppression are mentioned but these critiques are not included in the core of theorizing about poverty and theology.

In my earlier work, I have pointed out how issues of sexual and reproductive ethics have been lacking in liberation theology and how that lack touches the very core of liberation theology's central epistemological and ethical claims.[3] In

---

[3] E. Vuola, *Limits of Liberation. Feminist Theology and the Ethics of Poverty and Reproduction* (Sheffield and New York: Sheffield Academic Press and Continuum, 2002a).

development studies and gender studies, it has long been acknowledged that issues of sexuality, reproduction and poverty have to be analyzed and tackled simultaneously in order to reduce poverty. These questions are directly linked to issues of ecology, sustainable development and population growth.[4] In religious circles, and not just 'conservative' ones such as the Vatican, conservative Evangelicals or Muslims, but also otherwise critical and politically radical theologians such as liberation theologians, this fact has been almost totally left aside for intra-religious or intra-theological reasons. The main reason for this omission lies in the complex relationship of different religious traditions with human sexuality, reproduction and women. The problem is not exclusively Catholic, even in Latin America.[5]

II. Social Movements and Liberation Theology

The political alliances between environmental movements and liberation theological sectors of the churches are practically non-existent. At the same time, the importance of environmental and feminist movements in society can no longer be ignored, especially in the global south where both environmental degradation and gender inequalities most affect those that are poor. In liberation theology, nature is now mentioned together with women, indigenous people, Afro Latin Americans and children as being in need of liberation.

My point is not at all to trivialize this sensitivity to new issues that need to be included and taken seriously by liberation theologians. My somewhat critical point is that in today's liberation theology these social and political concerns do not have the status – either theoretically or practically – that social movements used to have in early liberation theology. The inclusion of different forms of oppression is not stemming from a dialogue with the corresponding social movements, theoretically or practically, or from an in-depth knowledge of the continent's (non-Christian or syncretistic) spiritual traditions. In the early days of liberation theology, theological concerns were tied to – or they even grew out of – concrete political struggles, such as the defence of human rights during the military dictatorships, land issues, labour unions and even early women's movements. Liberation theology was born out of the political and spiritual struggle of these groups. No such living, mutual relationship exists between today's liberation theology and new social movements. I am not suggesting that liberation theology has become depoliticized, but rather

---

[4] For example, Naila Kabeer states that, 'A population policy that is concerned with the needs of the poor, as well as with the preservation of the natural environment, has to break finally with the narrow fertility-reduction goals of the past and address the social conditions in which reproductive choices can be enhanced'. N. Kabeer, *Reversed Realities: Gender Hierarchies in Development Thought* (London: Verso, 1997), p. 204. See also several articles in N. Visvanathan, L. Duggan, L. Nisonoff and N. Wiegersma (eds), *The Women, Gender and Development Reader* (London: Zed Books, 1997).

[5] E. Vuola, 'Remaking Universals? Transnational Feminism(s) Challenging Fundamentalist Ecumenism', *Theory, Culture and Society* 19 (2002b), pp. 175–195.

that it is not sufficiently in contact with contemporary political struggles, which may envision the political and the public sphere in quite different terms than in the 1970s or 1980s.

The democratization of Latin America has given birth to new social and political movements. They are both the reason for and a product of democratization processes. In many countries, liberation theology is rightly counted among the theoretical and practical bases of these movements. For example, in Brazil both the early women's movement as well as the landless people's movement (MST) were born under the auspices of the Catholic church which used liberation theological language and analysis for the defence of the weak and marginalized.[6] However, the *basismo* type of activism, which I mentioned earlier, is no longer a reality, at least not in way it was before.

New social movements such as women's movements, environmental movements, antiracist, and indigenous rights movements as well as gay and lesbian rights movements, raise questions and demands that were impossible or very difficult to voice during the military dictatorships. In formally democratic countries, they also ask critical questions of the real depth and true content of democracy: why is it that some groups are still without full human and civil rights in society? Especially for feminist and gay and lesbian rights movements it is also about the conflict between the public and the private. As soon as the Brazilian feminist movement started to deal with issues of sexuality and reproduction, their alliance even with the liberation theology wing of the Catholic Church started to fail.

Bonnie Shepard speaks of a culture of *doble discurso* (double discourse), by which she means that in Latin American class societies, private practices (contraception, abortion, homosexuality, etc.) do not turn into public issues as long as the elites can get away with them without consequences; either with money, high quality health care services or protecting social networks. There is thus no pressure from the elites to change the current situation, for example, concerning decriminalization of abortion or securing sexual education in public schools. The result is that current political, legal and religious regulations affect most seriously those who already are the most marginalized in society.[7]

More precisely, for specific religious and theological reasons, issues concerning sexuality are also difficult to deal with for liberation theologians. The sexual ethical teaching of the Catholic Church has been questioned and reinterpreted by various Catholic theologians, mainly outside the most Catholic region of the world, Latin America. The role of religion and the churches is, however, central in issues related to sexuality, family and reproduction. Latin American liberation theologians

---

[6] See, for example, S. E. Alvarez, *Engendering Democracy in Brazil: Women's Movements in Transition Politics* (Princeton: Princeton University Press, 1990), pp. 59–70, on the relationship between the Church and the early women's movement; J. Burdick, *Legacies of Liberation. The Progressive Catholic Church in Brazil at the Start of a New Millennium* (Aldershot: Ashgate, 2004), pp. 101–114.

[7] B. Shepard, *Running the Obstacle Course to Sexual and Reproductive Health: Lessons from Latin America* (Westport: Praeger, 2006).

should and could be at the forefront of a critical self-analysis of that role both historically and today, especially in relation to poverty and marginalization. That is exactly what liberation theologians did earlier: their critique was not aimed only at society but also at Christian theology and the churches. Liberation theology was a critical and constructive attempt to interpret the meaning of Christianity in contemporary society.

Lack of dialogue and cooperation between liberation theology and new social movements may thus result in liberation theologians lack of credibility in major contemporary social issues, such as sexual ethics, racism, religious syncretism, environmental issues and popular religion; all relevant for women, indigenous, and African American people. The overall result is that liberation theology is seen by many as white, Western, patriarchal and anti-sexual. Or, in other words, that not even liberation theology can break away from the long legacy of Christian theology in legitimizing sexism and racism.

I believe that what is easily seen as mere 'adding' of new concerns to liberation theology reflects – and is possibly a result of – the lack of political engagement with contemporary social movements. The relationship of liberation theology with these movements is thin, and not as substantial and concrete as in the *basismo* type of activity earlier. I mean both the practical and theoretical aspects of these movements in the case of the feminist movement, sexism; in antiracist movements, racism; and so on. Liberation theologians have not been willing or able to create strategic alliances with them. The lack of dialogue and engagement has epistemological consequences for Latin American liberation theology today.

It is my understanding that the often presumed crisis of liberation theology today – if there is such – is not derived from the most often presented assumption of a causal relationship between the fall of socialism and today's liberation theology, as much as it is a result of the lack of engagement with the political demands, and the ways of theorizing them, of contemporary social movements in the continent. This is related to both a deeper and more nuanced understanding of democracy and, more specifically, to new forms of understanding the body and human bodiliness, including but not only in its sexual dimension but racially and ethnically as well. A theology of the body and a new theology of sexuality from a Latin American liberation theological perspective[8] could bridge some of the now yawning gaps of analysis between poverty, racism, sexism and ecology.

Some liberation theologians have been actively involved in the World Social Forum, creating in 2005 the World Forum for Liberation and Theology.[9] Globalization critique, or globalization from below, is potentially a new form of liberation theology from the South, which includes Latin America, aimed at establishing a broad-based network and encouraging cooperation between social

---

[8] See M. Althaus-Reid (ed.), *Liberation Theology and Sexuality: New Radicalism from Latin America* (London: Ashgate, 2006).

[9] See M. Althaus-Reid, I. Petrella, and L. C. Susin (eds), *Another Possible World* (London: SCM Press, 2007); J. J. Tamayo, 'Foro mundial de teología y libearción. Teología para otro mundo possible', *Pasos* 118 (2005), pp. 32–39.

movements and theologians. It is also noteworthy that this new context has attracted second- or third-generation liberation theologians, many of them also feminist theologians. According to Juan José Tamayo, corporality and religious pluralism (inter-religious dialogue) are central in contemporary Latin American liberation theology.[10]

It may be true that among younger generation liberation theologians issues concerning gender, religious diversity, and indigenous and African-American religions and cultures are more present than among the first- and second-generation theologians. In the context of liberation theology, [11] only a few younger generation theologians treat issues of sexual ethics explicitly as part of the supposed turn to corporality. But, interestingly, the development of an ecotheology from a liberation theological perspective seems to be primarily the interest of some of the first-generation theologians.

III. Nature and Liberation: Turn to Ecotheology

Liberation theologians such as Boff and Gebara, who explicitly work on ecological issues in more depth and who wish to develop a Latin American ecotheology, are not merely 'adding' ecological issues to liberation theology's agenda. Boff does, however, present nature or the earth as 'the great poor' (*el gran pobre*) in need of liberation, together with its condemned sons and daughters.[12] He also writes:

> In the preferential option for the poor and against poverty and for liberation – trademark of liberation theology – we include the Great Poor which is the Earth, the only common home we have to live in. A theology of liberation will only be integral if it incorporates into its reflection and practice the liberation of the Earth (…).[13]

Gebara and Boff represent a form of liberation theology which could be described both as a new assessment of the central liberation theological paradigm of liberation

---

[10] J. J. Tamayo, 'Foro mundial de teología y liberación. Teología para otro mundo possible', p. 35.

[11] See the essays in M. Althaus-Reid (ed.), *Liberation Theology and Sexuality: New Radicalism from Latin America*. The Brazilian black feminist theologian Silvia Regina de Lima Silva sees one characteristic of Latin American feminist theology in the affirmation of the body i.e., body as a theological locus, in both its gendered and racialized meaning. She however does not make any link between the centrality of the (female) body and sexual ethics. See S. R. Lima Silva, 'From within Ourselves. Afrodescendant Women on Paths of Theological Reflection in Latin America and the Caribbean', *Latin American Liberation Theology: The Next Generation* (I. Petrella (ed.); New York: Orbis Books, 2005), pp. 62–74 (67,70).

[12] L. Boff, 'Si no tenemos utopías, nos empantanamos en los intereses individuales', *Clarín* (August 2008), www.clarin.com/diario/2008/08/24/um/m-01745277.htm (accessed 14 May 2010).

[13] L. Boff, 'Two Urgent Utopias for the Twenty-First Century', *Another Possible World* (M. Althaus-Reid, I. Petrella, and L. C. Susin (eds); London: SCM Press, 2007), pp. 4–9 (5).

(now nature or the globe in need of liberation from human exploitation), and as a departure from classical liberation theology and its anthropocentric understanding of subjectivity and agency. In the latter case, their form of thinking distances itself not only from liberation theology, but also from some aspects of classical Christian theology more generally (for example, Christianity as universal truth, the centrality of Jesus, and the image of God). Leonardo Boff understands himself as a representative of liberation theology. For Gebara, as for Latin American feminist theologians more generally, the situation is more complicated. She both sees a continuum between liberation theology and her feminist theology, but she also has maintained a distance from liberation theology.

Ecofeminism is a name for a diverse group of thinkers and activists. It is understood both as an intellectual current, variably either a branch of feminist theory, development studies (especially in the South), or ecology, and as a political movement, again either as part of political feminism or of the ecological movement. It is impossible here to go into detail concerning the sometimes heated debate about ecofeminism's central discussions, even about its very core, and the relationship between women and nature. There is no consensus about it even among ecofeminists themselves.

Latin American feminist ecotheology is a growing field. Gebara is its most prominent – or, at least the best known – proponent. Her ecotheology reflects and includes most of the discussions that ecofeminists in other countries and regions have employed, and thus raises the question about what is specifically Latin American in her thinking. Obviously, it is the perspective of the impoverished South, especially its women, that arises from her own concrete experiences of working with poor urban women. However, it is difficult to see what makes her a specifically Latin American thinker, what her contribution to a Latin American ecofeminism would be, or what a specifically Latin American ecofeminism would look like. This is a relevant question because liberation theologians have always claimed that they think *desde América Latina* (from Latin America), from their own context, and thus understand their cultural and political context as an epistemic space, to paraphrase Arturo Escobar.[14]

I am by no means belittling Gebara's importance for developing Latin American liberation theology, feminist theology and ecotheology; however, I wish to point out two critical questions. They are both related to what I said above about liberation theologians' general lack of dialogue with new social and political movements.

These critical questions have to do, first, with the relationship of liberation theology with the indigenous cultures and popular religiosity (*religiosidad popular*) and, second, with the feminist movements and theorizing on the continent. Both Gebara and Boff take the nature wisdom of indigenous peoples and cultures for granted: they do this on a general level without giving much empirical evidence for what this supposed wisdom consists of or how it differs from non-indigenous groups and cultures. Anthropological research of indigenous cultures could give a

---

[14] A. Escobar, 'Worlds and Knowledges Otherwise: The Latin American Modernity/Coloniality Research Program', *Cultural Studies* 21 (2007), pp. 179–210 (190).

more detailed and varied image of their supposed nature wisdom and relationship to nature. In concrete terms, ecological concerns often lie at the centre of contemporary political struggles of indigenous peoples; however, these struggles do not form the social and practical base of today's liberation theology.

IV. Indigenous People and Liberation Theology

The distance between Christian liberation ecotheologians and the practices of the indigenous cultures may reflect a fear of what for centuries has been perceived as syncretism and non-Christian ('pagan') beliefs. The rich diversity of Latin America's religious landscape can be seen in the African-based religions (most notably *candomblé, umbanda, voudou, santería*), in the wide variety of indigenous religions, and in forms of popular Catholicism. These specifically Latin American forms of religiosity are practically non-existent in liberation theology, both in its earlier forms and in the ecotheological versions of it.[15]

There are some single exceptions such as Diego Irarrazával from Peru, who has worked on *teología indígena*, aiming at in-depth interreligious dialogue between indigenous religious systems and beliefs and Catholic (Christian) theology.[16] By and large, the thinness of liberation theologians' relationship to the indigenous cultures of their continent becomes clear when these are referred to so generally and homogenously, without paying attention to the differences between them or the possible conflicts and differences inside them.

What is usually called popular religiosity in Latin America has pejorative meanings attached to the concept itself (as do folk religion and syncretism), which may be one reason why the practices of popular Catholicism have never attained the interest of theologians, even liberation theologians. Ethnographic knowledge of local religious beliefs and cults is not included in theology, even when it is the 'common people' or 'Latin American' culture which are said to be the starting point of theology. This is true of practically all contemporary Latin American theology – be it liberation, feminist or ecological theology.

Robert A. Orsi – who has done ethnographic research on popular Catholicism in the United States, for example, the devotion of the Virgin Mary among contemporary Italian-descendant Catholics – stresses the importance of 'popular religion' and ethnographic methods for theology. He in fact questions the very use of terms such as popular religion as tendentious and unclear and instead uses the term 'lived religion', meaning 'religious practice and imagination in ongoing, dynamic relation

---

[15] For an exception, see for example S. R. Lima Silva, 'From within Ourselves. Afrodescendant Women on Paths of Theological Reflection in Latin America and the Caribbean', pp. 71–72.
[16] See D. Irarrazával, *Un Cristianismo Andino* (Quito: Abya-Yala, 1999); D. Irarrazával, *Inculturation: New Dawn of the Church in Latin America* (P. Berryman (trans.); Eugene, OR: Wipf and Stock Publishers, 2008); D. Irarrazával, *Raíces de la Esperanza* (Lima: CEP, 2004).

with the realities and structures of everyday life in particular times and places'.[17] His critique of the use of the term 'popular' is closely related to the hierarchies between the normative and the 'other' in academic studies of religion. Rethinking religion as a form of cultural work, according to Orsi, 'directs attention to institutions *and* persons, texts *and* rituals, practice *and* theology, things *and* ideas' and 'is concerned with what people *do* with religious idioms, how they use them, what they make of themselves and their worlds with them ... Religious practices and understandings have meaning only in relation to other cultural forms and in relation to the life experiences and actual circumstances of the people using them ...'[18]

Ethnographic methods in the study of religion have not been widely adopted by theologians. Feminist theology especially could work in closer contact with scholars who study religion as 'lived religion' and base some of its central claims about the sexism of patriarchal religions on women's concrete experiences, interpretations and agency within those traditions. Even in feminist theology, in which there has always been a keen interest in everyday, 'ordinary' experiences, there is striking gap between what is said about women's religious experiences, on the one hand, and the methods used to sustain that (the absence of ethnographic methods), on the other hand. The same of course could be said of indigenous and African-American religions: how much in fact is ethnographic and detailed knowledge of them used to sustain the claims of their relationship to nature? By and large, research done by anthropologists, especially on the cosmologies and practices of the indigenous cultures of the Americas, does not form an important source of knowledge for Latin American eco- and other theologians. Obviously, it could be used in a way similar to how social scientific and economic research was incorporated into liberation theology. It should be used when claims are made about indigenous people's knowledge, cosmologies, and religious practices.

There have been warnings of replacing Eurocentrism with 'indiocentrism' in liberation theology. Brazilian scholars Josué A. Sathler and Amós Nascimento take a critical look at the generalized view of the '*Indio*' in liberation theology, in many ways analogous to a feminist critique of 'women'. They also analyze how syncretism is understood in the traditional terms of mission and conversion in liberation theology, which justifies an asymmetric position between African-based religions and Christianity.[19] According to Sathler and Nascimento,

> ... there is a systematic rejection of the African and African-American element as constitutive of Brazilian multiculturalism, ethnic diversity and religious plurality. The great problem ... is the inability to conceive simultaneously Native, European, and African

---

[17] R. A. Orsi, *The Madonna of 115th Street: Faith and Community in Italian Harlem, 1880–1950* (New Haven and London: Yale University Press, 2002), pp. xiii–xiv.

[18] Ibid., pp. xix–xx.

[19] J. A. Sathler, and A. Nascimento, 'Black Masks on White Faces. Liberation Theology and the Quest for Syncretism in the Brazilian Context', *Liberation Theology, Postmodernity, and the Americas* (D. Batstone, E. Mendieta, L. A. Lorentzen, and D. N. Hopkins (eds); London and New York: Routledge, 1997), pp. 95–122 (100, 113).

cultures, without reducing them to something else that is, at the end, white, European, Catholic (Christian).[20]

Even inside formal Catholicism, popular religiosity or lived religion differs from 'official' doctrine and practises at least in the following issues:[21] the centrality of the body (in ritual, healing, dance etc.), the sacredness or sacrality of (all spheres of) life, relationship to nature (land, water, earth, sacred places), everyday life at the centre of religious activity (prayers, healing, miracles, relationships), concreteness and visuality (things such as *ex votos*, votive offerings) and often, but not always, greater ritual space for women. The latter is especially true in African-based religions. 'Popular religiosity' may be the only sphere where women have religious authority and right to interpretation. Finally, the relationship between the human and the divine is both closer and more diffuse: the human and the divine interact and influence each other. This interaction takes place in (relation to) the human body, through ritual, dance, trance and music. Elements such as water, flowers, fruits and different kinds of votive offerings, often in the form of the human body, are central in 'popular' Catholicism.

The need to value the sacramental character of life is something that most if not all ecotheologians stress. However, it is striking in the case of Latin American liberation theologians how unaware or dismissive they seem to be of the richness that the religious traditions of their continent offer.

V. Women, Gender, and Ecology

A similar omission of the continent's own traditions occurs with women and feminism: practically the only reference in, for example, Gebara's writings is to one ecofeminist group in the Southern Cone (*Con-Spirando* in Chile), a group which could best be described as cultural ecofeminism or ecofeminist spirituality. Other types of feminist activism, most notably that for sexual and reproductive rights, is lacking, and especially its relationship to ecological issues. Of all Latin American countries, these movements are most radical and broad-based in Brazil, Gebara's home country.

Unfortunately, critical analysis of the interplay between sexuality, reproduction, and religion is lacking in most of Latin American feminist theology. Feminist theorizing on issues of sexuality and reproduction is done by social scientists, not theologians. This may lead to a situation in which the role of religion in women's lives is not correctly understood.

---

[20] Ibid., p. 115.

[21] My own research has concentrated on 'popular' local cults of the Virgin Mary in Central America, especially Costa Rica. See for example E. Vuola, 'Patriarchal Ecumenism, Feminism, and Women's Religious Experiences in Costa Rica', *Gendering Religion and Politics. Untangling Modernities* (H. Herzog and A. Braude (eds); New York: Palgrave Macmillan, 2009), pp. 217–238.

Let me offer an example. The UN Conference on Environment and Development held in Rio de Janeiro, Brazil in 1992 made popular the notion that the 'population explosion' is the cause of the environmental destruction of the planet. Environmental activists and researchers joined women's groups in being critical of the mainstream arguments of population and environment. Both environmental and feminist activists challenge the current development model by arguing that we need to move away from solutions based on infinite growth. Nevertheless, alliances between women's groups and environmentalists falter because the policies proposed do not usually say anything about women. Women fear that in order to 'save the planet', they may again become targets of coercive population programmes, which do not take women's empowerment as the starting point but rather see them as objects to be controlled. Poor women are blamed for global consumption for which they are not responsible. As long as environmental degradation is seen principally as the result of (only) population growth, this argument may lay the groundwork for the re-emergence and intensification of top-down demographically driven population policies and programmes that are disrespectful of women, particularly women of colour, and their children.

A similar logic – even if with quite different presuppositions and goals – is the basis of traditional Catholic sexual ethics and teaching: women, especially, have to be told from above how to live their sexuality and reproductive potential.[22] In a Catholic continent like Latin America, this problem cannot be solved without a critical analysis of the role of the church and theology. Until now, neither traditional nor liberation theologians, including feminist and ecotheologians, have been able to do this.[23]

The variety and diversity of both indigenous cultures and feminist and women's movements in the continent is almost nowhere to be seen in Latin American liberation and ecotheologians' writings. These movements and cultures remain a vague reference point, which too easily takes for granted that there is a different

---

[22] See for example Congregation for the Doctrine of the Faith, *Instruction on Respect for Human Life in Its Origin and on the Dignity of Procreation: Replies to Certain Questions of the Day (Donum Vitae)* (Rome, 1987); John Paul II, *Evangelium Vitae* (Libreria Editrice Vaticana: Rome, 1995); Benedict XVI, *Caritas in Veritate* (Libreria Editrice Vaticana: Rome, 2009). It is impossible here to analyze in detail contemporary Roman Catholic teaching. Interestingly, it builds today on many insights from both feminist and liberation theology on women's dignity and poverty, for example. The result is a mixture of a language which, together with feminists, critiques disrespectful practices of demographic control, and, contrary to any feminist approach, does not approve 'artificial contraception' or abortion in any case. I analyze this in detail in the Latin American context in E. Vuola, *Limits of Liberation. Feminist Theology and the Ethics of Poverty and Reproduction*, pp. 188–228. In Latin America, Catholic bishops combine liberation theological language with the traditional view on sexuality and reproduction when speaking of demographic imperialism.

[23] See E. Vuola, *Limits of Liberation. Feminist Theology and the Ethics of Poverty and Reproduction*; E. Vuola, 'Remaking Universals? Transnational Feminism(s) Challenging Fundamentalist Ecumenism', p. 188.

relationship with and logic in both indigenous people's and women's relationship to nature from that of the *mestizo* or 'Western' culture or from men.

Boff's earlier works have been criticized by feminist theologians from both Latin America and elsewhere, including myself, concerning his romantic and binary view of gender and women. Among the first-generation liberation theologians, he is to be credited for taking gender issues seriously. In his later ecotheological writings, the critique of feminist theologians is met when he stresses the importance of women's roles and ecofeminism for ecotheology, even when he does not show how this in fact happens. However, by not taking the next step, Boff fails to meet the critique, which in fact is the core of the critique levelled at him by feminist theologians. The very constructions of gender, of 'men' and 'women', of the 'masculine' and the 'feminine', are not deconstructed by Boff. In this, he is siding with those ecofeminists who start from an assumption of gender difference, such as the assumption that women are more holistic, sensitive, and caring than men. Consequently, nature may become as romanticized as women.

Let me give an example of a possible reproduction of gender binaries in Boff's ecotheology. He distinguishes three different eras in the human relationship to nature: the pre-modern era of the spirit, the modern era of the body, and the third era, which we are entering now, is described as the era of life that connects body and spirit. According to Boff,

> the era of the spirit flourished in indigenous and ancestral cultures. [...] This grounding experience connected them in kinship with all things, creating a union mystique with beings and giving rise to a deep spiritual development. [...] That was the time when great myths were projected and the deities were born. [...] Second comes the era of the body. Human beings discover the body, the physical force of the Earth and the cosmos (...) when human beings became aware that they could manipulate that force for their advantage.[24]

Somewhat surprisingly, he equates the spirit with good and the body with evil, when the 'era of the body' is depicted in terms of systematic conquest of the Earth, the exploitation of its resources, and the loss of experience of its sacredness.[25] Many ecophilosophers would agree with this, especially concerning the modern era which has lost the sense of the sacrality of nature. To reframe this development in terms of spirit and body, however, may result in a reproduction of one of the most pervasive dualisms in Christian theology. Can this be reconciled with Boff's intention to value women, sexuality, bodiliness and human relationship to nature? I argue that it is in fact difficult to do because of the overall lack of a critical deconstruction of the spirit-body dualism itself. The result is alternately an attempt to value the spirit or the body, but the dualism itself is left intact in Boff's view of the human being, male and female, and of the culture-nature relationship. The spirit-body dualism or

---

[24] L. Boff, *Cry of the Earth, Cry of the Poor* (Phillip Berryman (trans.); New York: Orbis Books, 1997), pp. 76-77.
[25] Ibid.

dichotomy, as so many feminist theologians have pointed out, goes hand in hand with the male–female dichotomy, the West and the rest dualism, and the culture–nature dualism. These binary oppositions, as they are called in feminist theory, and their hierarchical relationship must be deconstructed. Otherwise there is a danger of either demonizing women and indigenous people (as classical and colonial theology did) or romanticizing them, as much ecotheology does, without taking seriously the real problems they are facing as bodily human beings and citizens. Needless to say, shifting the 'good' and 'bad' from one binary to another is not how a true deconstruction takes place. Most feminist theologians and philosophers have been insisting on the danger of reversing the dualisms or binaries.

A theology of the body – in the widest possible sense – in the Latin American context could simply start from the bodily realities of us being sexual and gendered beings, the body as our only way of being human in constant dependence on each other and on non-human nature. The diversity of being human includes not only gender, but ethnic, sexual, and other differences as well. In this sense, for me, an 'era of the body' is still to be waited for; it is not something *passé* as Boff sees it. A genuine respect for the body could be the starting point for an ecologically sound relationship to nature as well. Joining most feminist theologians, Gebara pays more attention to the devaluation of the human body, especially the female body in classical theology, and takes it, and not simply gender, as the starting point. The daily realities of urban poor women need to be resolved, but just as necessary is a critical evaluation of the religious and ethical constructions of the body, reproduction and sexuality in Christian theology.

VI. Drinking from Latin America's Own Wells

One of liberation theology's ideals has been 'drinking from our own wells'.[26] In the case of Latin American ecotheology, this could mean substantial knowledge of and engagement with the various indigenous cultures, their religious traditions, and their contemporary struggles. For Boff and Gebara, feminism has an important epistemological and political role; however, if feminism is indeed important to them, we would expect to see feminist theorizing and feminist politics at the core of their analysis of the Latin American situation. This is especially true for the analysis of the relationship between poverty and gender and their links to environmental issues. What is distinctive about Latin America is the classical class structure of its societies, on the one hand, and the predominance of Catholicism and its specific understanding and teaching of women, family, sexuality, sexual ethics and family planning, on the other hand. These are all issues that have direct relevance to ecological issues. The responsibility for critically analyzing and deconstructing the link between gender, ecological issues and poverty could be primarily that of politically, socially and ecologically sensitive theologians such as Gebara and Boff. Doing

---

[26] G. Gutiérrez, *Beber en su propio pozo. En el itinerario espiritual de un pueblo*, CEP: Lima, 3rd edn, 1989.

this would give a specific Latin American flavour to liberation theological ecotheology and re-establish its links to concrete political struggles in the continent. However, I am arguing that by and large this is not happening.

In the case of women, Catholic theologians such as Boff and Gebara need to be responsible for creating a new sexual and reproductive ethics which would be attentive to women, especially poor and ethnically or racially disadvantaged women, and ecological issues at the same time. Needless to say, that would mean a bold departure from mainstream Catholic teachings. A defence of 'life', which liberation theologians and Latin American ecotheologians claim to be doing, combined with an elaboration of the image of God as the god of life (*el dios de la vida*) and the moral requirement to defend life in all its forms, may in fact come close to traditional sexual ethical teaching of the Catholic church. This is probably not liberation theologians' intention, in fact I know it is not, but this is exactly my point. Without a well-based, explicit, and radical theorization of what is meant by 'life' and its defence, the liberation theological project faces the risk of sounding like the Vatican. Issues of reproduction, sexuality and family are at the core of possible solutions to ecological crises, especially in relation to poverty.

Movements defending sexual and reproductive rights in Latin America most often have the Catholic Church as their primary enemy. If progressive Catholic liberation theologians, including feminist theologians, do not explicitly distance themselves from the 'hierarchy' and side with ordinary people – as they did in the 1970s and 1980s – it will be very difficult for political activists to see any difference between the official and the dissenting or alternative parts of the Church.

In another book Boff presents 'care' and 'work' (care as feminine, work as masculine) as opposite ways of relating to life. He is probably relying on the work of some feminist ethicists, most notably Carol Gilligan whose theory about women's care-oriented ethics has been widely debated, but Boff does not mention these sources. Without discussing this further, I just point out how here again the problem of a too dualistic and binary view of gender may turn out to be very problematic. Without doubt, women in different parts of the world have been and are more oriented towards 'care' than men, professionally and inter-relationally. However, it is also a major problem for women. Men's abilities for care, fatherhood, sexual partnership and so on, are not mentioned by Boff. Human beings, both men and women, learn to care; care is not something essentially 'feminine'.

According to Boff, the contribution of ecofeminism lies in the fact that

> by instinct and by the unique way that they are constituted, women grasp and live out the complexity and interconnection of the real. By nature women are connected directly to what is most complex in the universe, namely life. [...] Women are related to life more by care than by labor. Care presupposes an ethic of respect, a basic stance required when facing the sacred. [...] It is primarily (though not exclusively) women who, with their presence as wives, mothers, companions, and counselors, handle this art and technique of the complex ...[27]

[27] L. Boff, *Essential Care: An Ethics of Human Nature* (Alexandre Guilherme (trans.); London: SPCK Books, 2007), pp. 26–27.

Boff's explicit aim is to overcome gender domination, but he takes no clue from either feminist political demands or feminist theories. He is relying here on the idea of complementarity of the sexes, which is the basis of Catholic teaching on men and women and their relationship, but also of many ecophilosophies. The problem with the complementarity model is that behaviour is seen as inherently gendered. Harmony and balance is thought to be obtained through this complementarity in which both the 'masculine' and the 'feminine' are valued. A deeper problem in the complementarity model is that the basic structure is never called into question. The binary oppositions male–female, masculine–feminine, remain intact. Both the traditional Catholic complementarity-of-the-sexes model and Boff's version of it are notably silent about issues of economy, population growth, production of food, family relationships, power and the lack of it, and sexual and reproductive rights when discussing 'the feminine' and 'the masculine'. It is important to note that Ivone Gebara does not build her ecotheology on the abstract complementarity model in the manner of Boff. She speaks of concrete men and women, not of masculinity and femininity as two sides of a coin.[28]

The reinforcement of the binary oppositions or dualisms is clear when women are thought to be closer by nature to life and care and when they are seen primarily in their roles as mothers and companions. In the case of indigenous people, it is important to remember that since the very beginning of the Conquest they were defined by nature as subordinate and less human than Europeans. This dehumanization had concrete effects such as slavery. The European Christian male has been the exemplary and normative human being for a long time. Turning this structure upside down – even to the extent of romanticizing women and indigenous people and their supposed closeness to nature and life – does nothing to change the real problems they are facing: lack of power, lack of civil, cultural and reproductive rights, land issues, and poverty, in addition to outright sexism and racism. An ecotheological approach that relies on the binary oppositions of male–female, spirit–body, Western–indigenous, sacred–profane, etc. by revaluing them differently does not change the dualism itself.

Christian theologians and liberation theologians have specific problems with women's and indigenous people's demands for autonomy and respect because of their long-held views of indigenous and Afro Latin American religions and cultures as syncretistic, non-Christian and pagan, on the one hand, and of human sexuality, gender and the body, on the other hand.

Empirically, it may be difficult to sustain the notion of indigenous and (Third World) women's greater care for nature vis-à-vis men.[29] In many regions and

---

[28] See I. Gebara, *Out of the Depths. Women's Experience of Evil and Salvation* (Ann Patrick Ware (trans.); Minneapolis: Fortress Press, 2002) in which she relates evil to concrete experiences of violence and suffering.

[29] See for example C. Nyamweru, 'Women and Sacred Groves in Coastal Kenya: A Contribution to the Ecofeminist Debate', *Ecofeminism and Globalization: Exploring Culture, Context, and Religion* (H. Eaton and L. A. Lorentzen (eds); Lanham: Rowman and Littlefield, 2003), pp. 41–56; L. Lorentzen, 'Indigenous Feet: Ecofeminism, Globalization, and the Case

cultures of the world, it is men rather than women who are associated with nature and who are seen as the primary caretakers and experts of the natural world. Women may be more likely to be identified with culture.[30] Thus, Lois Lorentzen warns of the tendency to romanticize indigenous and other so-called Third World women 'as the ultimate ecofeminists', and to replicate the dualism between the (white, Western, male) self and the (racialized, gendered) Other.[31]

VII. Concluding Remarks

In agreement with Lorentzen, my major overall criticism of Latin American liberation theologians' turn to ecotheology lies first in its lack of substantial analysis and its failure to critique the underlying dualisms or binaries in classical Christian theology. Even when ecotheologians such as Boff state that the problem of dualism is at the root of ecological crises. In fact, what we are seeing is a tendency to replicate those dualisms or binary oppositions. Second, I critique the tendency to include indigenous, gender and ecological concerns into the core of theology without applying the core of the practical and theoretical critique expressed by the corresponding social movements, which demand concrete political changes at the intersections of race, gender and sexuality, class, ethnicity, race, and ecology.[32] Third, I suggest that Latin American liberation theologians' self-understanding as intellectuals 'thinking from Latin America' is to some extent incomplete, partly because of the above-mentioned unwillingness to distance themselves from racist and sexist elements in classical Christian theology. And finally, I argue that this somewhat narrow view of what is 'Latin American' is partly a result of (Catholic) liberation theologians' lack of knowledge and interaction with indigenous spiritualities, popular Catholicism and Afro Latin American religions.

All this creates a somewhat contradictory situation in Latin American ecological liberation theology: it becomes overly theoretical and abstract, on the one hand, and not deeply elaborated theoretically, on the other hand. By the first I mean the already mentioned detachment from the realities of the struggles of new social

---

of Chiapas', *Ecofeminism and Globalization: Exploring Culture, Context, and Religion* (H. Eaton and L. A. Lorentzen (eds); Lanham: Rowman and Littlefield, 2003), pp. 57-71 (67).

[30] I think this holds true also for the Finnish culture, in which the wilderness, especially the forest, has been primarily the man's domain. Finnish masculinity even today is culturally constructed in relationship to and through nature.

[31] L. Lorentzen, 'Indigenous Feet: Ecofeminism, Globalization, and the Case of Chiapas', pp. 66-67.

[32] A somewhat similar argument is made by the younger generation liberation theologian Iván Petrella when he stresses the link between the theological and the political, which he sees as missing in the current forms of liberation theology. The notion of a 'historical project' was central in earlier liberation theology. I. Petrella, 'Latin American Liberation Theology, Globalization, and Historical Projects: From Critique to Construction', *Latin American Perspectives on Globalization: Ethics, Politics, and Alternative Visions* (M. Saénz (ed.); Lanham: Rowman & Littlefield, 2002), pp. 200-229 (210-211, 220).

movements and the people they represent. By the latter, I refer to the lack of critical elaboration of the complexity of claims about the human relationship to nature, be it that of indigenous people or women, which would go beyond mere generalizations. Theoretically, this reflects a lack or selectiveness of inter-disciplinarity in liberation theology. Anthropology and feminist theory are the principal fields from which to draw, if one wants to create a theological understanding of indigenous cultures and religions as well as of gender issues.

It seems that among the younger generation liberation theologians there is more elaboration and inclusion of insights from theories such as feminist theory and postcolonialism. They, however, have not worked on ecotheological issues as extensively as some first-generation liberation theologians like Gebara and Boff. In Latin American eco-liberation theology, the turn away from 'anthropocentrism' may have occurred too early in the eyes of Latin American women, indigenous peoples, and African Americans, when so many critical issues related to theological anthropology have been left practically intact in liberation theology. The *anthropos* in what has been named anthropocentrism may in fact have been the classical subject of Christian theology: white, male, and European. To move away too fast from reworking this *anthropos* from the perspective of colonialized, racialized and gendered subjects, also makes it difficult to reconceive human beings' relation to nature in radically new terms.

Bibliography

Althaus-Reid, M. (ed.), *Liberation Theology and Sexuality: New Radicalism from Latin America* (London: Ashgate, 2006).

Althaus-Reid, M., I. Petrella, and L. C. Susin (eds), *Another Possible World* (London: SCM Press, 2007).

Alvarez, S. E., *Engendering Democracy in Brazil: Women's Movements in Transition Politics* (Princeton: Princeton University Press, 1990).

Benedict XVI, *Caritas in Veritate* (Rome: Libreria Editrice Vaticana, 2009).

Boff, L., *Cry of the Earth, Cry of the Poor* (P. Berryman (trans.); New York: Orbis Books, 1997).

—*Essential Care: An Ethics of Human Nature* (A. Guilherme (trans.); London: SPCK Books, 2007).

—*Ética planetaria desde el Gran Sur* (J. F. D. García (trans.); Madrid: Editorial Trotta, 2001).

—'Si no tenemos utopías, nos empantanamos en los intereses individuales', *Clarín* (August 2008), www.clarin.com/diario/2008/08/24/um/m-01745277.htm (accessed 14 May 2010).

—'Two Urgent Utopias for the Twenty-First Century', *Another Possible World* (M. Althaus-Reid, I. Petrella, and L. C. Susin (eds); London: SCM Press, 2007), pp. 4–9.

Burdick, J., *Legacies of Liberation: The Progressive Catholic Church in Brazil at the Start of a New Millennium* (Aldershot: Ashgate, 2004).

Congregation for the Doctrine of the Faith, *Instruction on Respect for Human Life in Its Origin and on the Dignity of Procreation: Replies to Certain Questions of the Day* (*Donum Vitae*) (Rome, 1987).

Escobar, A., 'Worlds and Knowledges Otherwise: The Latin American Modernity/ Coloniality Research Program', *Cultural Studies* 21 (2007), pp. 179-210.

Gebara, I., 'Ecofeminism: An Ethics of Life', *Ecofeminism and Globalization. Exploring Culture, Context, and Religion* (H. Eaton and L.A. Lorentzen (eds); Lanham: Rowman and Littlefield, 2003), pp. 163-176.

—*Longing for Running Water: Ecofeminism and Liberation* (Minneapolis: Fortress Press, 1999).

—*Out of the Depths: Women's Experience of Evil and Salvation* (Ann Patrick Ware (trans.); Minneapolis: Fortress Press, 2002).

Gutiérrez, G., *Beber en su propio pozo. En el itinerario espiritual de un pueblo* (Lima: CEP, 3rd edn, 1989).

—*Teología de la liberación: Perspectivas* (Salamanca: Ediciones Sígueme, 14th rev. edn, 1990).

Irarrazával, D., *Un Cristianismo Andino* (Quito: Abya-Yala, 1999).

—*Inculturation: New Dawn of the Church in Latin America* (P. Berryman (trans.); Eugene, OR: Wipf and Stock Publishers, 2008).

—*Raíces de la Esperanza* (Lima: CEP, 2004).

John Paul II, *Evangelium Vitae* (Rome: Libreria Editrice Vaticana, 1995).

Kabeer, N., *Reversed Realities: Gender Hierarchies in Development Thought* (London: Verso, 1997).

Kainulainen, P., *Maan viisaus. Ivone Gebaran ekofeministinen käsitys tietämisestä ja teologiasta* ['The Wisdom of the Earth. Ivone Gebara's Ecofeminist Concept of Knowing and Theology'] (doctoral dissertation; University of Joensuu, 2005).

Lehmann, D., *Democracy and Development in Latin America: Economics, Politics and Religion in the Postwar Period* (Cambridge: Polity Press, 1990).

Lima Silva, S. R., 'From within Ourselves. Afrodescendant Women on Paths of Theological Reflection in Latin America and the Caribbean', *Latin American Liberation Theology: The Next Generation* (I. Petrella (ed.); New York: Orbis Books, 2005), pp. 62-74.

Lorentzen, L., 'Indigenous Feet: Ecofeminism, Globalization, and the Case of Chiapas', *Ecofeminism and Globalization: Exploring Culture, Context, and Religion* (H. Eaton and L. A. Lorentzen (eds); Lanham: Rowman and Littlefield, 2003), pp. 57-71.

Nyamweru, C., 'Women and Sacred Groves in Coastal Kenya: A Contribution to the Ecofeminist Debate', *Ecofeminism and Globalization: Exploring Culture, Context, and Religion* (H. Eaton and L. A. Lorentzen (eds); Lanham: Rowman and Littlefield, 2003), pp. 41-56.

Orsi, R. A., *The Madonna of 115th Street. Faith and Community in Italian Harlem, 1880-1950* (New Haven and London: Yale University Press, 2002).

Petrella, I., 'Latin American Liberation Theology, Globalization, and Historical Projects: From Critique to Construction', *Latin American Perspectives on Globalization: Ethics, Politics, and Alternative Visions* (M. Saénz (ed.); Lanham: Rowman & Littlefield, 2002), pp. 200-229.

Sathler, J. A., and A. Nascimento, 'Black Masks on White Faces. Liberation Theology and the Quest for Syncretism in the Brazilian Context', *Liberation Theology, Postmodernity, and the Americas* (D. Batstone, E. Mendieta, L. A. Lorentzen, and D. N. Hopkins (eds); London and New York: Routledge, 1997), pp. 95–122.

Shepard, B., *Running the Obstacle Course to Sexual and Reproductive Health: Lessons from Latin America* (Westport: Praeger, 2006).

Tamayo, J. J., 'Foro mundial de teología y liberación. Teología para otro mundo possible', *Pasos* 118 (2005), pp. 32–39.

Visvanathan, N., L. Duggan, L. Nisonoff, and N. Wiegersma (eds), *The Women, Gender and Development Reader* (London: Zed Books, 1997).

Vuola, E., *Limits of Liberation. Feminist Theology and the Ethics of Poverty and Reproduction* (Sheffield and New York: Sheffield Academic Press and Continuum, 2002a).

—'Patriarchal Ecumenism, Feminism, and Women's Religious Experiences in Costa Rica', *Gendering Religion and Politics. Untangling Modernities* (H. Herzog and A. Braude (eds); New York: Palgrave Macmillan, 2009), pp. 217–238.

—'Radical Eurocentrism. The Death, Crisis, and Recipes of Improvement of Latin American Liberation Theology', *Interpreting the Postmodern: Responses to Radical Orthodoxy* (M. Grau and R. Radford Ruether (eds); London and New York: T & T Clark and Continuum, 2006a), pp. 57–75.

—'Remaking Universals? Transnational Feminism(s) Challenging Fundamentalist Ecumenism', *Theory, Culture and Society* 19 (2002b), pp. 175–195.

—'Seriously Harmful for Your Health? Religion, Feminism and Sexuality in Latin America', *Liberation Theology and Sexuality: New Radicalism from Latin America* (M. Althaus-Reid (ed.); London: Ashgate, 2006b), pp. 137–162.

6 Geology vs. Theology? Uranium Prospecting and Theological Arguments in Northern Carelia 2006–2009

Pauliina Kainulainen
University of Eastern Finland, Joensuu

In my context in Northern Carelia, Finland, the role of Christian communities and their theological starting points is changing. The new phenomenon we face is uranium prospecting and the threatening possibility of a uranium mine in the neighbourhood. If some day a uranium mine opens 20 kilometres from my home, I am concerned that my drinking water could become polluted along with the water and air of tens of thousands of other people and animals in this region. In this remote area far from the national power centres, ecological issues intertwine with issues of justice, namely, the rights of the local people.

I. Uranium Prospecting in the Neighbourhood

Since 2006, international mining companies have been interested in the uranium ore in the ground of Northern Carelia and in other parts of my country. The richest uranium deposits are located in Southern Finland but, as those areas are densely populated, it has proved to be politically impossible to plan a mine there. The companies withdrew from those areas and have concentrated their explorations in Eastern and Northern Finland, where there are less people and supposedly less opposition to their plans.

I live in Kontiolahti in Northern Carelia. The neighbouring community is Eno, a town recently incorporated into the city of Joensuu in 2009. Exploring companies are active in the area of these communities. The most important of these mining companies is the French, state-owned Areva which has attained permission from the Finnish government to execute deep drilling explorations. Local communities have been powerless to prevent government permission because current mining laws, which have not been updated since 1965, grant considerable freedom to companies seeking to explore Finnish land.

In an effort to bring these laws up to date, the Finnish parliament proposed new mining legislation that was made public in December 2009, to be ready by the end of 2010. Environmentalists welcomed the proposal for many reasons, one being that it gives local communities more power to prevent uranium prospecting in their areas. However, the ongoing exploration is regulated by the old law, and the majority of people in Northern Carelia are alarmed by the prospect of a uranium mine in the future.

Finland is not a uranium-rich country but due to the rise in global uranium prices, mining companies are exploring all possible uranium resources. This rise in ore prices is attributed to renewed interest worldwide in nuclear power as an alleged solution to climate change. During the last several decades, Finland has been one of the few European countries to rely on nuclear energy: Areva is currently constructing a new reactor in Olkiluoto.[1] Because of Finland's reliance on nuclear reactors, some Finnish politicians have argued that it is hypocritical to oppose uranium mining in Finland since the uranium has to be mined from somewhere, so why not from Finnish soil? They also appeal to the possibility that uranium mines will bring jobs to areas that suffer from high unemployment.

Nevertheless, opposition movements have arisen in various parts of the country and I participate in the movement against uranium mines in Northern Carelia.[2] The popular movements tend to be non-sectarian and focused on non-competitive network building; they also bring together people from all walks of life: environmental activists, political activists (mostly green and left), artists, students, university teachers, farmers, church people and more. The opposition movements seek to remind people that uranium mining everywhere has caused serious environmental and health problems.[3] A full-scale uranium mine would be a major risk, as uranium is both radioactive and chemically poisonous. In particular, the tailings of abandoned uranium mines contain dangerous radioactive decay products such as thorium, radium, radon and polonium. Inhaled radioactive dust and polluted surface and ground waters could cause various kinds of cancer in humans. Moreover, the radiation would continue for tens of thousands of years. In addition, a uranium mine in Northern Carelia would probably destroy more jobs than it would create. Those who oppose uranium mining argue that this region relies heavily on tourism and that a uranium mine would pose a serious image problem. Agriculture would also suffer.

In this article, I aim to provide an insider analysis of the significance of these opposition movements and, in particular, to examine how local Lutheran

---

[1] For more on the unique features of Finnish nuclear policy, see M. Kojo, and T. Litmanen (eds), *The Renewal of Nuclear Power in Finland* (Energy, Climate and the Environment Series; Basingstoke: Palgrave Macmillan, 2009).

[2] See website of the movement; http://www.www.uraanitieto.net/ accessed 10th November 2010 (Mostly in Finnish).

[3] More information about the problems can be found at: http://www.ccnr.org/#topics, accessed 10th November 2010 (in English and French).

congregations participated in the discussion and took action. I will argue that the resulting new form of network building provides a fruitful base for creating a uniquely Finnish public theology based on traditional Finnish spirituality.

II. The Reaction of Local Congregations

The local discussion has been lively. The parish of Eno (5,500 members) has been very active in the public debate. In August 2008 the parish organized a special celebration of Creation Sunday. While Creation Sunday has been a common Lutheran practice in Finland since the 1990s, the celebration at Eno differed in two significant ways: first, the celebration developed in more contextual ways using old Finnish cultural traditions, and second, uranium mining became the main focus of the activities. Typically, celebrations involve a ten o'clock mass with an emphasis on creation and ecological issues; instead, the parish of Eno prepared a three-day celebration with various elements.

Several parishioners planned and prepared the event. During the celebration, Eno parishoners revived old traditional and ecological practices: for example, they constructed a wooden fence in the churchyard using traditional techniques and they prepared turnips in the old way by cooking them in a heated hole in the earth. Young famiies with babies in prams had a demonstration of these practices, local women prepared organic food for everyone, and there was an excursion to the site where Areva was exploring uranium ore.

The main event was the Sunday Mass. The habitual liturgy of Creation Sunday was used and the bishop of the diocese, Bishop Wille Riekkinen, preached. In his sermon Riekkinen stated, 'If Jesus were to live among us now, I think he would actively protect nature from pollution and protect the dignity of the human habitat. It is a sign of greed to believe that the small amount of money the uranium mines would bring to this area would be a source of happiness.'[4] According to Bishop Riekkinen, it is unwise to develop uranium mines.

Following the mass, environmental experts, a few major politicians[5] and the CEO of Areva in Finland gathered for a panel discussion. During the debate and through the audience participation it became clear that opinions differed even among members of the congregation. It was also made clear that the people resisting uranium mining do not categorically resist all mining; they stressed instead the particular problems associated with radioactive uranium ore.

After the three-day event, the debate in the local newspapers intensified. Many people expressed joy over the active role of the parish and found their sense of

---

[4] Author's translation; for the whole sermon in Finnish see, W. Riekkinen, 'Saarna Enon kirkossa luomakunnan sunnuntaina', http:\\www.kuopionhiippakunta.fi/piispa/puheet (17 August 2008) (accessed 7 June 2010).

[5] Of the many invited politicians, two participated: Tarja Cronberg, the chairwoman of the Green Party in Finland who lives in Northern Carelia; and Riitta Myller, a member of the European Parliament (Social Democrats), also originating from Northern Carelia.

belonging to the church growing stronger. People outside the church also appreciated the clear statements of the bishop and local pastors. Some people, however, were appalled by the new role of the congregation. Active parishioners who had ties with the pietistic movements in the church were angry with their pastors. A few people close to the Finnish mining industry attacked Bishop Riekkinen and scolded him publicly.

After the most agitated period, the pastors of Eno tried to widen perspectives by organizing opportunities to discuss the role of the Lutheran church and of individual Christians in environmental issues in general. I joined this endeavour by writing a newspaper article about the new national environmental activity in the Lutheran church and its basic theological assumptions. I also spoke about nature and Christian spirituality in an evening discussion at Eno parish hall.

The congregation of Kontiolahti (about 13,000 members) chose a different approach. The leaders of the congregation have not taken part in the public discussion about uranium exploring. Nevertheless, active parishioners together with some pastors organized liturgical actions that concretize the new ecological awareness of the Lutheran church in Northern Carelia. On summer solstice evening, 22 June 2009, the congregation held a forest prayer service incorporating an art work, with some participants actually standing on the rock carving depicting the sun. The carving, located in Kontiolahti in an area where exploration is going on, was created by an artist named Pessi Manner, who joined the critics of uranium mining. The location offered the perfect place for a nature prayer service with the theme of the *Canticle of the Sun* by Francis of Assisi. The idea of taking liturgy to the forest was not new; Finnish Lutherans have often thought that prayer or liturgy in nature reflects the traditional and, for many people, the living sense of the closeness of the sacred in creation. What was unique about this particular prayer service was the choice of location and its connection to the ongoing political discussion on uranium prospecting.

Throughout the years of uranium discussion, the support of the bishop has been crucial for local congregations. Some members of the popular movement against uranium mines have commented that the fearless action of the congregations in Northern Carelia has been decisive for many ordinary people, encouraging them to express their opinion and ask questions about this difficult ethical and political issue.

III. Theological Arguments

The new public role of theology in Northern Carelia is controversial. For background purposes it is useful to know that Lutheranism is the major denomination in Finland, which, since the eighteenth century, has had strong pietistic renewal movements. In general, Finnish Protestant theology has been anthropocentric with a highly individualistic concept of salvation. Salvation is understood as a matter of faith that mostly concerns the mind. Pietistic theology often focuses on transcendent dimensions of salvation, which has led to an indifference towards immanent, everyday issues like justice in society or the integrity of creation. In this Christian theological context, the idea of the sacredness of nature is unfamiliar and the mystical current within Christianity with its more holistic views has been downplayed.

The Lutheran church worldwide cannot always be proud of its history regarding the public role of theology. One possible explanation of this lies with the doctrine of the two kingdoms: something is lost when reality is divided into spiritual and profane spheres. The original intent of the doctrine was to emphasize that God's love is the guiding principle in both realms, but in practice this Lutheran teaching often results in passivity and in an uncritical stance on important ethical issues.[6] Moreover, in the Finnish context, the public and the private are frequently separated in the life of the church and its members; this has led to a silencing of the prophetic role of Christian communities. New insights concerning the public role of theology are needed. Doctrines must be evaluated in their changing contexts and attention must be paid to their ethical implications. While this type of theological reflection is often practiced in the global Lutheran community,[7] it has rarely reached the grassroots level of Finnish congregations.

In the discussions surrounding uranium prospecting and mining, church people have used different theological arguments. I shall briefly present here arguments made by three of the most vocal theologians in the discussion: Vicar Armi Rautavuori from Eno, Bishop Wille Riekkinen, and myself.

Rev. Armi Rautavuori frequently draws on traditional Lutheran ideas about the right and the responsibility to use natural reason when considering what is best for the community in the long term. Rev. Rautavuori wants to stress that Lutheran theology contains substantial resources for decision-making on ecological issues. She emphasizes the biblical command to serve and preserve the creation (Gen. 1:26)[8] alongside the basic idea of Christian responsibility for the neighbour, especially the neighbour whose voice is not heard. She also extends this responsibility to include future generations: 'this earth is a loan from our children'.[9]

Rev Rautavuori bases her argument on recent documents from the Finnish Evangelical Lutheran Church, such as the Strategy of the Church from February 2008 and the Climate Programme *Gratitude, Respect, Moderation* from June 2008.[10]

---

[6] See an interesting recent interpretation of Luther's theology and the concept of holistic salvation in V. Munyika, *A Holistic Soteriology in an African Context. Utilising Luther's Theology and the Owambo Traditions to Overcome a Spiritualised and Privatised Concept of Salvation in the Evangelical Lutheran Church of Namibia (ELCIN)* (Cluster Monograph Series; Pietermaritzburg: Cluster Publications, 2004).

[7] An example of this is U. Duchrow (ed.), *Lutheran Churches – Salt or Mirror of Society? Case Studies of the Theory and Practice of the Two Kingdoms Doctrine* (Geneva: WCC, 1977).

[8] The full statement can be found in 'Message by Ecumenical Patriarch Bartholomew for World Environment Day', 5th June 2009, see http://www.patriarchate.org/documents/world-environemnt-day-2009 (accessed 10 November 2009).

[9] See, for example, Armi Rautavuori's text in the newspaper of the movement against uranium mining: 'Luonnonsuojelu kuuluu kristityn kutsumukseen,' *Pekkerelli. Pohjois-Karjalan uraanikaivosten vastaisen kansalaisliikkeen lehti* (2009), p. 5. This and the following translations are mine.

[10] The English translation of the *Climate Programme of the Evangelical Lutheran Church*

These documents stress that it is the task of every Christian and every congregation to work for the realization of the basic values of justice, love of neighbour, and the integrity of creation. Rev. Rautavuori argues that, in her context, the implementation of these ideas in practice means resisting uranium mining; it means struggling against the 'sins of greed and indifference'.[11]

Bishop Riekkinen commented on the uranium situation for the first time in the Spring 2006 Diocesan magazine. Referring to Jesus' parable in the gospels – who would give a stone to a child who asks for bread? – Bishop Riekkinen writes, 'When the children are not yet even able to ask, would you give them a radiating future'?[12]

In his sermon in Eno in August 2008, Riekkinen, a renowned exegete, argued mainly from Scripture. He spoke about the role of humans as stewards of creation and about the values of the Kingdom of God, which he suggests are e.g. justice and the resistance of greed. Riekkinen criticized the consumerist culture in which we live. He took an unusually direct stand on the issue of uranium prospecting by suggesting that it presents too high a threat to nature and to the health of the people. Bishop Riekkinen also mentioned the idea of the sacredness of nature though he did not expound on the point.[13]

I have tried to introduce into the discussion the perspective of the sacredness of nature, in a panentheistic sense. By panentheism I refer to a concept of God that emphasizes God's immanent closeness in nature yet fully recognizes God's transcendent mystery.[14] For a long time this idea has been eclipsed in my church. However, there are some elements in the traditional Finnish nature-relationship that resonate beautifully with panentheistic thinking. A renewed sense of the intimate presence of God in nature reminds us that nature is sacred and therefore is, in a sense, inviolable. At its best, this kind of thinking can restrict human greed.

My first contribution to the discussion on uranium mining was also in spring 2006 in a local ecclesial newspaper. I urged congregations to participate in the public discussion about the issue. At that time I did not take a very strong stand on uranium; instead, I wrote in more general terms about the need to simplify our lifestyles, consume less and respect the nature around us.[15] Later, I argued more explicitly against uranium mining using biblical arguments about an appropriate nature-relationship and drawing on a theology of wisdom. By wisdom theology I refer to the mystical current in Christian theology that appreciates many ways

---

of Finland – Gratitude, Respect, Moderation can be found at http://evl.fi/EVLen.nsf/Documents/B843256B66E603EEC225730C003A7E1F?openDocument&lang=EN (accessed 29 May 2010).

[11] Interview of Rev Rautavuori by Aimo Salonen in 'Viljelty on, mutta onko varjeltu?', *Karjalan Heili* (27 July 2010), pp. 10–11.

[12] W. Riekkinen, 'Piisbailua', *Capitol: Kuopion hiippakuntalehti* 2(2006), p. 4.

[13] W. Riekkinen 'Saarna Enon kirkossa luomakunnan sunnuntaina', www.kuopionhiippakunta.fi/piispa/puheet (17 August 2008) (assessed 7 June 2010).

[14] More about panentheism in P. Clayton, and A. Peacocke (eds), *In Whom We Live and Move and Have Our Being: Panentheistic Reflections on God's Presence in a Scientific World.* (Grand Rapids, Michigan and Cambridge: Eerdmans, 2004).

[15] See my editorial in P. Kainulainen, 'Kirkko ja uraani', *Kirkkotie* 10 (2006), p. 2.

of knowing. It gives epistemic value to emotions, experience, and, in my context, to the age-old spiritual elements in the Finnish nature-relationship.[16] I wanted to encourage people to value their ways of knowing and their emotions as relevant bases for ethical and theological considerations.

We need a major shift in cosmology, of our underlying worldviews and of our concept of knowing, which is the ground of all theologizing. The dominant mechanistic concept of reality does not provide enough space for all the elements of a full-scale Christian theologizing, which should include rational and wisdom theological perspectives. A recovery of the sense of the sacredness of nature can only happen with a more holistic cosmology.[17]

Within my church there are signs of a shift in this direction. One sign is the growing interest in ecological issues. In concrete terms it is evident in the environmental diploma system, issued by The National Church Council, which has received a relatively positive welcome in the congregations over the last ten years. A Lutheran parish can obtain a diploma, valid for four years at a time, if it has systematically paid attention to ecological issues in all aspects of parish life: in energy solutions, educational work, kitchens, and cemeteries.

A more recent milestone is the *Climate Programme of the Evangelical Lutheran Church of Finland – Gratitude, Respect, Moderation* (2008). The programme contains biblical and theological arguments on why ecological responsibility concerns every Christian, every congregation, and the administration of the church as a whole. The theology of the programme combines traditional Lutheran emphases with elements from the global ecotheological discussion. It aims at strengthening the prophetic role of the church, a role long marginalized in Finnish Lutheran ecclesial life.[18] Having such a theological foundation opens up possibilities for new kinds of public theology in all environmental issues, not just in climate challenges, and theologians in Northern Carelia can now draw from this document in the discussion over uranium mining.

---

[16] For more on the concept of wisdom theology and other functions of theology, see S. B. Bevans, *Models of Contextual Theology* (Faith and Culture Series; Maryknoll, NY: Orbis Books, 7th edn, 2000); C. Deane-Drummond, *Creation Through Wisdom* (Edinburgh: T & T Clark, 2000). I have developed the idea of Finnish wisdom theology in my article P. Kainulainen, 'Wisdom Theology and Finnish Nature Spirituality: Reflections on Ivone Gebara's Ecofeminism', *Journal of the European Society of Women in Theological Research* 15 (2007), pp. 131–139.

[17] See, for example, R. Radford Ruether, *Gaia and God: An Ecofeminist Theology of Earth Healing* (London: SCM Press, 1993). This is one of the main points in my dissertation *Maan viisaus. Ivone Gebaran ekofeministinen käsitys tietämisestä ja teologiasta* [*The Wisdom of the Earth. Ivone Gebara's Ecofeminist Concept of Knowing and Theology*] (Joensuun yliopiston teologisia julkaisuja, 13. University of Joensuu, 2005).

[18] 'Environmental threats challenge Christian communities to reform spiritually and to return to the rich way to observe human relationship with nature that is based on the original sources. Based on them, they are to use their prophetic voice and call people to resistance against one-sided consumerism.' See, *Climate Programme of the Evangelical Lutheran Church of Finland – Gratitude, Respect, Moderation* p. 39.

IV. Geology vs Theology?

One of the vocal critics of this new role of the church has been a geologist named Toni Eerola, who works for one of the mining companies.[19] I cite some of his ideas here because in them I see the seeds for an important discussion about the way we understand 'knowing'.

Eerola has written in the newspapers about the movements against uranium mining, about the work of Finnish sociologists studying such movements, and about the role of the church.[20] He criticizes the sociological research for being uncritical and for not paying enough attention to the natural sciences when investigating the movements and their arguments. According to Eerola, the participation of Bishop Riekkinen and 'ecotheologians' in the discussion adds 'to this pseudo-scientific propaganda a new dimension'. Eerola seems to think that the only form of knowledge that can claim to be 'knowledge' is a natural science such as geology. Eerola and other representatives of the mining companies have repeatedly argued that there are no environmental risks in exploring and mining uranium and that the toxic waste can be safely stored for tens of thousands of years.

This tendency to focus on scientific knowledge is rooted in a prevailing Western mechanistic cosmology that privileges the natural sciences over any other perspective on reality. It now appears that this mechanistic cosmology is seriously inadequate: it has caused or been unable to prevent ethical problems, with ecological destruction as the most devastating result. In any case, serious dialogue between proponents of the natural sciences and other fields like sociology and theology is necessary. For such a dialogue to take place, all participants will need to be aware of the philosophical underpinnings of modern science.[21] However, for the church, theology is more than rational argumentation: it draws its semantic power from the power of emotions, liturgy, images and symbols.

One of the positive features of Finnish Lutheranism is its relatively unproblematic relationship with the principles and results of the natural sciences.[22] Contrary to Eerola's accusations, church-affiliated activists in the uranium movement do not argue against the basic findings of the natural sciences; instead, they argue for the value of local knowledge and for a more profound integration of ethics in the overall discussion over uranium mining. It would seem that the mining company

---

[19] The company was the Canadian Cooper Minerals Inc., under the name Namura Finland Oy in Finland.

[20] T. Eerola, 'Uraanin vastustus uskontona', *Luonnonsuojelija* (18 September 2008), p. 2. *Luonnonsuojelija* is a newspaper of a big nature conservation organization that regularly gives space for columns that represent ideas different from the organization's views. See also T. Eerola, 'Uraanikaivoksia vastustavien aktivismitutkimukset pseudotieteellistä propagandaa', *Luonnonsuojelija* (May 2008), p. 22.

[21] See Chapters on science and religion, especially 'Theology and the Physical Sciences', by Philip Clayton and 'Theology and the Biological Sciences' by Celia Deane-Drummond *The Modern Theologians* (D. Ford and R. Muers, eds., 2nd edn, Oxford: Blackwell/Wiley, 2005), pp. 342–356; 357–369.

[22] For example, the struggle about creationism is not a big issue in Finland, at least not so far.

representatives want to avoid ethical discussions in order to concentrate on economic issues.

There are plenty of possibilities for a significant dialogue between geology and theology in which both can deepen their understanding of each other's points of view. Rethinking the essence of knowing and its methods does not require us to underestimate the significance or the positive potential of Western science. What we need is this: an interaction between distinct knowledge systems, a new ranking of priorities in scientific work, and a redefinition of the problems. We need the sources of power to be united in the protection of the life on earth.[23]

V. Ecological Public Theology in Finland

At the beginning of 2010, it would seem that the popular movement against uranium mining in various parts of Finland has had an impact on society. New mining legislation has been proposed with stricter restrictions on uranium prospecting. The new law proposed still protects the right to prospect ore (including uranium) relatively freely; however, the law also incorporates modern environmental perspectives and accepts local people's right to be heard on the issues that affect their lives.

Public discussion concerning uranium mining in Northern Carelia is more open and widespread than other environmental issues in Finland. The ethical role of the Lutheran church and its theology is more visible than before. Due to changes in the global market and because of public opposition to mining, there is less interest (maybe only temporarily) in Finnish uranium. The Canadian mining company, Cooper Minerals Inc., announced that they were phasing out their uranium claims in Finland; Areva has reduced the area it is exploring. Nevertheless, the threat of a uranium mine has not disappeared from our neighbourhood.

The congregations in Northern Carelia have created a Finnish Ecological Public Theology by acting together with other groups in the popular movement. By Finnish Ecological Public Theology I mean the attempt to find a new and relevant way to voice theological arguments on important ecological issues in the Finnish political and spiritual context. Until now, there have been few examples in Finland of this type of theologizing happening from within a popular movement and as a part of a multidimensional network. The movement has benefited both from the interactions of very different kinds of people and from a shared leadership of men and women. It is a network that is non-hierarchical, non-sectarian and

---

[23] These emphases reflect the methodological thinking of the world's indigenous researchers, see L. T. Smith, *Decolonizing Methodologies: Research and Indigenous Peoples* (London: Zed Books, 1999), p. 193. See also R. Cooper, 'Through the Soles of my Feet: A Personal View of Creation', *Ecotheology: Voices from South and North* (D. G. Hallman (ed.); Geneva: WCC, 1994), pp. 207–212 (212): 'The coupling of technological, scientific and indigenous experiences and skills is not merely desirable but essential'.

non-competitive; as we face our present global and local problems, this kind of network building offers promise of a more effective activism.[24]

As one actor in the network, the church must abandon its triumphal attitudes of the past and find a new place for itself by participating humbly and, at the same time, with a clear vision of the possibilities of religious knowing. Symbols and rituals have the power to influence attitudes and values. The congregations of Eno and Kontiolahti have creatively used these possibilities in the Creation Sunday Mass and in other liturgical actions. Theological renewal can grow out of this kind of activity; new insights can arise that draw from the traditional Finnish nature-relationship and its spiritual sources: the spiritual elements found in our cultural relationship to trees, forest, sauna bathing, and the respect of silence.[25]

At the same time, theologians and pastors must consciously reflect the totality of Christian faith and try to maintain continuity with the core of the tradition, otherwise the potential for transformation within this tradition will get lost. I agree with Rosemary Radford Ruether who argues that, although the biblical and Christian tradition is not the only source for ecological ethics, it is a source that must remain central for people from a Christian background. The Christian tradition has magnificent themes that can inspire its followers. New visions have power when they find their mandates in those traditions that carry meaning and authority for Christians of all ages. One must not forget that Christianity is a major world religion and a world power. It is necessary to work for its renewal on ecological issues.[26]

At the same time, a meaningful transformation requires an awareness of the holistic elements of Christian theology, such as mystical theology, which has been unduly marginalized in Western theology. Consequently, many Protestants, in particular, have lost the power of mystical or wisdom theology to touch the reason *and feelings* of people. Wisdom theology prefers poetic language, metaphors and

---

[24] Rowan Williams has stated that Christians should develop some sort of critical identification with 'whatever political groupings speak for a serious and humane resistance to consumer pluralism and the administered society. These days, such groupings are less likely than ever to be found within mainstream political parties, though there are some countries happily, where moral imagination has not been so completely privatised.' R. Williams, *On Christian Theology* (Malden, Oxford, Victoria: Blackwell, 2000), p. 37.

[25] More about these features in P. Kainulainen, 'Wisdom Theology and Finnish Nature Spirituality. Reflections on Ivone Gebara's Ecofeminism', *Journal of the European Society of Women in Theological Research* 15 (2007), pp. 131–139. About the spiritual elements in the relationship of Finns with trees earlier and today see R. Kovalainen, and S. Seppo, *Tree People* (Oulu: Pohjoinen, 2006).

[26] R. Radford Ruether, 'Conclusion: Eco-Justice at the Center of the Church's Mission', *Christianity and Ecology. Seeking the Well-Being of Earth and Humans* (D. T. Hessel, and R. Radford Ruether (eds); Cambridge, Massachusetts: Harvard University Center for the Study of World Religions Publications, 2000), pp. 603–614 (604). Nevertheless, Ruether has not always worked consistently with this ideal, e.g. in her Biblical hermeneutics. Sometimes the reader gets an impression that her theology is more based on findings from earth sciences, etc. than on wrestling with the possibilities of the Scriptures and the Christian tradition.

stories. At its best it can create powerful symbols and ways of talking about the holy mystery; for example, there is ecological potential in the panentheistic concept of God who is both transcendent and immanent and intimately present in all creation. This is one way to recover the old intuition that the earth is sacred. In Christian theology, this notion is derived most often from the idea of the presence of God in the creation as Creator and as Spirit.[27]

The churches will be needed if Western people want to rediscover the sense of the sacredness of nature. If rightly understood, this sense can be deeply transformative and help limit our greedy inclinations to over-consume nature's resources. Christian churches should use their influence in the discussion on these values and base their arguments on both rational and wisdom-theological premises.

VI. Ecological Public Theology as Bridge Builder

In the Northern Carelia uranium debate, the interaction between those who base their views on geology (or natural sciences and technology) and those who represent theology has not been as constructive as one would hope. Both sides have written and spoken provocatively.

In the future we need deeper communication. We need someone to begin the laborious task of building a bridge between two very different cosmologies and epistemologies in the uranium discussion. The churches and their theologians can start by better defining their own assumptions. In Finland this means striving for a more coherent contextualization of Lutheran theology in the midst of the changing political and ecological situation. This kind of theologizing could benefit from ecumenical cooperation, especially with Orthodox Christians in eastern Finland. Global ecofeminist theology could also be a building block for a public theology that seeks a relevant relationship between spirituality and politics; ecofeminist theologians have also worked extensively on the science – theology debate and could be a valuable resource in the uranium discussions.[28]

In emerging global public theology, the spiritual aspects of Christian theology often receive little attention. In the Northern Carelia uranium debate, spirituality – liturgy, rites and symbols – is intertwined with the ethical role of the congregations. Symbolic power is derived from the old Finnish cosmology with its spiritual way of understanding the relationship between humans and the rest of nature; this traditional cosmology still influences the modern Finnish way of life, at least in fragments. In some respects, Finnish cosmology resembles the way the world's indigenous people understand the interaction of the spiritual, ecological and social dimensions of life. Ecological Public Theology can also be a bridge-builder to the

---

[27] See Jürgen Moltmann's trinitarian concept of panentheism in his *God in Creation: A New Theology of Creation and the Spirit of God,* The Gifford Lectures 1984–1985 (Margaret Kohl (trans.); San Francisco: HarperSanFrancisco, 1991).

[28] A concise guide to ecofeminist theology is H. Eaton, *Introducing Ecofeminist Theologies* (Introductions to Feminist Theology, 12; London & New York: T & T Clark, 2005).

important insights offered by indigenous peoples concerning cosmology and the role of knowing and science.[29] According to many indigenous thinkers, science and spirituality together can point towards the *transformation* and *healing* of dysfunctional ways of thinking and acting.[30] Those cultural gaps that divide, among others, natural scientists and theologians can begin to be bridged.

Bibliography

Bevans, S. B., *Models of Contextual Theology* (Faith and Culture Series; Maryknoll, NY: Orbis Books, 7th edn, 2000).

Clayton, P., 'Theology and the Physical Sciences', *The Modern Theologians* (D. Ford and R. Muers (eds); Oxford: Blackwell/Wiley, 2nd edn, 2005), pp. 342–356.

Clayton, P., and A. Peacocke (eds), *In Whom We Live and Move and Have Our Being: Panentheistic Reflections on God's Presence in a Scientific World*. (Grand Rapids, Michigan and Cambridge: Eerdmans, 2004).

Climate Programme of the Evangelical Lutheran Church of Finland: Gratitude, Respect, Moderation, http://evl.fi/EVLen.nsf/Documents/B843256B66E603EEC2 25730C003A7E1F?openDocument&lang=EN (accessed 29 May 2010).

Cooper, R., 'Through the Soles of my Feet: A Personal View of Creation', *Ecotheology: Voices from South and North* (D. G. Hallman (ed.); Geneva: WCC, 1994), pp. 207–212.

Deane-Drummond, C., *Creation Through Wisdom: Theology and the New Biology* (Edinburgh: T & T Clark, 2000).

—'Theology and the Biological Sciences', *The Modern Theologians* (D. Ford and R. Muers (eds); Oxford: Blackwell/Wiley, 2nd edn, 2005), pp. 342–356; 357–369.

Dillard, C. D., 'When the Ground is Black, the Ground is Fertile. Exploring Endarkened Feminist Epistemology and Healing Methodologies in the Spirit', *Handbook of Critical and Indigenous Methodologies* (N. K. Denzin, Y. S. Lincoln, and L. T. Smith (eds); Los Angeles, London, New Delhi, Singapore: Sage, 2008), pp. 277–292.

Duchrow, U. (ed.), *Lutheran Churches – Salt or Mirror of Society? Case Studies of the Theory and Practice of the Two Kingdoms Doctrine* (Geneva: WCC, 1977).

Eaton, H., *Introducing Ecofeminist Theologies* (Introductions to Feminist Theology, 12; London & New York: T & T Clark, 2005).

---

[29] Samis are an indigenous people with their own knowledge systems who live in Finland. See, E. Helander, and K. Kailo (eds), *No Beginning, No End – The Sami Speak Up* (Edmonton: Canadian Circumpolar Institute, 1998).

[30] Transformation and healing are common concepts in indigenous methodologies and ecofeminist philosophy and theology. See L. T. Smith, *Decolonizing Methodologies: Research and Indigenous Peoples* (London: Zed Books, 1999); K. J. Warren, *Ecofeminist Philosophy: A Western Perspective on What It is and Why It Matters* (Lanham, Boulder, New York, Oxford: Rowman & Littlefield, 2000); H. Eaton, *Introducing Ecofeminist Theologies* (Introductions to Feminist Theology, 12; London & New York: T & T Clark, 2005).

Eerola, T., 'Uraanin vastustus uskontona', *Luonnonsuojelija* (18 September 2008), p. 2.
—'Uraanikaivoksia vastustavien aktivismitutkimukset pseudotieteellistä propagandaa', *Luonnonsuojelija* (May 2008), p. 22.
Helander, E., and K. Kailo (eds), *No Beginning, No End – The Sami Speak Up* (Edmonton: Canadian Circumpolar Institute, 1998).
Kainulainen, P., 'Kirkko ja uraani', *Kirkkotie* 10 (2006), p. 2.
—'Maan viisaus. Ivone Gebaran ekofeministinen käsitys tietämisestä ja teologiasta' ['The Wisdom of the Earth. Ivone Gebara's Ecofeminist Concept of Knowing and Theology'] (doctoral dissertation; University of Joensuu, 2005).
—'Wisdom Theology and Finnish Nature Spirituality. Reflections on Ivone Gebara's Ecofeminism', *Journal of the European Society of Women in Theological Research* 15 (2007), pp. 131-139.
Kojo, M., and T. Litmanen (eds), *The Renewal of Nuclear Power in Finland* (Energy, Climate and the Environment Series; Basingstoke: Palgrave Macmillan, 2009).
Kovalainen, R., and S. Seppo, *Tree People* (Oulu: Pohjoinen, 2006).
Moltmann, J., *God in Creation: A New Theology of Creation and the Spirit of God*, The Gifford Lectures 1984-1985 (Margaret Kohl (trans); San Francisco: HarperSanFrancisco, 1991).
Munyika, V., *A Holistic Soteriology in an African Context. Utilising Luther's Theology and the Owambo Traditions to Overcome a Spiritualised and Privatised Concept of Salvation in the Evangelical Lutheran Church of Namibia (ELCIN)* (Cluster Monograph Series; Pietermaritzburg: Cluster Publications, 2004).
Radford Ruether, R., 'Conclusion: Eco-Justice at the Center of the Church's Mission', *Christianity and Ecology. Seeking the Well-Being of Earth and Humans* (D. T. Hessel, and R. R. Ruether (eds); Cambridge, Massachusetts: Harvard University Center for the Study of World Religions Publications, 2000), pp. 603-614.
—*Gaia and God: An Ecofeminist Theology of Earth Healing* (London: SCM Press, 1993).
Rautavuori, A., 'Luonnonsuojelu kuuluu kristityn kutsumukseen', *Pekkerelli. Pohjois-Karjalan uraanikaivosten vastaisen kansalaisliikkeen lehti* (2009), p. 5.
—'Viljelty on, mutta onko varjeltu?', *Karjalan Heili* (27 July 2010), pp. 10-11.
Riekkinen, W. 'Piisbailua', *Capitol: Kuopion hiippakuntalehti* 2(2006), p. 4.
—'Saarna Enon kirkossa luomakunnan sunnuntaina', (17 August 2008), www.kuopionhiippakunta.fi/piispa/puheet (assessed 7 June 2010).
Smith, L. T., *Decolonizing Methodologies: Research and Indigenous Peoples* (London: Zed Books, 1999).
Warren, K. J., *Ecofeminist Philosophy: A Western Perspective on What It is and Why It Matters* (Lanham, Boulder, New York, Oxford: Rowman & Littlefield, 2000).
Williams, R., *On Christian Theology* (Malden, Oxford, Victoria: Blackwell, 2000).

7 Towards an African Inculturated Sophiology: The Case of African Wisdom Traditions from Myths for Ecological Concerns

Loreen Maseno
Department of Religion, Theology & Philosophy,
Maseno University, Kenya

One of the many critiques of Christology is that the Christian understanding of the place and significance of Christ is too anthropocentric and thereby downplays the relation of Christ to the life of all creation. Yet, if that relation were taken seriously, it would have ramifications for the acute problems facing the created world, including, for example, the challenges of desertification, pollution, climate change, deforestation and even acid rain.[1] Theologians have suggested various ways to reconceptualize the meaning and significance of Christ so as to capture insights that will be useful for our interconnected world. Their contribution to and their articulation of the environment on various fronts in the public domain constitutes engagement in the public sphere.

Several approaches have been offered to help explore the intersection between Christology and ecology. Kwok Pui-Lan suggests three possibilities: first, the organic model for Christ, where organic images are consistently used in order to underscore the interrelatedness of the human and the natural realms; second, Jesus as the Wisdom of God, which draws upon the concept of Jesus as Sophia-God; and

---

[1] Ecological crises the world over are well documented. According to Radford-Ruether these crises include toxic air pollution, soil erosion and destruction of rain forests. All these remain are a threat to planetary life and their impacts are rapidly expanding exacerbated by the ever-increasing global human population. See R. Ruether, 'Ecofeminism and Healing Ourselves: Healing the Earth', *Feminist Theology* 3 (1995) pp. 51–62 (51). See also Sallie McFague, who maintains that the planet remains vulnerable to our destructive behaviour. S. McFague, 'An Earthly Theological Agenda', *Ecofeminism and the Sacred* (C. Adams (ed.); New York: Continuum, 1993).

third, Jesus as an epiphany, which identifies the Christic presence in and among humans.[2]

Jesus as Sophia remains underdeveloped within African Christology.[3] This chapter is an initial attempt to focus on Jesus as Sophia, as the Wisdom of God based on the wisdom traditions found in the myths of African peoples. It lies within a broader context that seeks wisdom from multiple traditions, in this case African indigenous mythology, in order to form an African inculturated Sophiology. Such an endeavour will use African categories taken from myths to articulate the wisdom of God.[4] In general, this chapter focuses on ancient African myths that retain contact with the earth and the sense of the sacred in nature, which is but one approach to Jesus Sophia within feminist theology. This chapter aims to articulate an African Sophiology that builds upon African wisdom traditions in light of ecological concerns.

---

[2] K. Pui-Lan, 'Ecology and Christology', *Feminist Theology* 5 (1997), pp. 113–125.

[3] To my knowledge there is significant work in religious circles in Africa that pays attention to creation and the environment in Africa. For example, J. Mugambi, and M. Vähäkangas (eds), *Christian Theology and Environmental Responsibility* (Nairobi: Acton, 2001). See also I. A. Phiri,'The Chisumphi Cult: The Role of Women in Preserving the Environment', *Women Healing Earth: Third World Women on Ecology, Feminism, and Religion* (R. Radford Ruether (ed.); Maryknoll: Orbis Books, 1996) pp. 161–171; J. Ongong'a, J. 'Towards an African Environmental Theology', *Theology of Reconstruction: Exploratory Essays* (M. N. Getui, and E. A. Obeng (eds); Nairobi: Acton 1999). Yet, what remains underdeveloped is the link between Christology and ecology and especially Jesus-Sophia. Scholars have examined Jesus in Africa in various ways. A survey of recent work on Christology in Africa includes Diane Stinton, who attempts to suggest plausible models for contemporary African Christology. She includes all those aspects of Jesus as creator, preserver, provider, planner, architect, healer and protector in her book *Jesus of Africa: Voices of Contemporary African Christology* (Maryknoll, NY: Orbis Books, 2004). See also R. J. Schreiter, *Faces of Jesus in Africa* (Maryknoll, NY: Orbis Books, 9th edn, 2005), pp. 128–149; T. Hinga, 'Jesus Christ and the Liberation of Women in Africa', *The Will to Arise: Women, Tradition, and the Church in Africa* (M. Oduyoye, and K. Kanyoro (eds); Maryknoll, NY: Orbis Books, 1992), pp. 183–194; W. Nasimiyu, 'Christology and an African Woman's Experience', *Faces of Jesus in Africa* (R, Schreiter (ed.); New York: Orbis Books, 9th edn, 2005); See D. A. Owusu, 'Jesus, The African Healer' (unpublished masters thesis; University of Oslo, 2001); M. A. Oduyoye, *Introducing African Women's Theology* (Sheffield, England: Sheffield Academic Press, 2001); L. Maseno, 'Widows' Christologies: A preliminary feminist analysis of Abanyole widows' Christologies considering kinship, gender and the power of naming' (doctoral dissertation; University of Oslo, 2008). However, none has considered Jesus as Sophia and especially not for ecological purposes. Thus this work serves as a formative step towards an African inculturated Sophiology.

[4] One objective of wisdom material and literature is to transmit lessons that nurture life. This is so even in the Old Testament and in the literature of other ancient Near Eastern civilizations, especially Egypt. See A. Clifford, *Introducing Feminist Theology* (Maryknoll, NY: Orbis Books, 2001), pp. 105–109.

I. Introduction

This chapter is an initial attempt towards an inculturated Sophiology in the African context. It has been suggested that it is through the concept of Jesus as Sophia that Christology and ecology intersect.[5] One approach to Jesus as Sophia in feminist theology is that of wisdom traditions stemming from the natural world, such as ancient cosmological myths which provide insight into the sense of the sacred in nature. I suggest that an African Sophiology could be gleaned from wisdom traditions, which attest to the sacredness in nature, within the various African cultures through inculturation;[6] such a Sophiology gives a contextual interpretation which takes African people's thought forms and worldviews seriously.

This approach is helpful for conceptualizing the significance of Christ in our contemporary world. According to Kwok Pui-Lan, Jesus as Sophia has implications for people in cultures around the world. Pui-Lan maintains that Asians have cultures and religions with strong wisdom traditions that use natural symbols such as the plant and the gardener, seasonal cycles, and the stream in their teachings about natural wisdom and human nature. For Pui-Lan, Jesus as Sophia appears in the wisdom traditions of various cultural contexts and is relevant cross-culturally for people struggling to find new language to speak about Christ.[7]

I will begin with a discussion on inculturation and how it has been redefined within the field of theology. In this work the primary focus will be on inculturation in Africa and the subject of inculturation will be Jesus. In the next part, I consider how the subject of inculturation has been reconstructed based on the idea that there is no absolute Jesus and that our image of Jesus is influenced by our cultural context. It is within this interpretative sphere that I consider Jesus as Sophia and draw a link between Sophia and the ancient wisdom traditions in Africa. In the final section, I will highlight some African myths and show how they provide insights into the sense of the sacred in nature.[8]

This chapter will not define culture, address the origins of the theology of inculturation in Africa, explore the debates on theories of myths[9], delve into Sophiology as a philosophical concept or consider deep ecology.[10] Instead, this chapter seeks to provide an interpretation of Jesus as Sophia in Africa as suggested through African myths. It explores these myths in order to creatively develop an African inculturated Sophiology that emphasizes ecological concerns. In so doing, meaning is made possible in the context of African culture and its historical periods. Such

---

[5] K. Pui-Lan, 'Ecology and Christology', pp. 113–125.
[6] Inculturation is discussed later on in the chapter.
[7] K. Pui-Lan, 'Ecology and Christology', p. 123.
[8] There are limits to inculturation such as capitulation to culture and the failure to recognize the authentic gospel in some local churches. Another limitation is that inculturation is ongoing since cultures are not static; thus, inculturation remains inadequate in itself.
[9] See 'Myth as Thought: Modern Theory and Myth', www.classics.uc.edu/~johnson/myth/theory.html (accessed 20 February 2010).
[10] D. Barnhill, and R. Gottlieb, *Deep Ecology and World Religions: New Essays on Sacred Ground* (Albany, NY: State University of New York Press, 2001).

reflection and description may encourage public debate among local communities and churches on environmental concerns, which are a public issue of contemporary society.

II. Inculturation

The reformulation and reinterpretation of the gospel so that it can be at home in African culture is an exercise that has been called by many names. Some of these include contextualization, localization, indigenization, inculturation and incarnation. Inculturation is a term whose meaning and use have yet to be standardized by frequent and repeated use. Furthermore, the meaning of inculturation is complicated because it is situated in both anthropology and theology; therefore, it is heavy with inference from both these areas of knowledge. What follows is one possible way to understand this term within the realm of theology.

According to the theologian Aylward Shorter, the very first recorded use of the word inculturation in the theological sense was made by Fr Joseph Masson of the Society of Jesus at the Gregorian University in Rome in 1962. He called for Catholicism to become inculturated in a variety of forms.[11] Inculturation in an African context is an attempt to reformulate and reinterpret the gospel so that it can be at home in African culture. This attempt is an ongoing process, which involves a dialogue between the gospel and culture, or cultures.[12] The two elements 'culture' and 'gospel' necessarily interact, and this interaction calls for a measure of re-interpretation.[13]

Inculturation calls for the interpretation of the gospel from the African people's thought forms and worldviews. Inculturation accepts a variety of possible ways of living and thinking. According to Stephen Bevans, 'In Africa ... Christians are becoming increasingly convinced that traditional approaches to theology do not really make sense within their own cultural patterns and thought forms.'[14] Inculturation in Africa is linked to a new understanding of culture where culture is not universal and static; consequently, no one theology is valid for all peoples and cultures.

It is necessary to distance ourselves from some of the common but inadequate ways of understanding inculturation. For some, inculturation primarily means

---

[11] A. Shorter, *Toward a Theology of Inculturation* (London: Geoffrey Chapman, 1998), p. 10).

[12] Given the geographical extent of Africa and the diversity of its people, Africa does not share in a single culture. There are varieties of cultures. Further, this study focuses on two regions of Africa, namely East and West Africa, which are indicative of the cultural variety. I do bear in mind the problem of broad generalizations; however, for practical purposes in this study reference is made to African culture.

[13] A. Shorter, *Toward a Theology of Inculturation* p. 10, 11, 60; L. Magesa, 'Authentic African Christianity', *32 Articles Evaluating Inculturation in Africa* (T. Okure, and P. van Thiel (eds); Spearhead Numbers 112–114; Port Harcourt: Gaba Publications, 1990), p. 112. See also J. Waliggo, *Inculturation: Its Meaning and Urgency* (Kampala, Uganda: St. Paul's Publications, 1986), p. 12.

[14] S. Bevans, *Inculturation and Healing* (Pietermaritzburg: Cluster Publications, 1995), p. 5.

finding suitable rituals or symbols in a given culture in order to express the Christian faith. However, inculturation does not simply mean finding suitable cultural expressions for the Christian faith.[15] Such an understanding is inadequate because it does not attend to all the aspects of human life and culture that engage with the gospel. Finding suitable expressions is only the *manifestation* of inculturation. According to the theologian Stuart Bate, definitions and understandings of inculturation revolve around the dynamic relationship of two elements: a religious one and a worldly one. The latter is often expressed as 'culture' or 'cultures'. The former is problematic and is often expressed diversely as the faith, the gospel, Jesus Christ, or the church.[16]

In his book *Christ and Culture* (1951), H. Richard Niebuhr examines how the relationship between Christ and culture has been perceived in the course of history. His intent is to present a treatment of the variety of ways in which Christ related to human cultural values and ideals. On this basis, he develops five types to explain how the relationship of Christ to culture may be understood.[17] These types are 'Christ above culture', 'Christ and culture in paradox', 'Christ the transformer of culture', 'Christ of culture' and 'Christ against culture'.[18]

The most radical of the five types is 'Christ against culture',[19] because this perspective does not see any interaction between the gospel and cultures. Human cultural values and ideals are at best viewed as unredeemable. In this type the believer focuses exclusively on a new order, the new society and its Lord.[20] However, its inability to see the relationship between cultures and the gospel makes this type unrealistic. The gospel message was, after all, revealed to us in human language by people in a particular culture. If human cultural values are unredeemable then it was improper of Jesus to become human and to be a part of Jewish cultural ideals and values. Whereas 'Christ and culture in paradox' places Christ and culture on two separate and conflicting paths, 'Christ above culture' manifests itself in an exclusive Christianity that is prone to radical biblicism. Consequently, the above three theological positions are not fruitful for this study and thus will not be used.

'Christ as the transformer of culture' suggests that Christ redirects, reinvigorates and regenerates all human works expressed in human life.[21] In effect, Christ enlivens human cultures from within. 'Christ of culture' examines cultural elements that are in agreement with Christ's work and person, and harmonizes these elements with Christ.[22] Both of these lines of thought on the relationship

---

[15] Ibid., p. 18.
[16] Ibid., p. 230.
[17] In developing his famous five types, Niebuhr was influenced by C. J. Jung's *Psychological Types* and Augustine's *City of God*; see H. R. Niebuhr, *Christ and Culture* (New York: Harper & Row, 1975), p. x.
[18] Ibid., pp. 45–190.
[19] Ibid., p. 66.
[20] Ibid., p. 48.
[21] Ibid., p. 209.
[22] Ibid., p. 83.

between Christ and culture are plausible; therefore, of Niebuhr's five types, the two that are fruitful for this chapter are: 'Christ of culture' and 'Christ the transformer of culture'. However, the relationship between Christ and culture in Africa has not been without contestation.

Bujo takes note of some voices raised against inculturation. For its critics, inculturation is empty rhetoric whose followers are adherents of a bourgeois Christianity. They also claim that inculturation is a product of an inferiority complex vis-à-vis the West and is coloured by an apologetic intent.[23] However, this perspective is unacceptable since African cultural heritage must be a part of a genuinely African theology that takes into account the contemporary African context. Only an inculturated gospel can be understood by the people of a specific culture. In order for African Christians to live out the new life of the gospel, the gospel must be communicated in a way that is understandable in their actual situation. Meaning is therefore made possible in the context of African culture and the historical period.

My claim is that inculturation leads to a suitable application of African culture by allowing a reciprocal and critical interaction between the gospel and African culture. Inculturated Christianity in Africa provides room for the growth of the identity of local churches. A truly authentic church is only possible through inculturation. Through inculturation, local churches are able to express their new consciousness of self-worth and develop their identity. This manifestation of identity expresses the public nature of faith in that the African Christian is now able to live out the new life in public. At the same time, African Christians in African churches are encouraged and strengthened to live faithfully in public life where there is no identity crisis.

According to Bate, inculturation is approached in a variety of ways depending on the subject of the inculturation process. The subject may first be the gospel, where the incarnation of the gospel in native cultures is examined. Second, the subject may be Jesus, where Jesus Christ becomes incarnated and is the real subject of inculturation. This second approach attempts to discover the Jesus who is already present in the culture and allows him to come to full view while transforming the Christ who has been preached within a Western cultural matrix. Third, the subject may be the people and, fourth, the subject could be the church.[24]

Leaning on the incarnational model for inculturation, Shorter suggests that inculturation is the process in which a human culture is in dialogue with the gospel; this process presupposes a measure of reformulation, or more accurately, re-interpretation. For Shorter, the gospel is the good news and Jesus is the good news; therefore, the gospel ought to be seen in terms of its ultimate essence: Jesus Christ. Consequently, what is inculturated is Jesus Christ himself.[25] The theologian Teresa Okure also uses this approach for inculturation. Shorter and Okure are both Catholics and their treatment of inculturation as Christ becoming 'incarnated' in a particular culture has been adopted extensively within the Catholic fraternity.

---

[23] B. Bujo, *African Theology in its Social Context* (Maryknoll, NY: Orbis Books, 1992), p. 15.
[24] S. Bate, *Inculturation and Healing*, pp. 231–235.
[25] A. Shorter, *Toward a Theology of Inculturation*, pp. 59–62.

However, according to the 1981 research seminar on missions, it was agreed that what is inculturated is the gospel, or more specifically, faith in the gospel.[26]

Clearly, to speak of the person of Jesus as the religious element for inculturation is problematic. Such a standpoint assumes that there is a consensus about the person of Christ. Indeed, it presupposes that there is what the theologian Jon Sobrino questioningly calls an 'absolutely absolute Jesus'.[27] It seems to imply that all people in a particular culture should have the same interpretation of the person of Jesus.

My point of departure for this chapter stems from this critique which opens up debates regarding the different images of Jesus Christ. While there are images of Jesus that suit the powerful or those who dominate others, other images are for the oppressed. Undeniably, understanding Jesus as Christ is already an interpretation. Choosing Jesus as the subject of inculturation in this chapter leaves room for a variety of contextual interpretations that may arise. It suggests that there are no absolutes, that our image of Jesus is necessarily influenced by our cultural context. Therefore the subject of inculturation in this study is taken to be Jesus Christ.[28] Indeed, according to the theologian Kwok Pui-Lan, 'there is no original or privileged understanding of Christ, whether at the beginning of the Christian religion or in the history of the church, that can be claimed as pure and foundational, not subject to the limitations of culture and history'.[29] As such, creative reconstructions of Christology[30] have been used in various ways with some theologians addressing the notion of Sophia.[31]

III. Sophia and Wisdom in Myths

In what follows, I will use African categories taken from myths and interviews to articulate the wisdom of God.[32] Myths are developed in order to explain and

---

[26] T. Okure, and P. van Thiel (eds), *32 Articles Evaluating Inculturation in Africa* (Spearhead Numbers 112-114; Port Harcourt: Gaba Publications, 1990), pp. 103-104.

[27] J. Sobrino, *Jesus the Liberator* (Maryknoll, NY: Orbis Books, 1993), p. 16.

[28] As mentioned, by taking Jesus as the subject of inculturation, this chapter is limited since it omits other possibilities, such as the gospel as the subject of inculturation. When the gospel is the subject of inculturation, there is room for a variety of contextual interpretations that arise to understand it.

[29] K. Pui-Lan, 'Engendering Christ', *Toward a New Heaven and a New Earth* (F. Segovia (ed.); Maryknoll, NY, Orbis Books, 2003), p. 309.

[30] M. Stevens, *Reconstructing the Christ Symbol: Essays in Feminist Christology* (New York: Paulist Press, 1993).

[31] K. Greene-McCreight, *Feminist Reconstructions of Christian Doctrine* (New York: Oxford Press, 2000).

[32] This link is the result of a reference to John Carmody in Celia Deane-Drummond's article where she dwells on various approaches to wisdom. Carmody describes the natural world as itself bearing wisdom. He stresses the Wisdom traditions of ancient cosmological myths that retain the sense of the sacred in nature. He argues that it is a mistake for Christian

answer questions about the meanings behind the historical events of a people's past, present and future.[33] Myths are sacred narratives explaining how the world and humankind came to be in their present form and are therefore closely linked to religion. The word 'myth' is used in various ways. In a broad sense, a myth refers to any traditional story. Myths explain various aspects of society and express realities that history does not fully account for. In Africa, there are many myths; these have often been told in the public sphere, passed on in the form of stories from generation to generation.

The female figure of wisdom in Hebrew (*Chokmah*) and Greek (*Sophia*) personifies the divine. In the Old Testament, divine wisdom or the figure of the wisdom of God is widely attested. It is described in various ways but its primary function is to mediate between God and world and, as such, is associated with the work of creation. The New Testament clearly associates wisdom with the person of Jesus Christ.

Concepts of Sophia are fluid and open to new developments. Sophia, who has a divine origin and dwells with God, existed before creation and played a role in creation. Identified with the divine spirit, Sophia is immanent in the world and is responsible for the coherence and permanence of the cosmos.[34] While Sophia was sidelined in patriarchal religion, she has now been reclaimed in a variety of ways. Kwok Pui-Lan suggests several possibilities for reconceptualizing the Christ symbol in our contemporary world. For her, religions with strong wisdom traditions, which are passed from one generation to another, can be compared and contrasted with wisdom traditions in the Bible. In general, Pui-Lan states that we need to move beyond innocence to wisdom; by learning wisdom, we thus find ways to be ethical agents of survival. This, she suggests, would be accomplished by returning to strong wisdom traditions.[35]

According to Celia Deane-Drummond, there are various approaches to Sophia in feminist theology. These primarily include the themes of wisdom as emancipatory wisdom,[36] wisdom as a new and helpful image of God,[37] wisdom as Jesus-Sophia with Christ as the wisdom of God in biblical passages,[38] and wisdom that stems

---

theology to be hostile to these sources of wisdom. See C. Deanne-Drummond, 'Sophia: The Feminine Face of God as a Metaphor for an Ecotheology', *Feminist Theology* 6 (1997), pp. 11-31 (25-25).

[33] J. Mugambi, J., and N. Kirima, *The African Religious Heritage* (Nairobi: Oxford University Press, 1989).

[34] A. O'Boyle, *Towards a Contemporary Wisdom Christology: Some Catholic Christologies in German, English and French 1965-1995* (Rome: Gregorian University Press, 2004), pp. 17-47.

[35] K. Pui-Lan, 'Ecology and Christology', p. 123.

[36] Celia Deane-Drummond investigates feminist approaches to the theme of wisdom by presenting various scholars, perspectives and interpretations. This is taken from her treatment of Catherine Keller. See C. Deane-Drummond, 'Sophia: The Feminine Face of God as a Metaphor for an Ecotheology', pp. 6, 19.

[37] Ibid., p. 19.

[38] Ibid., pp. 21-22.

from the natural world and looks to ancient cosmological myths for insights on the sense of the sacred in nature.[39] While these approaches indicate ways to gain a deeper understanding of wisdom, the latter is particularly welcome because it takes seriously the possibility of gaining insights into wisdom derived from other cultural contexts of the world, including Africa.[40]

Deane-Drummond draws upon Sergei Bulgakov's reflections on Sophia. For Bulgakov, Sophia is the intermediary between God and creation, the yearning love of God for creation. He uses both divine Sophia and creaturely Sophia to develop his theology; thus, in his view, Sophia is both divine and creaturely. In her creaturely mode, Sophia is visible in the creation.[41] Jesus as creaturely Sophia links God and creation, expressing a radical incarnation of God. Here, God-self is intimately connected with the earth, and as such becomes bound in human history and also in the ecological dynamics of planet earth. From the beginning, Sophia interpenetrates the whole creation even before the first days of creation. Thus, through wisdom, God created the world.[42] Creation, incarnation and redemption present a portrait of God as divine wisdom and of God as active in the world through creaturely Sophia.[43] In this way, the relationship between the natural world and God as revealed in Christ is made possible through the language of Sophia.[44] I now turn to a selection of African myths.

Among the Luo peoples of Africa, there is a myth that explains the origin of the lake *Simbi Nyaima*.[45] It is believed that there was once a very big village in which all the people belonged to the same clan. The people had plenty of water, food and land to till. After many years of living in harmony, hatred, disunity and animosity arose when a few people became greedy. A war broke out known as '*Goch Masira*', which means 'war of the angered' or 'war with a thorough beating'. The people forgot to continue farming, fishing and pottery-making and instead began cutting trees and spoiling their environment. Soon after, a severe drought came to the village and they believed that only God could save them. One day an old, weak woman came into the village and went from door to door begging for food. Nobody offered her food. She walked to the top of the hills (these are considered the Kisii highlands in

---

[39] Ibid., p. 25.

[40] Deane-Drummond indicates that there is a distinction between the 'natural wisdom' of ecology and the human 'cultural wisdom' of the sages of the Old Testament. She shows that the distinction is not as sharp as it may seem at first sight; yet wisdom is characterized by a unitary world in which the regularities in the human and the non-human realm are no different. Ibid., p. 28.

[41] C. Deane-Drummond, *Creation Through Wisdom: Theology and the New Biology* (Edinburgh: T & T Clark, 2000), p. 238.

[42] Ibid., 85.

[43] C. Deane-Drummond, *Christ and Evolution: Wonder and Wisdom* (Minneapolis: Fortress Press, 2009), p. 126.

[44] Ibid., pp. 95, 127.

[45] A. Odaga, *Simbi Nyaima* (Kisumu: Lake Publishers & Enterprises, 1983). See also the National Museum of Kenya website at http://www.museums.or.ke/content/view/119/10/ (accessed 20 February 2010).

present day) and sobbed, praying to God to restore the land and to bring rain and fertility to the land. Thunderstorms began and heavy rains followed which swept away the whole village and all that were in it. The only person who survived was this woman who later settled in the Kisii highlands. This is how *Simbi Nyaima* came to be and it can now be found in Kendu Bay in Kenya. It is a volcanic lake and it is thought to be connected to the ancestors, which is why many Luos pray beside the lake. It is believed that if a stone is thrown into the lake it will not fall far.

People draw water from this lake in bottles which they use for curative purposes. It is said that the lake is curative because the ancestors are directly involved when people pray for cures by the lake. Many skin diseases are cured and the lake is said to turn bloody or green or even is clear at some times.[46] When wishes and prayers are made around this lake, especially when there is drought, it is believed that the answers result from the ancestors in the lake having compassion on the people. Within this myth are insights into the sense of the sacred in *Simbi Nyaima*. This myth on the origins of the lake indicates the effects of carelessness with the planet earth and shows that such carelessness punishes an entire people. At the same time, the presence of ancestors in the lake serves as a deterrent to those Luos living around the lake who may want to pollute it. As such, this is a wisdom tradition whose emphasis is on the sacred in nature.

Among the Kisii peoples of Kenya, it is believed that long ago the tree known as *omontandege* was a shade provider and a place around which people gathered to pray to God to give them their daily needs. Then everyone decided to do whatever pleased them. One man came and cut some branches of the tree for firewood. Immediately, as a result of his interference with this tree, his body broke out in pimples. His remedy was to get an equivalent number of branches from another tree, place them at the foot of the tree, and then walk away without looking back.[47]

For the Kisii people there are species of trees that are not to be touched or converted for any use. The tree known as *Omonyia* is one such species of tree. From ancient times, it was believed to be an abomination to cut this kind of tree. The informant made it clear that such trees were often found in the specific areas where young boys were initiated. In clearing such trees, initiation grounds would be done away with and this would be disastrous. In all, these trees are instrumental because they make up and constitute particular sacred spaces for the Kisii people where their African religious and cultural rites may be practiced.[48]

The Agikuyu have a myth that in the beginning, Ngai (meaning God) called Gikuyu (the father of the tribe), and gave him a share of his land with rivers, rich forests, animals and fruits of all types. Ngai then went to live on the mountain

---

[46] Interview with a Luo elder informant on 26 October 2009. This information was verified during a lecture (21 January 2010) with fourth year Bachelor students of Religion and Theology at Maseno University who come from among the Luo.

[47] This was information given by an informant who is well versed with Kisii traditions during an interview carried out on 1 December 2009. Interviews took place in the Maseno area.

[48] This was information given by an informant who is well versed with Kisii traditions during an interview carried out on 12 December 2009. Interviews took place in the Maseno area.

Kirinyanga (Mount Kenya). One day Ngai took Gikuyu to the top of Kirinyanga and showed him a spot in the centre of the country where there were many *mugumo* (wild fig) trees. Ngai told him to go and build his homestead there. When Gikuyu went there he found a beautiful woman whom he took as his wife and named Mumbi. Together they had nine daughters. Gikuyu went to Ngai and asked for sons to marry his daughters. Ngai told him to take a lamb and a kid and to kill them under the big mugumo tree near the homestead and to pour the blood and the fat on the trunk of the tree. The family was to make a big fire under the tree and return to their house. Gikuyu then returned alone to the mugumo tree and found nine handsome men willing to marry his daughters.[49]

The mugumo tree among the Agikuyu people is known to be sacred. It is believed to have so much power that if anyone wants to change their gender all that is required is for the person to ride a sheep around the tree seven times without falling down as directed by the elders. When well performed, this ritual would result in a man becoming a woman and a woman becoming a man. Both the mugumo and omontandege display the power of the supernatural within trees. In cutting these trees, one was guilty of doing away with the sacredness of nature.

Through the language of Sophia, these myths inform a new creaturely Sophia by drawing directly from African sources. These African myths describe aspects of creation and identify the processes involved in creative activity. They communicate the dynamic interwovenness of the cosmos, humanity and the divine; they articulate, for instance, the human, social and cosmic[50] faces of wisdom and consider how humans relate to creation.

These myths reveal how God is Christ incarnate in the material world. They connect Jesus Sophia to the wider creation and move away from anthropocentricism. They attest to the wisdom involved in bringing Simbi Nyaima and the Mugumo tree into being. In summary, creaturely Sophia is informed by way of these myths as God-self is intimately connected with the earth by being bound up in ecological dynamics and in relation to humankind.

Rosemary Radford Ruether points to many local cultures of indigenous peoples in the Americas, Africa, Asia and the Pacific Islands who have on many occasions been scorned as pagans by monotheists. These peoples created their own bioregional culture that sustained the human community as a part of the community of animals, plants, earth, sky, past ancestors and future descendants.[51] Their restraints, regarding how trees can be cut or used and how trees in some areas are significant aspects of sacred spaces used for worship, depict sacredness in nature. Yet tensions remain in relating monotheistic religions to other religions. Clearly, the view of the divine in African religion is different from that of classical Christology, where divine Sophia and creaturely Sophia hold together. I believe there is room for an

---

[49] R. Mwangi, *Kikuyu's Folktales: Their Nature and Value* (Nairobi: Kenya Literature Bureau, 1983).

[50] C. Deane-Drummond, *Creation Through Wisdom: Theology and the New Biology*, pp. 20, 26.

[51] R. Radford Ruether, 'Ecofeminism and Healing Ourselves, Healing the Earth', pp. 51–62.

ongoing modification of the view of the divine in African traditional religion so as to resonate with Christology,[52] even as Christianity continues to be rooted in Africa.

IV. Conclusion

This chapter has examined Jesus as the subject of inculturation in relation to the wisdom of God in Africa. It has highlighted myths that help retain a sense of the sacred in nature for ecological purposes in communities within Africa. These myths promote healthy co-existence among all creation. At the fore of these within African Traditional Religion is the assumption that the sacred is everywhere and not limited to one place.

It has rearticulated the symbol and image of Sophia in the African context, opening up possibilities for further work in developing a critical praxis of reflective Sophiology. It has explored how creaturely Sophia links the natural world and God as revealed in Christ. An African inculturated Sophiology would involve a reinterpretation and re-articulation of the images of Sophia into African categories. This reinterpretation could create an emancipatory Christology in Africa that is sensitive to all creation and with Jesus as the incarnation of Sophia. Sophiology could be made functional within an African framework because wisdom traditions uphold the wholeness and health of the planet earth. Therefore, it is important for an African inculturated Sophiology to be further developed and for it to be critical, variegated and open-ended, while remaining engaged with a variety of African cultural contexts.

Bibliography

Barnhill, D., and R. Gottlieb, *Deep Ecology and World Religions: New Essays on Sacred Ground* (Albany: State University of New York Press, 2001).

Bate, S., *Inculturation and Healing* (Pietermaritzburg: Cluster Publications, 1995).

Bevans, S., *Models of Contextual Theology* (Maryknoll, NY: Orbis Books, 1999).

Bujo, B., *African Theology in its Social Context* (Maryknoll, NY: Orbis Books, 1992).

Clifford, A., *Introducing Feminist Theology* (Maryknoll, NY: Orbis Books, 2001).

Deane-Drummond. C., *Christ and Evolution: Wonder and Wisdom* (Minneapolis: Fortress Press, 2009).

—*Creation Through Wisdom: Theology and the New Biology* (Edinburgh: T & T Clark, 2000).

—'Sophia: The Feminine Face of God as a Metaphor for an Ecotheology', *Feminist Theology* 6 (1997), pp. 11–31.

---

[52] M. A. Oduyoye, *Introducing African Women's Theology*, pp. 51–66.

Greene-McCreight, K., *Feminist Reconstructions of Christian Doctrine* (New York: Oxford Press, 2000).

Hinga, T., 'Jesus Christ and the Liberation of Women in Africa', *The Will to Arise: Women, Tradition, and the Church in Africa* (M. Oduyoye and K. Kanyoro (eds); Maryknoll, NY: Orbis Books, 1992), pp. 183–194.

Magesa, L., 'Authentic African Christianity', *32 Articles Evaluating Inculturation in Africa* (T. Okure and P. van Thiel (eds); Spearhead Numbers 112–114; Port Harcourt: Gaba Publications, 1990).

Maseno, L., 'Widows' Christologies: A preliminary feminist analysis of Abanyole widows' Christologies considering kinship, gender and the power of naming' (doctoral dissertation; University of Oslo, 2008).

McFague, S., 'An Earthly Theological Agenda', *Ecofeminism and the Sacred* (C. Adams (ed.); NewYork: Continuum, 1993).

Mugambi, J., and N. Kirima, *The African Religious Heritage* (Nairobi: Oxford University Press, 1989).

Mugambi, J., and M. Vähäkangas (eds), *Christian Theology and Environmental Responsibility* (Nairobi: Acton, 2001).

Mwangi, R., *Kikuyu's Folktales: Their Nature and Value* (Nairobi: Kenya Literature Bureau, 1983).

'Myth as Thought: Modern Theory and Myth', www.classics.uc.edu/~johnson/myth/theory.html (accessed 20 February 2010).

Nasimiyu, W., 'Christology and an African Woman's Experience', *Faces of Jesus in Africa* (R, Schreiter (ed.); New York: Orbis Books, 9th edn, 2005).

Niebuhr, H. R., *Christ and Culture* (New York: Harper & Row, 1975).

O'Boyle, A., *Towards a Contemporary Wisdom Christology: Some Catholic Christologies in German, English and French 1965-1995* (Rome: Gregorian University Press, 2004).

Odaga A., *Simbi Nyaima* (Kisumu: Lake Publishers & Enterprises, 1983).

Oduyoye, M. A., *Introducing African Women's Theology* (Sheffield, England: Sheffield Academic Press, 2001).

Okure, T., and P. van Thiel (eds), *32 Articles Evaluating Inculturation in Africa* (Spearhead Numbers 112–114; Port Harcourt: Gaba Publications, 1990).

Ongong'a, J., 'Towards an African Environmental Theology', *Theology of Reconstruction: Exploratory Essays* (M.N. Getui and E.A. Obeng (eds); Nairobi: Acton Publishers, 1999).

Owusu, D. A., 'Jesus, The African Healer' (unpublished masters thesis; University of Oslo, 2001).

Phiri, I. A., 'The Chisumphi Cult: The Role of Women in Preserving the Environment', *Women Healing Earth: Third World Women on Ecology, Feminism, and Religion* (R. Radford Ruether (ed.); Maryknoll: Orbis Books, 1996) pp. 161–171.

Pui-Lan, K., 'Ecology and Christology', *Feminist Theology* 5 (1997), pp. 113–125.

—'Engendering Christ', *Toward a New Heaven and a New Earth* (F. Segovia (ed.); Maryknoll, NY, Orbis Books, 2003).

Radford Ruether, R., 'Ecofeminism and Healing Ourselves, Healing the Earth', *Feminist Theology* 3(1995), pp. 51–62.

Schreiter, R. J., *Faces of Jesus in Africa* (Maryknoll, NY: Orbis Books, 9th edn, 2005).
Shorter, A., *Toward a Theology of Inculturation* (London: Geoffrey Chapman, 1998).
Sobrino, J., *Jesus the Liberator* (Maryknoll, NY: Orbis Books, 1993).
Stevens, M., *Reconstructing the Christ Symbol: Essays in Feminist Christology* (New York: Paulist Press, 1993).
Stinton, D., *Jesus of Africa: Voices of Contemporary African Christology* (Maryknoll, NY: Orbis Books, 2004).
Waliggo, J., *Inculturation: Its Meaning and Urgency* (Kampala, Uganda: St. Paul's Publications, 1986).

Part III

Towards Public Theologies of Nature

8 Environmental Amnesia or the Memory of Place? The Need for Local Ethics of Memory in a Philosophical Theology of Place

Forrest Clingerman
Ohio Northern University, USA

Before the hemlocks of the Eastern US started dying from wooly adelgid, but after the ferns and forests had overtaken the stone walls and farmland of the early nineteenth century, I spent time walking along Shattuck Brook. For a few years, my family lived in a house where the yard met forest and stream in the foothills of the Berkshire Mountains in the Eastern United States. In a manner evocative of Heidegger's fourfold,[1] a footbridge across Shattuck Brook gathered the everyday routine and the imaginative possibility of childhood adventure. Playmates and I often entered its streambanks. Downstream was a small island, a secret meeting place for us. This locale transformed into hiding places, historic battles and mythological meetings. Further downstream the water current sped up, until it approached a sharp corner deeply incised into the bedrock. Granite rose to contain the water, forming walls which towered over our young frames. Moss and ferns grew in the crevices on the rock wall; lively green rested on the indifferent greyness

[1] In the essay 'Building Dwelling Thinking', Heidegger explains what he calls the *Geviert* or fourfold. This identifies four entities – earth, sky, gods and mortals – that make up a meaningful 'world' when gathered together. To explain this gathering of the fourfold, Heidegger gives a well-known example of a bridge. As he explains, a bridge connects the opposing banks of a river. In so doing, the banks come into being as banks by being set off from each other by the bridge. Further, the bridge is a gathering point for mortals, for it allows them to move as well as and linger at the river. Heidegger next explains how the bridge gathers the mortals before the divinities when humans give thanks or otherwise see a divine presence in the bridge. Finally, Heidegger explains that the bridge is also a meeting point of sky and earth. In sum, this simple bridge provides a 'site' or a place for the gathering of the fourfold. M. Heidegger, 'Building Dwelling Thinking', *Basic Writings* (D. Farrell (ed.); San Francisco: Harper San Francisco, 2nd edn, 1993), pp. 343–363 (353–60).

of the stone. These details created an altogether different atmosphere from school and home. Scrambling up we walked home through pastures or forest. Of course, turning upstream from our yard meant different woods, different adventures. There was an abandoned nineteenth century farmhouse with silent walls that never betrayed any secrets. Further down was a large pool, in which the currents endlessly swirled to make it deep enough to swim. Further still ...

Metaphorically stepping out of the banks of Shattuck Brook (still dripping with cool water), this essay starts with a simple claim: memory of place is profound and influential.[2] For example, by walking among hemlocks and ferns near Shattuck Brook, I encountered changes in the world in unique ways. My fragmentary memories take individual hours, days and months and press them into a vision of one place, and this place is identified as an instantiation of 'nature.' Thus the conceptualization of 'nature' is affected by personal memories of place: built or wild, pleasurable or uncomfortable, calm or violent. This influence is often ephemeral, unique, unsystematic and unrecognized. It might directly influence subjective descriptions or something that directly serves as a point of comparison. Or it might be indirect in its influence, with the lacuna of what is recollected affecting the sense of place. Both directly and indirectly, memory of nature becomes part of the present.

Taking this claim seriously, I wish to argue that memory deepens the perspective of environmental theology by introducing a local ethics of memory, which is an asset for religious thought in the 'green public square'.[3] My argument explains how memory deepens the understandings of place, and how theological reflection on the memory of place informs the public square through an ethics of locality. To situate this argument, I am approaching environmental theology as a *hermeneutically-oriented philosophical theology of place*. This way of theological reflection correlates theological and philosophical thinking on how we interpret and understand environments. Place is of primary concern, for the concept of place allows us to draw together nature as lived human experience, communal interpretations of space and time, and abstract understanding.[4]

From a hermeneutical perspective, the memory of place is not only important for environmental theology, but also for the public sphere. In both, memory provides

---

[2] For some examples of this influence, see K. Booth, 'Risdon Vale: Place, Memory, and Suburban Experience', *Ethics, Place and Environment* 11 (2008), pp. 299–311; M. Brocki, 'Landscapes of Memory—Narratives of Past Places', *Koht ja Paik/Place and Location* 6 (2008), pp. 219–225; C. Cooper-Marcus, 'Environmental Memories', *Place Attachment* (I. Altman, and S. M. Low (eds); New York: Plenum Press, 1992), pp. 87–112; F. Mathews, *Reinhabiting Reality: Towards a Recovery of Culture* (Albany, NY: SUNY Press, 2005).
[3] R. Gottlieb, *A Greener Faith: Religious Environmentalism and Our Planet's Future* (Oxford: Oxford University Press, 2006), pp. 235–238.
[4] See F. Clingerman, 'Reading the Book of Nature: A Hermeneutical Account of Nature for Philosophical Theology', *Worldviews: Global Religions, Culture, and Ecology* 13 (2009), pp. 72–91. For more on the relationship between philosophy and theology in light of an environmental hermeneutics, see F. Clingerman, 'Wilderness as the Place between Philosophy and Theology: Questioning Martin Drenthen on the Otherness of Nature', *Environmental Values* 19 (2010), pp. 211–232.

a basis for deepening our interpretations of the meaning of the past and present manifestations of specific places. The first section of this essay explains several facets of memory that relate to our understanding of place. In the second section I show that memory is crucial for deepening our theological understanding of place: we gather the particularity of our experiences in memory, the interpretations that emerge from our experience is informed by memory, and even our abstract conceptualization is influenced by memory. Importantly, this occurs both individually and communally, creating a dialogue between individual and communal memory. This dialogue presents a way for theological reflection to inform the public square in unique ways, as will be argued in the final section of the paper. Third, we see the underside of a memory of place: environmental amnesia. Environmental amnesia is not only a personal phenomenon, but also occurs in civil society. It is an ethical issue that can be addressed through theological reflection. And thus finally, through the discussion of memory we have confirmation that environmental theology is, as Heinrich Bedford-Strohm has argued, a public theology. Memory not only deepens our theological understanding, but it also illuminates the past and present of place for the community. 'Remembering place rightly' is an ethical responsibility for civil society. This intersection of environmental theology, the place of memory, and the public sphere is found in a local ethics of memory.

I. Defining Memory

To reminisce about Shattuck Brook is not the same as standing in the rush of water. Memory is not identical to the chill of its springtime current or the roots of maple trees that – like toes of an uncertain swimmer – dip into flowing water. But what, then, is memory? Is it simply gathering fragments of the past in the mind's eye? Or something more? To define memory is difficult, for it can be approached in a diversity of ways. The study of memory transcends the boundaries of many disciplines: it is studied by sciences such as neurophysiology, psychology and sociology, but it is also at the heart of reflections in humane disciplines such as art, literature and philosophy.

A starting point is to describe memory as the capacity to store and access information about the past. Westbury and Dennett, for example, state that '[m]emory in the fundamental sense is the ability to store useful information and to retrieve it in precisely those circumstances and that form which allow it to be useful'.[5] Insofar as we file away 'facts' about the past and also inevitably seek to retrieve them when the need arises, the capacity for memory furthermore presumes a peculiar process for remembering. Such an explanation is based on the fact that the work of memory is helpful – or even necessary – in order to allow humans to position themselves in time and to anticipate future events. Akin to the visual ability to

---

[5] C. Westbury and D. Dennett, 'Mining the Past to Construct the Future: Memory and Belief as Forms of Knowledge', *Memory, Brain and Belief* (D. Schacter, and E. Scarry (eds); Cambridge: Harvard University Press, 2000), pp. 11–32 (13).

track the movement of something across space, the process of memory provides us with the ability to identify events and things across time. But while Westbury and Dennett point out important facets of memory, this description of memory is not complete. Philosophical and theological discussions particularly benefit by expanding the concept of memory in three directions: through discussion of the inclusion of forgetting in memory, the relationship of memory and self-identity, and the cognitive character of memory.

First, memory requires that *someone* remembers. Memory illuminates and adds to the temporality of self-identity. Memory does not simply demarcate information storage but also includes our ability to reflect on the past's meaning in light of present circumstances; something true for individual and social memory. For both groups and individuals, therefore, memory undergirds the determination of *self-identity across time*.[6] There is a dialogue within the complex temporal relationship between who we are and who we were, between past and present: someone or something remembers because of who or what they are, and the same act of memory constructs the self-identity that remembers. Any being that seeks meaning therefore has a need for memory, in order to define and organize self-identity in light of the inevitable passage of time. Categorizing memory into different types (working memory, long term, semantic, episodic, etc.) or in terms of different modes of sensation (iconic memory, echoic, tactile, etc.) shows our need to approach the past in a myriad of ways in order to make sense of our lives in this way.

Through the process of memory we *become* individuals and communities. The temporality of self-identity is enclosed in the ever-changing boundaries between what is kept and what is forgotten. As Elie Wiesel writes, 'Memory is related to identity, the two feed one another. The existentialist action as a philosophy of life is only half-true; I am not only what I do, I am also what I remember. The life of memory is my own; when it dies, I also die. I mean: the only person in life that can say 'I' for me, the 'I' that is me dies the moment the light of and in my memory is extinguished'.[7] If memory allows the past to be present, it is possible because of a persistence of identity by one who remembers. This is true for social identity as well; communal memory (in forms such as memorials, histories and folklore) is essential for group cohesion and persistence. While groups do not possess the same

---

[6] The complex interrelationship between self-identity and memory reminds us of Augustine's vision of memory. 'Great is the power of memory, an awe-inspiring mystery, my God, a power of profound and infinite multiplicity. And this is mind, this is I myself. What then am I, my God?' *Confessions* X.xvii. The fact that memory is both passive and active comes out clearly in Augustine's view. Augustine, *Confessions* (H. Chadwick (trans.); Oxford: Oxford University Press, 1998), p. 194.

[7] E. Wiesel, *Ethics and Memory* (New York: Walter de Gruyter, 1997), p. 14. This is not taken to mean that memory is the sole constitutive factor of personhood. Rather, I take Wiesel to be writing here with a more poetic turn that does not attempt to address all of the elements of personhood. The importance of Wiesel's claim here is that memory is important for identifying 'me'. Certainly the loss of memory is not the destruction of *a* person, just the person *I* am now, the particular 'me' that remembers.

physical faculties for memory, they nonetheless still rely on memory to understand who they are.

Second, as we have seen in passing, there is a role for *forgetting* in memory. 'To remember everything' is a Sisyphean endeavour, for it would require pushing the limits of memory to the point of breaking. To remember every sight, sound and smell? Exact times and distances? Every feeling? Every individual perception of events? It is impossible to remember everything and, furthermore, it is not desirable to do so.[8] To be laden with a limitless recall of experiences at each instant would be unbearable.[9] If it is neither possible nor desirable to remember everything, then memory necessarily includes forgetting (whether forgetting here means not 'saving' things to memory, passively losing a specific memory, or the act of actively suppressing it). Thus Tzvetan Todorov defines memory as the selection between effacement and conservation.[10] This complexifies our assumptions about the goodness of memory. Todorov further writes:

> Memory should not be thought of as a mechanical recording of what has happened. It has many forms and functions, and we have to choose between them; it develops in stages, each of which can be distorted or disturbed; it can be possessed by different people who derive different moral attitudes from it. Is memory necessarily a good thing? Is forgetting always a curse? Does the past always help us to understand the present, or can it serve to confuse our view of the here and now?[11]

With such a complex interaction between memory and forgetting, it is apparent that here can be an inappropriate forgetting. Paul Ricoeur has noted this dynamic by pointing out the ethical and political dimensions of memory: not only might we have a 'duty to remember,' we also might have a 'duty to forget'.[12] Ricoeur highlights

---

[8] Not only should we admit the complexity of memory, but we must also recognize the complexity of forgetting. U. Neisser has pointed out some of the difficulties of explaining the cause of forgetting, and forgetting itself: 'Perhaps you fail to retrieve a piece of information that, by some standard, should have been available: you can't think of my name. At the same time, though, there is a lot that you are thinking of. What you do and what you think in every human situation has many causes at many levels, ranging from social convention to unconscious drive. What you do not do (i.e. think of my name) is an aspect of what you are doing, and has just as many causes. A great deal is going on. To point this out is not to argue that forgetting is due only to interference and not to decay. The matter is equally complex if the necessary information has decayed simply because you and I were introduced too long ago. Even then, its nonexistence would be a cause of remembering just as much as of forgetting – of what you do as well as of what you don't do.' U. Neisser, 'Memory: What are the Important Questions', *Memory Observed: Remembering in Natural Contexts* (U. Neisser (ed.); San Francisco: W. H. Freeman & Co., 1982), pp. 3–19 (9).

[9] A recent example is that of Jill Price. In her memoir, *The Woman Who Can't Forget* (New York: Free Press, 2008), Price notes several other cases of extraordinary memory.

[10] T. Todorov, 'The Abuses of Memory', *Common Knowledge* 5 (1996), pp. 6–26 (8).

[11] T. Todorov, *Hope and Memory: Lessons from the Twentieth Century* (Princeton: Princeton University Press, 2003), p. 3.

[12] P. Ricoeur, 'Memory, Forgetfulness, and History', *Iyyun: The Jerusalem Philosophical Quarterly* 45 (1996), pp. 13–24.

the fact that both memory and forgetting can either aid our understanding or distort it. The complexity of forgetting and ethics has great consequences: Ricoeur notes that while the *Shoah* demands an ethical response that includes memory, many instances of nationalistic violence require forgetting the past. Likewise, in the next section we will see that 'environmental amnesia' is another example of unethical forgetting.

Third, memory is a *form of knowing*. To be more specific, memory is an embodied form of knowledge that is tied to our hermeneutical consciousness. On the one hand, it is a knowledge of the self. From a Christian context, Miroslav Volf shows the need for the Christian community to remember rightly. This need makes a theological connection between salvation, identity and memory quite succinctly: '... salvation lies in memory insofar as that memory prevents us from distorting our essential selves and living a lie'.[13] On the other hand, memory serves as a knowledge of past activities, events or contexts. In both cases, it should be evident that our understanding always contains not only our present experience, but also our past interpretations, that is, our memories. We encounter and understand things through an interpretation of space *and time*; memory acts to help form knowledge of the past. For a theology of nature to be fully investigated, we must recognize that memory is one of the constitutive elements in a hermeneutics of place. In brief, *memory connects the past of the place with its presence or presentness*.

A key concept for explaining the way that memory manifests itself in the process of knowing is the 'trace'. Edward Casey gives this definition: 'the ordinary notion of the trace is that of a mere mark left by an entity or an event of which it is but the finite and fragile reflection. Its nature seems to consist in a self-surpassing operation whereby its meaning or value lies elsewhere, namely, in that of which it is the trace, that which the trace signifies by a self-suspension of its own being or happening'.[14] Through the trace, we can 'read' the past. In other words, 'reading' serves as a metaphor for this cognitive process of memory of place. The trace, in turn, is the manifestation of words and similar elements of the text of nature.

II. Memory, Place and Theology

In light of this discussion of memory, what is the connection between memory and place? This section explores how environmental theology approaches nature by addressing nature through place, more precisely, our 'emplacement' in place.[15] In

---

[13] M. Volf, *The End of Memory: Remembering Rightly in a Violent World* (Grand Rapids: Eerdmans, 2006), p. 24.

[14] E. Casey, 'Levinas on Memory and the Trace', *The Collegium Phaenomenologicum* (J. Sallis, G. Moneta, and J. Taminiaux (eds); Dordrecht: Kluwer, 1988), pp. 241–255 (241).

[15] F. Clingerman, 'Reading the Book of Nature: A Hermeneutical Account of Nature for Philosophical Theology.' *Worldviews: Global Religions, Culture, and Ecology* 13, no 1 (2009): pp. 72–91; F. Clingerman, 'Beyond the Flowers and the Stones: 'Emplacement' and the Modeling of Nature', *Philosophy in the Contemporary World* 11(2004), pp. 17–24.

other words, from the point of view of a hermeneutical theology of place, memory is not oriented toward nature: *place* is the more natural object of memory. Thus, memory of place is a dialectic of personal and communal memory.

The memory of place emerges in certain ways. In some cases, landscapes act as the background for a narrative or story – in effect a place dictates the possibility of memory – even though it is not the centre of the memory itself. In other cases, memory is explicitly focused on the place itself; in these cases our memory not only identifies the constitutive elements, but also weaves together the whole as a unique entity in its own right. This can be clarified by noting that there are at least two layers of the memory of place.

First, although not always explicitly recognized, environmental theology is built (at least in part and informally) on the *individual memory of place*. This claim rests on an assumption of what it means to reflect upon 'nature' as well as anecdotes found within theological literature. In terms of our reflections of 'nature', I have argued that we approach nature through place, that is, through reflection on the meaning of specific, concrete places as environments. Theologians discuss 'nature' in light of experience of places associated with nature (or at the very least places that, by being deemed 'unnatural', illuminate ways to identify nature). This is borne out anecdotally: in the last few years Mark Wallace's descriptions of the 'singing river' and Crumb Creek,[16] Sallie McFague's references to the Rockies,[17] Willis Jenkins' identification of his family connection to Old Rag Mountain in Virginia,[18] and H. Paul Santmire's walks along the Charles River[19] all show how theologians incorporate memory into theological reflection. All of these examples were not written as mere decoration, but use the memory of place – some positive, some negative – as a starting point for more systematic theological reflection.

Personal memory can provide a starting point for theologies of place quite readily. Foremost memory shows the interaction of subject and object, the self who remembers and the thing that is remembered. It also includes the process through which the individual highlights certain memories of places past, and forgets others. As an example, the present essay started with a personal example of memory. Such a starting point is inevitably partial and unique. My personal memories offer knowledge of concrete embodiments of the nature, identifying it as a temporal place (an object in memory). Due to this incomplete and individual basis, such

---

[16] M. Wallace, *Finding God in the Singing River* (Minneapolis: Fortress Press, 2005).

[17] This personal connection with several places runs through many of McFague's works, and for her personalizes more global concerns. For example, in her book on climate change, she writes, 'I wasn't thinking of the global consequences of submerged islands and coastal cities. Rather, I was thinking about myself. As a regular hiker in the Canadian Rockies, I saw the melting of glaciers as a personal loss: I loved those towering ice-covered mountains circling turquoise lakes.' S. McFague, *A New Climate For Theology: God, the World, and Global Warming* (Minneapolis: Fortress, 2008), p. 27. This is a clear example of how a personal memory of place informs our understanding of environmental policy.

[18] W. Jenkins, *Ecologies of Grace: Environmental Ethics and Christian Theology* (Oxford: Oxford University Press, 2008), pp. 25–27.

[19] H. P. Santmire, *Ritualizing Nature* (Minneapolis: Fortress, 2008), pp. xi–xii.

personal narratives are useful for approaching the meaning of place, but at the same time we must seek other forms of memory as well.

A common ground beyond personal memory is now necessary, for such a common ground would allow the discussion of memory to fit into a broader theological treatment of place. This common ground begins to emerge in the way that personal memories influence how one undertakes to conceptualize nature, not only betraying how one is situated in place but also showing how the temporality of place potentially infiltrates thinking about the natural world. In other words, the example given above highlights a dimension of place that emerges through memory: place is not exclusively spatial, but also inherently temporal. This temporal dimension of place requires tools to discover and interpret past manifestations of nature. We turn to memory, for memory provides us access to the 'pastness' of place, in the midst of its presence. The temporal dimensions of memory include both subject and object, self and place. In the pastness of memory, the self and place are like dance partners: moving together in step, responding to one another's movements, creating meaning in a unique pairing of particular individuals and places. Of course, this meaning is not exclusive to theology, but rather theology can provide a unique perspective of the spiritual depth of such memory.

Temporality shows that an exclusive focus on individual memory is insufficient for understanding place. In turn, a second claim concerning environmental theology serves to balance our focus on individual memory of place: the purpose of environmental theology is not just to understand systematically our religious experience and interpretation of place, but it also should offer a religious perspective that speaks for and to community and society.[20] In the next section of this essay, I correlate environmental theology with public theology, insofar as the former is a religious voice in the public sphere on environmental issues.

How is the move toward a communal memory oriented toward theological reflection? It is because individual memory is transformed when it enters into shared memory, to become theological reflection. Within Christian theology, a religious perspective is developed in light of a forward-looking, eschatological framework. That is to say, it contains the anticipation of a 'new world': a just, sustainable and flourishing future that is built upon a narrative sense of the past or tradition. But Christian religious thought is not confined to a future orientation; eschatological anticipation is found in tandem with anamnesis. Theology is rooted in remembrance of the past, because memory asserts a temporal richness to anticipation. Our finite memories are included within the sumptuousness of the eschatological memory of the community. In turn, communal recollection leads to the anticipation of wholeness within the infinite memory of the divine. This

---

[20] For a few different examples of this, see P. Scott, *A Political Theology of Nature* (Cambridge: Cambridge University Press, 2003), esp. Ch. 2; H. Bedford-Strohm, 'Tilling and Caring for the Earth: Public Theology and Ecology', *International Journal of Public Theology* 1 (2007), pp. 230–248; and R. Gottlieb, *A Spirituality of Resistance* (Lanham, MD: Rowman and Littlefield, 2003).

communal memory leads eventually to a spiritual memory. If this remembrance is important for Christian reflection as a whole, it is also important for theological reflection on the environment; a memory of place that is a spiritual memory combines a shared, communal memory with spiritual reflection on the infinite.

A fascinating relationship emerges in light of the two foregoing claims: theology reads nature through both individual memory and communal memory. But most importantly, a hermeneutically-oriented theology finds the depth of our memory – a spiritual memory – in the *interplay* between individual and communal memory; between private and public memories of place. Environmental theologies cannot exclusively dwell on private theological reflections and remembrances, but rather must move toward a communal vision, and a communal memory. Communal memory informs and illuminates, yet emerges from individual memory; because of this interaction, memory (as both individual and communal) is desirable for our ethical vision. This extends a point that has been argued by others; for example Rasmussen and Birch assert that 'agents of memory' are necessary for a well-functioning ethical community.[21]

Making explicit the hermeneutical roots of memory, the memory of place is – like other forms of memory – intersubjective. Francisco Delich comments, 'The dialectic of memory and forgetting thus includes the socialized individual and the individualized society: subjectivity and intersubjectivity are channels where memory is found, never perfect like a computer's because it remains ever open to a reinterpretation of actions'.[22] In fact, the process of memory and forgetting are a paradigmatic example of the complex interaction between self and other within place. Delich also writes:

> Memories are constructed in intersubjectivity. The most intimate memories, which are perceived as individual, have other eyes, sometimes created by ourselves, with which to see the same behavior but understand it in a different way. [...] Individual memory is an integral part of a social memory where reminiscences are constructed and also form a collective memory.[23]

The intersubjectivity of memory explains how *together* we build and inhabit place from individual reminiscences. Our emplacement, in other words, happens at the intersubjective intersection between the remembered and the forgotten. Knowledge of nature through memory is the dialectical movement in our intellectual engagement (alone and together) with the embodied, shared natural world. Another way of seeing the dialectical complexity of individual and communal memory, is to see how each is oriented toward memory in complementary but independent ways: while it is partly *built* upon memory, environmental theology

---

[21] B. Birch, and L. Rasmussen, *Bible and Ethics in the Christian Life* (Minneapolis: Augsburg, 1989), p. 109.
[22] F. Delich, 'The Social Construction of Memory and Forgetting,' *Diogenes* 201 (2004), pp. 65–75 (70).
[23] Ibid., p. 69.

has a *focus* on the task of being the religious voice in the public sphere on environmental issues.

III. Overcoming Environmental Amnesia

It should be clear that there is a place for memory in a hermeneutically-oriented, philosophical environmental theology from what has been argued thus far. To define this place more explicitly: memory of place, as a form of knowing, is *the task of holding a place in time*. This task is rooted in the acknowledgment that such work is imperative in the spiritual and ethical struggle against the environmental amnesia that confronts us. The memory of place, in other words, has an ethical dimension.

If memory is part of a theological and ethical framework for understanding nature, then part of the reason for this is that inappropriate forgetfulness creates the ethical problem: environmental amnesia.[24] Environmental amnesia is the underside of our memory of place. Since memory is a form of knowing, environmental amnesia is the lack of awareness or significant knowledge of nature. This is not only a lack of scientific or theoretical knowledge, but equally a lack of embodied exposure to the multiplicity of 'nature': as built or natural environments, as park or garden or wilderness, as cultivated or 'wild,' etc. Environmental amnesia has a number of causes, and is perhaps symptomatic of our contemporary existence (a fact illustrated by Marc Augé's 'non-places'[25] and Richard Louv's 'nature deficit disorder'[26]). Among others, an obvious cause is the lack of engagement with nature in daily life. While not as obvious, two other causes are equally significant. First is our excessive abstraction of 'nature', that is, the fact that we conceptualize nature to the point of divorcing 'nature' from lived experience. A second cause is the emphasis on individualism and the lack of communal participation in the natural world. These two difficulties should be addressed in an environmental theology that takes memory seriously.

Placing environmental amnesia in the context of the treatment of memory above, environmental amnesia is what is left when we continually fail to remember rightly the places of our past. *It is a present that does not include the presence of the pastness of nature*: that is, without the subtle influences of personal memories, a sense of natural history, or a recognition of evolutionary time. As individuals and communities, our understanding of place sometimes is distorted through unethical forgetfulness. This problem has been illustrated in a discussion of urban environ-

---

[24] For instance, S. Steingraber, 'Environmental Amnesia,' *Orion Magazine* (May/June 2008); S. Bergmann, 'Making Oneself at Home in Environments of Urban Amnesia,' *International Journal of Public Theology* 2 (2008), pp. 70–97.

[25] M. Augé, *Non-Places: Introduction to an Anthropology of Supermodernity* (New York: Verso, 1995).

[26] R. Louv, **Last Child in the Woods** (Chapel Hill, N.C.: Algonquin Books, 2005).

ments by Sigurd Bergmann. Bergmann notes that our erasure of the pastness of place is a characteristic of late modern urban space. As Bergmann writes,

> We need to account for the difference between what could be called good and bad amnesia. Or should we use two different terms? 'Natural oblivion' could circumscribe the process where spatial constructions must be demolished or left to decline naturally, while 'amnesia' – in accordance with the connotation in medicine—would describe the process where the intention to build something at a specific place displaces what is already there and violates the memories which are carried by the place.[27]

The environmental amnesia I seek to react against is that inappropriate forgetting that renders our experience of nature two-dimensional, ahistorical, individualistic and motivated by instrumental use.[28]

When memory works to hold place in time, however, it overcomes the above-mentioned difficulties that contribute to environmental amnesia. First, the conceptual separation of the past and present of actual experience is one of the reasons for environmental amnesia, that is, we forget the temporal fullness of nature, and no longer have a palpable understanding of it. The memory of nature is, in fact, the memory of place as experienced in space and time. As Peter Scott argues, we live in a 'camera obscura world': we have difficulty seeing or dealing with the 'far away' and our vision is distorted with an emphasis on the present.[29] Specific memories of place engage us, re-place us, and allow us to encounter nature in specific terms. More importantly, our reflection on memory shows us that particular instantiations of nature *can be seen otherwise,* thereby creating an openness toward our experience with the natural world. Housing lots are remembered as cornfield, and potentially in the broader shared memory as grassland or forest. Mountaintop removal mining destroys the West Virginia mountains and leaves behind pits, stone, tailings and toxic sludge, but the vanished mountains remain present in the shared memory of inhabitants, in collective wisdom and in the traces of the stones themselves. Likewise, the process of ecological restoration (a subject to which I will return) is predicated on the memory of a place as it once was; restorationists seek to allow the past of a place to speak in the present. Each of these examples illustrates how the struggle against environmental amnesia occurs in the work of holding the past of a particular place in the present.

In all these cases, memory is knowledge elicited through radically concrete, specific *traces* of the past. The trace actualizes memory; memory joins time to spatial manifestations of our memories through traces. Traces act as the temporal building blocks that constitute the meaning of place; in the case of environmental thinking, traces of memory are instantiations of nature as embodied in time, and

---

[27] S. Bergmann, 'Making Oneself at Home in Environments of Urban Amnesia', *International Journal of Public Theology* 2 (2008), pp. 70–97 (84).

[28] As Heinrich Bedford-Strohm reminded me, an obvious example of the ethical relevance of environmental amnesia can be found in current debates over climate change.

[29] P. Scott, 'Right Out of Time? Politics and Nature in a Postnatural Condition', in this volume.

as available for interpretation and experience. We find two types of traces in place. On one hand, there is the trace of the past *in our memory*; this is what is commonly debated and discussed as a form of 'trace': a signifier that stands in for the original. On the other hand, nature offers us a form of 'trace' *in its own physical embodiment*. The rings of a tree, decomposing leaves, watermarks and erosion patterns all offer this type of trace; unlike other traces, however, these are *instantiated* presences of the past. The past of nature is found in the trace of intellectual memory and physical memory: it is both in our cognition and in the physical environment. These two versions of the trace form our memory of nature, for together they explain the ways in which memory is emplaced, embodied within our cognition and embodied within nature itself. At the same time, recognition of the trace highlights the fact that we forget certain elements of place – just as we remember others – as an inevitable part of experience.

The second reason for environmental amnesia we identified involved the interaction between self and society. As intimated above, memory bridges individual and communal perspectives on place. It is not solely the task of the individual to rightly hold place in time; the community also is a participant in 'remembering rightly'.[30] Rather than seeing memory in purely solitary terms, we have seen that the relationship between memory and place is neither static nor one-dimensional; our memories are changing, as we both re-encounter places and have new experiences through which to judge the past. The place of memory in our thinking does not remain fixed in place, but *moves*. Memory is not simply an abstraction, a generalized imagination, or a vague presence of knowledge. Our memory of place becomes open and desirous of a multitude of perspectives, rather than offering a closed, exclusively personal perspective. And therefore, just as place draws together its inhabitants, the memory of place draws together a shared memory (which is at the heart of the communal narrative of place). The response to the multiplicity of the past is a weaving together a sense of the truth of a place – that is, a sense of place that admits a theological depth of meaning that transcends finite meanings and perspectives – in contrast to the ways in which place has been instrumentally forgotten.

Finding such truth inevitably coincides with the conceptions of nature found in our shared religious and philosophical worldviews. Our encounters with nature dive into a temporal flow rich with spiritual meaning; the places of our lives are captured in recollections and remembrances. Our hopes and expectations for the world are built upon memory. In fact, in many areas of theology a close connection between memory and eschatological expectation is both natural and pervasive. The most obvious example of this is the liturgy. As a framework through which the religious experience of the Christian community instantiates the theological task of Christological reflection, the liturgy provides a concrete way to manifest memory and expectation in place.[31] As we seek to understand our present experience in

---

[30] M. Volf, *The End of Memory: Remembering Rightly in a Violent World* (Grand Rapids: Eerdmans, 2006).
[31] Cf. A. Bieler, and L. Schottroff, *The Eucharist: Bodies, Bread, & Resurrection* (Minneapolis: Fortress, 2007); P. Atkins, *Liturgy and Memory* (Aldershot: Ashgate, 2004).

light of the traces of the past, an inevitable conclusion emerges: place envelops more than simply our individual selves. It is the site of dwelling for human and non-human alike. To theologically engage the work of memory of place means that we begin to systematically interpret particular memories with the view of a shared narrative of place, and this narrative includes a depth that interrogates superficial, private senses of place. This depth relates to both religious environmentalism and the theological reflection carried on in this essay. For both, God is present in the living richness carried in space and time. There are differences, however: whereas religious environmentalism can affirm this divine presence in its work on behalf of the environment, environmental theology seeks to reflect critically on the relationship between individual, community and place in ways that foster our understanding of this sacred richness. More forcefully, then, we can say that our work includes the process of carrying an otherwise missing richness of memory into the public square. With that, our personal memories intertwine with another's, and memory becomes a force that impacts our communal thinking of nature.

IV. Memory, Public Theology, and a Local Ethics of Memory

The present investigation not only aims to define memory and environmental amnesia, it also seeks to understand how memory participates in a public theology of nature. We have noticed the multivalent nature of memory, with its complex interaction between individual and communal identities. There is a dialogue between our personal memories and our shared memory and imagination (we could further this discussion to include our cultural history of nature as well). In the midst of this dialogue, we are able to frame the discussion of place in new ways, especially given the fact that individual narratives of the past are intertwined with communal expectation in the context of place. Thus our understanding of nature arises from individual and shared experience, and distortions of our understanding can arise from the lack of memory.

The theology of nature offers the unique setting for the interaction of individual memory and a communal ethics of memory to be enacted in the public sphere. In other words, the dynamics of individual and communal memory shows how a hermeneutical environmental theology is a form of public theology. Heinrich Bedford-Strohm has argued that environmental theology is a public theology insofar as the former manifests the task of the latter: '[i]ts [i.e. public theology] task is to give orientation to the public in questions of ethical significance, and by addressing such questions of public interest it adds the flesh to the secular constitutional bones of a pluralistic society'.[32] As a public task, theologians cannot concentrate exclusively on personal memories and situations. If theology rested on personal memory alone, it might become a theology of environmental amnesia. The public task of environmental theology demands the sharing of memories, in

---

[32] H. Bedford-Strohm, 'Tilling and Caring for the Earth: Public Theology and Ecology', p. 232.

ways that coincide with Bedford-Strohm's vision of the place of public theology in civil society.[33] With Scott, this public realm is influenced by traditions and might be defined as a version of 'weak secularity'.[34] The need to examine – and foster – collective memory emerges. This task is what leads the faith community from purely private visions of nature toward a spiritual memory that negates the social forgetfulness that is part of environmental amnesia. In turn, this fulfils some of the requirements necessary if this theology is to be 'liberation theology for a global civil society'.[35] This global civil society encompasses all of creation, thereby insisting on the inclusion of more than the human world in the collective memory.

Remembering place rightly – especially when part of a public theological thinking of nature – therefore means more than having nostalgia for the pristine wilderness of some mythic past. Of course, we should attend and hold dear to memory that uplifts and offers hope. But some memories of place distort or promote violence against nature; these are properly forgotten. In discussing memory and totalitarian regimes, Todorov notes that '… not even in the sphere of public life are all reminders of the past equally admirable; what nourishes the spirit of vengeance or of revenge itself need not be admired, in any case'.[36] In like manner, individual or social memories that are destructive of the place should not be the instantiated in our ethical judgements. Remembering rightly also means we can have solidarity and hope in the face of memory that cannot be instantiated: memory of places lost, never to be regained.

Sensing such theological resistance to environmental amnesia allows us to reiterate this important point: memory of place is pivotal in our understanding of environmental theology as public theology. There is a political nature to memory, which is implicit in the intersubjective nature of memory and the role of memory in ethical judgement. Memory works to build individual and group self-identity; it offers material through which society can more deeply appreciate the meaning of nature. Memory informs societal responsibilities toward the natural world, even as it is informed by present debates over the status of the natural world.

> Memory has been constituted as a different object of study with different political functions within different academic discourses. There are, however, certain commonalities shared [by diverse scholars] …: namely, a concern with seeing memory as a process through which identities are constructed or re-constituted in the present by actively articulating a relationship with the past.[37]

In other words, memory – as a mode of holding the past of a place in time – allows for the manifestation of a temporal depth of nature to emerge in present discussions

---

[33] H. Bedford-Strohm, 'Public Theology of Ecology and Civil Society', in this volume.
[34] P. Scott, 'Right Out of Time? Politics and Nature in a Postnatural Condition', in this volume.
[35] H. Bedford-Strohm, 'Public Theology of Ecology and Civil Society', in this volume.
[36] T. Todorov, 'The Abuses of Memory', p. 13.
[37] T. Robins, 'Remembering the Future: The Cultural Study of Memory', *Theorizing Culture: An Interdisciplinary Critique After Postmodernism* (B. Adam, and S. Allen (eds); New York: New York University Press, 1995), p. 209.

in the public sphere. Theology can attend to this temporal depth in unique ways, associated with its identification of the sacred in the world.

A public theology of the environment – at least, one that takes memory seriously and is hermeneutically informed – finds support in the creation of a *local ethics of memory* or alternately stated, an *ethics of locality*. Foremost, this local ethics of memory is inextricably tied to a hermeneutical experience of the world; it is a reflection on how we interpret place in light of our relationship with nature over space and time. Simultaneously it is the application of the idea of an ethics of memory as a response to the places in which we live, dwell and experience.

An ethics of locality is an ethics of memory. As Pamela Sue Anderson argues, 'An ethics of memory is exposed in the human activity of making narrative sense of our lives'.[38] Our sense of place makes narrative connections within space and time; such an ethical sensibility is constructed in light of how we hold the past and future of a place in the present. At the same time, memories force us to reflect on whether an individual self truly neither changes nor errs. Finally, as Avishai Margalit and others have pointed out, an ethics of memory draws from shared memory. 'A shared memory ... is not a simple aggregate of individual memories. It requires communication. A shared memory integrates and calibrates the different perspectives of those who remember the episode ...'.[39] Because ethics is a shared enterprise, we see that our memory of nature is forced toward the interaction of competing senses of the past, and toward a communal, critical memory.

A local ethics of memory desires to remember the place rightly, and thereby seeks the truth of place in light of our individual and shared memories. Individual and social memories show a place *as otherwise*. They illuminate the violence of the present against the environment, and also the present degradation. And in so doing, they call the community to account and encourage it to remember a place more fully. In other words, a local ethics draws on both shared and personal memory to allow us to see place in ways that speak to the public sphere. Just as memories are essential for telling the stories of success and failure of life, and an *ethics of* memory makes possible our ability to live good – and presumably just – narratives in common. Likewise, if our knowledge of nature is constituted by *our past in the place* (or is it *our place in the past*?), it is inevitable that we look back in *remembrance* to discover a way forward in *expectation* through these places and locales. Such a spatial and temporal situatedness requires recollection, forgetting and expectation; that is, we are called to have a fullness of memory that might be called a spiritual memory.

What has been argued challenges us to re-imagine the terms and outcomes of a theological environmental ethics, in order to fulfil the place of memory in a theology of place. How might this be manifested concretely? To illustrate, we can

---

[38] P. Anderson, 'An Ethics of Memory: Promising, Forgiving, Yearning', *The Blackwell Companion to Postmodern Theology* (G. Ward (ed.); Malden, MA: Blackwell, 2005), pp. 231–248 (234).

[39] A. Margalit, *The Ethics of Memory* (Cambridge, MA: Harvard University Press, 2002), p. 51.

briefly examine a concept that has been widely discussed and debated as a public response to local environmental degradation: ecological restoration. As an option for public policy, ecological restoration seeks to return a particular ecosystem or place to a predetermined prior state. This might be a state 'before human contact', or at least be one prior to the impairment or destruction of a robust ecosystem. It often includes the reestablishment of native plant and animal species, hydrological features, and the assessment of given functions and values of the ecosystem. Of course, restoration uses novel, 'non-natural' means in order to re-establish communities and processes (for instance, using herbicides to get rid of stubborn invasive species), but at the same time restoration projects actively mimic nature as well (for instance, prairie burning). Some of the questions of ecological restoration coincide with the deliberations concerning wilderness, for both must find a balance between human intervention and an independence from human effects.

But how do we decide whether ecological restoration is appropriate? This provides an example of how the theological investigation of the memory of place can contribute to the public discussion. For environmental theology, restoration efforts are not primarily debates over technique or practice (what Higgs refers to as 'technological restoration'[40]). Instead, informed by an understanding of place and memory, environmental theology reframes and supplements discussions of ecological restoration as a process of ethical deliberation, seeking to answer questions raised by an interpretation of a communal, spiritual memory of place. As Bill Jordan writes in *The Sunflower Forest*, ecological restoration becomes a spiritual and religious task of communion with place.

Restoration ecology (or at least many types of ecological restoration) can be considered a response stemming from an ethics of memory, when memories challenge the state of the present.[41] The desire of restoration is to renew a particular place, based on an interpretation of how earlier alterations have led to an unhealthy state. A restoration project can be a small prairie remnant or large wetland complex. It can include the reintroduction of large predators or merely add diversity to local plant species. The steps taken, however, are always focused on a particular place, instead of some general abstract notion of 'nature'. In short, ecological restoration can be defined as *a process of interpretation and recollection*

---

[40] E. Higgs, *Nature By Design: People, Natural Process, and Ecological Restoration* (Cambridge: MIT Press, 2003), p. 2.

[41] Of course, as Harris, et al. point out, climate change creates challenges for this type of historically minded restoration. Because of these expected changes have direct impact of the health of individual species and ecosystems, 'Conservation schemes tying assemblages to one place may actually lead to ossification of those ecosystems—in effect making them more fragile and less resilient by not providing space for the elements of the total gene pool on the fringes of the bell-curve niche space for occasional regeneration, and thereby reducing or eliminating the ability of the species and ecosystem to adapt to changes in biophysical regime' (p. 171). This argument does not negate the use of historical references – or as I am arguing, the memory of place – in restoration, but it does transform it. J. Harris, R. Hobbes, E. Higgs and J. Aronson, 'Ecological Restoration and Global Climate Change', *Restoration Ecology* 14 (June 2006), pp. 170–176 (173).

of the past in the present: our interpretations of place move to the past state of a place and seek to embody this recollection. If restoration is an ethical process of interpretation and recollection, then it means that we move backwards in time in order to establish the presence of memory of a place long forgotten. Restoration is the act of asking forgiveness to an embodiment of nature's past, and thereby takes on spiritual dimensions. In so doing, it becomes an example of how a local ethics of memory can interact with theology, as an embodied individual and communal practice.

Memory of places – places as different as Shattuck Brook or the riverbanks of Abo – inform our understanding of the latent meaning of environments. Starting from the crisp coolness of such waters (acting as an antidote to the river Lethe?), the foregoing has argued for a particular understanding of memory in theology, before suggesting how individual and communal memory serves to enact a public theology. This ethical, political theology counteracts environmental amnesia and leads us toward a local ethics of memory, or an ethics of locality. In theological terms, we can end with a suggestion: an ethics of locality gathers together the community of God and instantiates a version of remembrance that can be tied to the eschatological memory of Christianity. Thus the community holds the memory of place for both human and more than human, and this memory is held both in the imagination and in the physical place itself. Environmental theology, in sum, is built upon memory: in terms of an individual memory of place, the communal memory of shared environments, and finally the spiritual memory that confronts environmental amnesia in the public sphere.

Acknowledgments

I benefited from a summer Ohio Northern University Faculty Development Grant for the revision of this essay. In addition, my thanks go to several colleagues who offered useful comments on the ideas of this paper, including Sarah Fredrickson (Texas Christian University), Verna Ehret (Mercyhurst College), and many of the participants of the conference from which this volume emerged.

Bibliography

Anderson, P., 'Ethics and Hermeneutics: A Question of Memory', *Literary Canons and Religious Identity* (E. Borgmann, B. Philipsen, and L. Verstricht (eds); Aldershot: Ashgate, 2004), pp. 79–96.

—'Ethics, Hermeneutics and Politics: A Critical Standpoint on Memory', *The Sacred and the Profane* (J. Keuss (ed.); Aldershot: Ashgate, 2003), pp. 109–125.

—'An Ethics of Memory: Promising, Forgiving, Yearning', *The Blackwell Companion to Postmodern Theology* (G. Ward (ed.); Malden, MA: Blackwell, 2005), pp. 231–248.

Atkins, P., *Liturgy and Memory* (Aldershot: Ashgate, 2004).
Augé, M., *Non-Places: Introduction to an Anthropology of Supermodernity* (New York: Verso, 1995).
Augustine, *Confessions* (H. Chadwick (trans.); Oxford: Oxford University Press, 1998).
Bedford-Strohm, H., 'Public Theology of Ecology and Civil Society', *Religion and Ecology in the Public Sphere* (C. Deane-Drummond, and H. Bedford-Strohm (eds); London: Continuum, 2011), pp. 39–56.
—'Tilling and Caring for the Earth: Public Theology and Ecology', *International Journal of Public Theology* 1 (2007), pp. 230–248.
Bergmann, S., 'Making Oneself at Home in Environments of Urban Amnesia', *International Journal of Public Theology* 2 (2008), pp. 70–97.
Bieler, A., and L. Schottroff, *The Eucharist: Bodies, Bread, & Resurrection* (Minneapolis: Fortress, 2007).
Birch, B., and L. Rasmussen, *Bible and Ethics in the Christian Life* (Minneapolis: Augsburg, 1989).
Booth, K., 'Risdon Vale: Place, Memory, and Suburban Experience', *Ethics, Place and Environment* 11 (2008), pp. 299–311.
Brocki, M., 'Landscapes of Memory – Narratives of Past Places', *Koht ja Paik/Place and Location* 6 (2008), pp. 219–225.
Casey, E., 'Levinas on Memory and the Trace', *The Collegium Phaenomenologicum* (J. Sallis, G. Moneta, and J. Taminiaux (eds); Dordrecht: Kluwer, 1988), pp. 241–255.
Clingerman, F., 'Beyond the Flowers and the Stones: 'Emplacement' and the Modeling of Nature', *Philosophy in the Contemporary World* 11 (2004), pp. 17–24.
—'Reading the Book of Nature: A Hermeneutical Account of Nature for Philosophical Theology', *Worldviews: Global Religions, Culture, and Ecology* 13 (2009), pp. 72–91.
—'Wilderness as the Place between Philosophy and Theology: Questioning Martin Drenthen on the Otherness of Nature', *Environmental Values* 19 (2010), pp. 211–232.
Cooper-Marcus, C., 'Environmental Memories', *Place Attachment* (I. Altman, and S. M. Low (eds); New York: Plenum Press, 1992), pp. 87–112.
Delich, F., 'The Social Construction of Memory and Forgetting', *Diogenes* 201 (2004), pp. 65–75.
Gottlieb, R., *A Greener Faith: Religious Environmentalism and Our Planet's Future* (Oxford: Oxford University Press, 2006).
—*A Spirituality of Resistance* (Lanham, MD: Rowman and Littlefield, 2003).
Harris, J., R. Hobbes, E. Higgs, and J. Aronson, 'Ecological Restoration and Global Climate Change', *Restoration Ecology* 14 (2006), pp. 170–176.
Heidegger, M., 'Building Dwelling Thinking', *Basic Writings* (D. Farrell (ed.); San Francisco: Harper San Francisco, 2nd edn, 1993), pp. 343–363.
Higgs, E., *Nature By Design: People, Natural Process, and Ecological Restoration* (Cambridge: MIT Press, 2003).
Jenkins, W., *Ecologies of Grace: Environmental Ethics and Christian Theology* (Oxford: Oxford University Press, 2008).

Jordan, W., *The Sunflower Forest: Ecological Restoration and the New Communion with Nature* (Berkeley: University of California Press, 2003).
Louv, R., *Last Child in the Woods: Saving our Children from Nature-Deficit Disorder* (Chapel Hill, N.C.: Algonquin Books, 2005).
Margalit, A., *The Ethics of Memory* (Cambridge, MA: Harvard University Press, 2002).
Mathews, F., *Reinhabiting Reality: Towards a Recovery of Culture* (Albany, NY: SUNY Press, 2005).
McFague, S., *A New Climate For Theology: God, the World, and Global Warming* (Minneapolis: Fortress, 2008).
Neisser, U., 'Memory: What are the Important Questions?', *Memory Observed: Remembering in Natural Contexts* (U. Neisser (ed.); San Francisco: W.H. Freeman & Co., 1982), pp. 3–19.
Price, J., *The Woman Who Can't Forget* (New York: Free Press, 2008).
Ricoeur, P., 'Memory and Forgetting', *Questioning Ethics: Contemporary Debates in Philosophy* (R. Kearney, and M. Dooley (eds); New York: Routledge, 1999), pp. 5–11.
—'Memory, Forgetfulness, and History', *Iyyun: The Jerusalem Philosophical Quarterly* 45 (1996), pp. 13–24.
Robins, T., 'Remembering the Future: The Cultural Study of Memory', *Theorizing Culture: An Interdisciplinary Critique After Postmodernism* (B. Adam, and S. Allen (eds); New York: New York University Press, 1995).
Santmire, H. P., *Ritualizing Nature* (Minneapolis: Fortress, 2008).
Scott, P., *A Political Theology of Nature* (Cambridge: Cambridge University Press, 2003).
—'Right Out of Time? Politics and Nature in a Postnatural Condition', *Religion and Ecology in the Public Sphere* (C. Deane-Drummond, and H. Bedford-Strohm (eds); London: Continuum, 2011), pp. 57–76.
Steingraber, S., 'Environmental Amnesia', *Orion Magazine* (May/June 2008).
Todorov, T., 'The Abuses of Memory', *Common Knowledge* 5 (1996), pp. 6–26.
—*Hope and Memory: Lessons from the Twentieth Century* (Princeton: Princeton University Press, 2003).
Volf, M., *The End of Memory: Remembering Rightly in a Violent World* (Grand Rapids: Eerdmans, 2006).
Wallace, M., *Finding God in the Singing River* (Minneapolis: Fortress Press, 2005).
Westbury, C., and D. Dennett, 'Mining the Past to Construct the Future: Memory and Belief as Forms of Knowledge', *Memory, Brain and Belief* (D. Schacter, and E. Scarry (eds); Cambridge: Harvard University Press, 2000), pp. 11–32.
Wiesel, E., *Ethics and Memory* (New York: Walter de Gruyter, 1997).

9 Public Theology as a Substantial Contribution to an Ecumenical and Ecological Culture

Daniel Munteanu
Otto-Friedrich University of Bamberg, Germany

Global warming, holes in the ozone layer, toxic wastes, oil spills, acid rain, drinking water contamination, over-flowing landfills, top-soil erosion, species extinction, destruction of the rain forests, leakage of nuclear waste, lead poisoning, desertification, smog [are the] bald-faced reality of contemporary life in the world today.[1]

I. Eco- and Ecumenical Theology as Part of Public Theology

The ecological crisis is a crisis of human culture, i.e. a spiritual crisis. Ecotheology is, in this sense, a response to the environmental crisis, to the human destructiveness (biocide) of the natural world. It answers the question of how to avoid devastation and offers a new perspective on nature. In my opinion, ecotheology contributes substantially to the process of overcoming the environmental crisis. From an orthodox point of view, it involves a *resacralization of nature* in terms of a sensitivity to the immanence of God in the world. Creation is a gift from God and should be treasured as such. Ecotheology offers a moral code that is rooted in a *pneumatological worldview*. According to a Christian understanding of the world, the Holy Spirit permeates the entire creation: 'Spiritus ubique diffusus'. God's presence in the world through the energies of his Spirit allows us to speak about the theological dignity of matter and of creatures. This presence of God in the world constitutes the 'pneumatological grammar'[2] of ecotheology.

In this chapter, I intend to map out the inner connection between *ecotheology*, *ecumenical theology*, and *public theology*. How might we understand the link

---

[1] S. Bouma-Prediger, *The Greening of Theology: the Ecological Models of Rosemary Radford Ruether, Joseph Sittler, and Jürgen Moltmann* (Atlanta: Scholars Press, 1995), p. 3.

[2] S. Bergmann, *Creation Set Free: The Spirit as Liberator of Nature* (D. Stott (trans.); Grand Rapids and Cambridge: William B. Eerdmans Publishing Company, 2005).p. 308.

between ecotheology and ecumenism? The Greek word οἰκουμένη refers to the *whole inhabited earth*. The metaphor of οἶκος (household) clarifies the relation between ecological and ecumenical theology:

> The oikumene is furthermore related to the global political and economic realities, critically discussed from the perspective of the political economy of the Holy Spirit, as well as to the habitable earth and, in fact, the whole of creation and ecology. The oikos of church, political economy and earth all together form part of the one household of life in the economy of the living Triune God.[3]

In Germany, Jürgen Moltmann, Wolfgang Huber and Heinrich Bedford-Strohm link public theology with ecumenism. Huber affirms an 'ecumenism of profiles',[4] whereas Moltmann interprets ecumenical culture as a culture of acceptance of the other in his otherness.[5] Huber emphasizes on his part that public theology leads to a *responsibility ethic*, which contributes to the *humanization of the society* and her social structures.[6] Bedford-Strohm not only points to the need for a 'public theology', but also for an 'ecumenical social teaching', a contemporary form in which the church fulfils her vocation 'to be salt of the earth and light of the world'.[7]

Moltmann aims to exceed narrow, particular Christian traditions in favour of a comprehensive *ecumenical horizon*. In his opinion, one of the strengths of ecumenical thought lies in the fact that 'knowledge of one's own imperfection awakens longing for the other': 'To be Protestant in an ecumenical age does not mean to isolate yourself, but to bring the Gospel into the world and to trust in its own effects'.[8] For Moltmann, public theology involves the political responsibility of any theology, i.e. participation in society with the critical and prophetic theology of hope.[9] Moltmann is not only a point of reference in regard to ecumenical and public theology, but also for ecotheology. According to him, human culture must be 'environmentally compatible'.

---

[3] D. Smit, *Essays in Public Theology. Collected Essays 1* (E. Conradie (ed.); Study Guides in Religion and Theology 12; Stellenbosch: SUN Press, 2007), p. 259.

[4] W. Huber, *Im Geist der Freiheit: Für eine Ökumene der Profile* (Freiburg im Breisgau, Basel, Wien: Herder, 2007); W. Huber, 'Ökumene der Profile. Vortrag zur Eröffnung der Dietrich-Bonhoeffer-Forschungsstelle für Öffentliche Theologie', 29 January 2008 at Otto Friedrich University of Bamberg, http://www.uni-bamberg.de/fileadmin/uni/fakultaeten/ppp_lehrstuehle/evangelische_theologie_1/pdf_Dateien/Vortrag_WHuber_Oekumene_der_Profile_080129.pdf (accessed 16 July 2010).

[5] J. Moltmann, *Gott im Projekt der modernen Welt: Beiträge zur öffentlichen Relevanz der Theologie* (Gütersloh: Kaiser, 1997), pp. 126–135.

[6] W. Huber, *Konflikt und Konsens: Studien zur Ethik der Verantwortung* (München: Kaiser, 1990), pp. 231–239.

[7] H. Bedford-Strohm, 'Öffentliche Theologie in der Zivilgesellschaft', *Politik und Theologie in Europa. Perspektiven ökumenischer Sozialethik* (I. Gabriel (ed.); Ostfildern: Matthias-Grünewalt-Verlag, 2008), pp. 340–366.

[8] J. Moltmann *Gott im Projekt der modernen Welt*, p. 168.

[9] Ibid., p. 15.

Public theology, in my opinion, can help to solve the ecological crisis in a concrete and decisive way. We have to take into account that this is a global crisis and that it concerns all humanity. This is the reason why I understand *ecotheology to be a new platform for an ecumenical public theology*. A contemporary ecotheology is an opportunity for a new ecumenical and public theology; it can be a source of convergence and ecumenical reconciliation.

The ecumenical dimension of theology enables us to find a common and authentic public voice in a pluralistic society. On the other hand, public theology forms a common and complex horizon of activity and encourages a *culture of ecological and ecumenical responsibility*. Ecumenism, as a fundamental orientation, gives Christianity credibility as a powerful factor in our society. Ecumenical presence requires an authentic public voice and the public involvement of Christianity. Ecumenical statements can have a greater impact and influence on the sphere of public affairs than can isolated churches. The ecological crisis challenges both the unity of the Church as vocation and the unity of Christian values.

II. Public Theology as a New Paradigm of Theology

Public theology is greatly significant for our common human future. Today, it is one of the most important paradigms of theology[10] and results from the growing

---

[10] On 5 May 2007 a 'Global Network for Public Theology' (GNPT) was founded in Princeton which should link up different research centres and research programs on the subject of 'public theology'. See 'Global Network for Public Theology', Charles Sturt University, http://www.csu.edu.au/special/accc/about/gnpt/ (accessed 16 July 2010); 'Public Theology', http://www.public-theology.de (accessed 16 July 2010); see 'Centre for Public Theology', Huron University College, http://www.publictheology.org (accessed 16 July 2010). Concerning the public dimension of theology, see H. Bedford-Strohm, 'Poverty and Public Theology: Advocacy of the Church in Pluralistic Society', *International Journal of Public Theology* 2 (2008), pp. 144–162; H. Bedford-Strohm, 'Tilling and Caring for the Earth. Public Theology and Ecology', *International Journal of Public Theology* 1 (2007), pp. 230–248; H. Bedford-Strohm, 'Public Theology and the Global Economy: Ecumenical Social Thinking between Fundamental Criticism and Reform', *Ned Geref Theologiese Tydskrif* 48 (2007), pp. 8–24; H. Bedford-Strohm, 'Kirche – Ethik – Öffentlichkeit. Zur ethischen Dimension der Ekklesiologie' (VuF 51, Heft 2, 2006), pp. 4–19; H. Bedford-Strohm, 'Kirche in Zivilgesellschaft', *Was hat die Kirche heute zu sagen? Auftrag und Freiheit der Kirche in der pluralistischen Gesellschaft* (R. Weth (ed.); Neukirchen-Vluyn: Neukirchener Verlag, 1998), pp. 92-108; M. Higton, *Christ, Providence and History: Hans W. Frei's Public Theology* (London: T & T Clark International, 2004), pp. 1–3; H.-J. Grosse Kracht, *Kirche in ziviler Gesellschaft. Studien zur Konfliktgeschichte von katholischer Kirche und demokratischer Öffentlichkeit* (Paderborn, München, Wien, Zürich: Schöningh, 1997); C. Aarsbergen-Ligtvoet, 'Harry Kuitert and the Possibility of a Public Witness of the Church', *Theology between Church, University, and Society* (M. E. Brinkman, N. F. M. Schreurs, H. M. Vroom, and C. J. Wethmar (eds); Van Gorkum: Koninklijke, 2003), pp. 194–223 (194–205); R. F. Thiemann, *Constructing a Public Theology. The Church in a Pluralistic Culture* (Louisville, Westminster: John Knox Press, 1991); H. Cox, *Religion in the Secular City: Toward a*

consciousness that theology must react to the needs and primary questions of contemporary society.[11] Christian theology is a theology of 'interference and lawyership',[12] i.e. it is always *public*[13] because of its basic values,[14] and it embodies among other things a socio-critical dimension.[15] Moreover, it deals with the future questions of humanity and fights for human rights as well as for social and ecological justice.

Public theology is 'the reflection on actions and effects of Christianity in public, in society'.[16] The topic of 'public theology' is relatively new in Europe, although European theology has never lacked a public dimension. Each theology is based on 'narratives of public circumstance, of action and interaction in public spaces' so that it never was purely a 'private matter'.[17] The concept of 'public theology' was introduced into the discussion by Ronald F. Thiemann and Max Stackhouse, as well as by David Tracy in the United States, Duncan Forrester and William Storrar in the United Kingdom, by John W. De Gruchy and Dirk Smit in South Africa.[18]

In this chapter I intend to show that public theology always concerns the culture of the time. All theologians who focus on the role of public theology point to the

---

Postmodern Theology (New York: Simon and Schuster 1984); D. S. Browning, and F. Schüssler Fiorenza (eds.), *Habermas, Modernity, and Public Theology* (New York: Crossroad, 1992); W. Huber, *Kirche und Öffentlichkeit* (Stuttgart: Klett, 1973).

[11] See S. Kim, 'Editorial', *International Journal of Public Theology* 1 (2007), pp. 1-4 (1).

[12] M. Heimbach-Steins, 'Einmischung und Anwaltschaft. Die sozialethische Verantwortung der Kirche', *Kirche - lebenswichtig. Was Kirche zu geben und zu lernen hat* (V. Eid (ed.); München: Don Bosco, 1999), pp. 78-104; I. Mörth, and G. Fröhlich, 'Auf Spurensuche nach der "informellen Logik tatsächlichen Lebens"', *Symbolische Anthropologie der Moderne. Kulturanalysen nach Clifford Geertz* (G. Fröhlich, and I. Mörth (eds); Frankfurt am Main: Campus-Verl., 1998), pp. 7-50 (13-20).

[13] See H. R. Niebuhr, *Christ and Culture* (New York: Harper Collins, 2001), p. 93: 'Christ belongs in culture, because culture itself, without 'sense and taste for the infinite', without a 'holy music' accompanying all its work, becomes sterile and corrupt'; K. Rahner, 'Die Kirche und die heutige Wirklichkeit. Theologische Aspekte', *Universitas* 34 (1979), pp. 811-817 (813).

[14] See M. Heimbach-Steins, "Angst vor der eigenen Courage'? Theologie zwischen gesellschaftlich-politischem Engagement und ekklesialer Verbindlichkeit', *Bulletin ET* 15 (2004), pp. 51-65.

[15] See H. Bedford-Strohm, Vorrang für die Armen. Auf dem Weg zu einer theologischen Theorie der Gerechtigkeit (Öffentliche Theologie, 4, Gütersloh: Kaiser, 1993), pp. 300-325; M. Higton, *Christ, Providence and History: Hans W. Frei's Public Theology*, pp. 1-6: The language of Christian theology influences the public discourse or the public culture.

[16] See W. Vögele, *Menschenwürde zwischen Recht und Theologie. Begründungen von Menschenrechten in der Perspektive öffentlicher Theologie* (Gütersloh: Kaiser, Gütersloher Verlagshaus, 2000), pp. 23-29.

[17] M. Higton, *Christ, Providence and History*, pp. 1-5.

[18] I would like to mention also two representative theologians of public theology in Australia: James Haire and Clive Pearson. Unfortunately I cannot analyze their theology in this short paper, but I do want to underline their substantial contribution for contemporary public theology.

significance of Christian culture in transforming society. Always possessing a cultural dimension, public theology contributes to the positive changes in public culture through the values of the Christian worldview.

Ronald F. Thiemann, a leading theologian on the role of religion and ethics in the United States, has analyzed the public role of Christianity in a pluralistic society.[19] Thiemann understands public theology as 'faith seeking to understand the relation between Christian convictions and the broader social and cultural context within which the Christian community lives'.[20] Christian theology not only exercises a critical function in society, but it is also open to criticism. 'Theology rightly conceived is a communal, formative, critical and public activity'.[21] Thiemann points to the connection between *identity* and *culture*. Identity would not exist without the influence of the 'matrix of roles and structures that constitute a society'.[22] This is the reason why it is necessary for theology to take part in the education of religious identity through a common, formative, critical and public activity.[23]

Max L. Stackhouse is a member of the 'Societé Européenne de Culture' and author of numerous essays concerning the public relevance of theology.[24] In his book *Apologia: Contextualization and Mission*, he describes ecumenism as a central task of future theological education.[25] He develops a public theology which stresses the role of 'interculturality' in terms of the interdependence of culture, religion, family, and society: 'Humanly nature is social as well as biological, moral as well as cultural, and spiritual as well as material'.[26] His thesis is that 'common life in a global era' disposes of 'moral roots'.[27] For Stackhouse, the real vocation of public theology is: 'To form or reform the inner moral fabric of the globalization process'.[28] Consequently, public theology embodies a cultural transformative power in the world because Christianity is a missionary religion that brings the message

---

[19] See R. F. Thiemann, *Religion in Public Life. A Dilemma for Democracy* (Washington, D.C.: Georgetown University Press, 1996).
[20] Ibid., p. 21.
[21] Ibid., p. 167.
[22] Ibid., p. 169.
[23] Ibid., pp. 170–173.
[24] See M. L. Stackhouse, *Public Theology and Political Economy, Christian Stewardship in Modern Society* (Michigan: Grand Rapids, 1991); M. L. Stackhouse, *Christian Social Ethics in a Global Era* (Nashville: Abingdon, 1995); M. L. Stackhouse, *Covenant and Commitments: Faith, Family and Economic Life* (Louisville, Kentucky: John Knox Press, 1997); M. L. Stackhouse, *Apologia: Contextualization, Globalization and Mission in Theological Education* (Michigan: Grand Rapids, 1988); M. L. Stackhouse, T. Dearborn, S. Paeth (eds), *The Local Church in a Global Era: Reflection for a New Century* (Michigan: Grand Rapids, 2000).
[25] M. L. Stackhouse, *Apologia*, p. 31.
[26] M. L. Stackhouse, *Covenant and Commitments*, p. 3.
[27] M. L. Stackhouse, 'The Moral Roots of the Common Life in a Global Era', *Loving God with Our Minds: The Pastor as Theologian* (M. Welker, and C. A. Jarvis (eds); Michigan: Grand Rapids, 2004), pp. 50–61.
[28] See 'Max Stackhouse', Gordon College, Center for Christian Studies, http://www.gordon.edu/ccs/usaspeakers/maxstackhouse (accessed 16 July 2010), p. 1.

of reconciliation and peace into the world.[29] Christianity can serve 'as the decisive resource for the future'.[30] 'Religion is decisive as an unifying and universally human reality'[31] that contributes in history to a *process of civilization*. Religion is for Stackhouse 'the inner guidance system of civilizations'.[32]

David Tracy, professor of theology at the Divinity School at the University of Chicago, explores the public character of theology and considers the religious nature of theological truth as well as the meaning of theological pluralism.[33] Religion is not a 'private option' as long as 'any seriously theocentric construal of reality demands publicness. To speak and mean God-language is to speak publicly and mean it'.[34] Tracy distinguishes three public spheres, namely 'a public of society', 'a public of academy' and 'a public of church'.[35] As an academic discipline, theology always remains linked to these three distinct public spheres. In his opinion, public theology is a theology developed in the context of a cultural, theological and religious pluralism, all which enrich the human mind.[36]

Duncan B. Forrester, emeritus professor of the chair of ethics and practical theology at the Faculty of Divinity at the University of Edinburgh, is the author of several works that have shaped the face of public theology.[37] In his book *Apocalypse Now? Reflections on Faith in a Time of Terror*, Forrester deals with the question of how Christian faith should be preached in an age of terrorism.[38] According to him, the Christian tradition forms an inexhaustible resource for a *culture of peace*,

---

[29] See M. L. Stackhouse, 'Reflections on How and Why We Go Public', *International Journal of Public Theology* 1 (2007), pp. 421–430 (427).

[30] See M. L. Stackhouse, 'Introduction: Foundations and Purposes', *On Moral Business. Classical and Contemporary Resources for Ethics in Economic Life* (M. L. Stackhouse, D. P. McCann, S. J. Roels and P. N. Williams (eds); Michigan: Grand Rapids, 1995), pp. 10–34 (34).

[31] Ibid., p. 56.

[32] Ibid., p. 30.

[33] See D. Tracy, 'Defending the Public Character of Theology', http://www.religion-online.org/showarticle.asp?title=1720 (accessed 17 July 2010).

[34] Ibid.

[35] Ibid.

[36] Ibid. See also D. Tracy, *Blessed Rage for Order: The New Pluralism in Theology* (Chicago: The University of Chicago Press, 1996); D. Tracy, *Plurality and Ambiguity: Hermeneutics, Religion, Hope* (Chicago: The University of Chicago Press, 1994).

[37] See D. B. Forrester, *Caste and Christianity: Attitudes and Policies on Caste of Anglo-Saxon Protestant Mission in India* (London: Curzon Press, 1980); D. B. Forrester, *Christianity and the Future of Welfare* (London: Epworth Press, 1985); D. B. Forrester, *Beliefs, Values and Politics: Conviction Politics in a Secular Age* (Oxford: Clarendon, 1989); D. B. Forrester, *Studies in the History of Worship in Scotland* (Edinburgh: T. & T. Clark, 1984); D. B. Forrester, *Christian Justice and Public Policy* (Cambridge: Cambridge University Press, 1997); D. B. Forrester, *On Human Worth: A Christian Vindication of Equality* (London: SCM Press, 2001).

[38] D. B. Forrester, *Apocalypse Now? Reflections on Faith in a Time of Terror* (Aldershot: Ashgate, 2005), p. 11.

forgiveness and reconciliation.[39] Public theology is a part of practical theology and is pursued today in a multicultural context.[40]

William F. Storrar, head of the Center of Theological Inquiry of Princeton and initiator of the Global Network for Public Theology, examines as a central theme the role of public theology in the twenty-first century.[41] Christian theology bears *responsibility* 'to participate in global public sphere as well as criticising the economic, social, political and environmental disruptions of globalization'.[42]

John W. De Gruchy is the former chair of Christian studies and director of the Graduate School in Humanities at the University of Cape Town.[43] He focuses on subjects like 'multicultural identity'[44] and the role of Christianity for a *culture of peace*.[45] He links public theology, in an original manner, with art and analyses the aesthetic dimension of religious art in public.[46] Christian art is always public: this is an unmistakeable message that exercises transformative power in a society. He stresses that 'Public theology is … a form of Christian witness in the secular world that arises out of theological reflection and the life and worship of the church'.[47]

Dirk Smit, professor for systematic theology at Stellenbosch University, is 'one of South Africa's most significant and influential theologians over the last few decades' and 'one of the world's leading theologians'.[48] He took part in the birth of the 'Confession of Belhar' (1982/1986), which addressed the ecumenical unity of the church, reconciliation, and justice in the church and society.[49] According

---

[39] Ibid., p. 109.
[40] D. B. Forrester, *Theological Fragments: Explorations in Unsystematic Theology* (London: T. & T. Clark, 2005), p. x.
[41] W. Storrar, and A. Morton (eds), *Public Theology for the 21st Century: Essays in Honour of Duncan B. Forrester* (New York: T & T Clark, 2004).
[42] W. Storrar, 'A Kairos Moment for Public Theology', *International Journal of Public Theology* 1 (2007), pp. 5–25 (25). See also W. Storrar, P. Donald, and A. Morton (eds), *God in Society: Doing Social Theology in Scotland Today* (Edinburgh: Saint Andrew Press, 2003).
[43] See J. W. De Gruchy, *The Church Struggle in South Africa* (London: SCM Press, 2005); J. W. De Gruchy, *Liberating Reformed Theology: a South African Contribution to an Ecumenical Debate* (Michigan: Grand Rapids, 1991); J. W. De Gruchy, *Christianity and Democracy: A Theology for a Just World Order* (Cambridge Studies in Ideology and Religion, Cambridge: Cambridge University Press, 1995); J. W. De Gruchy, *The Cambridge Companion to Dietrich Bonhoeffer* (Cambridge: Cambridge University Press, 1999); J. W. De Gruchy, *Christianity, Art, and Transformation: Theological Aesthetics in the Struggle for Justice* (Cambridge: Cambridge University Press, 2001).
[44] J. W. De Gruchy, 'An Euro-African Theologian Looks at his Ancestral Home', *On the Making of Europe: A Distant View* (J. Wiersma (ed.); Kampen: Kok Pharos Publishing House, 1997), pp. 24–45.
[45] J. W. De Gruchy, *Christianity and Democracy*, pp. 225–278.
[46] J. W. De Gruchy, *Christianity, Art, and Transformation*, pp. 122–135.
[47] J. W. De Gruchy, 'Public Theology as Christian Witness: Exploring the Genre', *International Journal of Public Theology* 1 (2007), pp. 26–41 (28).
[48] E. Conradie, 'Editor's Foreword', Essays in Public Theology: Collected Essays (E. Conradie (ed.); vol. 1; Stellenbosch: Sun Press 2007), pp. iii–xv (iii).
[49] Ibid., p. iv.

to Smit, theology is always theology 'in re publica' because the church exists in the world and as part of the world: 'The church exists always as an integral part of human life in the world; it is interwoven always with public life in society and community'.[50] This is why the direct influence of theology on public life must be examined. Theology has an *impact on culture, education, and public life*, i.e. through its engagement for justice.[51] 'Public Theology deals with the place of the church in public life, the social form of the church and the role of the church in the society'.[52]

III. Public Theology and Culture

How can a *public* and *ecumenical ecotheology* become a field of cultural gravity[53] and take part in the *transformation of the society*? How can it contribute to the *renewal of an ecumenical culture marked by ecological responsibility*?

In my opinion, the most important aspect is the fundamental cultural role of public theology in society. Human beings are different from animals because of their highly developed culture,[54] i.e. through their 'ability to use systems of communication'.[55] For Ernst Cassirer, culture reveals the whole reality of the human being. As *animal symbolicum*, a person needs culture as a system of production and interpretation of meaning.[56] In the present 'crisis of meaning' (*Sinnkrise*),[57] public theology manifests the *real meaning of the human life* and contributes to

---

[50] D. Smit, 'Notions of the Public and Doing Theology', *International Journal of Public Theology* 1 (2007), pp. 431–454 (441).

[51] D. Smit, '" ... The Doing of the Little Righteousness": On Justice in Barth's View of the Christian Life', *Loving God with Our Minds: The Pastor as Theologian* (M. Welker, and C. A. Jarvis (eds); Michigan: Grand Rapids, 2004), pp. 120–145.

[52] D. Smit, 'Notions of the Public and Doing Theology', *International Journal of Public Theology* 1 (2007), pp. 431–454 (438–443).

[53] See P. Bourdieu, *Zur Soziologie der symbolischen Formen* (Frankfurt am Main: Suhrkamp, 6th ed., 1997), pp. 75–84: he shows the connections between the intellectual and the cultural force field.

About the cultural identity, see H.-O. Mühleisen, T. Stammen, and M. Ungethüm (eds), *Anthropologie und kulturelle Identität. Friedemann Maurer zum 65. Geburtstag* (Lindenberg: Fink, Beuron: Beuroner Kunstverlag, 2005).

[54] See W. H. Sewell, *Logics of History: Social Theory and Social Transformation* (Chicago: The University of Chicago Press, 2005), p. 157.

[55] U. Volli, *Semiotik. Eine Einführung in ihre Grundbegriffe* (Tübingen: Francke, 2002), p. 275. The complexity of human culture does not exclude, in my opinion, animal systems of communication. All creatures have an ability to communicate and possess in this way an ontological communion with the Logos.

[56] B. Recki, *Kultur als Praxis. Eine Einführung in Ernst Cassirers Philosophie der symbolischen Formen* (Berlin: Akademie Verlag, 2004), pp. 31–36.

[57] P. L. Berger, T. Luckmann, *Modernität, Pluralismus und Sinnkrise. Die Orientierung des modernen Menschen* (Gütersloh: Kaiser, 1995), pp. 9–23, 63: mention the 'decay of culture', the 'estrangement of person', the 'inflation of sense in the society' and the 'disorientation' of today's human being.

its orientation. For instance, the *ecumenical-ecological culture* is socially relevant because culture is a system of signs, of symbolic meaning in society. No society exists without culture and no culture without society. Culture, as the 'totality of the sign systems and meaning structures in a society'[58] and as the 'pulse of consciousness',[59] is the 'grammar'[60] or the 'substance of the society'.[61]

The *ecumenical-ecological culture* as an ideological orientation is based on the Christian faith and contributes to 'cultural interpretation and cultural creation'.[62] Besides, faith forms the basic dimension of human life and it has a social function.[63] No culture exists without social function. Also an ecumenical-ecological culture disposes of such a function. Cultures and social systems embody different aspects of the same phenomena,[64] which is why Geertz, one of the most famous American anthropologists, understood culture as 'logical-sense-donating' and social system as 'causal-functional'.[65] Culture subsists as 'socially established structures of meaning' through which people communicate with each other: 'Culture is the fabric of meaning in terms of which human beings interpret their experience and guide their action; social structure is the form that action takes, the actually existing network of social relations'.[66]

Finally, we can consider public theology as a *symbolic source of light and orientation in the world*. Inspired by the 'theology of hope', by 'political theology' and by 'liberation theology', public theology stresses *political responsibility* in the here and now of history. In the social-economic and political situation of today's society, public theology accentuates the global responsibility of Christian culture concerning the present ecological crisis. In its eschatological hope, as hope for the history of humanity, public theology exercises a creative influence on society and promotes a *culture of public and ecological participation*.

If a Christian is a 'transformer of culture', then an ecumenical-ecological culture has the same transformative function and responsibility to reform the different confessional cultures towards an *ecological spirituality*. Culture is characterized by

---

[58] T. Aklemeyer, 'Semiotische Aspekte der Soziologie: Soziosemiotik', *Semiotik: Ein Handbuch zu den zeichentheoretischen Grundlagen von Natur und Kultur* (R. Posner, and K. Robering (eds); volume 3; Berlin: W. de Gruyter, 2003), pp. 2758–2846 (2778).

[59] B. Recki, *Kultur als Praxis*, p. 56.

[60] C. Schwöbel, *Christlicher Glaube im Pluralismus: Studien zu einer Theologie der Kultur* (Tübingen: Mohr Siebeck, 2003), p. 263.

[61] U. Di Fabio, *Die Kultur der Freiheit* (München: Beck, 2005), p. 1, 21: Culture as an 'identity sign of the society'.

[62] C. Schwöbel, *Christlicher Glaube im Pluralismus*, p. 272.

[63] Ibid., p. 290.

[64] See F. Steger, 'Einleitung. Kultur: Ein Netz von Bedeutungen', *Kultur. Ein Netz von Bedeutungen: Analysen zur symbolischen Kulturanthropologie* (F. Steger, (ed.); Würzburg: Verlag Königshausen & Neumann, 2002), pp. 11–24(12): The social behaviour is connected with the cultural self-interpretation.

[65] C. Geertz, *The Interpretation of Cultures: Selected Essays* (New York: Basic Books, 1973), p. 145; see T. Aklemeyer, 'Semiotische Aspekte der Soziologie', p. 2778.

[66] C. Geertz, *The Interpretation of Cultures*, p. 145.

the 'unity of style, logical implications, meaning and value',[67] which is why it cannot be separated from symbolic-social discourse.[68]

What role does public theology play for an *ecumenical-ecological culture*? We can describe public theology as communicative competence, as the cultural matrix of meanings and the grammar of interconfessional and intercultural communication, and as intersubjective action[69] which is possible through an 'agreement of participants on the validity of a statement'.[70]

In this context the acceptance of public theology offers the base for such an agreement because it follows the meaning of the symbolic systems.[71] 'Men communicate by means of symbols and signs', so that all areas of culture are 'pregnant with meaning'.[72] This fine and determining effect of culture also appears in its definition as 'silent language', which is based on the fact that traditions and conventions are often 'silent' or unaware.[73] Also the ecumenical-ecological culture can become a 'silent language' which also forms the subconsciousness of Christians. As I have noted, an essential part of this culture is a public theology which as 'common language' and as a source of the symbolic order can exercise a creative force on the organization of the society.[74]

---

[67] Ibid.

[68] J. D. Moore, *Visions of Culture: An Introduction to Anthropological Theories and Theorists* (Oxford: Alta Mira Press, 2nd ed., 2004), p. 264.

[69] The symbolic forms are embedded in historical and socially structured contexts, so that without social context, individuality and identity remain incomprehensible: see T. Aklemeyer, 'Semiotische Aspekte der Soziologie', p. 2790; see J. Schwarte, *Der werdende Mensch. Persönlichkeitsentwicklung und Gesellschaft heute* (Wiesbaden: Westdeutscher Verlag, 2002), pp. 330-350; see E. Tramsen, 'Semiotische Aspekte der Religionswissenschaft: Religionssemiotik', *Semiotik: Ein Handbuch zu den zeichentheoretischen Grundlagen von Natur und Kultur* (R. Posner, and K. Robering (eds); 3 Teilband; Berlin: W. de Gruyter, 2003), pp. 3301-3343 (3314).

[70] T. Aklemeyer, 'Semiotische Aspekte der Soziologie', p. 2798.

[71] See C. Morris, 'Sprechen und menschliches Handeln', *Philosophische Anthropologie* (H.-G. Gadamer, and P. Vogler (eds); Band 7, München: Dt. Taschenbuch Verl., 1975), pp. 23-251 (249): 'Human behaviour is to a very high degree a symbolic-controlled behaviour'.

[72] I. Rossi, 'Intellectual Antecedents of Lévi-Strauss' Notion of Unconscious', *Perspectives in Cultural Anthropology* (H. Applebaum (ed.); New York: State University of New York Press, 1987), pp. 416-424 (419); see A. N. Whitehead, *Symbolism: Its Meaning and Effect* (Cambridge, Cambridge University Press, 1959), pp. 7-8: 'The human mind is functioning symbolically'.

[73] J. L. Peacock, *The Anthropological Lens: Harsh Light, Soft Focus* (Cambridge: Cambridge University Press, 2002), p. 4.

[74] This does not mean that Christian rationality oppresses or ignores the role of the secular rationality in society. Anyway, the society is not always determined only by power, but also by rituals and symbols. One can speak of a 'power' which expresses itself as a *rule on the available symbols*: see C. Geertz, *Negara: The Theatre State in Nineteenth-century Bali* (Princeton: Princeton University Press, 1980); see R. A. Shweder, and B. Good (eds), *Clifford Geertz by His Colleagues* (Chicago: The University of Chicago Press, 2005).

Culture is communication, i.e. a sign system with public relevance.[75] Human thinking is basically 'social as well as public'. Culture exists on account of 'socially established meaning structures' which steer the behaviour of the person.[76] The symbolic function of its language is universal because culture belongs to humankind.[77] The symbols which constitute a culture are vehicles of meanings, so that the symbolic, cultural sentences determine all social activities.[78] 'Culture is neither a particular kind of practise nor practise that takes place in a particular social location. It is, rather, the *semiotic dimension of human social practise* in general'.[79] Culture is a *semiotic structured universe which forms the practise*.[80]

Culture as 'extrinsic information coded in symbols' is a condition of the survival of the human being.[81] It plays a determining role in human life because a person needs the symbolic strength of culture to steer his behaviour: 'Without orientation by cultural pattern – organized systems of significant symbols – the behaviour of the person would be virtually uncontrollable, a perfect chaos of aimless actions and eruptive feelings'.[82]

The human being is 'the animal most desperately dependent on such extragenetic control mechanisms, such cultural programs for ordering his behaviour'.[83] The symbols-system is necessary for orientation, communication and self-control.[84]

> By submitting himself to governance by symbolically mediated programs for producing artefacts, organizing social life, or expressing emotions, man determined, if unwittingly, the culminating stage of his own biological destiny. Quite literally, though quite inadvertently, he created himself.[85]

---

[75] A. Duranti, *Linguistic Anthropology* (Cambridge: Cambridge University Press, 2002), p. 33.

[76] C. Geertz, *The Interpretation of Cultures*: p. 12: speaks about 'socially established structures of meaning'; p. 28: 'Society's forms are culture's substance'.

[77] C. Geertz, 'Thick Description: Toward an Interpretive Theory of Culture', *Anthropology in Theory: Issues in Epistemology* (H. L. Moore, T. Sanders (eds); Malden: Blackwell Publishing Ltd., 2006), pp. 236–257 (236–245); see A. Kuper, *Culture: The Anthropologists' Account* (Harvard: Harvard University Press, 2000), p. 98.

[78] A. Kuper, *Culture: The Anthropologists' Account*, p. 99.

[79] W. H. Sewell, *Logics of History*, p. 164.

[80] Ibid., p. 165.

[81] W. H. Sewell, 'Geertz, cultural systems, and history: from synchrony to transformation', *Historiography: Critical Concepts in Historical Studies* (R. M. Burns (ed.); vol. 4 Culture; New York: Routledge, 2006), pp. 116–137 (125).

[82] C. Geertz, 'Kulturbegriff und Menschenbild', *Kulturphilosophie* (F.-P. Burkard (ed.); Frankfurt: Alber, 2000), pp. 189–243 (221): Therefore, the culture is a 'necessary condition of human existence'; see C. Geertz, 'The Impact of the Concept of Culture on the Concept of Man', *Schooling the Symbolic Animal: Social and Cultural Dimensions of Educations* (B. A. U. Levinson, K. M. Borman, and M. Eisenhart (eds); Lanham, Maryland: Rowman & Littlefield Publischers, Inc., 2000), pp. 33–54 (26).

[83] C. Geertz, 'The Impact of the Concept of Culture on the Concept of Man', p. 25.

[84] Ibid., p. 28.

[85] Ibid.

Culture refers, like religion, to the integral reality of the human being as *animal symbolicum*,[86] as *homo significans*,[87] i.e. as a being that is looking for the sense of his existence. Culture is a system of meanings and an 'ensemble of symbolic systems'.[88] It is the semiotic system of 'socially agreed meaning structures', the 'meaning fabric', in which people are involved.[89] Therefore, culture has also been described as the totality of symbols which surrounds the human being in a society,[90] as a 'highly complicated whole', as a 'whole life style of people', as a 'map, sieve and matrix'.[91] Culture can be described as a 'process of progressive self-freeing of the person',[92] as well as an 'aggregation of symbolic aid to behavioural control' and as a 'system of extra-somatic sources of information'.[93]

---

[86] E. Cassirer, *Versuch über den Menschen. Einführung in eine Philosophie der Kultur* (R. Kaiser (trans.); Hamburg: Meiner, 1996), p. 51; see G. Hartung, 'Anthropologische Grundlegung der Kulturphilosophie – Zur Entstehungsgeschichte von Ernst Cassirer's Essay on Man', *Kulturwissenschaftliche Studien* (H.-J. Lachmann, and U. Kösser (eds); Kulturphilosophische und ästhetische Reihe, Band 6, Leipzig: Passage-Verlag, 2001), pp. 2–18.; H. Wahl, *Glaube und symbolische Erfahrung. Eine praktisch-theologische Symboltheorie* (Freiburg, Basel, Wien: Herder, 1994); J. Splett, '"Realsymbol". Zur Anthropologie des Sakramentalen', *Raum-zeitliche Vermittlung der Transzendenz. Zur 'sakramentalen' Dimension religiöser Tradition. Arbeitsdokumentation eines Symposiums* (G. Oberhammer, and M. Schmücker (eds); Wien: Verlag der Österreichischen Akademie der Wissenschaften, 1999), pp. 325–351.

[87] C. Schwöbel, *Christlicher Glaube im Pluralismus*, p. 261.

[88] C. Lévi-Strauss, Das Nahe und das Ferne. Eine Autobiographie in Gesprächen (D. Eribon (trans.); Frankfurt am Main: S. Fischer, 1989), p. 15; P. Tillich, 'Kirche und Kultur', P. Tillich, Gesammelte Werke, Die Religiöse Substanz der Kultur: Schriften zur Theologie der Kultur (R. Albrecht (ed.); Band 9; Stuttgart: Evangel. Verl.-Werk, 1967), pp. 30–46 (34): For Tillich, theology is always 'cultural theology'; see H. Tillich, 'Das Neue Sein als Zentralbegriff einer christlichen Theologie', *P. Tillich, Gesammelte Werke, Schriften zur Theologie, Offenbarung und Glaube* (R. Albrecht (ed.); Band 8; Stuttgart: Evangel. Verl.-Werk, 1970), pp. 220–239; see E. Sturm, 'Das absolute Paradox als Prinzip der Theologie und Kultur in Paul Tillichs "Rechtfertigung und Zweifel" von 1919', *The Theological Paradox: Interdisciplinary Reflections on the Centre of Paul Tillich's Thought: Proceedings of the V. International Paul Tillich Symposium hold in Frankfurt/Main 1994* (G. Hummel (ed.); Theologische Bibliothek Töpelmann 74 ; Berlin: W. de Gryter & Co., 1995), pp. 32–45: speaks about Tillich's Theology of culture; P. Steinacker, 'Passion und Paradox – Der Expressionismus als Verstehenshintergrund der theologischen Anfänge Paul Tillichs. Ein Versuch', *God and Being: the Problem of Ontology in the Philosophical Theology of Paul Tillich: Contributions made to the II. International Paul Tillich Symposium held in Frankfurt 1988* (G. Hummel (ed.); Berlin, New York: W. de Gruyter, 1989), pp. 59–99 (87).

[89] C. Geertz, 'Primordial Loyalties and Standing Entities: Anthropological Reflections on the Politics of Identity', http://www.colbud.hu/main_old/PubArchive/PL/PL07-Geertz.pdf (accessed 16 July 2010).

[90] T. Alkemeyer, 'Semiotische Aspekte der Soziologie: Soziosemiotik', p. 2777.

[91] C. Geertz, *Dichte Beschreibung: Beiträge zum Verstehen kultureller Systeme* (B. Luchesi (trans.); Frankfurt am Main: Suhrkamp, 2007), p. 9.

[92] B. Recki, *Kultur als Praxis*, p. 66.

[93] C. Geertz, 'Kulturbegriff und Menschenbild', p. 228.

Clifford Geertz[94] has strongly influenced our understanding of culture. He described 'religion as a cultural system'.[95] For him, sacred symbols generate an ethos, an emotional tone and an ensemble of feelings.[96] Therefore, Geertz views the human being as 'suspended in webs of meaning'.[97] He unfolds a 'symbolic or interpretative anthropology', which describes the human being as a cultural being.[98] Culture is for him a 'sensory connection' or a 'sign system';[99] he writes, 'there is no such thing as a human nature independent of culture'.[100]

Christian culture is marked by the dynamism of creative change.[101] Its field of action cannot be limited by cultural borders; it has the potential to fuse cultures with itself. This fusion requires, in my opinion, a *process of education*. There is no ecological culture without ecological education. For instance, public theology promotes the education of the person as the *art of transformation*.[102] The understanding of culture as a *cultivation* underlines the role of education[103] in

---

[94] W. H. Sewell, *Logics of History*, p. 175.

[95] C. Geertz, *The Interpretation of Cultures*, pp. 87–125; see M. Lambek (ed.), *A Reader in the Anthropology of Religion* (Malden: Blackwell Publishing Ltd, 3rd ed., 2003), pp. 61–82; D. L. Pals, *Seven Theories of Religion* (Oxford: Oxford University Press, 1996), pp. 233–244; V. Samuel, 'Die Religion in der Gesellschaft und die Weltreligionen', *Zeugnis im Dialog der Religionen und der Postmoderne* (R. Pechmann, and M. Reppenhagen (eds); Neukirchen-Vluyn: Neukirchener Verlag, 1999), pp. 202–213 (203): 'All religions are cultural-linguistic systems'.

[96] A. Swindler, 'Geertz's Ambiguous Legacy', *Required Reading: Sociology's Most Influential Books* (D. Clawson (ed.); Massachusetts: The University of Massachusetts Press, 1998), pp. 79–84 (80).

[97] C. Geertz, *Available Light: Anthropological Reflections on Philosophical Topics* (Princeton: Princeton University Press, 3rd edition, 2001), p. 17.

[98] C. Geertz, 'Kulturbegriff und Menschenbild', p. 217.

[99] C. Geertz, *Available Light*, p. 17.

[100] C. Geertz, 'The Impact of the Concept of Culture on the Concept of Man', p. 28.

[101] See K. H. Hörning, and J. Reuter, 'Doing Culture: Kultur als Praxis', *Doing Culture. Neue Positionen zum Verhältnis von Kultur und sozialer Praxis* (K. H. Hörning, and J. Reuter (eds); Bielefeld: transcript Verlag, 2004), pp. 9–18 (9): 'Culture is dynamic, it is *in action* ... The mainspring of cultural transformation' is the human being as cultural being.

[102] K. Jaspers, *Was ist Erziehung? Ein Lesebuch* (München, Zürich: Piper, 1977), p. 47.

[103] See M. Heimbach-Steins, 'Bildung als Menschenrecht', *Erziehung und Bildung heute* (H.-E. Tenortz, M. Hüther, and M. Heimbach-Steins (eds); Berlin: Verlag der GDA, 2006), pp. 47–70; M. Heimbach-Steins, 'Bildung und Chancengleichheit', *Christliche Sozialethik. Ein Lehrbuch, Band 2: Konkretionen* (M. Heimbach-Steins (ed.); Regensburg: Pustet, 2005), pp. 50–81; M. Heimbach-Steins, 'Menschenbild und Menschenrecht auf Bildung. Bausteine für eine Sozialethik der Bildung', *Bildung und Beteiligungsgerechtigkeit. Sozialethische Sondierungen* (M. Heimbach-Steins, G. Kruip (eds); Bielefeld: Bertelsman, 2003), pp. 23–43; M. Heimbach-Steins, 'Bildung für die Weltgesellschaft. Sozialethische Sondierungen', *Stimmen der Zeit* 127 (2002), pp. 371–382; M. Heimbach-Steins, 'Bildung und Beteiligungsgerechtigkeit. Bildungspolitische und sozialethische Anfragen', *Zwischen Sicherheitskalkül, Interesse und Moral. Beiträge zur Entwicklungspolitik* (K. Hirsch, and K. Seitz (eds); Frankfurt am Main: IKO Verlag für Interkulturelle Kommunikation, 2005), pp. 257–272; see H. Bedford-Strohm, 'Bildung, Gerechtigkeit, Teilhabe – Kommentar

society.[104] The crossing *from humus to homo* happens through culture or 'cultivation'.[105] The same process of cultivation is necessary if we want to achieve an ecological culture. In my opinion, an ecological culture is one of the main issues concerning an authentic human life. The human being ceases to be 'humus' when it practices an ecological life-style. *Ecological culture* is in this case not only a process of education[106] but also a *life-style*.[107] This life-style has to do with a new kind of communication: an ecological and ecumenical culture is a culture of healing communication. An ecumenical-ecological culture inspired by public theology leads to ecumenical-ecological action. The human being becomes active in his/her social system which is formed, thanks to the ecumenical-ecological culture, by the *paradigm of communication*.[108] As a *cultural force-field* it exercises a 'catalytical

---

zum Beitrag von Gerhard Kruip', *Bildung und Beteiligungsgerechtigkeit* (M. Heimbach-Steins, and Gerhard Kruip (eds); Bielefeld: Bertelsman, 2003), pp. 131–136; 'Das Sozialwort des ÖRK Österreich, 1 Bildung: Orientierung und Beteiligung', http://www.sozialwort.at/ (assessed 16 July 2010), pp. 17–42; see H.-J. Fraas, *Bildung und Menschenbild in theologischer Perspektive* (Göttingen: Vandenhoeck & Ruprecht, 2000); H. Timm, *Diesseits des Himmels. Von Welt- und Menschenbildung. Facetten der Religionskultur* (Gütersloh: Kaiser, Gütersloher Verlagshaus, 1988); Aristoteles, *Über die Seele, griechisch-deutsch* (W. Biehl, and O. Apelt (eds); W. Theiler (trans.); Hamburg: F. Meiner Verlag, 1995), p. 3. The first sentence of Aristotelis tract is: 'All people strive from nature for knowledge'.

[104] T. J. Gorringe, *Furthering Humanity: A Theology of Culture* (Aldershot: Ashgate, 2004), p. 4; see A. Wimmer, *Kultur als Prozess: Zur Dynamik des Aushandelns von Bedeutungen* (Wiesbaden: VS Verlag für Sozialwissenschaften, 2005), p. 14; J. Hüllen, *Mensch sein – human werden: Grundzüge kritischer Anthropologie* (Frankfurt am Main, Bern, New York: Peter Lang, 1985), pp. 41–49; B. Malinowski, *Kultur und Freiheit* (Stuttgart: Humbold, 1951), p. 143: 'The consideration of education as a cultural process reveals that this explains one of the most powerful tools of democracy. Its cultural value lies in the fact that it removes prerogatives of birth and offers the extensive possibility to promote real talents.'; W. Haubeck, W. Heinrichs, and M. Schröder (eds), *Mensch sein – Mensch werden. Impulse christlicher Anthropologie* (Witten: Bundes-Verl., 2001).

[105] G. Hartmann, *The Fateful Question of Culture* (New York: Columbia University Press, 1997), p. 172; see H. R. Niebuhr, *Christ and Culture*, p. 69: 'Christ claims no man as a purely natural being, but always as one who has become human in culture; who is not only culture, but into whom culture has penetrated. Man not only speaks but thinks with the aid of the language of culture'.

[106] R. Williams, *Resources of Hope: Culture, Democracy, Socialism* (London: Verso, 1989), p. 37; see D. B. Hegeman, *Plowing in Hope. Towards a Biblical Theology of Culture* (Moscow: Canon Press, 2nd edition, 2007), pp. 4350; J. M. Hull, *Studies in Religion and Education* (London, New York: Falmer Press, 1984).

[107] H. R. Niebuhr, *Christ and Culture*, p, 69; see M. Percy, *Engaging with Contemporary Culture: Christianity, Theology and the Concrete Church* (Chippenham: Ashgate, 2005), pp. 43–45.

[108] About the paradigm of communication see T. Luckmann, *Lebenswelt, Identität und Gesellschaft* (Konstanz: UVK Verlagsgesellschaft, 2007), pp. 91–109, 255–253; H. Kraemer, *Die Kommunikation des christlichen Glaubens* (Zürich: Zwingli-Verlag, 1958).

function'[109] in the political process, in terms of protecting creation, by promoting a culture of solidarity.[110]

The values of culture[111] can change the ethos of the society[112] while becoming part of the public discourse. 'This is what human culture can be – a transformed human life in and to the glory of God ... the Christian life is cultural life converted by the regeneration of man's spirit'.[113]

IV. Liturgy as Ecotheology – Main Aspects of an Orthodox Public Theology

a. Liturgical Spirituality

This issue of liturgy is central for an orthodox understanding of public theology and ecotheology. I will show this by analyzing Ion Bria's ecumenical theology. Needless to say, nowadays a liturgical worldview tends to be treated as common sense in ecumenical dialogue. For instance, in order to emphasize the public character of theology, Forrester points to liturgy and describes '*liturgical anthropology*' as the base of today's public theology. [114] He is not the only one supporting the idea of a *liturgical dimension of public theology*. Smit shows the connection between *lex orandi, lex credendi* and *lex convivendi*,[115] while Thiemann underlines the link between 'liturgy and public responsibility'.[116] In addition, Patrick R. Keifert argues that Christianity needs a *liturgical-cultural contextualization* in order to renew the public dimension of Christian liturgy.[117]

Ion Bria, a world-famous Romanian-Orthodox theologian of the twentieth century, dedicated his life to ecumenism. His ecumenical theology is liturgical and ecological at the same time. He developed a public theology as *liturgical spirituality*.

---

[109] See G. Müller-Fahrenholz, *Phantasie für das Reich Gottes. Die Theologie Jürgen Moltmanns. Eine Einführung* (Gütersloh: Kaiser, Gütersloher Verlag, 2000), pp. 75–86.

[110] K. Rahner, *Politische Dimensionen des Christentums. Ausgewählte Texte zu Fragen der Zeit* (H. Vorgrimler (ed.); München: Kösel, 1986), p. 56: 'In theology, dogmatics and fundamental theology the society-political background of the life of the people must be always considered.' The succession of Christ has a 'mystic and a social component'.

[111] See H. R. Niebuhr, *Christ and Culture*, p. 34: 'The world of culture is a *world of values*'.

[112] T. J. Gorringe, *Furthering Humanity*, p. 48.

[113] H. R. Niebuhr, *Christ and Culture*, p. 196, 205.

[114] D. B. Forrester, *Theological Fragments*, pp. 95–97.

[115] D. Smit, 'Lex orandi, lex credendi, lex (con)vivendi? – Orienterende inleiding tot liturgie en etiek', http://academic.sun.ac.za/buvton/Navorsing/liturgie.en.etiek.buvton.doc (accessed 17 July 2010).

[116] R. F. Thiemann, *Constructing a Public Theology*, pp. 112–128.

[117] P. R. Keifert, *Welcoming the Stranger: A Public Theology of Worship and Evangelism* (Minneapolis: Fortress, 1992), pp. 52–59: The liturgical hospitality creates a public space that encloses the strangers.

Bria describes the Christian life as '*Liturgy after the Liturgy*'.[118] Christian theology is based on an indivisible unity between *lex orandi* and *lex credendi*. The celebration of the resurrection remains at the centre of the Christian liturgy.[119] Liturgy and resurrection are unified because Jesus Christ, who is resurrected and present in liturgy, is an open door to the intimate life of the Holy Trinity.[120] The theology of resurrection is fundamental for an orthodox ecotheology because it underlines the eschatological dignity of the entire creation, of all ecosystems that are going to become part of the new creation (2 Cor. 5.17). Each orthodox liturgy has as its centre the Eucharist and is, as such, a celebration or anticipation of the resurrection, i.e. of the new creation.

The eucharistic liturgy is 'the best way of access to the heart of the Orthodox Church'.[121] As a medium of communication with God and as a space for the highest intimacy with the Holy Trinity,[122] it is a synthesis of the fundamental elements of the Orthodox faith.[123] Liturgy means a participation in the divine koinonia, a sacramental communication with the incomprehensible infinity of the divine truth, and an anticipation of the kingdom of God.[124] There is no Christian identity apart from belonging to a liturgical community.[125] Christian life is a life in communion, in dialogue with God, and in communion with the resurrected body of Christ: 'Here and now, on earth and in time, the liturgy inaugurates the eschatological community of the redeemed'.[126] Christ is the source of life because he communi-

---

[118] I. Bria, 'Celebrating Life in the Liturgy', *Jesus Christ – the Life of the World: An Orthodox Contribution to the Vancouver Theme* (I. Bria (ed.); Geneva: World Council of Churches, 1982), pp. 75–87 (85); I. Bria, *Romania: Orthodox Identity at a Crossroads of Europe* (Geneva: WCC Publications, 1995), p. 23, 47; I. Bria, *The Liturgy after the Liturgy. Mission and Witness from an Orthodox Perspective* (Geneva: WCC Publications, 1996), p. 9.

[119] I. Bria, *Mari sărbători și praznice creștine, praznice împărătești. Meditații teologice* (Sibiu: Ed. Popasuri Duhovnicesti, 2004), p. 7; I. Bria, *Tratat de teologie dogmatică și ecumenică* (Bucuresti: Ed. Romania Crestina, 1999), p. 284: 'The Eucharist inspire a 'liturgical spirituality' and encourage towards a culture of solidarity, based on justice, peace, freedom and respect of creation'.

[120] I. Bria, *Mari sărbători și praznice creștine, praznice împărătești*, p. 17.

[121] I. Bria, 'Celebrating Life in the Liturgy', p. 85: 'If people would like to know what Orthodox Christian believe in, whom they worship and how they live, they should penetrate the form and substance of the liturgy'; I. Bria, *The Liturgy after the Liturgy*, p. 9: 'The most appropriate way to experience and communicate the message is to celebrate the faith through doxological hymns and prayers and sacramental symbolism'.

[122] I. Bria, *Mari sărbători și praznice creștine, praznice împărătești*, p. 16.

[123] I. Bria, 'Aspecte dogmatice ale unirii Bisericilor creștine', *Studii Teologice* 1–2 (1968), pp. 12–24 (17).

[124] I. Bria, 'Celebrating Life in the Liturgy', pp. 86–87; I. Bria, *The Liturgy after the Liturgy*, p. 31: 'Liturgy opens the horizon of the kingdom of God for all humanity in the midst of history'.

[125] I. Bria, *The Liturgy after the Liturgy*, p. 74: 'The divine communion determines the quality of the human community ... The community of the Holy Trinity [is] a reality which holds together human society and orders common life. The new life is life within community'.

[126] Ibid., p. 16.

cates to us the divine life as well as his Spirit of Life. Thanks to the work of the Holy Spirit, the liturgy is a medium for the cosmic transfiguration of the world.[127] The liturgy is an initiation into the glory of the kingdom of God and an anticipation of eternal life.[128] This consciousness of God's presence in the world contributes to an *ecological culture*, which has its roots in a liturgical worldview. To understand the world in a liturgical way is to respect the theological dignity of creation. The world is a field of dialogue between creator and creatures. If the human being takes responsibility for the creation as a gift of God and does not destroy or try to possess it, then s/he practices an *eucharistical way of being*, a *liturgical way of existence*, i.e. *the liturgy after the liturgy*.

b. Liturgical Anthropology

According to Orthodox theology, the vocation of the human being is to grow up in and deepen communion with the Creator.[129] Through his/her movement towards God, the human being participates in the beauty of the uncreated light of the divine life.[130] *Theosis* not only means *imitatio Christi* but, primarily, real participation (*metousia*) in the fullness of the divine life.[131] Liturgy or liturgical prayer becomes the new *modus vivendi* of a Christian. The human being can participate in a personal way in the holiness of God.[132] This participation involves a transfiguration of the human being into a space where the Holy Spirit and the glory of the coming Kingdom of God indwell.[133] There is no liturgy without *epiclesis*, i.e. without the transformative work of the Holy Spirit who opens the eschatological dimension of the new creation.[134]

The human being has a cosmic responsibility because s/he can contribute to the restoration or destruction of the entire world.[135] If the human being lives liturgically, s/he is connected with the Holy Spirit who is present in the entire universe as Spirit of Life. The human being becomes more and more communicative, more and more sensitive to others and to the world.

---

[127] I. Bria, *Dicţionar de Teologie Ortodoxă* (Bucuresti: Editura Institutului Biblic si de Misiune al Bisericii Ortodoxe Romane, 2nd ed., 1994), p. 100; I. Bria, *The Sense of Ecumenical Tradition: The Ecumenical Witness and Vision of the Orthodox* (Geneva: WCC Publications, 1991), pp. 38–40.

[128] I. Bria, 'Introduction', *Martyria/Mission. The Witness of the Orthodox Churches Today* (I. Bria (ed.); Geneva: Commission on World Mission and Evangelism, 1980), pp. 5–12 (10).

[129] I. Bria, Comentariu la Catehismul Ortodox: 12 Sinteze Catehetice (Sibiu: Editura Oastea Domnului, 2000), p. 14.

[130] I. Bria, 'La vie. Un avenir déterminé par le Salut du monde', *L'Orthodoxie Hier-Demain* (M. A. Costa de Beauregard, I. Bria, and T. de Foucauld (eds); Paris: Ed. du Cerf, 1979), pp. 189–199; I. Bria, *Tratat de teologie dogmatică şi ecumenică*, p. 109.

[131] I. Bria, *Tratat de teologie dogmatică şi ecumenică*, p. 83.

[132] Ibid., p. 182.

[133] Ibid.,, p. 206.

[134] I. Bria, 'La vie. Un avenir déterminé par le Salut du monde', p. 197; I. Bria, *The Liturgy after the Liturgy*, p. 9.

[135] I. Bria, *Tratat de teologie dogmatică şi ecumenică*, p. 116.

c. Christian Culture as Culture of Holiness

The Orthodox understanding of liturgy underlines the importance of a culture of holiness. Orthodox liturgical theology contributes to a culture 'of unification and of sanctification'.[136] A faith marked by love is the foundation of an ethos or a lifestyle connected with the 'sanctification of the universe'.[137] Christian culture is not only interpretative but also unifying, like the Christological synthesis.[138]

Culture is related to 'cult' (liturgy); they both converge in the process of the transfiguration of the world.[139] Culture is not an aim in itself but a way of participation in the divine life, a way of making the Gospel of Christ accessible in the world[140]: 'Culture is the 'stylistic matrix' of the good news, making it transparent and alive, able to enter the experience of the whole people'.[141]

Christian culture is liturgical because the liturgy is the medium of sanctification for the human being as well as for the entire world. The liturgy involves immediate participation in Jesus Christ, the spring of holiness.[142] A Christian theology of culture is a theology of the Logos, [143] a sanctifying, apophatic, and doxological culture.[144] Without liturgy, sanctification is impossible. The transformative element of the Christian culture consists in its intimate union with Jesus Christ as the light of resurrection and the spring of eternal life in communion with God. The resurrected Lord liberates matter from death,[145] and his resurrection is an event of cosmic significance. On account of his resurrection everything is called to eternal life.[146]

Liturgical culture can be understood as a way toward sanctification and the transfiguration of the cosmos.[147] Through liturgy and liturgical culture the world becomes more and more transparent to divine beauty. Christian soteriology is cosmic and underlines the values of the material world in its liturgical and sanctifying communion with God.[148] A Christian liturgical culture plays a crucial role in this cosmic soteriology because it is the medium of civilization and humanization

---

[136] I. Bria, *Mari sărbători și praznice creștine, praznice împărătești*, p. 6.

[137] I. Bria, *Romania*, p. 28.

[138] Ibid., p. 30: 'Culture ... is a symbol unifying two realities in one'.

[139] Ibid., p. 25.

[140] Ibid., p. 37.

[141] Ibid., p. 31.

[142] I. Bria, *Dicționar de teologie ortodoxă*, p. 325.

[143] I. Bria, 'Ion Coman 1902–1987', *Ecumenical Pilgrims: Profiles of Pioneers in Christian Reconciliation* (I. Bria, and D. Heller (eds); Geneva: WCC Publications, 1995), pp. 50–64 (64); Ion Bria, *Teologia Ortodoxă în România contemporană* (Iași: Trinitas, 2003), p. 92.

[144] I. Bria, *Romania*, p. 38.

[145] I. Bria, *Mari sărbători și praznice creștine, praznice împărătești*, p. 12.

[146] Ibid., p. 29.

[147] I. Bria, *Tratat de teologie dogmatică și ecumenică*, p. 286.

[148] I. Bria, 'Sanctification de la Création', *Dictionnaire Oecuménique de Missiologie. Cent mots pour la Mission* (I. Bria, P. Chanson, J. Gadille, and M. Spindler (eds); Paris: Cerf, 2001), pp. 290–315 (315).

of society and the entire world.[149] Liturgy, as an ecological, eschatological, and ecumenical life-style, helps us to see the world differently, i.e. with a sensibility for the new creation and for the inhabitation of God.

d. Christian Culture as Historical and Eschatological at the Same Time

Christian culture can bring into history the light of the resurrection. The resurrection of Jesus Christ marks the beginning of a cosmic transfiguration of the world.[150] Christian life as 'life in Christ' is eschatological because it is an anticipation of God's Kingdom.[151] It is a new way of existence in communion with the source of life.[152] In its historical form, Christian culture is a way of renewing of the world; in this sense, it is indeed a genuine *public culture*.

> Is it possible to believe in Jesus Christ – the Life of the World – if the church keeps silent over the issue of violence and the extermination of others? The theology of peace and the ethic of social justice and solidarity are an essential part of the Christian commitment, especially today! The churches have to be involved in the struggle for human rights where the spiritual and cultural freedom of persons and communities are violated by various exclusive ideologies, by all forms of dictatorship, political imperialism and technological domination.[153]

In conclusion, we can say that an orthodox public theology, which offers a substantial contribution to an ecumenical-ecological culture, involves a doxological dimension. It can be described as a 'politics' of healing communication and as an attempt to sanctify the world. Last, but not least, public theology as ecumenical ecotheology means to rediscover and practice a cosmic love, a 'cosmic liturgy', by respecting the transcendental dignity of all creatures and of the whole world.[154] Orthodox spirituality, with its sensitivity to God's immanence in the world, directly contributes to the overcoming of our contemporary ecological crisis and has, as such, a public dimension. It encourages us to a culture of love in terms of respect and responsibility for God's creation. The entire world can become a cosmic liturgy in which the ecological crisis has been resolved through a green, i.e. ecological, spirituality.

---

[149] I. Bria, *Romania*, pp. 42–43, 54.
[150] I. Bria, *Mari sărbători și praznice creștine, praznice împărătești*, p. 32.
[151] I. Bria, 'The Significance of the Theme: Some Preliminary Observations', *Jesus Christ – the Life of the World: An Orthodox Contribution to the Vancouver Theme* (I. Bria (ed.); Geneva: WCC Publications, 1982), pp. 11–19 (17).
[152] I. Bria, 'La vie. Un avenir déterminé par le Salut du monde', p. 194.
[153] I. Bria, 'The Significance of the Theme: Some Preliminary Observations', p. 19.
[154] F. Dostoyevsky, Dostoyevsky, F., *The Brothers Karamasov* (New York: New American Library, 1999), p. 309: 'Love all of God's creation, the whole and every grain of sand in it. Love every leaf, every ray of God's light. Love the animals, love the plants, love everything. If you love everything, you will perceive the divine mystery in things'.

Bibliography

Aarsbergen-Ligtvoet, C., 'Harry Kuitert and the Possibility of a Public Witness of the Church', *Theology between Church, University, and Society* (M. E. Brinkman, N. F.M. Schreurs, H. M. Vroom, and C. J. Wethmar (eds); Van Gorkum: Koninklijke, 2003), pp. 194–223.

Alkemeyer, T., 'Semiotische Aspekte der Soziologie: Soziosemiotik', *Semiotik: Ein Handbuch zu den zeichentheoretischen Grundlagen von Natur und Kultur* (R. Posner, and K. Robering (eds); volume 3; Berlin: W. de Gruyter, 2003), pp. 2758–2846.

Aristoteles, *Über die Seele, griechisch-deutsch* (W. Biehl, and O. Apelt (eds); W. Theiler (trans.); Hamburg: F. Meiner Verlag, 1995).

Bedford-Strohm, H., 'Bildung, Gerechtigkeit, Teilhabe – Kommentar zum Beitrag von Gerhard Kruip', *Bildung und Beteiligungsgerechtigkeit* (M. Heimbach-Steins, and Gerhard Kruip (eds); Bielefeld: Bertelsman, 2003), pp. 131–136.

—'Kirche – Ethik – Öffentlichkeit. Zur ethischen Dimension der Ekklesiologie' *Verkündigung und Forschung* 51 (2006), pp. 4–19.

—'Kirche in Zivilgesellschaft', *Was hat die Kirche heute zu sagen? Auftrag und Freiheit der Kirche in der pluralistischen Gesellschaft* (R. Weth (ed.); Neukirchen-Vluyn: Neukirchener Verlag, 1998), pp. 92–108.

—'Öffentliche Theologie in der Zivilgesellschaft', *Politik und Theologie in Europa. Perspektiven ökumenischer Sozialethik* (I. Gabriel (ed.); Ostfildern: Matthias-Grünewalt-Verlag, 2008), pp. 340–366.

—'Poverty and Public Theology: Advocacy of the Church in Pluralistic Society', *International Journal of Public Theology* 2 (2008), pp. 144–162.

—'Public Theology and the Global Economy: Ecumenical Social Thinking between Fundamental Criticism and Reform', *Ned Geref Theologiese Tydskrif* 48 (2007), pp. 8–24.

—'Tilling and Caring for the Earth. Public Theology and Ecology', *International Journal of Public Theology* 1 (2007), pp. 230–248.

—*Vorrang für die Armen. Auf dem Weg zu einer theologischen Theorie der Gerechtigkeit* (Öffentliche Theologie, 4, Gütersloh: Kaiser, 1993).

Berger, P. L., and T. Luckmann, *Modernität, Pluralismus und Sinnkrise. Die Orientierung des modernen Menschen* (Gütersloh: Kaiser, 1995).

Bergmann, S., *Creation Set Free: The Spirit as Liberator of Nature* (D. Stott (trans.); Grand Rapids and Cambridge: William B. Eerdmans Publishing Company, 2005).

Bouma-Prediger, S., *The Greening of Theology: the Ecological Models of Rosemary Radford Ruether, Joseph Sittler, and Jürgen Moltmann* (Atlanta: Scholars Press, 1995).

Bourdieu, P., *Zur Soziologie der symbolischen Formen* (Frankfurt am Main: Suhrkamp, 6th ed., 1997).

Bria, I., 'Aspecte dogmatice ale unirii Bisericilor creștine', *Studii Teologice* 1–2 (1968), pp. 12–24.

—'Celebrating Life in the Liturgy', *Jesus Christ – the Life of the World: An Orthodox Contribution to the Vancouver Theme* (I. Bria (ed.); Geneva: World Council of Churches, 1982), pp. 75–87.

—*Comentariu la Catehismul Ortodox: 12 Sinteze Catehetice* (Sibiu: Editura Oastea Domnului, 2000).
—*Dicționar de Teologie Ortodoxă* (Bucuresti: Editura Institutului Biblic si de Misiune al Bisericii Ortodoxe Romane, 2nd ed., 1994).
—'Introduction', *Martyria/Mission. The Witness of the Orthodox Churches Today* (I. Bria (ed.); Geneva: Commission on World Mission and Evangelism, 1980), pp. 5–12.
—'Ion Coman 1902-1987', *Ecumenical Pilgrims: Profiles of Pioneers in Christian Reconciliation* (I. Bria, and D. Heller (eds); Geneva: WCC Publications, 1995), pp. 50–64.
—*The Liturgy after the Liturgy. Mission and Witness from an Orthodox Perspective* (Geneva: WCC Publications, 1996).
—*Mari sărbători și praznice creștine, praznice împărătești. Meditații teologice* (Sibiu: Ed. Popasuri Duhovnicesti, 2004).
—*Romania: Orthodox Identity at a Crossroads of Europe* (Geneva: WCC Publications, 1995).
—'Sanctification de la Création', *Dictionnaire Oecuménique de Missiologie. Cent mots pour la Mission* (I. Bria, P. Chanson, J. Gadille, and M. Spindler (eds); Paris: Cerf.
—*The Sense of Ecumenical Tradition: The Ecumenical Witness and Vision of the Orthodox* (Geneva: WCC Publications, 1991).
—'The Significance of the Theme: Some Preliminary Observations', *Jesus Christ – the Life of the World: An Orthodox Contribution to the Vancouver Theme* (I. Bria (ed.); Geneva: WCC Publications, 1982), pp. 11–19.
—*Teologia Ortodoxă în România contemporană* (Iași: Trinitas, 2003).
—*Tratat de teologie dogmatică și ecumenică* (Bucuresti: Ed. Romania Crestina, 1999).
—'La vie. Un avenir déterminé par le Salut du monde', *L'Orthodoxie Hier-Demain* (M. 'A. Costa de Beauregard, I. Bria, and T. de Foucauld (eds); Paris: Ed. du Cerf, 1979), pp. 189–199.
Browning, D. S., and F. Schussler Fiorenza (eds), *Habermas, Modernity, and Public Theology* (New York: Crossroad, 1992).
Cassirer, E., *Versuch über den Menschen. Einführung in eine Philosophie der Kultur* (R. Kaiser (trans.); Hamburg: Meiner, 1996).
'Centre for Public Theology', Huron University College, http://www.publictheology.org (accessed 16 July 2010).
Conradie, E., 'Editor's Foreword', *Essays in Public Theology: Collected Essays* (E. Conradie (ed.); vol. 1; Stellenbosch: Sun Press 2007), pp. iii–xv.
Cox, H., *Religion in the Secular City: Toward a Postmodern Theology* (New York: Simon and Schuster, 1984).
De Gruchy, J. W., *The Cambridge Companion to Dietrich Bonhoeffer* (Cambridge: Cambridge University Press, 1999).
—*Christianity and Democracy: A Theology for a Just World Order*, (Cambridge Studies in Ideology and Religion, Cambridge: Cambridge University Press, 1995).

—*Christianity, Art, and Transformation: Theological Aesthetics in the Struggle for Justice* (Cambridge: Cambridge University Press, 2001).
—*The Church Struggle in South Africa* (London: SCM Press, 2005).
—'An Euro-African Theologian Looks at his Ancestral Home', *On the Making of Europe: A Distant View* (J. Wiersma (ed.); Kampen: Kok Pharos Publishing House, 1997), pp. 24–45.
—*Liberating Reformed Theology: a South African Contribution to an Ecumenical Debate* (Michigan: Grand Rapids, 1991).
—'Public Theology as Christian Witness: Exploring the Genre', *International Journal of Public Theology* 1 (2007), pp. 26–41.
Di Fabio, U., *Die Kultur der Freiheit* (München: Beck, 2005).
Dostoyevsky, F., *The Brothers Karamasov* (New York: New American Library, 1999).
Duranti, A., *Linguistic Anthropology* (Cambridge: Cambridge University Press, 2002).
Forrester, D. B., *Apocalypse Now? Reflections on Faith in a Time of Terror* (Aldershot: Ashgate, 2005).
—*Beliefs, Values and Politics: Conviction Politics in a Secular Age* (Oxford: Clarendon, 1989).
—*Caste and Christianity: Attitudes and Policies on Caste of Anglo-Saxon Protestant Mission in India* (London: Curzon Press, 1980).
—*Christian Justice and Public Policy* (Cambridge: Cambridge University Press, 1997).
—*Christianity and the Future of Welfare* (London: Epworth Press, 1985).
—*On Human Worth: A Christian Vindication of Equality* (London: SCM Press, 2001).
—*Studies in the History of Worship in Scotland* (Edinburgh: T. & T. Clark, 1984).
—*Theological Fragments: Explorations in Unsystematic Theology* (London: T. & T. Clark, 2005).
Fraas, H.-J., *Bildung und Menschenbild in theologischer Perspektive* (Göttingen: Vandenhoeck & Ruprecht, 2000).
Geertz, C., *Available Light: Anthropological Reflections on Philosophical Topics* (Princeton: Princeton University Press, 3rd edn, 2001).
—*Dichte Beschreibung: Beiträge zum Verstehen kultureller Systeme* (B. Luchesi (trans.); Frankfurt am Main: Suhrkamp, 2007).
—'The Impact of the Concept of Culture on the Concept of Man', *Schooling the Symbolic Animal: Social and Cultural Dimensions of Educations* (B. A. U. Levinson, K. M. Borman, and M. Eisenhart (eds); Lanham, Maryland: Rowman & Littlefield Publischers, Inc., 2000), pp. 33–54.
—*The Interpretation of Cultures: Selected Essays* (New York: Basic Books, 1973).
—'Kulturbegriff und Menschenbild', *Kulturphilosophie* (F.-P. Burkard (ed.); Frankfurt: Alber, 2000), pp. 189–243.
—*Negara: The Theatre State in Nineteenth-century Bali* (Princeton: Princeton University Press, 1980).
—'Primordial Loyalties and Standing Entities: Anthropological Reflections on the Politics of Identity', http://www.colbud.hu/main_old/PubArchive/PL/PL07-Geertz.pdf (accessed 16 July 2010).

—'Thick Description: Toward an Interpretive Theory of Culture', *Anthropology in Theory: Issues in Epistemology* (H. L. Moore, T. Sanders (eds); Malden: Blackwell Publishing Ltd., 2006), pp. 236–257.

'Global Network for Public Theology', Charles Sturt University, http://www.csu.edu.au/special/accc/about/gnpt/ (accessed 16 July 2010).

Gorringe, T. J., *Furthering Humanity: A Theology of Culture* (Aldershot: Ashgate, 2004).

Grosse Kracht, H.-J., *Kirche in ziviler Gesellschaft. Studien zur Konfliktgeschichte von katholischer Kirche und demokratischer Öffentlichkeit* (Paderborn, München, Wien, Zürich: Schöningh, 1997).

Hartmann, G., *The Fateful Question of Culture* (New York: Columbia University Press, 1997).

Hartung, G., 'Anthropologische Grundlegung der Kulturphilosophie – Zur Entstehungsgeschichte von Ernst Cassierers Essay on Man', *Kulturwissenschaftliche Studien* (H.-J. Lachmann, and U. Kösser (eds); Kulturphilosophische und ästhetische Reihe, Band 6, Leipzig: Passage-Verlag, 2001), pp. 2–18.

Haubeck, W., W. Heinrichs, M. Schröder (eds), *Mensch sein – Mensch werden. Impulse christlicher Anthropologie* (Witten: Bundes-Verl., 2001).

Hegeman, D. B., *Plowing in Hope. Towards a Biblical Theology of Culture* (Moscow: Canon Press, 2nd edn, 2007).

Heimbach-Steins, M., '"Angst vor der eigenen Courage"? Theologie zwischen gesellschaftlich-politischem Engagement und ekklesialer Verbindlichkeit', *Bulletin ET* 15 (2004), pp. 51–65.

—'Bildung als Menschenrecht', *Erziehung und Bildung heute* (H.-E. Tenortz, M. Hüther, and M. Heimbach-Steins (eds); Berlin: Verlag der GDA, 2006), pp. 47–70.

—'Bildung für die Weltgesellschaft. Sozialethische Sondierungen', *Stimmen der Zeit* 127 (2002), pp. 371–382.

—'Bildung und Beteiligungsgerechtigkeit. Bildungspolitische und sozialethische Anfragen', *Zwischen Sicherheitskalkül, Interesse und Moral. Beiträge zur Entwicklungspolitik* (K. Hirsch, and K. Seitz (eds); Frankfurt am Main: IKO Verlag für Interkulturelle Kommunikation, 2005), pp. 257–272.

—'Bildung und Chancengleichheit', *Christliche Sozialethik. Ein Lehrbuch, Band 2: Konkretionen* (M. Heimbach-Steins (ed.); Regensburg: Pustet, 2005), pp. 50–81.

—'Einmischung und Anwaltschaft. Die sozialethische Verantwortung der Kirche', *Kirche – lebenswichtig. Was Kirche zu geben und zu lernen hat* (V. Eid (ed.); München: Don Bosco, 1999), pp. 78–104.

—'Menschenbild und Menschenrecht auf Bildung. Bausteine für eine Sozialethik der Bildung', *Bildung und Beteiligungsgerechtigkeit. Sozialethische Sondierungen* (M. Heimbach-Steins, G. Kruip (eds); Bielefeld: Bertelsman, 2003), pp. 23–43.

Higton, M., *Christ, Providence and History: Hans W. Frei's Public Theology* (London: T & T Clark International, 2004).

Hörning, K. H., and J. Reuter, 'Doing Culture: Kultur als Praxis', *Doing Culture. Neue Positionen zum Verhältnis von Kultur und sozialer Praxis* (K. H. Hörning, and J. Reuter (eds); Bielefeld: transcript Verlag, 2004), pp. 9–18.

Huber, W., *Im Geist der Freiheit: Für eine Ökumene der Profile* (Freiburg im Breisgau, Basel, Wien: Herder, 2007).
—*Kirche und Öffentlichkeit* (Stuttgart: Klett, 197—*Konflikt und Konsens: Studien zur Ethik der Verantwortung* (München: Kaiser, 1990).
—'Ökumene der Profile. Vortrag zur Eröffnung der Dietrich-Bonhoeffer-Forschungsstelle für Öffentliche Theologie', 29 January 2008 at Otto Friedrich University of Bamberg, http://www.uni-bamberg.de/fileadmin/uni/fakultaeten/ppp_lehrstuehle/evangelische_theologie_1/pdf_Dateien/Vortrag_WHuber_Oekumene_der_Profile_080129.pdf (accessed 16 July 2010).
Hull, J. M., *Studies in Religion and Education* (London, New York: Falmer Press, 1984).
Hüllen, J., *Mensch sein – human werden: Grundzüge kritischer Anthropologie* (Frankfurt am Main, Bern, New York: Peter Lang, 1985).
Jaspers, K., *Was ist Erziehung? Ein Lesebuch* (München, Zürich: Piper, 1977).
Keifert, P. R., *Welcoming the Stranger: A Public Theology of Worship and Evangelism* (Minneapolis: Fortress, 1992).
Kim, S., 'Editorial', *International Journal of Public Theology* 1 (2007), pp. 1–4.
Kraemer, H., *Die Kommunikation des christlichen Glaubens* (Zürich: Zwingli-Verlag, 1958).
Kuper, A., *Culture: The Anthropologists' Account* (Harvard: Harvard University Press, 2000).
Lambek, M. (ed.), *A Reader in the Anthropology of Religion* (Malden: Blackwell Publishing Ltd, 3rd edn, 2003).
Lévi-Strauss, C., *Das Nahe und das Ferne. Eine Autobiographie in Gesprächen* (D. Eribon (trans.); Frankfurt am Main: S. Fischer, 1989).
Luckmann, T., *Lebenswelt, Identität und Gesellschaft* (Konstanz: UVK Verlagsgesellschaft, 2007).
Malinowski, B., *Kultur und Freiheit* (Stuttgart: Humbold, 1951).
'Max Stackhouse', Gordon College, Center for Christian Studies, http://www.gordon.edu/ccs/usaspeakers/maxstackhouse (accessed 16 July 2010).
Moltmann, J., *Gott im Projekt der modernen Welt: Beiträge zur öffentlichen Relevanz der Theologie* (Gütersloh: Kaiser, 1997).
Moore, J. D., *Visions of Culture: An Introduction to Anthropological Theories and Theorists* (Oxford: Alta Mira Press, 2nd edn, 2004).
Morris, C., 'Sprechen und menschliches Handeln', *Philosophische Anthropologie* (H.-G. Gadamer, and P. Vogler (eds); Band 7, München: Dt. Taschenbuch Verl., 1975), pp. 23–251.
Mörth, I., and G. Fröhlich, 'Auf Spurensuche nach der "informellen Logik tatsächlichen Lebens"', *Symbolische Anthropologie der Moderne. Kulturanalysen nach Clifford Geertz* (G. Fröhlich, and I. Mörth (eds); Frankfurt am Main: Campus-Verl., 1998), pp. 7–50.
Mühleisen, H.-O., T. Stammen, M. Ungethüm, (eds), *Anthropologie und kulturelle Identität. Friedemann Maurer zum 65. Geburtstag* (Lindenberg: Fink, Beuron: Beuroner Kunstverlag, 2005).
Müller-Fahrenholz, G., *Phantasie für das Reich Gottes. Die Theologie Jürgen Moltmanns. Eine Einführung* (Gütersloh: Kaiser, Gütersloher Verlag, 2000).

Niebuhr, H. R., *Christ and Culture* (New York: Harper Collins, 2001).
Pals, D. L., *Seven Theories of Religion* (Oxford: Oxford University Press, 1996).
Peacock, J. L., *The Anthropological Lens: Harsh Light, Soft Focus* (Cambridge: Cambridge University Press, 2002).
Percy, M., *Engaging with Contemporary Culture: Christianity, Theology and the Concrete Church* (Chippenham: Ashgate, 2005).
'Public Theology', http://www.public-theology.de (accessed 16 July 2010).
Rahner, K., 'Die Kirche und die heutige Wirklichkeit. Theologische Aspekte', *Universitas* 34 (1979), pp. 811–817.
—*Politische Dimensionen des Christentums. Ausgewählte Texte zu Fragen der Zeit* (H. Vorgrimler (ed.); München: Kösel, 1986).
Recki, B., *Kultur als Praxis. Eine Einführung in Ernst Cassirers Philosophie der symbolischen Formen* (Berlin: Akademie Verlag, 2004).
Rossi, I., 'Intellectual Antecedents of Lévi-Strauss' Notion of Unconscious', *Perspectives in Cultural Anthropology* (H. Applebaum (ed.); New York: State University of New York Press, 1987), pp. 416–424.
Samuel, V., 'Die Religion in der Gesellschaft und die Weltreligionen', *Zeugnis im Dialog der Religionen und der Postmoderne* (R. Pechmann, and M. Reppenhagen (eds); Neukirchen-Vluyn: Neukirchener Verlag, 1999), pp. 202–213.
Schwarte, J., *Der werdende Mensch. Persönlichkeitsentwicklung und Gesellschaft heute* (Wiesbaden: Westdeutscher Verlag, 2002).
Schwöbel, C., *Christlicher Glaube im Pluralismus: Studien zu einer Theologie der Kultur* (Tübingen: Mohr Siebeck, 2003).
Sewell, W. H., 'Geertz, cultural systems, and history: from synchrony to transformation', *Historiography: Critical Concepts in Historical Studies* (R. M. Burns (ed.); vol. 4 Culture; New York: Routledge, 2006), pp. 116–137.
—*Logics of History: Social Theory and Social Transformation* (Chicago: The University of Chicago Press, 2005).
Shweder, R. A., and B. Good (eds), *Clifford Geertz by His Colleagues* (Chicago: The University of Chicago Press, 2005).
Smit, D., '"… The Doing of the Little Righteousness": On Justice in Barth's View of the Christian Life', *Loving God with Our Minds: The Pastor as Theologian* (M. Welker, and C. A. Jarvis (eds); Michigan: Grand Rapids, 2004), pp. 120–145.
—*Essays in Public Theology: Collected Essays 1* (E. Conradie (ed.); Publications of the Western Cape, Stellenbosch: Sun Academic Press, 2007).
—'Lex orandi, lex credendi, lex (con)vivendi? - Orienterende inleiding tot liturgie en etiek', http://academic.sun.ac.za/buvton/Navorsing/liturgie.en.etiek.buvton.doc (accessed 17 July 2010).
—'Notions of the Public and Doing Theology', *International Journal of Public Theology* 1 (2007), pp. 431–454.
Das Sozialwort des OÅNRK OÅNsterreich, 1 Bildung: Orientierung und Beteiligung', http://www.sozialwort.at/ (assessed 16 July 2010).
Splett, J., '"Realsymbol". Zur Anthropologie des Sakramentalen', *Raum-zeitliche Vermittlung der Transzendenz. Zur 'sakramentalen' Dimension religiöser Tradition. Arbeitsdokumentation eines Symposiums* (G. Oberhammer, and M. Schmücker

(eds); Wien: Verlag der Österreichischen Akademie der Wissenschaften, 1999), pp. 325–351.

Stackhouse, M. L., *Apologia: Contextualization, Globalization and Mission in Theological Education* (Michigan: Grand Rapids, 1988).

—*Christian Social Ethics in a Global Era* (Nashville: Abingdon, 1995).

—*Covenant and Commitments: Faith, Family and Economic Life* (Louisville, Kentucky: John Knox Press, 1997).

—'Introduction: Foundations and Purposes', *On Moral Business. Classical and Contemporary Resources for Ethics in Economic Life* (M. L. Stackhouse, D. P. McCann, S. J. Roels, and P. N. Williams (eds); Michigan: Grand Rapids, 1995), pp. 10–34.

—'The Moral Roots of the Common Life in a Global Era', *Loving God with Our Minds: The Pastor as Theologian* (M. Welker, and C. A. Jarvis (eds); Michigan: Grand Rapids, 2004), pp. 50–61.

—*Public Theology and Political Economy, Christian Stewardship in Modern Society* (Michigan: Grand Rapids, 1991).

—'Reflections on How and Why We Go Public', *International Journal of Public Theology* 1 (2007), pp. 421-430.

Stackhourse, M. L., T. Dearborn, and S. Paeth (eds), *The Local Church in a Global Era: Reflection for a New Century* (Michigan: Grand Rapids, 2000).

Steger, F., 'Einleitung. Kultur: Ein Netz von Bedeutungen', *Kultur. Ein Netz von Bedeutungen: Analysen zur symbolischen Kulturanthropologie* (F. Steger, (ed.); Würzburg: Verlag Königshausen & Neumann, 2002), pp. 11–24.

Steinacker, P., 'Passion und Paradox – Der Expressionismus als Verstehenshintergrund der theologischen Anfänge Paul Tillichs. Ein Versuch', *God and Being: the Problem of Ontology in the Philosophical Theology of Paul Tillich: Contributions made to the II. International Paul Tillich Symposium held in Frankfurt 1988* (G. Hummel (ed.); Berlin, New York: W. de Gruyter, 1989), pp. 59–99.

Storrar, W., 'A Kairos Moment for Public Theology', *International Journal of Public Theology* 1 (2007), pp. 5–25.

Storrar, W., A. Morton (eds), *Public Theology for the 21st Century: Essays in Honour of Duncan B. Forrester* (New York: T & T Clark, 2004).

Storrar, W., P. Donald, and A. Morton (eds), *God in Society: Doing Social Theology in Scotland Today* (Edinburgh: Saint Andrew Press, 2003).

Sturm, E., 'Das absolute Paradox als Prinzip der Theologie und Kultur in Paul Tillichs 'Rechtfertigung und Zweifel' von 1919', *The Theological Paradox: Interdisciplinary Reflections on the Centre of Paul Tillich's Thought: Proceedings of the V. International Paul Tillich Symposium hold in Frankfurt/Main 1994* (G. Hummel (ed.); Theologische Bibliothek Töpelmann 74 ; Berlin: W. de Gryter & Co., 1995), pp. 32–45.

Swindler, A., 'Geertz's Ambiguous Legacy', *Required Reading: Sociology's Most Influential Books* (D. Clawson (ed.); Massachusetts: The University of Massachusetts Press, 1998), pp. 79–84.

Thiemann, R. F., *Constructing a Public Theology: The Church in a Pluralistic Culture* (Louisville, Westminster: John Knox Press, 1991).

—*Religion in Public Life: A Dilemma for Democracy* (Washington, D.C.: Georgetown University Press, 1996).

Tillich, H., 'Das Neue Sein als Zentralbegriff einer christlichen Theologie', *P. Tillich, Gesammelte Werke, Schriften zur Theologie, Offenbarung und Glaube* (R. Albrecht (ed.); Band 8; Stuttgart: Evangel. Verl.-Werk, 1970), pp. 220-239.

Tillich, P., 'Kirche und Kultur', *P. Tillich, Gesammelte Werke, Die Religiöse Substanz der Kultur: Schriften zur Theologie der Kultur* (R. Albrecht (ed.); Band 9; Stuttgart: Evangel. Verl.-Werk, 1967), pp. 30-46.

Timm, H., *Diesseits des Himmels. Von Welt- und Menschenbildung. Facetten der Religionskultur* (Gütersloh: Kaiser, Gütersloher Verlagshaus, 1988).

Tracy, D., *Blessed Rage for Order: The New Pluralism in Theology* (Chicago: The University of Chicago Press, 1996).

—'Defending the Public Character of Theology', http://www.religion-online.org/showarticle.asp?title=1720 (accessed 17 July 2010).

—*Plurality and Ambiguity: Hermeneutics, Religion, Hope* (Chicago: The University of Chicago Press, 1994).

Tramsen, E., 'Semiotische Aspekte der Religionswissenschaft: Religionssemiotik', *Semiotik: Ein Handbuch zu den zeichentheoretischen Grundlagen von Natur und Kultur* (R. Posner, and K. Robering (eds); 3 Teilband; Berlin: W. de Gruyter, 2003), pp. 3301-3343.

Vögele, W., *Menschenwürde zwischen Recht und Theologie. Begründungen von Menschenrechten in der Perspektive öffentlicher Theologie* (Gütersloh: Kaiser, Gütersloher Verlagshaus, 2000).

Volli, U., *Semiotik. Eine Einführung in ihre Grundbegriffe* (Tübingen: Francke, 2002).

Wahl, H., *Glaube und symbolische Erfahrung. Eine praktisch-theologische Symboltheorie* (Freiburg, Basel, Wien: Herder, 1994).

Whitehead, A. N., *Symbolism: Its Meaning and Effect* (Cambridge, Cambridge University Press, 1959).

Williams, R., *Resources of Hope: Culture, Democracy, Socialism* (London: Verso, 1989).

Wimmer, A., *Kultur als Prozess: Zur Dynamik des Aushandelns von Bedeutungen* (Wiesbaden: VS Verlag für Sozialwissenschaften, 2005).

10 Public Theology as Contested Ground: Arguments for Climate Justice

Celia Deane-Drummond
Department of Theology and Religious Studies, University of Chester, UK

'Climate change is the greatest humanitarian challenge facing humankind today. And it is a challenge that has a grave injustice at its heart'.

Kofi Annan[1]

Public discussion over climate issues has received relatively higher media attention in the last few years, not least because of high level international meetings taking place through the United Nations framework convention meetings on climate change (UNFCCC). This public and political process works in parallel with the ongoing international cooperative work on the scientific aspects of climate impacts alongside possible mitigating and adaptive strategies. Yet the attention paid to cultural and religious aspects of climate negotiations is still comparatively sparse. Although there have been public debates about the extent of scientific consensus on this matter, those living in those parts of the world most affected by climate change make the reality of climate change all the more evident, often naming such changes in terms of their religious beliefs. Drawing on my experience of working alongside a development agency, the Catholic Fund for Overseas Development (CAFOD), I will suggest that social justice requires a commitment to address climate injustice between developed and developing nations situated in the context of acknowledging the interdependence of all of life. I will argue that Martha Nussbaum's capability approach is particularly promising, but there are shortcomings in it that need to be addressed. I will suggest that proper attention to the virtues of charity and prudence, sets forth the kind of justice making that is vitally needed at the individual, structural and global level. Core theological ideas around human flour-

---

[1] Cited in GBM *The Green Belt Movement Approach, Responding to Climate Change from the Grassroots* (London/Washington: GBM International, 2009), p. 4.

ishing, solidarity and the common good need to inform the shape of such global justice making.

I. The UNFCCC Context for Climate Negotiations

The United Nations Framework Convention on Climate Change (UNFCCC) represents a slow and somewhat drawn out process to try and come to an internationally binding treaty on climate issues. The UNFCCC began in Rio in 1992, and was the first international agreement on climate change. The Kyoto Protocol, which was adopted in 1996, set binding emission targets for developing countries. The refusal of the USA to sign up to this agreement was a crucial weakness of this Protocol. At the thirteenth meeting in Bali in 2007, the US agreed to discuss the possibility of adopting emission reductions. The fifteenth meeting of the Conference of Parties in Copenhagen, COP 15, that met in Copenhagen in December 2009, was the occasion when a new international agreement should have been reached, amid a flurry of high-level political and public support.

Given the variety of political governance across the world, does it even make sense to use the rhetoric of global justice to describe such a process? As one privileged to take part in COP 15 as a delegate for CAFOD, a charitable non-government agency (NGO)[2], at least until the doors were almost completely shut to such agencies in the last few days, I will begin with some personal reflections as a way of bringing this process to life. My first impression on arriving at Copenhagen for the COP 15 negotiations was a sense of intensity alongside almost a party atmosphere. The side shows and campaign stunts were carefully crafted to generate the biggest impact, and on arrival we were greeted by a group chanting 'Don't Kill Kyoto, Climate Justice Now!!'. This had the effect of a mantra, repeated again and again by a group in unison with almost religious fervour. The first commitment period for the Kyoto Protocol will end in 2012. The completion of negotiations on emission targets for the second commitment period for the Kyoto Protocol was one of the goals of the COP 15 process. But behind this almost carnival atmosphere there were serious issues at stake. Denmark, the host country, intended to offer a neutral position yet proved unable to provide such a platform by means of the circulation, even in the first week of talks, of a draft text known as the Danish text, in collaboration with some other like-minded nations. Alternatives, named as the African text, BASIC (Brazil, South Africa, India, China) and AOSIS (small island communities) texts started circulating at the same time. The tension was highlighted in the second week by efforts to introduce new texts for both negotiating tracks by the Danish Presidency, which essentially replaced the texts prepared by the working groups over the previous days. The two negotiating tracks were (a) the long-term cooperative action track and (b) the second commitment period for Kyoto protocol. At

---

[2] From 1 July 2009 until 1 July 2010 I was on a secondment to the Catholic Fund for Overseas Development (CAFOD). I am grateful to both CAFOD and the University of Chester for the opportunities that this secondment provided.

the time, Brazil, supported by a number of other countries, objected to the Danish introduction of new texts, coming apparently 'out of the blue' without consultation with the working parties, and allegedly in order to deliver results.

In spite of its rhetoric that the EU would 'pay its fair share', decisions from the European Council to repackage existing ODA development funds for climate impacts in the developing world still fell far short of what was required by earlier agreements and what was desirable based on the principle of fairness. This is because it failed to meet the agreement reached under both the 1992 UNFCCC agreement (Art 4.3) and the Bali Action Plan at COP 13 that developed countries would meet the agreed incremental cost of climate change in developing countries. Grouped vested national interests and impatience at the ability to deliver concrete proposals appeared to supersede any desire to work for genuine justice making in the global sphere. That is why protesters at the COP meeting were chanting 'Don't Kill Kyoto', for Kyoto, though insufficient, at least had governance compliance mechanisms in place.

It was obvious even at the time that if the international negotiations stalled before any such agreement was reached, then a political agreement with heads of state would be weaker – and not legally binding. In the end this is what happened. At this meeting, the developing world, spearheaded by Africa, showed itself to be far more resilient compared with past negotiations. Of course, Africa, in pressing for global 1.5°C rise as a target for the legal and policy negotiations on climate, was conscious of the fact that even a global average 2°C rise would threaten to make large parts of Africa virtually uninhabitable. This resistance was, of course, all the more remarkable because throughout the process developing nations were only able to support and send a relatively small number of delegates to the United Nations framework conventions that had met on a regular basis for the last seventeen years. While the stronger representation by NGOs, who were determined to support their interests, heightened the media interest in these questions, the overall failure to reach legally binding agreements was very disappointing, but perhaps not unexpected.

The build up of public support in the United Kingdom for some concrete action on climate issues at Copenhagen emerged in the effervescence of large public demonstrations. One was held in London on 5 December 2009, known as *The Wave*, where around 50,000 demonstrators took part.[3] Over 3,000 participants attended an ecumenical service, where the Archbishop of Westminster, Vincent Nicholls, and the Archbishop of Canterbury, Rowan Williams, among other leaders of the Methodist and Baptist churches, addressed a packed congregation. The demonstration on 5 December, like the even larger one of 100,000 participants in Copenhagen itself on 12 December, and other parallel events all around the world, showed the degree of global public frustration. In the United Kingdom, *The Wave* was a culmination of efforts by ordinary people to make their views known, and other smaller demonstrations on the same topic were held across the country earlier in the year. The slogan that united environmental agencies, development

---

[3] Reports of the numbers vary depending on the source. However, as one of the many thousands who took part in this demonstration, I can witness to the fact that the scale of this event suggested that the larger estimates were more likely to be accurate.

agencies, and religious groups from a diversity of religious traditions was that of climate justice, namely, the disproportionate impact of climate effects on the world's poorest communities, combined, of course, with devastating impacts on the natural environment. The culmination of all this public energy and effort in an international meeting that failed to arrive at a legally binding agreement has led to a feeling of intense public disappointment. While the process has not completely collapsed, given that, at the time of writing this chapter, the UNFCCC meetings are set to continue in Mexico in 2010, the moment may have passed, at least for the time being, when public opinion will be engaged in climate issues to the extent that it was in the build up to the Copenhagen Summit.

The problematic nature of these negotiations highlight just how hard it is to envisage any effective internationally negotiated system of climate response without some notion of the common good. The difficulty, of course, is that what seems just, fair and good to one nation or society may not to another. This is where negotiations at the global level become extremely difficult, but attempts to build an overlapping consensus that protects the basic needs of all peoples are important for global security. In climate terms this means a drastic cutting back by wealthier nations in order to allow a minimal standard of development in poorer or developing nations. A refashioning of what might count for the good life in Western societies, that resists the present emphasis on consumerism, is crucial. Envisaging the meaning of the common good also needs to go beyond the confines of the human community and include other creaturely kinds in order that economic patterns mesh with the carrying capacity of a finite planet, supporting biodiversity and enabling flourishing of other creaturely kinds. In this chapter, I will argue that the capability approach, developed by Martha Nussbaum, provides a useful theoretical starting point for envisioning what global human flourishing might look like. While I suggest that an application of the capability idea may be fruitful in the area of global economics, the main critical concern of this chapter will be in the area of international global negotiations.[4]

Michael Northcott's critical commentary on climate discourse is more sceptical about the possibility of economic instruments that favour ecological responsibility. He also points to the self-interested arguments by individual nations in other contexts to that of COP 15 alluded to above. Drawing on the biblical notion of a

---

[4] Tim Jackson has used the capability approach in order to argue for a different way of conceiving the economy as a whole, so that the measure of human flourishing is not tied into consumerism, and the economy functions well without being linked to growth. T. Jackson, *Prosperity without Growth: Economics for a Finite Planet* (London: Earthscan, 2009). While Herman Daly had pointed to the possibility of a steady state economy within ecological limits some 30 years earlier, he had not yet envisaged *how* that economy might stabilize within those limits. Jackson argues that our notion of prosperity needs to change from one based in consumerism, to one that is rooted in human flourishing, including social participation (p. 143). The resonance of such a view with theological critiques of consumerism is clear. The difference is that Jackson has worked out how such principles might be applied to macroeconomics. Given what he calls a faulty social logic, he recommends going back to tradition, but not in such a way that all innovation is obscured (p. 204).

'cloud of witnesses', he argues specifically in favour of a return to what he terms the 'communion of the saints' as a way of affirming the spiritual communion between peoples of past, present and future.[5] Such an attitude that, somewhat oddly, draws its historical roots from the powerful cosmopolis of the Roman Empire, would certainly be an effective antidote to relentless consumerism. Northcott clearly wishes to distance himself from the structures of power of the Empire itself, which may be one reason why he has described such a communion as a spiritual reality 'beyond space and time'.[6] But such a vision of the cosmopolis seems to encourage a spiritual affiliation with other persons somehow detached from the immediate needs of the present, and, equally as important, detached from the embodied nature of human lives in the natural world. This jars somewhat unevenly with Northcott's clear intention to develop forms of institutions and patterns of Christian living that address the real needs of climate injustice.

II. Science and Story Telling: What is the Reality of Climate Change?

The work of the UNFCCC draws heavily on the work of the Intergovernmental Panel on Climate Change (IPCC) in order to help set its policy and its negotiating targets. While there were attempts to block its credibility which I will refer to below, the chequered history of the IPCC highlights the resistance in the Western world to dealing with the responsibility of climate impacts. The first assessment report of the IPCC was released in 1990, two years before the UN Rio Summit. Almost immediately after the IPCC released its first report, a US based lobbying campaign, known as the Information Council on the Environment (ICE) and supported by the coal and oil industries, pressed against any political regulation of greenhouse gases. Steve Vanderheiden puts this succinctly:

> Following a strategy that remains dominant among industry-orchestrated anti-Kyoto campaigns, modeled {sic} on the successful tobacco industry effort to discredit the scientific link between smoking and cancer, the ICE aimed to discredit the scientific basis of climate change research with the general public ... claiming that climate change predictions were nothing more than a hoax perpetuated by environmental groups using fear-mongering as a fundraising technique, and asserting that GHG abatement efforts would raise gas prices by more than a dollar per gallon and cripple the domestic economy.[7]

ICE then produced a video entitled *The Greening of Planet Earth* arguing for the supposed benefits of global warming; they suggested that rising carbon dioxide

---

[5] M. Northcott, 'Atmospheric Space, Climate Change and the Communion of Saints', *Nature, Space and the Sacred* (S. Bergmann, P.M. Scott, M. Jansdotter Samuelsson, and H. Bedford-Strom (eds); Farnham: Ashgate, 2009), pp. 57–74. See also, Michael Northcott, *A Moral Climate: The Ethics of Global Warming* (London: Darton, Longman and Todd, 2007).

[6] Northcott, 'Atmospheric Space', p. 72.

[7] S. Vanderheiden, *Atmospheric Justice: A Political Theory of Climate Change* (Oxford: Oxford University Press, 2008), p. 31.

levels would result in a 60 per cent increase in crop yields, which would be enough to feed the world's poorest communities. This is unscientific misinformation, but it sounded sufficiently reasonable to the uninitiated. Plant physiologists conducting experiments in laboratory conditions have found that altering carbon dioxide initially stimulates the growth of crops; however, it also negatively affects the crops' ability to take up and use nitrogen, thus reducing nutritional quality. The ICE's claim of a yield increase is a gross distortion. Further, the negative climate impacts of an increase in greenhouse gases in the most vulnerable areas of the world would more than offset any possible stimulation of crop physiological processes. While the yields of some crops in some places may be enhanced through climate change, any claim for a new age of agricultural abundance that will be of benefit to the world's poorest is mythological rather than scientific. This half-truth might seem almost laughable if it were not for the fact that this video was supposedly a favourite of John Sununu, President George H. W. Bush's Chief of Staff.[8]

The work of the ICE was eventually discredited, but this did not prevent the launch of another campaign group in 1994 called the Global Climate Coalition (GCC), headed by Exxon Mobil along with 53 other fossil fuel and chemical industry opponents of carbon taxes or regulation, and formed in anticipation of the COP meeting in Berlin in 1995. Like the ICE, this group directed its attention to discrediting the work of the IPCC. Like the ICE, this group also exercised considerable influence over US climate policy. Such lobbying was not confined to the US. A parallel group in Europe was formed in March 1996, called the European Science and Environment Forum. The success of the GCC in blocking approval of the Kyoto Protocol in the US was short lived, since public criticism followed, and several companies then left from 1997 onwards.[9] The shift in public opinion against climate scepticism risked a loss in credibility for those companies that continued publicly to deny climate change. Even after the demise of the GCC, Exxon Mobil has continued to pour funds into campaigns denying climate science and opposing climate regulation, including religious groups. The continued attempts by opponents of regulating greenhouse gas emissions to suppress and manipulate scientific evidence that conflicts with their political goals is deeply disturbing.

Particular case studies from those parts of the world where climate change is having its largest impacts illustrate the point that as far as the poorest communities are concerned, changes in climate, leading to changes in food security and water resources, are a real and present threat to survival. These stories represent only a tiny fraction of the possible problems triggered by climate disruptions around the world. I am going to use two representative case studies as a way of filling out this account in narrative terms. The first comes from the Amazon basin, reflecting the experience of indigenous peoples. The second comes from a farming community living in the Arctic region of Siberia. The first is from a partner organization to

---

[8] Vanderheiden, *Atmospheric Justice*, p. 31.

[9] Since then a new coalition that admits climate change has formed called the Business Environmental Leadership Council. Several former GCC members have joined, including Shell, BP Amoco and DuPont.

CAFOD working with an indigenous community in the Amazon basin. The second is a result of a more academic study by an American anthropologist.

David Kopenawa is a Yanomani from the Amazon who is President of the Hulukara Yanomani Association. This association, like many other similar groups, is a partner to CAFOD. In an interview conducted for CAFOD on 10 July 2009, he made the following comments:

> Climate change for us Yanomani has meant that the rains have changed. Now the rains start in the summer in our community, it's weak rain but it rains a lot. We get lots of rain filling the rivers and not much sun in the summer. January and February is summer. With all this rain we can't work, we have to wait until the sun arrives to dry the crops. The Yanomani are affected, the destruction of the forest has increased to plant soya, sugar cane and the earth is cracking. The destruction of the forest is making us ill. [...] The men in cities, we want them to listen and believe in us, to look to the future, and the past, to see what is happening, to see the pollution, poverty and illness. [...] People in the industrialised world are starting to worry. We always warned them, they would not listen.[10]

David Kopenawa had heard of climate change and was able to express his anxiety in a way that made sense to the Western world. He also recognized the need for global cooperation between indigenous people and world government. Many of those in the poorest regions of the world are less conscious of *why* the climate is changing in the way it is. In some cases, such as the indigenous Indonesian people living in vulnerable coastal regions of Central Java and the nearby coral fringed atolls, there are widely held beliefs that the changes in weather and environmental conditions that they are experiencing, such as rise in sea levels, coral bleaching or tropical storms, are a result of either divine punishment from their gods, or disapproval of their activities by their ancestors[11]

The impact of climate change is not simply on those living in low lying or tropical regions. Anthropologist Professor Susan Crate has studied the impact of climate change for the native Viliui Sakha people living in Siberia in the aftermath of the collapse of the Soviet Union.[12] One of the main impacts is an increase in water on

---

[10] The full text of this exchange can be found on You Tube, http://www.youtube.com/watch?v=QO_Fd4AbNbU (accessed 18 January 2010).

[11] U. U. Frömming, and C. Reichel, 'Indigenous People Under Climate Change: Regional Examples From Indonesia', presentation given to the PIK/EFSRE workshop *Religion in Global Environmental and Climate Change: Sufferings, Values and Lifestyles*, Potsdam, Germany, 11 January 2010.

[12] From the 1930s the Viliui Sakha changed from being agropastoralists to collectivized industrial producers of meat, milk and crops to feed those working in the diamond mines nearby. In the 1980s the farms lost their state subsidy and were seized by clan-based networks or 'mafias'. Contemporary Viliui remain dependent on the mines for cash payment from the republican government, while wanting to revive their pre-collectivist forms. For a fascinating account, see S. Crate, 'Gone the Bull of Winter? Grappling with the Cultural Implications of and Anthropology's Role(s) in Global Climate Change', *Current Anthropology*, 49(2008), pp. 569–595.

the land, interfering with the sustainable life style that the Sakha people have built up over generations. The coming of deeply freezing conditions; minus 60 degrees C from early or mid December to late February or March has held religious and mythological significance. Narratives are therefore told about the coming of the bull of winter. Using focus groups, participants of all ages observed warmer winters and colder summers. In the winter, due to the rise in temperature, noxious mushrooms are growing in the basements of simple accommodation that in colder conditions once acted as natural freezers. In the summer heavy rain is preventing harvesting of hay. The slow thaw that used to take place in the spring was described in the imagery of the bull losing its horns. Now the bull only appears for one week instead of many months and so the people express anxiety that the bull of winter has gone. The increase in snowfall in the warmer temperatures means that the community has to undertake repeated snow clearance that uses up energy and reserves. The horses starve as they cannot reach the grass where ice is forming. The Sakha communities struggle to maintain the standard traditional practices of storing food and rearing cattle and horses in these waterlogged conditions. An ancient religious mythology claims that the people 'will survive until the day when the Arctic Ocean melts'. Of course, this is literally coming true.

What such stories illustrate is not simply the physical problems associated with climate change, but the importance of the political and social contexts where such changes are taking place. David Kopenawa's comments on the need for negotiations are telling: those in power are not yet feeling the impact of the changes such that their basic ability to survive is being eroded and undermined. The attempt by the GCC to block negotiations and discredit scientific claims for climate change show that particular political vested interests overcame other goals in a way that was morally reprehensible and socially irresponsible. Just before the COP 15 meeting, media reports, suggesting that climate change was some sort of 'hoax' because of the way statistics were presented by the University of East Anglia Climate Research Group, unsettled a sense of public responsibility on the issues. Descriptions such as 'Climategate', implying a cover up due to vested interests, were deliberately inflationary.[13] Many of the multinational companies have an even larger turnover than some nation states, so the stakes are high. The US oil industrial multinational giants are not the only culprits. The experience of Canada suggests that some countries are actually shifting to even more polluting sources of energy, rather than the reverse.[14] The promotion of tar sands in Canada as a source of 'dirty' oil that creates

---

[13] Even well-respected newspapers such as the *Daily Telegraph* presented exaggerated reports on this issue, with headlines such as 'Climate Change: This is the Worst Scientific Scandal of Our Generation', reported on 28 November 2009, by Christopher Booker, just before COP 15. See http://www.telegraph.co.uk/comment/columnists/christopherbooker/6679082/Climate-change-this-is-the-worst-scientific-scandal-of-our-generation.html (accessed 7 April 2010).

[14] T. Leduc, 'A Case for An Intercultural IPCC', PIK/EFSRE workshop, *Religion in Global Environmental and Climate Change: Sufferings, Values and Lifestyles*, Potsdam, Germany, 12 January 2010.

two times more emissions compared with conventional methods of oil extraction may sabotage any new climate deal. About 80 per cent of the Canadian oil supply is exported to the USA, which considers Canada a safer trading partner given the instability of other oil producing nations.

III. Rough Justice: Expanding the Scope of Justice Making

There seems, then, an enormous conceptual gap between political negotiations at the international level that have largely failed to reach agreement, and the case studies above which demonstrate the disproportionate impact of climate change on the lives of some of the most vulnerable people in the world. The question then becomes, how might this gap be filled in order to transform such negotiations so that they are more effectively grounded in the lives of ordinary citizens? Political scientist Steve Vanderheiden points out that the UNFCCC does include normative statements about a requirement for justice in negotiations. He argues that these normative statements are important as they set the agenda for the way legal and policy instruments are worked through subsequently, and are particularly obvious in the 1992 statement.[15] The language used here is that of differentiated responsibilities and capabilities, based on a principle of fairness that the developed nations need to take the lead in reducing their emissions. Vanderheiden believes that only if a climate regime is widely perceived to be *fair* will all members sign up to it, and it also has to be sufficiently robust to prevent more powerful nations taking advantage of developing nations. There is a discrepancy here between the rhetorical claims for fairness and the evident lack of procedural fairness in representation. Smaller or less powerful nations have fewer representatives, may suffer from weak governance and thus do not have adequate infrastructure to train those representatives. Nation states have also consistently pressed for their own national interests in climate negotiations. Given such practices, it would be tempting for grass roots movements in the Western world to give up on seeking reform at the global level and put all efforts into reform of local governance. It is also worth pointing out that the Bush administration alleged that the Kyoto Protocol was unfair, because it did not expect the developing world to cap its emissions. Yet this is more about efficacy, rather than fairness, given the disproportionate contribution of USA to emissions.[16] A reply to such a position is that developing nations also have a right to develop, and therefore produce what might be termed 'survival' emissions. The UNFCCC uses criteria of equity, historical responsibility and capability to reduce emissions. National capability is understood in terms of national wealth, current greenhouse gas emissions and potential for improvement in energy and transport infrastructure.

Martha Nussbaum's capability approach is a theory of justice that deliberately attempts to work across national boundaries and in situations where there is

---

[15] Vanderheiden, *Atmospheric Justice*, pp. 56–57.
[16] Vanderheiden, *Atmospheric Justice*, pp. 63–69.

gross global inequality of opportunity between nations.[17] Unlike the weak sense of capabilities already inherent in social contract theory, Nussbaum focuses specifically on *outcomes*, and ways to arrive at certain outcomes by promoting individual capabilities for flourishing. Importantly, she highlights the relative lack of capacity among women in the developing world. They are not only habitually subject to the disadvantages in Western society in terms of physical violence and discrimination, but they are also relatively more illiterate, less well nourished and compared with men lack the possibility of participation in political life.[18] Her philosophical position is aligned in many respects with the work of economist Amartya Sen, whose capability theory challenged previous attempts to posit development just in terms of crude GDP estimates. In *Frontiers of Justice*, Nussbaum argues that the capability approach will work for those with disabilities, across national boundaries and animal species other than humans. She draws up a list of basic goods that she believes all individual persons are entitled to and that would be commonly agreed across different cultural settings. This relies on a version of Grotius' theory of natural law and has certain affinities with the idea of basic human rights. The difference is that responsibility for enabling such capabilities to exist is stressed, rather than beginning with the idea of rights. Amartya Sen parts company with Nussbaum in this respect, for he believes that such goods need to be worked out in local contexts according to the needs of a deliberative democracy.[19] Sen is also closer to Rawls in his resistance to a particular universal list of goods to be attained.

Although Nussbaum rejects the idea that her theory leads to any sense of fixity in outcomes, her approach provides a richer theory of justice compared with a purely procedural one that does not include a specific *goal to be reached* in the manner of her particular version of capability theory.[20] Nussbaum's theory of goods to be sought for individual persons sets the stage for the list of goods to be arrived both at a global

---

[17] While Nussbaum is in some respects indebted to John Rawls' liberal theory of justice, she argues that Rawls attempted to tackle the problem of justice between nations in his later work, such as *The Law of Peoples*, but maintains it remained an unsolved problem of justice. M. Nussbaum, *Frontiers of Justice: Disability, Nationality, Species Membership* (Cambridge: Harvard University Press/Belknap, 2006), pp. 3, 23.

[18] Although she did not undertake such an analysis, the disproportionate impact of climate change on women in particular could be added to this list of relative inequalities. See M. Nussbaum, *Women and Human Development: The Capabilities Approach* (New York: Cambridge University Press, 2000).

[19] A. Sen, *Development as Freedom* (Oxford: Oxford University Press, 1999); A. Sen *The Idea of Justice* (London: Penguin, 2009).

[20] Nussbaum parts company from Rawls in this respect, though there are common threads, such as the concept of overlapping consensus. Rawls, according to Nussbaum, aims to generate political principles based on 'pure procedural justice'. Unlike other social contract theories, Rawls resists the historical idea that human beings have natural rights in the state of nature. Nussbaum, *Frontiers of Justice*, p. 12. See also Peter Scott, 'Right Out of Time? Politics and Nature in a Postnatural Condition', this volume. The difference is that while Rawls puts most emphasis on a fair procedure, the capability approach begins with an outcome that is 'an intuitive grasp of a particular content, as having a necessary connection to a life worthy

scale for other nations and also for other animal species. For she argues that in order for human dignity to be realized, nations have an obligation to meet the basic requirements of its citizens. Furthermore, while her Aristotelian capability approach refuses to distinguish natural and political, one might question why she does not explicitly name environmental goods in her framing of ten principles for a global structure across national boundaries.[21] Yet her emphasis on *relationships* as a goal is vitally important, since it parts company from a social theory of justice that aims purely at *mutual advantage*.[22] This is crucially important in the context of international climate negotiations, where the assumed goal of mutual advantage in climate negotiations seems to have dominated, leading to a breakdown of negotiations.

David Kronlid has analysed what he terms the *moral landscape* of IPCC in as much as how far it coheres with the capability approach in ethical decision-making.[23] He therefore begins to address the way in which a particular international organization functions in terms of how far they are consistent with such an ethical theory. [24] He argues that the assumption by policy makers and others is that they are working with a theory of distributive justice. His analysis looks specifically at the themes of mitigation, adaptation and vulnerability, all of which are key issues in the IPCC's fourth assessment report. He believes that it is a mistake to assume ethical focus just on the model of distributive justice, and 'lock climate change ethics into a particular paradigm' while ignoring other possible frameworks for thinking through what justice making might entail. He puts forward what he terms a 'tentative list' of capabilities that seem to be under threat by climate change according to the IPCC reports. He is critical of Nussbaum's list of goods as too fixed, though this seems overdrawn, as her list is still subject to revision or enlargement.

Importantly, Kronlid suggests that the capacity for knowledge in indigenous communities is compromised by climate change, as numerous examples and the case studies cited above testify. He also argues that climate change threatens modern knowledge, since climate change reminds modernity of the uncertainty of its knowledge base. I suggest that this is not strictly accurate, since what is threatened is not so much modern knowledge, as the *trust* given to that knowledge by members of the public. Climate scientists are, perhaps, being forced to be more open about

---

of human dignity', Nussbaum, *Frontiers of Justice*, p. 82. A full discussion of Rawls' views is outside the scope of this chapter.

[21] Nussbaum, *Frontiers of Justice*, pp. 85–86.

[22] Nussbaum attributes such a view to Rawls and is therefore critical of his theory in this respect. The assumptions of free equality of parties and mutual advantage as the overall purpose also apply to other social contract theories. See Nussbaum, *Frontiers of Justice*, pp. 29–35. I have also discussed this aspect in C. Deane-Drummond, 'Does Sustainable Development Have a Future?', *Theology, Religion and Exclusion: Towards Transformation* (H. Bacon, and W. Morris (eds); London: T & T Clark/Continuum, *in press*, 2011).

[23] D. Kronlid, 'Mapping the Moral Landscape of IPCC', *Ecological Ethics: Exploring Religion, Ethics and Aesthetics* (S. Bergmann, and H. Eaton (eds); LIT, *in press*, 2010).

[24] Steve Vanderheiden, cited above, tries to do something similar with respect to the workings of international governance according to John Rawls' theory. A discussion of this aspect is outside the scope of this chapter.

the uncertainty of their knowledge, and this undermines what is, arguably, a false sense of security in that knowledge. The so-called Climategate scandal seemed to be more an argument about what might be publishable in a scientific journal called *Climate Research*, thus weakening scientific credibility, but it was blown up by the media to imply scientists are deliberately deceiving the public. Although Kronlid believes that contingency in climate change 'positions indigenous knowledge and Western knowledge on an equal scale of reference', this claim exaggerates the extent to which the Western world still relies on Western knowledge and, in spite of some undermining of trust in scientists, still finds it a reliable source for practical decision making.[25] The open religious explanation for their observed local changes in weather patterns in those indigenous communities unaware of Western explanations contrasts with the scientific model presupposed in the IPCC statements and incorporated into the UNFCCC negotiations. Hence, Kronlid's analysis examines an aspect of climate discourse filtered through the IPCC, that is itself reliant on scientific methodological approaches. Kronlid is aware of this limitation, so 'The IPCC leaves [those] abilities [that are] key to human wellbeing and dignified life – appreciation of beauty, play, friendship, self-integration, coherent self-determination – unnoticed'.[26] The challenge remains as to how to integrate indigenous knowledge with more sophisticated cultural and social analysis that foregrounds these abilities, and what is required to secure them on a scale that mirrors that of the IPCC.[27] But here we need to ask *why* Kronlid implies that the role of IPCC is to mirror such a broad vision of the good life, given that their brief is much more limited, namely, to offer an international scientific consensus on climate change and its impacts. This issue is, however, important for international negotiations, so the question then becomes, *how* can such indigenous knowledge, and stories around climate impacts become integrated into international processes and goals. Hence while the research of the IPCC is crucial for the workings of the UNFCCC, the importance of a more expansive notion of climate justice in reassessing what justice making between *nations* requires should not be overlooked. The dilemma exists that as long as there are disparate versions of what the good might be, and what justice making requires, there is likely to be limited consensus. Yet achieving some sort of overlapping consensus is vital if international agreements are to have any meaning and the global commons of climate health is to be addressed.[28]

Nussbaum suggests ten principles for global structure, all of which are relevant to climate change debates, though disappointingly she does not address the environment or climate as such. First is an insistence on domestic responsibility. She

---

[25] Kronlid, 'Mapping the Moral Landscape of IPCC'.
[26] Ibid.
[27] Timothy Leduc raises the interesting possibility that a close examination of different cultural responses to climate change requires the same sort of scale of operations as the IPCC with respect to scientific research. The methodology adopted would be different. See T. Leduc, 'A Case for Intercultural IPCC'.
[28] That is exactly Rawls' point in his article 'The Idea of an Overlapping Consensus', *Oxford Journal of Legal Studies* 7(1987), pp. 1–25.

argues that global injustice exists 'if poorer nations have to struggle against greater obstacles than rich nations in order to meet their fundamental commitments'.[29] Second, global agreement does not need to undermine national sovereignty, a concern that was aired by pressure groups demonstrating at the COP 15 Summit meeting in 2009. Third, prosperous nations have the responsibility to give a substantial portion of their GDP to poorer nations. Nussbaum argues that the disproportionate gap between the luxurious consumption in some nations compared with the lack of basic requirements for survival needs to be addressed. She suggests that given the corruption of some nations, funnelling support through non-government aid agencies may be an option. The gross inequality is particularly crucial in climate change politics, since without additional support the possibility of nations reaching a minimal subsistence level is compromised.

Fourth, and crucially, multinational companies have a responsibility for promoting human capabilities where they operate. Fifth, Nussbaum argues that the main structures of the global economic system should be designed to be fair to poor and developing countries. The relative balancing of economic growth with the carrying capacity of the planet is not an issue that she considers. Sixth, she argues for a thin, decentralized, yet forceful, global public sphere. This would have at least some coercive powers. Seventh, all nations should focus on the problem of the disadvantaged, including discrimination against particular groups. The importance of women in carrying the greatest burden in adaptation to climate change needs to be highlighted. Eighth, care of the ill, elderly, children and disabled should be guaranteed. This is particularly challenging in the context of climate change where the most vulnerable are always the worst affected. Ninth, the family should be treated as a sphere that is precious, but not private. Nussbaum believes that the world has been far too slow in addressing the discrimination against girls by family members among those cultures that do not give equal respect to male and female offspring. As climate change impacts on basic resources in the poorest regions of the world, such discrimination is likely to worsen unless strong measures are put in place. Finally, the importance of education for those who are disempowered is vitally important, both in addressing ignorance over climate change impacts and in building up resilience.

While Nussbaum's map of goods to be sought is relevant to envisaging the kind of global structure that is required, and points towards a process for achieving this, she fails to address adequately the deeper *motivation* for making these global changes, and *why* the particular list of goods that she lists needs to be adopted on a universal scale. It seems that her list is arrived at by intuition, but given the impact of social factors in shaping what form that intuition might take, it is unlikely to be sufficient. While she compares her capability approach with social contract theory by allowing for the inclusion of 'moral sentiments', including sympathy and benevolence,[30] it is not clear how such sentiments might be fostered in her scheme.

---

[29] Nussbaum, *Frontiers of Justice*, p. 316
[30] This is addressed in the final chapter of her *Frontiers of Justice*, pp. 408–415, but compared with the detailed treatment of capability theory as such, her attention to the sentiments is

It also seems that she believes that compassion is engendered through telling stories, and in this respect I have some sympathy with her approach, though it is not entirely clear from the very limited treatment of this topic. She does, however, in earlier writing positively allow for the possibility of religious belief in the list of capability goods, and rejects what she terms a comprehensive map of secular feminism that seeks deliberately to exclude the religious dimension in the list of capabilities to be fostered.[31] Yet I suggest that her place for religion in the list of capabilities is still too limited, and is connected with freedom of choice, alongside other choices such as that towards literary or musical preferences.[32] In her book *Women and Human Development*, she also argues that religion is important in affirming the principle of each person as an end, in giving meaning to life and in affirming moral standards. Of course, the clash between religious views and those accepted by liberal societies creates a tension that she seems content to be settled through courts of law.[33] In other words, although she claims that her vision of the good can be adapted to different contexts, the account of what that global good might entail is not necessarily self-evident to all people.

It is here that a more explicit public theology plays a role in speaking to a heavily contested ground. While those most likely to listen to theological statements are members of particular religions, it offers a way of expanding on Nussbaum's capability approach and critiquing aspects of it. Capabilities are therefore first of all truncated if they do not address the religious nature of human existence understood *not simply* as an added dimension to human imagination, but as a ground of being and human meaning. In a similar way, Nussbaum seemingly *adds on* the environmental dimension to her list of goods for human flourishing, rather than seeing the natural world as the ground in which all of life depends and without which nothing could exist.[34] Her lack of attention to this comes through in a more obvious way in her principles for a global structure named above. Although she is sympathetic to the plight of non-human animals, this is not the point I am making here, for her

---

relatively thin, though her emphasis on the importance of imaginatively entering into the situation of another in distress is pertinent. She hints that another book that she is currently writing, *Compassion and Capabilities*, is likely to address this concern, but to date it remains unpublished.

[31] Religion is named as one capability alongside others in a model of political liberalism, for example, Nussbaum, *Women and Human Development*, pp. 167–240. She does give a place for what she terms traditionalist feminism, which seeks to affirm women through traditional roles in given religious structures. Her analysis is heavily influenced by her experience of India.

[32] Nussbaum, *Frontiers of Justice*, p. 76. Religion is included under the category of Senses, Imagination and Thought.

[33] Nussbaum, *Women and Human Development*, p. 270.

[34] In the list of central human capabilities, 'other species' is named as eighth in the list, and living in concern for and in relation to animals, plants and the world of nature is included together. Hence, this facet seems to extend outwards from those creatures most similar to human beings, that is, other animals. It is also telling that she names 'control over one's environment' as a tenth capacity, which implies a particular attitude to the natural world.

inclusion of other animals is a way of *expanding* the notion of capabilities so that it applies to other animals, rather like the expansion of human rights to animal rights. I suggest that the list of capabilities needs to be revised so that it takes much greater account of the religious and natural ground of human life, and in that way it is likely to connect more readily with the epistemology of non-Western societies. This might help establish a rather better platform for the possibility of mutual fellowship in international negotiations that Nussbaum has named as a central goal in establishing a partial theory of justice. Fellowship is intended as an inclusive term and implies mutual affirmation of all the others involved in the negotiations. Further, highlighting the religious and natural ground for human flourishing helps to articulate *why* there has been a failure in understanding between nation states, as well as pointing to a tradition that *motivates* a much deeper sense of global climate responsibility.

IV. Charity, Justice Making and Practical Wisdom

The context of widespread environmental collapse, along with the suffering of the most vulnerable communities and the specific problems associated with climate change, has provided the occasion for public declarations by senior religious leaders calling for greater moral responsibility. The latest encyclical *Caritas in Veritate* by Pope Benedict XVI, for example, tackled the need for environmental responsibility along with a critical examination of what might be termed economism, scientism and technologism – the belief that economics, science and technology work in an inevitable way according to pre-set norms.[35] Mention of climate change in Pope Benedict XVI's World Day Message of Peace took the following form: 'Can we remain indifferent before the problems associated with such realities as climate change, desertification, the deterioration and loss of productivity in vast agricultural areas, the pollution of rivers and aquifers, the loss of biodiversity, the increase of natural catastrophes and the deforestation of equatorial and tropical regions?'[36] This was followed by a comment on environmental refugees and the actual and likely conflicts over scarce resources. The message sought to strengthen the theological basis of why creation care is important and to challenge economics to become more environmentally sensitive. However, other than calling for technologically advanced societies to adopt simpler lifestyles and improve energy efficiency,[37] there was no specific attention paid to the relatively drastic nature of the social and political changes that are necessary in order to address climate change. This

---

[35] Pope Benedict XVI, *Caritas in Veritate*, http://www.vatican.va/holy_father/benedict_xvi/encyclicals/documents/hf_ben-xvi_enc_20090629_caritas-in-veritate_en.html (accessed 14 January 2010).
[36] Pope Benedict XVI, *World Day Message of Peace*, January 2010, paragraph 4, http://www.vatican.va/holy_father/benedict_xvi/messages/peace/documents/hf_ben-xvi_mes_20091208_xliii-world-day-peace_en.html (accessed 30 January 2010).
[37] Ibid., paragraph 9.

global change is inclusive of those changes that are forced by natural cycles as well as those that can be mapped onto anthropogenic impacts. Christian theology can name the breakdown in such international negotiations discussed earlier as a form of structural and institutional sin, but it needs to go further than this in articulating ways to motivate and change behaviour that is locked into habits of mind that are destructive, that is, in traditional parlance: vices of arrogance, pride, indulgence and excessive self-interest.

The key for Pope Benedict XVI seems to be to focus on valuing the special dignity of each human person within institutional structures of power, and as a way of seeking to transform those structures. In *Caritas in Veritate* Pope Benedict XVI also spoke of the need to reform United Nations organizations so that the idea of the family of nations is real and poorer nations have an effective voice in decision-making. He presses here for a 'true world political authority' regulated by law, and committed to securing 'authentic' human development marked by a particular Christian vision of charity and truth.[38] But does this mean a weakening of plurality of nations, given his particular interpretation of charity and truth? The problem not adequately addressed in this encyclical is how strong theological statements, that make sense in the context of the Christian community, can become the basis for a globalized structure, without appearing to others to be acts of hegemony. While I would certainly support, for example, the concept of deep incarnation as a way of expressing from the standpoint of Christian belief why it is so crucial that the natural world is protected,[39] translating such ideas into forms that make sense practically in the political sphere is rather more problematic. The best we might hope for is an approach that uses themes that are more widely recognized as having value, such as the need for fellowship, the need to protect the needs of the most vulnerable in society and the promotion of virtues rather than self-interest in order to promote social transformation. Although stewardship is popular among many writers from Christian traditions, including in Roman Catholic social teaching, it tends to give the impression that environmental issues are simply additional problems that the human community is able to address, if only we manage our affairs correctly.

As an alternative that complements and critiques aspects of capability theory, I suggest that proper attention to the virtues as informed by the central virtue of charity needs to take priority, as long as this is understood in such a way that virtues are not just individualistic, that is, they are expressed at different social levels, including the level of the individual, family, civic society and political structural level. In the Christian community these virtues are understood as being not just learnt, but also given by the grace of the Holy Spirit working in the lives of ordinary believers. The virtues are also orientated towards the common good,

---

[38] Pope Benedict XVI, *Caritas in Veritate*, paragraph 67.

[39] I have argued that ecological concerns are at the heart of Christian faith once the full significance of the incarnation is appreciated. See C. Deane-Drummond, 'Deep Incarnation and Eco-Justice as Theodrama', *Ecological Ethics: Exploring Religion, Ethics and Aesthetics* (S. Bergmann, and H. Eaton (eds); LIT, *in press*, 2010).

understood on the broadest possible scale to include the most vulnerable societies in different nations. Such attention to the virtues therefore *goes beyond simply recommending a procedure or process*, even if it includes the procedural by naming *prudence* as virtue. The list of goods drawn up by Nussbaum may be used, as long as this list is revised by giving greater attention to religious and natural life as the ground for human flourishing. Further, the Holy Spirit may also be recognized by Christians as active in a cross-cultural sense. Justice as virtue takes justice making further than distributive justice requires, for it is about matching outer action with inner integrity of purpose. In this scenario justice becomes a particular habit of mind.[40]

What sort of shape might negotiations at the different COP meetings have taken if the priority given to the delegates was less on how to represent the interests of a particular nation state and more on how to express justice as virtue? Would the list of global goods that Martha Nussbaum's capability theory has suggested have come closer to being expressed or not? Is overlapping consensus only really possible if negotiators are prepared to situate themselves in another's place when drawing up what is due to whom? Alongside justice, the importance of the ability to connect with another and express charity and compassion in *mutual fellowship* is vitally important if justice making is to move beyond the narrow constraint of national interests. The need for such charity, justice and peace making is characteristic of many religious traditions and cultures. While a comparative cultural exercise on how different religious traditions are responding and might respond to climate pressures has yet to be carried out, the possibility of an overlapping global international consensus where the needs of the most vulnerable are met seems reasonable. It has been the basis for other global movements of the United Nations, such as that of human rights. However, what is called for now is a global movement that stresses *human responsibilities* to act according to the value of each human being, understood as embedded in the natural world, rather than apart from it.

Nussbaum resists relativism in virtue theory by naming a list of goods as the minimal requirement across national boundaries. But she does not spell out how the desired outcome of these negotiations might be reached. In other words, not only are there problems in motivation, there are also practical procedural difficulties in her theory; precisely how might nations come together to reach these kinds of agreements? It is here that the Aristotelian virtue of prudence or practical wisdom would be not only helpful, but would also fit in with her conceptual scheme readily, since she is also indebted to an Aristotelian approach. Practical wisdom, understood in the classic Aristotelian sense as the ability to deliberate, judge and act aright not only between individuals, but also at the level of justice making, can apply to political as well as individual contexts. Prudence has as one of its elements *solertia*, the ability to act well in the face of the unexpected. Given

---

[40] I have written on justice as virtue and practical wisdom/prudence in Aquinas in numerous different contexts, such as C. Deane-Drummond, *The Ethics of Nature* (Oxford: Blackwell, 2004). I am not intending to rehearse this again here; rather, the intention is to flag up the relevance of justice as virtue and practical wisdom to climate negotiations.

the contingencies associated with climate change, the ability of nation states to act well in response to particular emergencies, the ability of other nations to cooperate in providing support, all this requires *solertia*. In addition, *memoria*, the accurate remembrance of the past is critical to many indigenous communities faced with the possibility of their traditions being eroded or challenged through climate impacts. Other elements such as insight are important, and cannot easily be pre-judged. One of the difficulties of the UNFCCC's seeming reliance on IPCC data is that already hinted at by David Kronlid: the way the IPCC has been set up relies on scientific methodology that stresses prediction and what Aquinas called foresight. If this, along with circumspection, or accurate reading of current data, is all that impinges on decision-making, then the richness of what different cultural traditions might bring to a discussion is lost. In this way practical wisdom gives some clues as to what it might mean to act justly, where competing demands and interests complicate matters under discussion. This raises the question of what might be reasonable goods to support according to such a procedure.

V. Can There Ever Be a *Jus Gentium?* Solidarity and the Common Good

Is justice between the nations a realistic aspiration? Given the prevalence of vested interests evident in international deliberations, are such aspirations worth retaining? The argument of this chapter so far has been that the temptation to shape justice just in distributive ways needs at least to be qualified by proper attention to a revised list of capabilities that are informed and motivated by proper attention to the virtues. The priority in Roman Catholic social teaching for creating a more just global society for those that have the least advantages in that society resonates with much of Martha Nussbaum's analysis. The difference is that the Catholic social tradition is clear about reasons *why* the poor take priority based on the special attention given to the value of each and every human being as made in the image of God and the value of the natural world as the Creator's gift.

In the Catholic tradition the idea of justice with solidarity across peoples and nations is commonplace, from the first encyclical on social justice issues, *Rerum Novarum*, published in 1898, through to the present day. Solidarity as traditionally understood is that which inclines human beings to identify with those who are in other communities in other parts of the world, based on a shared sense of humanity. Yet, as *Caritas in Veritate* makes clear, solidarity at best combines with subsidiarity, that is, a principle that allows only that structure of governance that is strictly required, and fosters the greatest level of human freedom possible.[41] Subsidiarity therefore prevents solidarity becoming a form of paternalism, since it aims at empowerment of those who are receiving aid, rather than dependency. The goal of fellowship in Nussbaum's analysis offers some parallels to this approach that puts particular emphasis on the need for mutual respect. Solidarity and subsidiarity in climate change politics implies local systems of governance to manage

[41] Pope Benedict XVI, *Caritas in Veritate*, p. 57–58.

adaptation to climate stress. While subsidarity does not apply to other creaturely kinds, the notion of solidarity could stretch to include other creatures; only this time it is solidarity with all life forms, rather than solidarity just with human creatures. Further, given the closeness of the interweaving of human and other life forms, then the idea of solidarity with all life makes sense even if our primary concern is for humanity, for, as indigenous cultures and ecological science has insisted, humanity is to be thought of as embodied in a close and intricate web of ecological networks and relationships. The tragedy of many Western cultures in particular is that humanity has lost that sense of being embodied and embedded in the natural world.

VI. Conclusions

I have attempted in this chapter to set the scene for a form of public theology that makes sense, given the particular controversies over climate justice, and the difficulties at arriving at global consensus on such issues. After exposing some of the ways in which those with particular vested interests have tried to suppress information about climate change in order to stall regulation, I have argued that the voices of those who are at the margins of global society need to be taken into account. This is of particular importance if the interests of these groups and other vulnerable people are going to be addressed. I suggest that the capability approach of Martha Nussbaum is promising, but it fails to address the reasons for adopting such a concrete list of goods. Further, in the Christian community the depth of theological reasoning as to *why* such a position is needed can be recognized and affirmed as a way of encouraging public engagement.[42] Hence, I have argued that while the means of reaching the possibility of such a consensus is rooted in the virtues that themselves are understood as grace laden in the Christian context, realism about the plural nature of human communities requires an overlapping consensus in the interests of the least developed nations. Adjusting the economy in the West so that it follows a more sustainable model is a major challenge, but not an impossible one. If theology in the public sphere is to make sense, then not only must it be prepared to speak out into the public domain, but also it needs to connect with and allow for public debate about what justice requires. This chapter is an attempt to offer a theological approach according to this model in the contested field of international negotiations over climate change.

---

[42] I have attempted to do this in a popular accessible work that is specifically for use in Christian communities, including short reflections, stories, prayers and discussion questions. C. Deane-Drummond, *Seeds of Hope: Facing the Challenge of Climate Justice* (London: CAFOD, 2009).

Bibliography

Bacon, H., and W. Morris (eds), *Theology, Religion and Exclusion: Towards Transformation* (London: T & T Clark/Continuum, *in press*, 2011).

Benedict XVI, *Caritas in Veritate* (Rome: Libreria Editrice Vaticana, 2009); http://www.vatican.va/holy_father/benedict_xvi/encyclicals/documents/hf_ben-xvi_enc_20090629_caritas-in-veritate_en.html (accessed 14 January 2010).

—*World Day Message of Peace*, January 2010, http://www.vatican.va/holy_father/benedict_xvi/messages/peace/documents/hf_ben-xvi_mes_20091208_xliii-world-day-peace_en.html (accessed 30 January 2010).

Bergmann, S., and H. Eaton (eds), *Ecological Ethics: Exploring Religion, Ethics and Aesthetics* LIT, *in press*, 2010).

Bergmann, S., P. M. Scott, M. Jansdotter Samuelsson, and H. Bedford-Strom (eds), *Nature, Space and the Sacred* (Farnham: Ashgate, 2009), pp. 57–74.

Booker, C., 'Climate change: This is the Worst Scientific Scandal of Our Generation', *Daily Telegraph* (28 November 2009), http://www.telegraph.co.uk/comment/columnists/christopherbooker/6679082/Climate-change-this-is-the-worst-scientific-scandal-of-our-generation.html (accessed 7 April 2010).

Crate, S., 'Gone the Bull of Winter? Grappling with the Cultural Implications of and Anthropology's Role(s) in Global Climate Change', *Current Anthropology* 49 (2008), pp. 569–595.

Deane-Drummond, C., 'Deep Incarnation and Eco-Justice as Theodrama', *Ecological Ethics: Exploring Religion, Ethics and Aesthetics* (S. Bergmann, and H. Eaton (eds); LIT, *in press*, 2010).

—'Does Sustainable Development Have a Future?', *Theology, Religion and Exclusion: Towards Transformation* (H. Bacon, and W. Morris (eds); London: T & T Clark/Continuum, *in press*, 2011).

—*The Ethics of Nature* (Oxford: Blackwell, 2004).

—*Seeds of Hope: Facing the Challenge of Climate Justice* (London: CAFOD, 2009).

Frömming, U. U., and C. Reichel, 'Indigenous People Under Climate Change: Regional Examples From Indonesia', PIK/EFSRE workshop, *Religion in Global Environmental and Climate Change: Sufferings, Values and Lifestyles*, Potsdam, Germany, 11 January 2010.

Green Belt Movement, *The Green Belt Movement Approach, Responding to Climate Change from the Grassroots* (London/Washington: GBM International, 2009).

Jackson, T., *Prosperity without Growth: Economics for a Finite Planet* (London: Earthscan, 2009).

Kronlid, D., 'Mapping the Moral Landscape of IPCC', *Ecological Ethics: Exploring Religion, Ethics and Aesthetics* (S. Bergmann, and H. Eaton (eds); LIT, *in press*, 2010).

Leduc, T., 'A Case for An Intercultural IPCC', PIK/EFSRE workshop, *Religion in Global Environmental and Climate Change: Sufferings, Values and Lifestyles*, Potsdam, Germany, 12 January 2010.

Northcott, M., *A Moral Climate: The Ethics of Global Warming* (London: Darton, Longman and Todd, 2007).

—'Atmospheric Space, Climate Change and the Communion of Saints', *Nature, Space and the Sacred* (S. Bergmann, P.M. Scott, M. Jansdotter Samuelsson, and H. Bedford-Strom (eds); Farnham: Ashgate, 2009), pp. 57–74.

Nussbaum, M., *Frontiers of Justice: Disability, Nationality, Species Membership* (Cambridge: Harvard University Press/Belknap, 2006).

—*Women and Human Development: The Capabilities Approach* (New York: Cambridge University Press, 2000).

Rawls, J., 'The Idea of an Overlapping Consensus', *Oxford Journal of Legal Studies* 7(1987), pp. 1–25.

—*The Law of Peoples* (Cambridge, MA and London: Harvard University Press, 2001).

Sen, A., *Development as Freedom* (Oxford: Oxford University Press, 1999).

—*The Idea of Justice* (London: Penguin, 2009).

Vanderheiden, S., *Atmospheric Justice: A Political Theory of Climate Change* (Oxford: Oxford University Press, 2008).

Bibliography

Aarsbergen-Ligtvoet, C., 'Harry Kuitert and the Possibility of a Public Witness of the Church', *Theology between Church, University, and Society* (M. E. Brinkman, N. F. M. Schreurs, H. M. Vroom, and C. J. Wethmar (eds); Van Gorkum: Koninklijke, 2003), pp. 194–223.

Alkemeyer, T., 'Semiotische Aspekte der Soziologie: Soziosemiotik', *Semiotik: Ein Handbuch zu den zeichentheoretischen Grundlagen von Natur und Kultur* (R. Posner, and K. Robering (eds); volume 3; Berlin: W. de Gruyter, 2003), pp. 2758–2846.

Alleyne, R., 'Maybe Religion is the Answer Claims Atheist Scientist', *Daily Telegraph* (7 September 2009), http://www.telegraph.co.uk/journalists/richard-alleyne/6146656/Maybe-religion-is-the-answer-claims-atheist-scientist.html (accessed 20 July 2010).

Althaus-Reid, M. (ed.), *Liberation Theology and Sexuality: New Radicalism from Latin America* (London: Ashgate, 2006).

Althaus-Reid, M., I. Petrella, and L. C. Susin (eds), *Another Possible World* (London: SCM Press, 2007).

Altner G., *Schöpfung am Abgrund. Die Theologie vor der Umweltfrage* (Neukirchen-Vluyn: Neukirchener Verlag, 1974).

Alvarez, S. E., *Engendering Democracy in Brazil: Women's Movements in Transition Politics* (Princeton: Princeton University Press, 1990).

Amery C., *Das Ende der Vorsehung. Die gnadenlosen folgen des Christentums* (Reinbek: Rowohlt, 1972).

Anderson, P., 'Ethics and Hermeneutics: A Question of Memory', *Literary Canons and Religious Identity* (E. Borgmann, B. Philipsen, and L. Verstricht (eds); Aldershot: Ashgate, 2004), pp. 79–96.

—'Ethics, Hermeneutics and Politics: A Critical Standpoint on Memory', *The Sacred and the Profane* (J. Keuss (ed.); Aldershot: Ashgate, 2003), pp. 109–125.

—'An Ethics of Memory: Promising, Forgiving, Yearning', *The Blackwell Companion to Postmodern Theology* (G. Ward (ed.); Malden, MA: Blackwell, 2005), pp. 231–248.

Aristoteles, *Über die Seele, griechisch-deutsch* (W. Biehl, and O. Apelt (eds); W. Theiler (trans.); Hamburg: F. Meiner Verlag, 1995).

Atkins, P., *Liturgy and Memory* (Aldershot: Ashgate, 2004).

Augé, M., *Non-Places: Introduction to an Anthropology of Supermodernity* (New York: Verso, 1995).

Augustine, *Confessions* (H. Chadwick (trans.); Oxford: Oxford University Press, 1998).

Bacon, H., and W. Morris (eds), *Theology, Religion and Exclusion: Towards Transformation* (London: T & T Clark/Continuum, in press, 2011).

Badiner, A. H. (ed.), *Dharma Gaia: A Harvest of Essays in Buddhism and Ecology* (Berkeley, CA: Parallax, 1990).

Balagangadhara, S.N., *'The Heathen in His Blindness ...': Asia, the West, and the Dynamic of Religion* (Leiden: E.J. Brill, 1994).

Barnhill, D., and R. Gottlieb, *Deep Ecology and World Religions: New Essays on Sacred Ground* (Albany: State University of New York Press, 2001).

Bate, S., *Inculturation and Healing* (Pietermaritzburg: Cluster Publications, 1995).

Bayerisches Staatsministerium für Umwelt und Gesundheit, http://www.stmug.bayern.de/umwelt/klimaschutz/allianz/ (assessed 15 March 2010).

Beck, U., 'Climate for Change, or How to Create a Green Modernity', *Theory, Culture and Society* 27 (2010), pp. 254–266.

Bedford-Strohm, H., 'Bildung, Gerechtigkeit, Teilhabe – Kommentar zum Beitrag von Gerhard Kruip', *Bildung und Beteiligungsgerechtigkeit* (M. Heimbach-Steins, and Gerhard Kruip (eds); Bielefeld: Bertelsman, 2003), pp. 131–136.

—'Die Entdeckung der Ökologie in der ökumenischen Bewegung', *Hoffnungswege. Wegweisende Impulse des Ökumenischen Rates der Kirchen aus sechs Jahrzehnten* (H.G. Link and G. Müller-Fahrenholz (eds); Frankfurt: Otto Lembeck, 2008), pp. 321–347.

—'Kirche – Ethik – Öffentlichkeit. Zur ethischen Dimension der Ekklesiologie', *Verkündigung und Forschung* 51 (2006), pp. 4–19.

—'Kirche in Zivilgesellschaft', *Was hat die Kirche heute zu sagen? Auftrag und Freiheit der Kirche in der pluralistischen Gesellschaft* (R. Weth (ed.); Neukirchen-Vluyn: Neukirchener Verlag, 1998), pp. 92–108.

—'Nurturing Reason: The Public Role of Religion in the Liberal State', *Ned Geref Theologiese Tydskrif* 48 (2007), pp. 25–41.

—'Öffentliche Theologie in der Zivilgesellschaft', *Politik und Theologie in Europa. Perspektiven ökumenischer Sozialethik* (I. Gabriel (ed.); Ostfildern: Matthias-Grünewalt-Verlag, 2008), pp. 340–366.

—'Poverty and Public Theology: Advocacy of the Church in Pluralistic Society', *International Journal of Public Theology* 2 (2008), pp. 144–162.

—'Public Theology and the Global Economy: Ecumenical Social Thinking between Fundamental Criticism and Reform', *Ned Geref Theologiese Tydskrif* 48 (2007), pp. 8–24.

—*Schöpfung* (Göttingen: Vandenhoeck & Ruprecht, 2001).

—'Theological Ethics and the Church: Reconsidering the Boundaries Between Practical Theology and Theological Ethics in Light of the Debate on Liberalism and Communitarianism', *Reconsidering the Boundaries Between Theological Disciplines. Zur Neubestimmung der Grenzen zwischen den theologischen Disziplinen* (M. Welker and F. Schweitzer (eds); Münster: Lit, 2005), pp. 175–186.

—'Tilling and Caring for the Earth: Public Theology and Ecology', *International Journal of Public Theology* 1 (2007), pp. 230–248.

—*Vorrang für die Armen. Auf dem Weg zu einer theologischen Theorie der Gerechtigkeit* (Öffentliche Theologie, 4; Gütersloh: Kaiser, 1993).

Bellah, R. N., R. Madsen, W. Sullivan, A. Swidler, and S. Tipton, *Habits of the Heart: Individualism and Commitment in American Life* (Berkeley, Los Angeles and London: University of California Press, 1985).

Benedict XVI, *Caritas in Veritate* (Rome: Libreria Editrice Vaticana, 2009); http://www.vatican.va/holy_father/benedict_xvi/encyclicals/documents/hf_ben-xvi_enc_20090629_caritas-in-veritate_en.html (accessed 14 January 2010).

—*World Day Message of Peace*, January 2010, http://www.vatican.va/holy_father/benedict_xvi/messages/peace/documents/hf_ben-xvi_mes_20091208_xliii-world-day-peace_en.html (accessed 30 January 2010).

Berger, P. L., and T. Luckmann, *Modernität, Pluralismus und Sinnkrise. Die Orientierung des modernen Menschen* (Gütersloh: Kaiser, 1995).

Bergmann, S., *Creation Set Free: The Spirit as Liberator of Nature* (D. Stott (trans.); Grand Rapids and Cambridge: William B. Eerdmans Publishing Company, 2005).

—'Making Oneself at Home in Environments of Urban Amnesia', *International Journal of Public Theology* 2 (2008), pp. 70–97.

Bergmann, S., and H. Eaton (eds), *Ecological Ethics: Exploring Religion, Ethics and Aesthetics* LIT, *in press*, 2010).

Bergmann, S., P. M. Scott, M. Jansdotter Samuelsson, and H. Bedford-Strom (eds), *Nature, Space and the Sacred* (Farnham: Ashgate, 2009), pp. 57–74.

Bevans, S., *Models of Contextual Theology* (Maryknoll, NY: Orbis Books, 1999).

—*Models of Contextual Theology* (Faith and Culture Series; Maryknoll, NY: Orbis Books, 7th edn, 2000).

Beyer, P., 'The Global Environment as a Religious Issue: A Sociological Analysis', *Religion* 22 (1992), pp. 1–21.

—*Religion and Globalization* (London: Sage, 1994).

—*Religions in Global Society* (London: Routledge, 2006).

Bieler, A., and L. Schottroff, *The Eucharist: Bodies, Bread, & Resurrection* (Minneapolis: Fortress, 2007).

Birch, B., and L. Rasmussen, *Bible and Ethics in the Christian Life* (Minneapolis: Augsburg, 1989).

Bobbio, N., *Democracy and Dictatorship* (Cambridge: Polity, 1989).

Böckenförde, E.W, 'Fundamente der Freiheit', *Was hält die moderne Gesellschaft zusammen?* (E. Teufel (ed.); Frankfurt: Suhrkamp, 1996), pp. 89–99.

—*Recht, Staat, Freiheit. Studien zur Rechtsphilosophie, Staatstheorie und Verfassungsgeschichte* (Frankfurt: Suhrkamp, 2nd edn, 1992).

—*Säkularisation und Utopie. Ebracher Studien. Ernst Forsthoff zum 65. Geburtstag* (Stuttgart: Kohlhammer, 1967).

Boff, L., *Cry of the Earth, Cry of the Poor* (P. Berryman (trans.); New York: Orbis Books, 1997).

—*Essential Care: An Ethics of Human Nature* (A. Guilherme (trans.); London: SPCK Books, 2007).

—*Ética planetaria desde el Gran Sur* (J. F. D. García (trans.); Madrid: Editorial Trotta, 2001).

—'Si no tenemos utopías, nos empantanamos en los intereses individuales', *Clarín*

(August 2008), www.clarin.com/diario/2008/08/24/um/m-01745277.htm (accessed 14 May 2010).
—'Two Urgent Utopias for the Twenty-First Century', *Another Possible World* (M. Althaus-Reid, I. Petrella, and L. C. Susin (eds); London: SCM Press, 2007), pp. 4–9.
Booker, C., 'Climate Change: This is the Worst Scientific Scandal of Our Generation', *Daily Telegraph* (28 November 2009), http://www.telegraph.co.uk/comment/columnists/christopherbooker/6679082/Climate-change-this-is-the-worst-scientific-scandal-of-our-generation.html (accessed 7 April 2010).
Booth, K., 'Risdon Vale: Place, Memory, and Suburban Experience', *Ethics, Place and Environment* 11 (2008), pp. 299–311.
Bouma-Prediger, S., *The Greening of Theology: the Ecological Models of Rosemary Radford Ruether, Joseph Sittler, and Jürgen Moltmann* (Atlanta: Scholars Press, 1995).
Bourdieu, P., *Zur Soziologie der symbolischen Formen* (Frankfurt am Main: Suhrkamp, 6th ed., 1997).
Brague, R., *The Law of God: The Philosophical History of an Idea* (Chicago & London: University of Chicago Press, 2008).
Breitmaier, I., *Das Thema der Schöpfung in der Ökumenischen Bewegung 1948 bis 1988* (Frankfurt et al.: Peter Lang, 1995).
Bria, I., 'Aspecte dogmatice ale unirii Bisericilor creștine', *Studii Teologice* 1–2 (1968), pp. 12–24.
—'Celebrating Life in the Liturgy', *Jesus Christ – the Life of the World: An Orthodox Contribution to the Vancouver Theme* (I. Bria (ed.); Geneva: World Council of Churches, 1982), pp. 75–87.
—*Comentariu la Catehismul Ortodox: 12 Sinteze Catehetice* (Sibiu: Editura Oastea Domnului, 2000).
—*Dicționar de Teologie Ortodoxă* (Bucuresti: Editura Institutului Biblic si de Misiune al Bisericii Ortodoxe Romane, 2nd ed., 1994).
—'Introduction', *Martyria/Mission. The Witness of the Orthodox Churches Today* (I. Bria (ed.); Geneva: Commission on World Mission and Evangelism, 1980), pp. 5–12.
—'Ion Coman 1902-1987', *Ecumenical Pilgrims: Profiles of Pioneers in Christian Reconciliation* (I. Bria, and D. Heller (eds); Geneva: WCC Publications, 1995), pp. 50-64.
—*The Liturgy after the Liturgy. Mission and Witness from an Orthodox Perspective* (Geneva: WCC Publications, 1996).
—*Mari sărbători și praznice creștine, praznice împărătești. Meditații teologice* (Sibiu: Ed. Popasuri Duhovnicesti, 2004).
—*Romania: Orthodox Identity at a Crossroads of Europe* (Geneva: WCC Publications, 1995).
—'Sanctification de la Création', *Dictionnaire Oecuménique de Missiologie. Cent mots pour la Mission* (I. Bria, P. Chanson, J. Gadille, and M. Spindler (eds); Paris: Cerf, 2001), pp. 290–315.
—*The Sense of Ecumenical Tradition: The Ecumenical Witness and Vision of the Orthodox* (Geneva: WCC Publications, 1991).

—'The Significance of the Theme: Some Preliminary Observations', *Jesus Christ – the Life of the World: An Orthodox Contribution to the Vancouver Theme* (I. Bria (ed.); Geneva: WCC Publications, 1982), pp. 11–19.
—*Teologia Ortodoxă în România contemporană* (Iaşi: Trinitas, 2003).
—*Tratat de teologie dogmatică şi ecumenică* (Bucuresti: Ed. Romania Crestina, 1999).
—'La vie. Un avenir déterminé par le Salut du monde', *L'Orthodoxie Hier-Demain* (M. A. Costa de Beauregard, I. Bria, and T. de Foucauld (eds); Paris: Ed. du Cerf, 1979), pp. 189–199.
Brocki, M., 'Landscapes of Memory – Narratives of Past Places', *Koht ja Paik/Place and Location* 6 (2008), pp. 219–225.
Browning, D. S., and F. Schussler Fiorenza (eds), *Habermas, Modernity, and Public Theology* (New York: Crossroad, 1992).
Bujo, B., *African Theology in its Social Context* (Maryknoll, NY: Orbis Books, 1992).
Burdick, J., *Legacies of Liberation: The Progressive Catholic Church in Brazil at the Start of a New Millennium* (Aldershot: Ashgate, 2004).
Carson, R., *Silent Spring* (Boston: Houghton Mifflin, 1962).
Casey, E., 'Levinas on Memory and the Trace', *The Collegium Phaenomenologicum* (J. Sallis, G. Moneta, and J. Taminiaux (eds); Dordrecht: Kluwer, 1988), pp. 241–255.
Cassierer, E., *Versuch über den Menschen. Einführung in eine Philosophie der Kultur* (R. Kaiser (trans.); Hamburg: Meiner, 1996).
'Centre for Public Theology', Huron University College, http://www.publictheology.org (accessed 16 July 2010).
Chapple, C. K. (ed.), *Jainism and Ecology: Nonviolence in the Web of Life* (Cambridge, MA: Center for the Study of World Religions and Harvard University Press, 2002).
Christopher, J., *No Blade of Grass* (New York: Avon, 1956).
Clayton, P., 'Theology and the Physical Sciences', *The Modern Theologians* (D. Ford and R. Muers (eds); Oxford: Blackwell/Wiley, 2nd edn, 2005), pp. 342–356.
Clayton, P., and A. Peacocke (eds), *In Whom We Live and Move and Have Our Being: Panentheistic Reflections on God's Presence in a Scientific World* (Grand Rapids, Michigan and Cambridge: Eerdmans, 2004).
Clifford, A., *Introducing Feminist Theology* (Maryknoll, NY: Orbis Books, 2001).
Climate Programme of the Evangelical Lutheran Church of Finland: Gratitude, Respect, Moderation, http://evl.fi/EVLen.nsf/Documents/B843256B66E603EEC225730C003A7E1F?openDocument&lang=EN (accessed 29 May 2010).
Clingerman, F., 'Beyond the Flowers and the Stones: 'Emplacement' and the Modeling of Nature', *Philosophy in the Contemporary World* 11 (2004), pp. 17–24.
—'Reading the Book of Nature: A Hermeneutical Account of Nature for Philosophical Theology', *Worldviews: Global Religions, Culture, and Ecology* 13 (2009), pp. 72–91.
—'Wilderness as the Place between Philosophy and Theology: Questioning Martin Drenthen on the Otherness of Nature', *Environmental Values* 19 (2010), pp. 211–232.

Cobb, C. W., 'The Index for Sustainable Economic Welfare', *For the Common Good. Redirecting the Economy Toward Community, the Environment and a Sustainable Future* (H. E. Daly, and J. B. Cobb, Jr (eds); Boston: Beacon Press, 1989), p. 416 (Appendix).

Congregation for the Doctrine of the Faith, *Instruction on Respect for Human Life in Its Origin and on the Dignity of Procreation: Replies to Certain Questions of the Day* (*Donum Vitae*) (Rome, 1987).

Conradie, E., *Christianity and Ecological Theology. Resources for Further Research* (Stellenbosch: Sun Press, 2006).

—'Editor's Foreword', *Essays in Public Theology: Collected Essays* (E. Conradie (ed.); vol. 1; Stellenbosch: Sun Press 2007), pp. iii–xv.

Cooper, R., 'Through the Soles of my Feet: A Personal View of Creation', *Ecotheology: Voices from South and North* (D. G. Hallman (ed.); Geneva: WCC, 1994), pp. 207–212.

Cooper-Marcus, C., 'Environmental Memories', *Place Attachment* (I. Altman, and S. M. Low (eds); New York: Plenum Press, 1992), pp. 87–112.

Cox, H., *Religion in the Secular City: Toward a Postmodern Theology* (New York: Simon and Schuster, 1984).

Crate, S., 'Gone the Bull of Winter? Grappling with the Cultural Implications of and Anthropology's Role(s) in Global Climate Change', *Current Anthropology* 49 (2008), pp. 569–595.

Daston, L., 'The World in Order', *Without Nature: A New Condition for Theology* (D. Albertson and C. King (eds); New York: Fordham University Press, 2010), pp. 15–33.

Deane-Drummond. C., *Christ and Evolution: Wonder and Wisdom* (Minneapolis: Fortress Press, 2009).

—*Creation Through Wisdom: Theology and the New Biology* (Edinburgh: T & T Clark, 2000).

—'Deep Incarnation and Eco-Justice as Theodrama', *Ecological Ethics: Exploring Religion, Ethics and Aesthetics* (S. Bergmann, and H. Eaton (eds); LIT, *in press*, 2010).

—'Does Sustainable Development Have a Future?', *Theology, Religion and Exclusion: Towards Transformation* (H. Bacon, and W. Morris (eds); London: T & T Clark/Continuum, *in press*, 2011).

—*The Ethics of Nature* (Oxford: Blackwell, 2004).

—*Seeds of Hope: Facing the Challenge of Climate Justice* (London: CAFOD, 2009).

—'Sophia: The Feminine Face of God as a Metaphor for an Ecotheology', *Feminist Theology* 6 (1997), pp. 11–31.

—'Theology and the Biological Sciences', *The Modern Theologians* (D. Ford and R. Muers (eds); Oxford: Blackwell/Wiley, 2nd edn, 2005), pp. 342–356; 357–369.

D'Entrèves, A. P., *Natural Law: An Historical Survey* (New York: Harper Torchbooks, 1951).

De Gruchy, J. W., *The Cambridge Companion to Dietrich Bonhoeffer* (Cambridge: Cambridge University Press, 1999).

—*Christianity and Democracy: A Theology for a Just World Order*, (Cambridge Studies in Ideology and Religion, Cambridge: Cambridge University Press, 1995).

—*Christianity, Art, and Transformation: Theological Aesthetics in the Struggle for Justice* (Cambridge: Cambridge University Press, 2001).
—*The Church Struggle in South Africa* (London: SCM Press, 2005).
—'An Euro-African Theologian Looks at his Ancestral Home', *On the Making of Europe: A Distant View* (J. Wiersma (ed.); Kampen: Kok Pharos Publishing House, 1997), pp. 24–45.
—*Liberating Reformed Theology: a South African Contribution to an Ecumenical Debate* (Michigan: Grand Rapids, 1991).
—'Public Theology as Christian Witness: Exploring the Genre', *International Journal of Public Theology* 1 (2007), pp. 26–41.
De Lange, H., and B. Goudzwaard, *Economie van het genoeg* (Kampen: Kok Agora, 1985).
Delich, F., 'The Social Construction of Memory and Forgetting', *Diogenes* 201 (2004), pp. 65–75.
De Vries, H., 'Introduction: Before, Around and Beyond the Theologico-Political', *Political Theologies: Public Religions in a Post-Secular World* (H. de Vries, and L. E. Sullivan (eds); Fordham: Fordham University Press, 2006), pp. 1–88.
Diefenbacher, H., 'A Different Kind of Globalization – Resistance and Opportunities', *Globalisierung. Wirtschaft im Dienst des Lebens – Stellungnahme der Evangelischen Kirche von Westfalen zum Soesterberg-Brief* (Evangelische Kirche von Westfalen (ed.); Bielefeld: EKvW, 2006), pp. 123–139.
Di Fabio, U., *Die Kultur der Freiheit* (München: Beck, 2005).
Dillard, C. D., 'When the Ground is Black, the Ground is Fertile. Exploring Endarkened Feminist Epistemology and Healing Methodologies in the Spirit', *Handbook of Critical and Indigenous Methodologies* (N. K. Denzin, Y. S. Lincoln, and L. T. Smith (eds); Los Angeles, London, New Delhi, Singapore: Sage, 2008), pp. 277–292.
Dostoyevsky, F., *The Brothers Karamasov* (New York: New American Library, 1999).
Douthwaite, R. *The Growth Illusion* (Hartland, Devon: Green Books, 1992).
Duchrow, U. (ed.), *Lutheran Churches – Salt or Mirror of Society? Case Studies of the Theory and Practice of the Two Kingdoms Doctrine* (Geneva: WCC, 1977).
Dupré, L., *Passage to Modernity: An Essay in the Hermeneutics of Nature and Culture* (New Haven and London: Yale University Press, 1993).
Duranti, A., *Linguistic Anthropology* (Cambridge: Cambridge University Press, 2002).
Dwiwedi, O. P., and B. N. Tiwari, *Environmental Crisis and the Hindu Religion* (New Delhi: Gitanjali, 1987).
Eagleton, T., *Trouble with Strangers* (Oxford: Blackwell, 2009).
Eaton, H., *Introducing Ecofeminist Theologies* (Introductions to Feminist Theology, 12; London & New York: T & T Clark, 2005).
Eerola, T., 'Uraanin vastustus uskontona', *Luonnonsuojelija* (18 September 2008), p. 2.
—'Uraanikaivoksia vastustavien aktivismitutkimukset pseudotieteellistä propagandaa', *Luonnonsuojelija* (May 2008), p. 22.
El Serafy, S., 'The Proper Calculation of Income from Depletable Natural Resources', *Environmental and Resource Accounting and their Relevance to the Measurement*

of Sustainable Income (E. Lutz and S. El Serafy (eds); Washington, D.C.: World Bank, 1988).

Ely, J., 'Ernst Bloch, Natural Right and the Greens', *Minding Nature: The Philosophers of Ecology* (D. Macauley (ed.); New York: Guilford, 1996), pp. 134–166.

Escobar, A., 'Worlds and Knowledges Otherwise: The Latin American Modernity/Coloniality Research Program', *Cultural Studies* 21 (2007), pp. 179–210.

Ferguson, A., *Versuch über die Geschichte der bürgerlichen Gesellschaft* (Frankfurt: Suhrkamp, 1988).

Finnis, J., *Natural Law and Natural Rights* (Oxford: Clarendon, 1980).

Fitzgerald, T., 'A Critique of 'Religion' as a Cross-Cultural Category', *Method & Theory in the Study of Religion* 9 (1997), pp. 91–110.

Foltz, R C., F. M. Denny, and A. Baharuddin (eds), *Islam and Ecology: A Bestowed Trust* (Cambridge, MA: Center for the Study of World Religions and Harvard University Press, 2003).

Forrester, D. B., *Apocalypse Now? Reflections on Faith in a Time of Terror* (Aldershot: Ashgate, 2005).

—*Beliefs, Values and Politics: Conviction Politics in a Secular Age* (Oxford: Clarendon, 1989).

—*Caste and Christianity: Attitudes and Policies on Caste of Anglo-Saxon Protestant Mission in India* (London: Curzon Press, 1980).

—*Christian Justice and Public Policy* (Cambridge: Cambridge University Press, 1997).

—*Christianity and the Future of Welfare* (London: Epworth Press, 1985).

—*On Human Worth: A Christian Vindication of Equality* (London: SCM Press, 2001).

—*Studies in the History of Worship in Scotland* (Edinburgh: T. & T. Clark, 1984).

—*Theological Fragments: Explorations in Unsystematic Theology* (London: T. & T. Clark, 2005).

Fox, M., *The Coming of the Cosmic Christ: The Healing of Mother Earth and the Birth of a Global Renaissance* (San Francisco: Harper & Row, 1988).

Fraas, H.-J., *Bildung und Menschenbild in theologischer Perspektive* (Göttingen: Vandenhoeck & Ruprecht, 2000).

Frömming, U. U., and C. Reichel, 'Indigenous People Under Climate Change: Regional Examples From Indonesia', PIK/EFSRE workshop, *Religion in Global Environmental and Climate Change: Sufferings, Values and Lifestyles*, Potsdam, Germany, 11 January 2010.

Gebara, I., 'Ecofeminism: An Ethics of Life', *Ecofeminism and Globalization. Exploring Culture, Context, and Religion* (H. Eaton and L. A. Lorentzen (eds); Lanham: Rowman and Littlefield, 2003), pp. 163–176.

—*Longing for Running Water: Ecofeminism and Liberation* (Minneapolis: Fortress Press, 1999).

—*Out of the Depths: Women's Experience of Evil and Salvation* (Ann Patrick Ware (trans.); Minneapolis: Fortress Press, 2002).

Geertz, C., *Available Light: Anthropological Reflections on Philosophical Topics* (Princeton: Princeton University Press, 3rd edn, 2001).

—*Dichte Beschreibung: Beiträge zum Verstehen kultureller Systeme* (B. Luchesi (trans.); Frankfurt am Main: Suhrkamp, 2007).
—'The Impact of the Concept of Culture on the Concept of Man', *Schooling the Symbolic Animal: Social and Cultural Dimensions of Educations* (B. A. U. Levinson, K. M. Borman, and M. Eisenhart (eds); Lanham, Maryland: Rowman & Littlefield Publischers, Inc., 2000), pp. 33–54.
—*The Interpretation of Cultures: Selected Essays* (New York: Basic Books, 1973).
—'Kulturbegriff und Menschenbild', *Kulturphilosophie* (F.-P. Burkard (ed.); Frankfurt: Alber, 2000), pp. 189–243.
—*Negara: The Theatre State in Nineteenth-century Bali* (Princeton: Princeton University Press, 1980).
—'Primordial Loyalties and Standing Entities: Anthropological Reflections on the Politics of Identity', http://www.colbud.hu/main_old/PubArchive/PL/PL07-Geertz.pdf (accessed 16 July 2010).
—'Thick Description: Toward an Interpretive Theory of Culture', *Anthropology in Theory: Issues in Epistemology* (H. L. Moore, T. Sanders (eds); Malden: Blackwell Publishing Ltd., 2006), pp. 236-257.
Gellner, E., *Bedingungen der Freiheit. Die Zivilgesellschaft und ihre Rivalen* (Stuttgart: Klett-Cotta, 1995).
Geuss, R., *History and Illusion in Politics* (Cambridge: Cambridge University Press, 2001).
—*Philosophy and Real Politics* (Princeton: Princeton University Press, 2008).
Gill, S., *Mother Earth: An American Story* (Chicago: University of Chicago Press, 1987).
'Global Network for Public Theology', Charles Sturt University,
http://www.csu.edu.au/special/accc/about/gnpt/ (accessed 16 July 2010).
Gore, A., *An Inconvenient Truth* (Hollywood, CA: Parmount, 2006).
Gorringe, T. J., *Furthering Humanity: A Theology of Culture* (Aldershot: Ashgate, 2004).
Gosling, D., *A New Earth, Covenanting for Justice: Peace and the Integrity of Creation* (London: CCBI, 1992).
Gottlieb, R., *A Greener Faith: Religious Environmentalism and Our Planet's Future* (Oxford: Oxford University Press, 2006).
—*A Spirituality of Resistance* (Lanham, MD: Rowman and Littlefield, 2003).
Green Belt Movement, *The Green Belt Movement Approach, Responding to Climate Change from the Grassroots* (London/Washington: GBM International, 2009).
Greene-McCreight, K., *Feminist Reconstructions of Christian Doctrine* (New York: Oxford Press, 2000).
Greil, A. L., and D. G. Bromley (eds), *Defining Religion: Investigating the Boundaries between Sacred and Secular, Religion and the Social Order* (vol. 3; London: Elsevier Scientific, 2003).
Grosse Kracht, H.-J., *Kirche in ziviler Gesellschaft. Studien zur Konfliktgeschichte von katholischer Kirche und demokratischer Öffentlichkeit* (Paderborn, München, Wien, Zürich: Schöningh, 1997).
Gutiérrez, G., *Beber en su propio pozo. En el itinerario espiritual de un pueblo* (Lima: CEP, 3rd edn, 1989).

—*Teología de la liberación: Perspectivas* (Salamanca: Ediciones Sígueme, 14th rev. edn, 1990).
Habermas, J., *Faktizität und Geltung. Beiträge zur Diskurstheorie des Rechts und des demokratischen Rechtsstaates* (Frankfurt: Suhrkamp, 1992).
—*Glauben und Wissen* (Frankfurt: Suhrkamp, 2001).
—*Zwischen Naturalismus und Religion. Philosophische Aufsätze* (Frankfurt: Suhrkamp, 2005).
Habermas, J., and J. Ratzinger, *Dialektik der Säkularisierung. Über Vernunft und Religion* (Freiburg, Basel, and Wien: Herder, 2005).
Harasta, E., 'Karl Barth, A Public Theologian? The One Word and Theological 'Bilinguality", *International Journal of Public Theology* 3 (2009), pp. 188–203.
Harris, J., R. Hobbes, E. Higgs, and J. Aronson, 'Ecological Restoration and Global Climate Change', *Restoration Ecology* 14 (2006), pp. 170–176.
Hartmann, G., *The Fateful Question of Culture* (New York: Columbia University Press, 1997).
Hartung, G., 'Anthropologische Grundlegung der Kulturphilosophie – Zur Entstehungsgeschichte von Ernst Cassierers Essay on Man', *Kulturwissenschaftliche Studien* (H.-J. Lachmann, and U. Kösser (eds); Kulturphilosophische und ästhetische Reihe, Band 6, Leipzig: Passage-Verlag, 2001), pp. 2–18.
Haubeck, W., W. Heinrichs, M. Schröder (eds), *Mensch sein – Mensch werden. Impulse christlicher Anthropologie* (Witten: Bundes-Verl., 2001).
Hegeman, D. B., *Plowing in Hope. Towards a Biblical Theology of Culture* (Moscow: Canon Press, 2nd edn, 2007).
Heidegger, M., 'Building Dwelling Thinking', *Basic Writings* (D. Farrell (ed.); San Francisco: Harper San Francisco, 2nd edn, 1993), pp. 343-363.
Heimbach-Steins, M., '"Angst vor der eigenen Courage'? Theologie zwischen gesellschaftlich-politischem Engagement und ekklesialer Verbindlichkeit', *Bulletin ET* 15 (2004), pp. 51–65.
—'Bildung als Menschenrecht', *Erziehung und Bildung heute* (H.-E. Tenortz, M. Hüther, and M. Heimbach-Steins (eds); Berlin: Verlag der GDA, 2006), pp. 47–70.
—'Bildung für die Weltgesellschaft. Sozialethische Sondierungen', *Stimmen der Zeit* 127 (2002), pp. 371–382.
—'Bildung und Beteiligungsgerechtigkeit. Bildungspolitische und sozialethische Anfragen', *Zwischen Sicherheitskalkül, Interesse und Moral. Beiträge zur Entwicklungspolitik* (K. Hirsch, and K. Seitz (eds); Frankfurt am Main: IKO Verlag für Interkulturelle Kommunikation, 2005), pp. 257–272.
—'Bildung und Chancengleichheit', *Christliche Sozialethik. Ein Lehrbuch, Band 2: Konkretionen* (M. Heimbach-Steins (ed.); Regensburg: Pustet, 2005), pp. 50–81.
—'Einmischung und Anwaltschaft. Die sozialethische Verantwortung der Kirche', *Kirche – lebenswichtig. Was Kirche zu geben und zu lernen hat* (V. Eid (ed.); München: Don Bosco, 1999), pp. 78–104.
—'Menschenbild und Menschenrecht auf Bildung. Bausteine für eine Sozialethik der Bildung', *Bildung und Beteiligungsgerechtigkeit. Sozialethische Sondierungen* (M. Heimbach-Steins, G. Kruip (eds); Bielefeld: Bertelsman, 2003), pp. 23–43.

Helander, E., and K. Kailo (eds), *No Beginning, No End – The Sami Speak Up* (Edmonton: Canadian Circumpolar Institute, 1998).

Higgs, E., *Nature By Design: People, Natural Process, and Ecological Restoration* (Cambridge: MIT Press, 2003).

Higton, M., *Christ, Providence and History: Hans W. Frei's Public Theology* (London: T & T Clark International, 2004).

Hinga, T., 'Jesus Christ and the Liberation of Women in Africa', *The Will to Arise: Women, Tradition, and the Church in Africa* (M. Oduyoye and K. Kanyoro (eds); Maryknoll, NY: Orbis Books, 1992), pp. 183–194.

HM Treasury, *Stern Review on the Economics of Climate Change* (1976), http://www.hm-treasury.gov.uk/stern_review_report.htm (accessed 14 May 2010).

—UK Budget 2009 Report, *Building Britain's Future*, www.hm-treasury.gov.uk/bud_bud09_index.htm (accessed 21 June 2010).

Hoekstra, K., 'Hobbes on the Natural Condition of Mankind', *The Cambridge Companion to Hobbes's Leviathan* (P. Springborg (ed.); Cambridge: Cambridge University Press, 2007), pp. 109–127.

Hörning, K. H., and J. Reuter, 'Doing Culture: Kultur als Praxis', *Doing Culture. Neue Positionen zum Verhältnis von Kultur und sozialer Praxis* (K. H. Hörning, and J. Reuter (eds); Bielefeld: transcript Verlag, 2004), pp. 9–18.

Horrell, D., C. Hunt, C. Southgate, and F. Stavrakopoulou (eds), *Ecological Hermeneutics: Biblical, Historical and Theological Perspectives* (London: T & T Clark/Continuum, 2010).

Huber, W., *Im Geist der Freiheit: Für eine Ökumene der Profile* (Freiburg im Breisgau, Basel, Wien: Herder, 2007).

—*Kirche und Öffentlichkeit* (Stuttgart: Klett, 1973).

—*Konflikt und Konsens: Studien zur Ethik der Verantwortung* (München: Kaiser, 1990).

—'Ökumene der Profile. Vortrag zur Eröffnung der Dietrich-Bonhoeffer-Forschungsstelle für Öffentliche Theologie', 29 January 2008 at Otto Friedrich University of Bamberg, http://www.uni-bamberg.de/fileadmin/uni/fakultaeten/ppp_lehrstuehle/evangelische_theologie_1/pdf_Dateien/Vortrag_WHuber_Oekumene_der_Profile_080129.pdf (accessed 16 July 2010).

Hull, J. M., *Studies in Religion and Education* (London, New York: Falmer Press, 1984).

Hüllen, J., *Mensch sein – human werden: Grundzüge kritischer Anthropologie* (Frankfurt am Main, Bern, New York: Peter Lang, 1985).

Immler, H., *Natur in der ökonomischen Theorie* (Opladen: Westdeutscher Verlag, 1985).

Irarrazával, D., *Un Cristianismo Andino* (Quito: Abya-Yala, 1999).

—*Inculturation: New Dawn of the Church in Latin America* (P. Berryman (trans.); Eugene, OR: Wipf and Stock Publishers, 2008).

—*Raíces de la Esperanza* (Lima: CEP, 2004).

Jackson, T. *Prosperity without Growth: Economics for a Finite Planet* (London: Earthscan, 2009).

Jaspers, K., *Was ist Erziehung? Ein Lesebuch* (München, Zürich: Piper, 1977).

Jenkins, W., *Ecologies of Grace: Environmental Ethics and Christian Theology* (Oxford: Oxford University Press, 2008).

Jenson, R. W., 'Is There an Ordering Principle?', *Essays in the Theology of Culture* (Grand Rapids, MI: Eerdmans, 1995), pp. 67–75.
Joas, H., 'Die religiöse Situation in den USA', *Woran glaubt die Welt? Analysen und Kommentare zum Religionsmonitor 2008* (Bertelsmann Stiftung (ed.); Gütersloh: Verlag Bertelsmann-Stiftung, 2009), pp. 329–347.
John Paul II, *Evangelium Vitae* (Rome: Libreria Editrice Vaticana, 1995).
Jordan, W., *The Sunflower Forest: Ecological Restoration and the New Communion with Nature* (Berkeley: University of California Press, 2003).
Kabeer, N., *Reversed Realities: Gender Hierarchies in Development Thought* (London: Verso, 1997).
Kainulainen, P., 'Kirkko ja uraani', *Kirkkotie* 10 (2006), p. 2.
—'Maan viisaus. Ivone Gebaran ekofeministinen käsitys tietämisestä ja teologiasta' ['The Wisdom of the Earth. Ivone Gebara's Ecofeminist Concept of Knowing and Theology'] (doctoral dissertation; University of Joensuu, 2005).
—'Wisdom Theology and Finnish Nature Spirituality. Reflections on Ivone Gebara's Ecofeminism', *Journal of the European Society of Women in Theological Research* 15 (2007), pp. 131–139.
Kearns, L., 'Religion and Ecology in the Context of Globalization', *Religion, Globalization and Culture* (P. Beyer and L. Beaman (eds); Leiden: Brill Academic Publishers, 2007), pp. 305–344.
—'Saving the Creation: Christian Environmentalism in the United States', *Sociology of Religion* 57 (1996), pp. 55–70.
Keifert, P. R., *Welcoming the Stranger: A Public Theology of Worship and Evangelism* (Minneapolis: Fortress, 1992).
Kersting, W., 'Politics, Freedom and Order: Kant's Political Philosophy', *The Cambridge Companion to Kant* (P. Guyer (ed.); Cambridge: Cambridge University Press, 1992), pp. 342–366.
Kim, S., 'Editorial', *International Journal of Public Theology* 1 (2007), pp. 1–4.
Klandermans, B., H. Kriesi, and S. Tarrow (eds), *From Structure to Action: Comparing Social Movement Research Across Cultures, International Social Movement Research: A Research Annual* (vol. 3; Greenwich, CT: JAI Press, 1988).
Kojo, M., and T. Litmanen (eds), *The Renewal of Nuclear Power in Finland* (Energy, Climate and the Environment Series; Basingstoke: Palgrave Macmillan, 2009).
Kovalainen, R., and S. Seppo, *Tree People* (Oulu: Pohjoinen, 2006).
Kraemer, H., *Die Kommunikation des christlichen Glaubens* (Zürich: Zwingli-Verlag, 1958).
Kronlid, D., 'Mapping the Moral Landscape of IPCC', *Ecological Ethics: Exploring Religion, Ethics and Aesthetics* (S. Bergmann, and H. Eaton (eds); LIT, *in press*, 2010).
Kuckartz, U., 'Leben im Einklang mit der Natur. Einsichten aus der Sozialwissenschaft', *Und Gott sah, dass es gut war: Schöpfung und Endlichkeit im Zeitalter der Klimakatastrophe* (H. Bedford-Strohm (ed.); Neukirchen-Vluyn: Neukirchener Verlag, 2009), pp. 59–69.
Kuper, A., *Culture: The Anthropologists' Account* (Harvard: Harvard University Press, 2000).

Lambek, M. (ed.), *A Reader in the Anthropology of Religion* (Malden: Blackwell Publishing Ltd, 3rd edn, 2003).

Leduc, T. 'A Case for An Intercultural IPCC', PIK/EFSRE workshop, *Religion in Global Environmental and Climate Change: Sufferings, Values and Lifestyles*, Potsdam, Germany, 12 January 2010.

Lehmann, D., *Democracy and Development in Latin America: Economics, Politics and Religion in the Postwar Period* (Cambridge: Polity Press, 1990).

Leipert, C., 'Ist 'humaner Wohlstand' möglich?', *Universitas* 41 (1986), pp. 1109-1120.

Lévi-Strauss, C., *Das Nahe und das Ferne. Eine Autobiographie in Gesprächen* (D. Eribon (trans.); Frankfurt am Main: S. Fischer, 1989).

Lewis, C. S., *Studies in Words* (Cambridge: Cambridge University Press, 2nd edn, 1967).

Liedke G., *Im Bauch des Fisches: Ökologische Theologie* (Stuttgart: Kreuz, 1979).

Lienemann-Perrin, C., and W. Lienemann (eds), *Kirche und Öffentlichkeit in Transformationsgesellschaften* (Stuttgart: Kohlhammer-Verlag, 2006).

Lima Silva, S. R., 'From within Ourselves. Afrodescendant Women on Paths of Theological Reflection in Latin America and the Caribbean', *Latin American Liberation Theology: The Next Generation* (I. Petrella (ed.); New York: Orbis Books, 2005), pp. 62-74.

Lorentzen, L., 'Indigenous Feet: Ecofeminism, Globalization, and the Case of Chiapas', *Ecofeminism and Globalization: Exploring Culture, Context, and Religion* (H. Eaton and L. A. Lorentzen (eds); Lanham: Rowman and Littlefield, 2003), pp. 57-71.

Louv, R., *Last Child in the Woods: Saving our Children from Nature-Deficit Disorder* (Chapel Hill, N.C.: Algonquin Books, 2005).

Lovelock, J. E., *Gaia: A New Look at Life on Earth* (Oxford: Oxford University Press, 1987).

Luckmann, T., *Lebenswelt, Identität und Gesellschaft* (Konstanz: UVK Verlagsgesellschaft, 2007).

Luhmann, N., 'Die Ausdifferenzierung der Religion', *Gesellschaftsstruktur und Semantik: Studien zur Wissenssoziologie der modernen Gesellschaft* (Vol. 3; Frankfurt: Suhrkamp, 1989), pp. 259-357.

—*Social Systems* (J. Bednarz, Jr. and D. Baecker (trans.); Stanford, CA: Stanford University Press, 1995).

Macpherson, C. B., *The Political Theory of Possessive Individualism* (Oxford and New York: OUP, 1964 paperback).

Magesa, L., 'Authentic African Christianity', *32 Articles Evaluating Inculturation in Africa* (T. Okure and P. van Thiel (eds); Spearhead Numbers 112-114; Port Harcourt: Gaba Publications, 1990).

Malinowski, B., *Kultur und Freiheit* (Stuttgart: Humbold, 1951).

Margalit, A., *The Ethics of Memory* (Cambridge, MA: Harvard University Press, 2002).

Martinich, A. P., *Hobbes: A Biography* (Cambridge: Cambridge University Press, 1999).

Marx, K., and F. Engels, *The German Ideology* (London: Lawrence & Wishart, 2nd edn, 1974).
Maseno, L., 'Widows' Christologies: A preliminary feminist analysis of Abanyole widows' Christologies considering kinship, gender and the power of naming' (doctoral dissertation; University of Oslo, 2008).
Mathews, F., *Reinhabiting Reality: Towards a Recovery of Culture* (Albany, NY: SUNY Press, 2005).
'Max Stackhouse', Gordon College, Center for Christian Studies, http://www.gordon.edu/ccs/usaspeakers/maxstackhouse (accessed 16 July 2010).
McFague, S., 'An Earthly Theological Agenda', *Ecofeminism and the Sacred* (C. Adams (ed.); NewYork: Continuum, 1993).
—*A New Climate For Theology: God, the World, and Global Warming* (Minneapolis: Fortress, 2008).
Mishan, E.J., 'GNP – Measurement or Mirage', *National Westminster Bank Quarterly Review* (1984), p. 13.
Moltmann J., *God in Creation: A New Theology of Creation and the Spirit of God*, The Gifford Lectures 1984-1985 (Margaret Kohl (trans); San Francisco: HarperSanFrancisco, 1991).
—*Gott im Projekt der modernen Welt: Beiträge zur öffentlichen Relevanz der Theologie* (Gütersloh: Kaiser, 1997).
—*Gott in der Schöpfung: Ökologische Schöpfungslehre* (München: Kaiser, 1985).
'Le Monde Diplomatique', *Atlas der Globalisierung*, (Berlin: Le Monde Diplomatique/ taz Verlag, 2009)
Moore, J. D., *Visions of Culture: An Introduction to Anthropological Theories and Theorists* (Oxford: Alta Mira Press, 2nd edn, 2004).
Morris, C., 'Sprechen und menschliches Handeln', *Philosophische Anthropologie* (H.-G. Gadamer, and P. Vogler (eds); Band 7, München: Dt. Taschenbuch Verl., 1975), pp. 23–251.
Mörth, I., and G. Fröhlich, 'Auf Spurensuche nach der 'informellen Logik tatsächlichen Lebens", *Symbolische Anthropologie der Moderne. Kulturanalysen nach Clifford Geertz* (G. Fröhlich, and I. Mörth (eds); Frankfurt am Main: Campus-Verl., 1998), pp. 7–50.
Mugambi, J., and M. Vähäkangas (eds), *Christian Theology and Environmental Responsibility* (Nairobi: Acton, 2001).
Mugambi, J., and N. Kirima, *The African Religious Heritage* (Nairobi: Oxford University Press, 1989).
Mühleisen, H.-O., T. Stammen, M. Ungethüm, (eds), *Anthropologie und kulturelle Identität. Friedemann Maurer zum 65. Geburtstag* (Lindenberg: Fink, Beuron: Beuroner Kunstverlag, 2005).
Müller-Fahrenholz, G., *Phantasie für das Reich Gottes. Die Theologie Jürgen Moltmanns. Eine Einführung* (Gütersloh: Kaiser, Gütersloher Verlag, 2000).
Müller-Wenk, R., *Die ökologische Buchhaltung – ein Informations- und Steuerungsinstrument für umweltkonforme Unternehmenspolitik* (Frankfurt: Campus-Verlag, 1978).
Munyika, V., *A Holistic Soteriology in an African Context. Utilising Luther's Theology*

and the Owambo Traditions to Overcome a Spiritualised and Privatised Concept of Salvation in the Evangelical Lutheran Church of Namibia (ELCIN) (Cluster Monograph Series; Pietermaritzburg: Cluster Publications, 2004).

Murray, R., *The Cosmic Covenant: Biblical Themes of Justice, Peace and the Integrity of Creation* (Piscataway, N.J.: Gorgias Press, 2007).

Mwangi, R., *Kikuyu's Folktales: Their Nature and Value* (Nairobi: Kenya Literature Bureau, 1983).

'Myth as Thought: Modern Theory and Myth', www.classics.uc.edu/~johnson/myth/theory.html (accessed 20 February 2010).

Nasimiyu, W., 'Christology and an African Woman's Experience', *Faces of Jesus in Africa* (R, Schreiter (ed.); New York: Orbis Books, 9th edn, 2005).

Neisser, U., 'Memory: What are the Important Questions', *Memory Observed: Remembering in Natural Contexts* (U. Neisser (ed.); San Francisco: W.H. Freeman & Co., 1982), pp. 3–19.

Niebuhr, H.R., *Christ and Culture* (New York: Harper & Row, 1975).

—*Christ and Culture* (New York: Harper Collins, 2001).

Northcott, M., *A Moral Climate: The Ethics of Global Warming* (London: Darton, Longman and Todd, 2007).

—'Atmospheric Space, Climate Change and the Communion of Saints', *Nature, Space and the Sacred* (S. Bergmann, P. M. Scott, M. Jansdotter Samuelsson, and H. Bedford-Strom (eds); Farnham: Ashgate, 2009), pp. 57–74.

Nussbaum, M., *Frontiers of Justice: Disability, Nationality, Species Membership* (Cambridge: Harvard University Press/Belknap, 2006).

—*Women and Human Development: The Capabilities Approach* (New York: Cambridge University Press, 2000).

Nyamweru, C., 'Women and Sacred Groves in Coastal Kenya: A Contribution to the Ecofeminist Debate', *Ecofeminism and Globalization: Exploring Culture, Context, and Religion* (H. Eaton and L.A. Lorentzen (eds); Lanham: Rowman and Littlefield, 2003), pp. 41–56.

O'Boyle, A., *Towards a Contemporary Wisdom Christology: Some Catholic Christologies in German, English and French 1965-1995* (Rome: Gregorian University Press, 2004).

Odaga A., *Simbi Nyaima* (Kisumu: Lake Publishers & Enterprises, 1983).

Oduyoye, M. A., *Introducing African Women's Theology* (Sheffield, England: Sheffield Academic Press, 2001).

Okure, T., and P. van Thiel (eds), *32 Articles Evaluating Inculturation in Africa* (Spearhead Numbers 112–114; Port Harcourt: Gaba Publications, 1990).

Ongong'a, J., 'Towards an African Environmental Theology', *Theology of Reconstruction: Exploratory Essays* (M. N. Getui and E.A. Obeng (eds); Nairobi: Acton Publishers, 1999).

Orsi, R. A., *The Madonna of 115th Street. Faith and Community in Italian Harlem, 1880-1950* (New Haven and London: Yale University Press, 2002).

Owusu, D. A., 'Jesus, The African Healer' (unpublished masters thesis; University of Oslo, 2001).

Pals, D. L., *Seven Theories of Religion* (Oxford: Oxford University Press, 1996).

Peacock, J. L., *The Anthropological Lens: Harsh Light, Soft Focus* (Cambridge: Cambridge University Press, 2002).
Percy, M., *Engaging with Contemporary Culture: Christianity, Theology and the Concrete Church* (Chippenham: Ashgate, 2005).
Petrella, I., 'Latin American Liberation Theology, Globalization, and Historical Projects: From Critique to Construction', *Latin American Perspectives on Globalization: Ethics, Politics, and Alternative Visions* (M. Saénz (ed.); Lanham: Rowman & Littlefield, 2002), pp. 200–229.
Phiri, I.A., 'The Chisumphi Cult: The Role of Women in Preserving the Environment', *Women Healing Earth: Third World Women on Ecology, Feminism, and Religion* (R. Radford Ruether (ed.); Maryknoll: Orbis Books, 1996) pp. 161–171.
Price, J., *The Woman Who Can't Forget* (New York: Free Press, 2008).
'Public Theology', http://www.public-theology.de (accessed 16 July 2010).
Pui-Lan, K., 'Ecology and Christology', *Feminist Theology* 5 (1997), pp. 113–125.
—'Engendering Christ', *Toward a New Heaven and a New Earth* (F. Segovia (ed.); Maryknoll, NY, Orbis Books, 2003).
Radford Ruether, R., 'Conclusion: Eco-Justice at the Center of the Church's Mission', *Christianity and Ecology. Seeking the Well-Being of Earth and Humans* (D. T. Hessel, and R. R. Ruether (eds); Cambridge, Massachusetts: Harvard University Center for the Study of World Religions Publications, 2000), pp. 603–614.
—'Ecofeminism and Healing Ourselves, Healing the Earth', *Feminist Theology* 3(1995), pp. 51–62.
—*Gaia and God: An Ecofeminist Theology of Earth Healing* (London: SCM Press, 1993).
Rahner, K., 'Die Kirche und die heutige Wirklichkeit. Theologische Aspekte', *Universitas* 34 (1979), pp. 811–817.
—*Politische Dimensionen des Christentums. Ausgewählte Texte zu Fragen der Zeit* (H. Vorgrimler (ed.); München: Kösel, 1986).
Rasmussen L., *Earth Community, Earth Ethics* (Geneva: WCC Publications, 1996).
Rautavuori, A., 'Luonnonsuojelu kuuluu kristityn kutsumukseen', *Pekkerelli. Pohjois-Karjalan uraanikaivosten vastaisen kansalaisliikkeen lehti* (2009), p. 5.
—'Viljelty on, mutta onko varjeltu?', *Karjalan Heili* (27 July 2010), pp. 10–11.
Rawls, J., *Collected Papers* (S. Freeman (ed.); Cambridge: Harvard University Press, 1999).
—'The Idea of an Overlapping Consensus', *Oxford Journal of Legal Studies* 7(1987), pp. 1–25.
—*The Law of Peoples* (Cambridge, MA and London: Harvard University Press, 2001).
Recki, B., *Kultur als Praxis. Eine Einführung in Ernst Cassirers Philosophie der symbolischen Formen* (Berlin: Akademie Verlag, 2004).
Reich, U. P., and C. Stahmer (eds), *Gesamtwirtschaftliche Wohlfahrtsmessung und Umweltqualität* (Frankfurt: Campus-Verlag, 1983).
Ricoeur, P., 'Memory and Forgetting', *Questioning Ethics: Contemporary Debates in Philosophy* (R. Kearney, and M. Dooley (eds); New York: Routledge, 1999), pp. 5–11.

—'Memory, Forgetfulness, and History', *Iyyun: The Jerusalem Philosophical Quarterly* 45 (1996), pp. 13–24.
Riekkinen, W. 'Piisbailua', *Capitol: Kuopion hiippakuntalehti* 2(2006), p. 4.
—'Saarna Enon kirkossa luomakunnan sunnuntaina', (17 August 2008), www.kuopionhiippakunta.fi/piispa/puheet (assessed 7 June 2010).
Robins, T., 'Remembering the Future: The Cultural Study of Memory', *Theorizing Culture: An Interdisciplinary Critique After Postmodernism* (B. Adam, and S. Allen (eds); New York: New York University Press, 1995).
Rossi, I., 'Intellectual Antecedents of Lévi-Strauss' Notion of Unconscious', *Perspectives in Cultural Anthropology* (H. Applebaum (ed.); New York: State University of New York Press, 1987), pp. 416–424.
Rubik, F., 'Das Bruttosozialprodukt als Indikator für Lebensqualität? Kritik und Alternativen', *Arbeiten im Einklang mit der Natur* (Projektgruppe Ökologische Wirtschaft (ed.); Freiburg: Dreisam-Verlag, 1985), pp. 145–176.
Russell, C., and Z. Nyssa, 'The Tipping Point Trend in Climate Change Communication', *Global Environmental Change* 19 (2009), pp. 336–344.
Samuel, V., 'Die Religion in der Gesellschaft und die Weltreligionen', *Zeugnis im Dialog der Religionen und der Postmoderne* (R. Pechmann, and M. Reppenhagen (eds); Neukirchen-Vluyn: Neukirchener Verlag, 1999), pp. 202–213.
Santmire, H. P., *Ritualizing Nature* (Minneapolis: Fortress, 2008).
Sathler, J. A., and A. Nascimento, 'Black Masks on White Faces. Liberation Theology and the Quest for Syncretism in the Brazilian Context', *Liberation Theology, Postmodernity, and the Americas* (D. Batstone, E. Mendieta, L. A. Lorentzen, and D. N. Hopkins (eds); London and New York: Routledge, 1997), pp. 95–122.
Scholte, J. A., *Globalization: A Critical Introduction* (London: Palgrave Macmillan, 2nd edn, 2005).
Schreiter, R. J., *Faces of Jesus in Africa* (Maryknoll, NY: Orbis Books, 9th edn, 2005).
Schwarte, J., *Der werdende Mensch. Persönlichkeitsentwicklung und Gesellschaft heute* (Wiesbaden: Westdeutscher Verlag, 2002).
Schwöbel, C., *Christlicher Glaube im Pluralismus: Studien zu einer Theologie der Kultur* (Tübingen: Mohr Siebeck, 2003).
Scott, P. M., 'The City's Grace? Recycling the Urban Ecology', *International Journal of Public Theology* 2 (2008), pp. 119–135.
—*A Political Theology of Nature* (Cambridge: Cambridge University Press, 2003).
—'Politics and the New Visibility of Theology', *The New Visibility of Religion* (G. Ward and M. Hoelzl (eds); London: Continuum, 2008), pp. 170–186.
Sen, A., *Development as Freedom* (Oxford: Oxford University Press, 1999).
—*The Idea of Justice* (London: Penguin, 2009).
Sewell, W. H., 'Geertz, cultural systems, and history: from synchrony to transformation', *Historiography: Critical Concepts in Historical Studies* (R. M. Burns (ed.); vol. 4 Culture; New York: Routledge, 2006), pp. 116–137.
—*Logics of History: Social Theory and Social Transformation* (Chicago: The University of Chicago Press, 2005).
Shepard, B., *Running the Obstacle Course to Sexual and Reproductive Health: Lessons from Latin America* (Westport: Praeger, 2006).

Shorter, A., *Toward a Theology of Inculturation* (London: Geoffrey Chapman, 1998).
Shweder, R. A., and B. Good (eds), *Clifford Geertz by His Colleagues* (Chicago: The University of Chicago Press, 2005).
Skrimshire, S. (ed.), *Future Ethics: Climate Change and Political Action* (London: Continuum, 2010).
Smit, D., '"...The Doing of the Little Righteousness": On Justice in Barth's View of the Christian Life', *Loving God with Our Minds: The Pastor as Theologian* (M. Welker, and C. A. Jarvis (eds); Michigan: Grand Rapids, 2004), pp. 120–145.
—*Essays in Public Theology: Collected Essays 1* (E. Conradie (ed.); Publications of the Western Cape, Stellenbosch: Sun Academic Press, 2007).
—'Lex orandi, lex credendi, lex (con)vivendi? – Orienterende inleiding tot liturgie en etiek', http://academic.sun.ac.za/buvton/Navorsing/liturgie.en.etiek.buvton.doc (accessed 17 July 2010).
—'Notions of the Public and Doing Theology', *International Journal of Public Theology* 1 (2007), pp. 431–454.
Smith, L. T., *Decolonizing Methodologies: Research and Indigenous Peoples* (London: Zed Books, 1999).
Sobrino, J., *Jesus the Liberator* (Maryknoll, NY: Orbis Books, 1993).
Solow, R. 'Intergenerational Equity and Exhaustible Resources', *Review of Economic Studies* 41 (1974 supplement), pp. 29–45.
Soosten, J. v., 'Civil Society: Zum Auftakt der neueren demokratietheoretischen Debatte mit einem Seitenblick auf Religion, Kirche und Öffentlichkeit (Literaturbericht)', *ZEE* 37 (1993), pp. 139–157.
'Das Sozialwort des ÖRK Österreich, 1 Bildung: Orientierung und Beteiligung', http://www.sozialwort.at/ (assessed 16 July 2010).
Splett, J., '"Realsymbol". Zur Anthropologie des Sakramentalen', *Raum-zeitliche Vermittlung der Transzendenz. Zur 'sakramentalen' Dimension religiöser Tradition. Arbeitsdokumentation eines Symposiums* (G. Oberhammer, and M. Schmücker (eds); Wien: Verlag der Österreichischen Akademie der Wissenschaften, 1999), pp. 325–351.
Stackhouse, M. L., *Apologia: Contextualization, Globalization and Mission in Theological Education* (Michigan: Grand Rapids, 1988).
—*Christian Social Ethics in a Global Era* (Nashville: Abingdon, 1995).
—*Covenant and Commitments: Faith, Family and Economic Life* (Louisville, Kentucky: John Knox Press, 1997).
—'Introduction: Foundations and Purposes', *On Moral Business. Classical and Contemporary Resources for Ethics in Economic Life* (M. L. Stackhouse, D. P. McCann, S. J. Roels, and P. N. Williams (eds); Michigan: Grand Rapids, 1995), pp. 10–34.
—'The Moral Roots of the Common Life in a Global Era', *Loving God with Our Minds: The Pastor as Theologian* (M. Welker, and C. A. Jarvis (eds); Michigan: Grand Rapids, 2004), pp. 50–61.
—*Public Theology and Political Economy, Christian Stewardship in Modern Society* (Michigan: Grand Rapids, 1991).
—'Reflections on How and Why We Go Public', *International Journal of Public Theology* 1 (2007), pp. 421–430.

Stackhourse, M. L., T. Dearborn, and S. Paeth (eds), *The Local Church in a Global Era: Reflection for a New Century* (Michigan: Grand Rapids, 2000).

Steger, F., 'Einleitung. Kultur: Ein Netz von Bedeutungen', *Kultur. Ein Netz von Bedeutungen: Analysen zur symbolischen Kulturanthropologie* (F. Steger, (ed.); Würzburg: Verlag Königshausen & Neumann, 2002), pp. 11–24.

Steinacker, P., 'Passion und Paradox – Der Expressionismus als Verstehenshintergrund der theologischen Anfänge Paul Tillichs. Ein Versuch', *God and Being: the Problem of Ontology in the Philosophical Theology of Paul Tillich: Contributions made to the II. International Paul Tillich Symposium held in Frankfurt 1988* (G. Hummel (ed.); Berlin, New York: W. de Gruyter, 1989), pp. 59–99.

Steingraber, S., 'Environmental Amnesia', *Orion Magazine* (May/June 2008).

Stevens, M., *Reconstructing the Christ Symbol: Essays in Feminist Christology* (New York: Paulist Press, 1993).

Stichweh, R., 'Science in the System of World Society', *Social Science Information* 35 (1996), pp. 327–340.

Stinton, D., *Jesus of Africa: Voices of Contemporary African Christology* (Maryknoll, NY: Orbis Books, 2004).

Storrar, W. F., 'A Kairos Moment for Public Theology', *International Journal of Public Theology* 1 (2007), pp. 5–25.

Storrar, W. F., and A. R. Morton, *Public Theology for the 21st Century: Essays in Honour of Duncan Forrester* (London and New York: T&T Clark, 2004).

Storrar, W., P. Donald, and A. Morton (eds), *God in Society: Doing Social Theology in Scotland Today* (Edinburgh: Saint Andrew Press, 2003).

Sturm, E., 'Das absolute Paradox als Prinzip der Theologie und Kultur in Paul Tillichs "Rechtfertigung und Zweifel" von 1919', *The Theological Paradox: Interdisciplinary Reflections on the Centre of Paul Tillich's Thought: Proceedings of the V. International Paul Tillich Symposium hold in Frankfurt/Main 1994* (G. Hummel (ed.); Theologische Bibliothek Töpelmann 74 ; Berlin: W. de Gryter & Co., 1995), pp. 32–45.

Swindler, A., 'Geertz's Ambiguous Legacy', *Required Reading: Sociology's Most Influential Books* (D. Clawson (ed.); Massachusetts: The University of Massachusetts Press, 1998), pp. 79–84.

Tamayo, J. J., 'Foro mundial de teología y liberación. Teología para otro mundo posible', *Pasos* 118 (2005), pp. 32–39.

Tanner, K., 'Creation, Environmental Justice, and Ecological Justice', *Reconstructing Christian Theology* (R. Chopp, and M. L. Taylor (eds); Minneapolis: Fortress Press, 1994), pp. 99–123.

Theobald, A., *Das Ökosozialprodukt – Lebensqualität als Volkseinkommen* (Osnabrück: Verlag A. Fromm, 1985).

Thiemann, R., *Constructing a Public Theology: The Church in a Pluralistic Culture* (Louisville: Westminster/John Knox Press, 1991).

—*Religion in Public Life: A Dilemma for Democracy* (Washington D.C.: Georgetown University Press, 1996).

Thomas, K., 'The Social Origin of Hobbes's Political Thought', *Hobbes Studies* (K. C. Brown (ed.); Oxford: Blackwell, 1985), pp. 185–236.

Tillich, H., 'Das Neue Sein als Zentralbegriff einer christlichen Theologie', *P. Tillich,*

Gesammelte Werke, Schriften zur Theologie, Offenbarung und Glaube (R. Albrecht (ed.); Band 8; Stuttgart: Evangel. Verl.-Werk, 1970), pp. 220–239.

Tillich, P., 'Kirche und Kultur', *P. Tillich, Gesammelte Werke, Die Religiöse Substanz der Kultur: Schriften zur Theologie der Kultur* (R. Albrecht (ed.); Band 9; Stuttgart: Evangel. Verl.-Werk, 1967), pp. 30–46.

Timm, H., *Diesseits des Himmels. Von Welt- und Menschenbildung. Facetten der Religionskultur* (Gütersloh: Kaiser, Gütersloher Verlagshaus, 1988).

Tirosh-Samuelson, H. (ed.), *Judaism and Ecology: Created World and Revealed Word* (Cambridge, MA: Center for the Study of World Religions and Harvard University Press, 2002).

Todorov, T., 'The Abuses of Memory', *Common Knowledge* 5 (1996), pp. 6–26.

—*Hope and Memory: Lessons from the Twentieth Century* (Princeton: Princeton University Press, 2003).

Tracy, D., *Blessed Rage for Order: The New Pluralism in Theology* (Chicago: The University of Chicago Press, 1996).

—'Defending the Public Character of Theology', http://www.religion-online.org/showarticle.asp?title=1720 (accessed 17 July 2010).

—*Plurality and Ambiguity: Hermeneutics, Religion, Hope* (Chicago: The University of Chicago Press, 1994).

Tramsen, E., 'Semiotische Aspekte der Religionswissenschaft: Religionssemiotik', *Semiotik: Ein Handbuch zu den zeichentheoretischen Grundlagen von Natur und Kultur* (R. Posner, and K. Robering (eds); 3 Teilband; Berlin: W. de Gruyter, 2003), pp. 3301–3343.

Tucker, M. E., and J. Grim, 'Series Foreword', *Christianity and Ecology:Seeking the Well-Being of Earth and Humans* (D.T. Hessel, and R. Radford-Ruether (eds); Cambridge: Harvard University Press 2000), pp. xv–xxxii.

Vanderheiden, S., *Atmospheric Justice: A Political Theory of Climate Change* (Oxford: Oxford University Press, 2008).

Vester, F., *Der Wert eines Vogels* (München: Kösel-Verlag, 1983).

Visvanathan, N., L. Duggan, L. Nisonoff, and N. Wiegersma (eds), *The Women, Gender and Development Reader* (London: Zed Books, 1997).

Vögele, W., *Menschenwürde zwischen Recht und Theologie. Begründungen von Menschenrechten in der Perspektive öffentlicher Theologie* (Gütersloh: Kaiser, Gütersloher Verlagshaus, 2000).

—*Zivilreligion in der Bundesrepublik Deutschland* (Gütersloh: Gütersloher Verlagshaus, 1994).

Volf, M., *The End of Memory: Remembering Rightly in a Violent World* (Grand Rapids: Eerdmans, 2006).

Volli, U., *Semiotik. Eine Einführung in ihre Grundbegriffe* (Tübingen: Francke, 2002).

Vuola, E., *Limits of Liberation. Feminist Theology and the Ethics of Poverty and Reproduction* (Sheffield and New York: Sheffield Academic Press and Continuum, 2002a).

—'Patriarchal Ecumenism, Feminism, and Women's Religious Experiences in Costa Rica', *Gendering Religion and Politics. Untangling Modernities* (H. Herzog and A. Braude (eds); New York: Palgrave Macmillan, 2009), pp. 217–238.

—'Radical Eurocentrism. The Death, Crisis, and Recipes of Improvement of Latin American Liberation Theology', *Interpreting the Postmodern: Responses to Radical Orthodoxy* (M. Grau and R. Radford Ruether (eds); London and New York: T & T Clark and Continuum, 2006a), pp. 57–75.
—'Remaking Universals? Transnational Feminism(s) Challenging Fundamentalist Ecumenism', *Theory, Culture and Society* 19 (2002b), pp. 175–195.
—'Seriously Harmful for Your Health? Religion, Feminism and Sexuality in Latin America', *Liberation Theology and Sexuality: New Radicalism from Latin America* (M. Althaus-Reid (ed.); London: Ashgate, 2006b), pp. 137–162.
Wahl, H., *Glaube und symbolische Erfahrung. Eine praktisch-theologische Symboltheorie* (Freiburg, Basel, Wien: Herder, 1994).
Waliggo, J., *Inculturation: Its Meaning and Urgency* (Kampala, Uganda: St. Paul's Publications, 1986).
Wallace, M., *Finding God in the Singing River* (Minneapolis: Fortress Press, 2005).
'Wanted: A Public Theology Dedicated to Sustainable Development, http://www.bertelsmann-stiftung.de/cps/rde/xchg/SID-0968CF92-55BE9599/bst_engl/hs.xsl/nachrichten_100592.htm (accessed 20 July 2010).
Ward, G., *The Politics of Discipleship: Becoming Postmaterial Citizens* (Grand Rapids, MI: Baker Academic, 2009).
Warren, K. J., *Ecofeminist Philosophy: A Western Perspective on What It is and Why It Matters* (Lanham, Boulder, New York, Oxford: Rowman & Littlefield, 2000).
Weeramantry, C. G., *Tread Lightly on the Earth: Religion, the Environment and the Human Future* (Pannipitiya: Stamford Lake Ltd., 2009).
Wehner, U., 'Ökologische soziale Kosten und volkswirtschaftliche Gesamtrechnung' (unpublished doctoral dissertation; University of Köln, 1976).
Welker, M., *Kirche im Pluralismus* (Gütersloh: Gütersloher Verlagshaus, 1995).
Westbury, C., and D. Dennett, 'Mining the Past to Construct the Future: Memory and Belief as Forms of Knowledge', *Memory, Brain and Belief* (D. Schacter, and E. Scarry (eds); Cambridge: Harvard University Press, 2000), pp. 11–32.
Westermann C., *Genesis 1–11* (Minneapolis: Augsburg Fortress Press, 1994).
White, L., 'The Historical Roots of Our Ecological Crisis', *Science* 155 (1967), pp. 1203–1207.
Whitehead, A. N., *Symbolism: Its Meaning and Effect* (Cambridge, Cambridge University Press, 1959).
Wiesel, E., *Ethics and Memory* (New York: Walter de Gruyter, 1997).
Williams, R., *On Christian Theology* (Malden, Oxford, Victoria: Blackwell, 2000).
—*Resources of Hope: Culture, Democracy, Socialism* (London: Verso, 1989).
—'Secularism, Faith and Freedom', *The New Visibility of Religion* (G. Ward, and M. Hoelzl (eds); London: Continuum, 2008), pp. 45–56.
Wimmer, A., *Kultur als Prozess: Zur Dynamik des Aushandelns von Bedeutungen* (Wiesbaden: VS Verlag für Sozialwissenschaften, 2005).

Index of Subjects

aboriginal peoples 26–7, *see also* indigenous peoples
abortion 95, 102n. 22
action 3, 6, 33, 70, 72–3, 81, 87, 113–14, 164, 169, 173–4, 190–1, 205
activism 27, 40, 95, 98, 101–2, 105, 112, 118, 120
African Americans 96–7, 100, 108
African context 3, 10, 47, 125–36
African National Congress 47
Agikuyu people 134–5
animals 40, 51, 64, 69–70, 72, 84, 111, 134–5, 156, 168, 171–2, 179, 198–9, 202–3, *see also* creatures
humans as political animals 62–3, 79
anthropocentrism 10, 50, 49, 52, 68–9, 71, 91–2, 98, 108, 114, 125, 135
anthropogenic impacts 17, 204
anthropology 98, 100, 108, 128, 169, 173, 195
liturgical 175, 177
antislavery 45
art 24–5, 30–1, 33–5, 114, 143, 167
authority 8, 10, 64, 101, 120, 204
autonomy 59, 106

Baltic Marine Environmental Protection Commission (HELCOM) 17–18
Baltic Sea 7, 16–18
Baltic Sea Action Plan (BSAP) 18
basismo 92, 95–6
beauty 177–8, 200
belief 10, 53, 84, 202–4
Bible/Scripture 1n. 2, 2n. 2, 43, 45, 47–51, 64, 115–17, 120, 132, 126n. 3, 132, 192
biblicism 129
biodiversity 3, 13, 15, 18
body 22, 96, 97n. 11, 101, 103–4, 106, 134, 176
Brazil 12, 47, 95, 100–2, 190–1

CAFOD, *see* Catholic Fund for Overseas Development
camera obscura 8, 57–8, 68–70, 151
Canada 196–7
capability approach 189, 192, 197–207
capitalism 24–5, 27–9, 46, 67
carbon emissions (CO2) 58, 61, 79
levels 193–4
care 105–6, 201, 203
Catholic Fund for Overseas Development (CAFOD) 189–90, 195
Catholicism 12, 45, 63, 92, 94–5, 99, 101–2, 104–7, 128, 130, 204, 206
charity 189, 203–5
children 93–4, 102, 115–16, 201
Christian Social Union 39
Christianity 5, 61, 91, 120, 163–7
and environmental crisis 26–7, 34, 49
Christology 10, 125–7, 131, 135–6
church 5, 8, 10, 39–41, 43, 47, 49, 53–4, 92–6, 102, 105, 114–21, 128–31, 146, 152–5, 157, 162–3, 165–8, 176, 179, 204, 207
citizen 18, 44–5, 68, 104, 197, 199
civil society 3, 5, 8, 13, 39–46, 48, 52–4, 92, 143, 154
class 95, 104, 107
climate change 3–7, 9, 11–13, 17–18, 29, 39, 49, 54, 58, 61, 77, 81–2, 84–7, 112, 125, 151n. 28, 156n. 41, 189–201, 203, 206–7
skepticism 13, 194, 196, 200
see also global warming
colonialism 31, 108
common good 9, 60, 63, 190, 192, 204, 206–7
commonwealth 65–7
communication 11–12, 21–25, 31–5, 121, 155, 168–77, 179
communism 42

community 47, 71, 73, 135, 148–9, 152–5, 157, 168, 176, 204
consensus 41, 44, 48, 60, 84, 192, 198n. 20, 200, 205, 207
Con-Spirando 101
consumerism 117n. 18, 192–3
consumption 79, 82, 84, 86, 102, 201
COP 15, *see* United Nations Summit on Climate Change
Copenhagen, *see* United Nations Summit on Climate Change
covenant 66
creation 4, 28, 39–40, 50–1, 54, 64, 66, 73, 113–16, 121, 125, 132–3, 135–6, 154, 161–2, 176–7, 179
  care of 28, 50, 175, 203, *see also* stewardship
  gift of God 4, 66, 161, 177, 206
  integrity of 28, 40, 79, 114, 116
creatures 50–1, 58–9, 65, 70–2, 161, 168n. 55, 177, 179, 192, 202n. 34, 207
  see also animals
culture 69, 103–4, 128–30, 173, 175
  Christian 162, 165–7, 169, 173, 178–9
  ecological 162–3, 169–70, 173–4, 177
  as sign system 11, 168–75

democracy 42–3, 44n. 16, 92, 95–6, 174n. 104, 198
Denmark 190–1
desire 68–9
Dietrich Bonhoeffer Research Centre for Public Theology 46
domination 49, 106, 131, 179
dominion 27, 49–50, 64
dualism 103–7

Eastern Europe 93
Eastern Orthodoxy 11, 161, 175–9
ecofeminism and theology 91, 98, 101, 103, 105–7, 121, 122n. 30
ecological restoration 151, 156–7, 177
ecology, concept of 1–2, 21–2, 26, 28, 61–2
  and economy 77–87
economics 7–11, 15–16, 24, 28–31, 33, 42–3, 77–87, 92–3, 162, 192, 201, 203
  and ecology 78–87
  growth 46, 78–9, 85–6, 102, 192n. 4, 201
  value of nature 77–87

ecosystems 15–18, 156, 176
ecotheology 8, 97, 103–7, 142–3, 146–50, 153–4, 156–7, 161–3, 168, 175–6, 179
ecumenism 11–12, 121, 161–70, 174–5, 179, 191
Eden, Garden of 65, 69
education 24, 30, 95, 165, 168, 173–4, 201
eikos, *see* oikos
emotion 117–18, 120, 171, 173
energy 2, 29, 52–3, 84, 86, 112, 196–7, 203
environment, idea of 21–2, 26, 28–9, 58
environmental degradation 94, 102, 155–6
environmental movements 2, 33–5, 94–5, 98, 101, 112–14, 118–19, 205
environmental theology, *see* ecotheology
equality 71–2
eschatology 51, 54, 70, 148, 152, 157, 169, 176–7, 179
ethics 4, 8, 12–13, 17, 45–7, 52–3, 93, 115, 117–21, 132, 162, 179, 199
  of locality 142–3, 145–6, 149–51, 153–7
  sexual 95–7, 102, 104–5
EU, *see* European Union
Eucharist 176–7
eurocentrism 100
European Forum for the Study of Religion and the Environment 7, 12
European Science and Environment Forum 194
European Union (EU) 18, 40, 58, 61–2, 191
evil 103
exchange 24–5, 71, 79
external effects, theory of 78–82, 86

faith 43, 114, 129–31, 165, 169, 176n. 121, 178
family 95, 104–6, 165, 201, 204
femininity 103, 105–6
feminism and feminist theology 50, 91, 96–106, 108, 121, 126–7, 132, 202
  see also ecofeminism
Finland 7, 10, 111–22
flourishing 7, 9, 11, 60, 62, 148, 192, 198, 202–3, 205
food 40, 51, 82, 106, 113, 133, 194, 196
forgiveness 157, 167
freedom 62, 66, 71
  of religion 44
future generations 79–80, 82, 84–5, 87, 115

Index of Subjects

Gaia hypothesis 26–8
GCC, *see* Global Climate Coalition
GDP, *see* gross domestic product
gender 91–4, 97, 101–8
genetically modified (GM) crops 40, 54
geology 118–19, 121
German Free Democratic Party 42
  ecological movement 2, 40, 53
Germany 2–3, 39–40, 48, 83, 162
Global Climate Coalition (GCC) 194, 196
Global Network for Public Theology 46, 163n. 10, 167
global warming 161, 193, 196
  see also climate change
globalization 24, 31, 79, 96, 165, 167
GM crops, *see* genetically modified crops
GNP, *see* gross national product
God, communion with 175–9
  and creation 27–8, 50, 66, 116, 121, 132–3, 153, 161, 177
  sovereignty of 64–5
  transcendence/immanence of 116, 121, 161, 179
good life 60, 72, 192, 200
gospel 127n. 8, 128–31, 162, 178
governance 47, 61, 80, 171, 197, 206
  of God 65
grace 64–5, 67, 204, 207
greed 113, 116
greenhouse gases 58n. 4, 77, 82, 193–4, 197
Greenpeace 40
gross domestic product (GDP) 11, 78, 198, 201
gross national product (GNP) 82–6

health, environmental effects on 16, 112, 116, 156n. 41
  healthcare 84, 95
hermeneutics, and ecology 142–57
Holy Spirit 121, 161–2, 177, 204–5
hope 152, 154
  theology of 162, 169
humanism 73

ICE, *see* Information Council on the Environment
identity 144, 146, 154, 165, 167, 170n. 69
  Christian 130, 176
image of God 50, 93, 105, 132, 206
  of Christ 10, 177
images, *see* symbols
incarnation 133, 136, 204
inculturation 127–31, 136
indigenous peoples 135, 194–5, 206–7
  cosmology 100, 121–2
  knowledge 199–200
inequality 6–7, 86, 94, 198, 201
Information Council on the Environment (ICE) 193–4
injustice 28, 189, 193, 201
Intergovernmental Panel on Climate Change (IPCC) 193–4, 199–200, 206
International Journal of Public Theology 46
IPCC, *see* Intergovernmental Panel on Climate Change
Islam 3, 27, 94

Jesus 176–9
  and inculturation 127–31, 136
  as Sophia/wisdom of God 10, 125–7, 131–3, 135–6
judgment 152, 154, 205
justice 28, 45, 72, 111, 114, 116, 167–8, 176n. 119, 189–93, 197–207

Kenya 134–5
kingdom
  of God 47, 116, 176–7, 179
  two kingdoms 115
kingship 50
Kisii people 134
knowledge 7–9, 30, 32, 100, 116–20, 122, 174n.103, 199–200
  and memory 146–57
  ways of 116–20, 122
Kyoto Protocol 190–1, 193–4, 197

language 4, 8, 23, 43, 45, 47, 52, 54, 92, 95, 127, 166, 170–1
Latin America 9, 46–7, 91–108
  democratization 92, 95
  see also liberation theology
law 29–30, 60–9
liberation theology 8, 9, 28, 39, 46–7, 91–7, 131, 154, 169
  and indigenous 91, 93–100, 102–4, 106–8

and nature 9, 94, 97–9, 103–7
and women 46, 91, 93–8, 100–8
liberty 63, 66–7, 69, 72
limitations 50, 52, 65, 68–9, 79–81, 86–7, 121, 145, 192n. 4
liturgy 113–14, 118, 121, 152, 175–9
love 178–9
   of God 115, 133,
   of neighbour 116
Luo people 133–4
Lutheran church 10, 12, 39–40, 112–21

marginalization 43, 95–6
Marxism 92–3
Mary, Virgin 99
masculinity 103, 105–6, 107n. 30
memory 11, 142–57, 206
metousia 177
Mexico, Gulf of 15–17
military regimes 92, 94–5
mining industry 111–19, 151
mitigation 81–2
modernity 6, 7, 10, 42, 44, 71, 199
modernization 6
Monsanto 40
multiculturalism 167
Muslims, *see* Islam
mystery of God 116, 121, 179
mysticism 115–16, 120
myth(s) 10, 103, 126–7, 131–6

narrative 47, 69, 132, 147–8, 152–3, 155, 164, 194, 196, 202
nation-state, *see* state
natural capital 84–5
natural history 150
natural law 60, 62–3, 67, 69, 198
natural resources 2–3, 6, 16, 18, 58, 79, 98, 103, 112, 121, 194, 201
   non-renewable 61, 81, 84–6
nature 51, 62–71, 147–8, 150, 153
   conflict with humans 51
   connection with/dependence on 8, 10–11, 57–8, 104, 133–5, 189
   destruction/exploitation of 2, 46, 49–50, 77–9, 98, 102–3, 118, 125, 156, 161, 177, 195
   harmony with 51
   institutionization of 62, 67, 69, 71

   relationship to 99–101, 103, 107n. 30, 108, 116–17, 121, 155
   romantic view of 51, 103
neoliberalism 31
NGO, *see* non-governmental organization
non-governmental organization (NGO) 190–1
North Korea 31
Northern Carelia 111–14, 117, 119, 121
nuclear, energy 2, 112
   waste 161
   weapons 24, 31

oikos 21, 62, 162
oil 2, 15–16, 81, 193, 196–7
otherness 162
   of nature 68, 72

panentheism 116, 121
participation, in divine life 176–8
peace 51, 65, 166–7, 176n. 119, 179, 205
pietism 114
piety 44
place 11, 142–57
plants 40, 84, 127, 135, 156, 179n. 154, 194, 202n. 34
pluralism 4, 8, 12, 41, 44–5, 47, 120n. 24, 153, 163, 165, 207
   religious 97, 100, 166
policy 4, 7, 12, 42, 77
   economic 79, 82–3, 86
   environmental 147, 156, 191, 193–4, 197, 199
polity 59, 61–2, 69
pollution 16, 79, 111–13, 125, 195–6, 203
poor 3, 28, 43, 80, 93–4, 98, 102, 104–5, 192, 194–5, 201, 204, 206
   as the earth 97
   option for the poor 28, 45, 48, 97
   see also poverty
population, control 102
   growth 94, 102, 106, 125n. 1
postcolonialism 108
postnatural condition 9, 59, 62–4, 67–73
poverty 42, 92–4, 96–7, 102n. 22, 104–6
   see also poor
power 7, 26, 29–35, 47, 51, 61, 64, 66, 106, 118–21, 126n. 3, 131, 170n. 74, 193, 201, 204, 206

Index of Subjects

and Christianity 163, 165, 167
economic 24, 26, 40, 43, 80
lack of 106, 111, 197, 201
private sphere 43–5, 95, 115, 149, 153, 164, 166, 201
prophetic role 13, 47, 115, 117, 162
Protestantism 27, 92, 114, 120, 162
prudence 189, 205
public sphere 5, 7–13, 39, 42–3, 59–62, 70–3, 77, 92, 95, 115, 125, 132, 142–3, 148, 150, 153–5, 157, 163, 166–7, 201, 207
public theology 4–5, 8, 11–13, 39–41, 46–9, 92, 143, 161–70, 202, 207
and ecology 4, 13, 49–53, 148, 153–5, 157, 174–5, 179
Finnish 113, 117, 119–21

racism 92–3, 95–6, 106–7
reason 43–5, 47–8, 59, 65, 72–3, 115, 120
reconciliation 163, 166–7
redemption 43, 66, 129, 133, 176
reform 52–3, 165, 169, 197, 204
religion, popular 92, 96, 98–101
traditional 3, 136
reproduction 94–5, 101–2, 104–5
contraception 95, 102n. 22
family planning 104
resistance 47, 113–16, 117n. 18, 120n. 24
responsibility 18, 28, 42, 52, 78–9, 115, 117, 143, 162–3, 167–9, 196–201, 205
ecological 117, 154, 175, 177, 179, 192–3, 203
restoration, *see* ecological restoration
resurrection 71, 176, 178–9
revelation 59
rights 42, 47, 50, 111, 115, 119, 198
human 92, 94–5, 164, 179, 198, 203, 205
indigenous 95
natural 62–9
postnatural 59, 70–3
reproductive 101, 105–6
of women 95, 101
ritual practices 35, 100–1, 120, 129, 135, 170n. 74

sacred 25, 101, 105–6, 132, 155
of nature 103, 114–17, 121, 126–7, 131n. 32, 133–6, 161

salvation 61, 114, 146
sanctification 178–9
science 13, 18, 31, 47, 203, 207
climate 13, 58n. 4, 194
as communication 23–30
as knowledge 118–22
secular 10, 25–9, 43–4, 47, 48, 59–61, 71, 73, 154, 167, 170
sexism 93, 96, 100, 106
sexuality 92–7, 101–7
sin 204
social contract theory 62, 66–7, 198, 201
social justice 28, 48, 164, 179, 189, 206
socialism 2, 31, 92–3, 96
sociality 72–3
sociology 5–7, 32, 118, 143
soil erosion 125n. 1, 161
solidarity 5, 42, 154, 175, 176n. 119, 179, 190, 206–7
Sophia, *see* Jesus as Sophia
sovereignty
of God 64
of monarch 60, 62, 67
of nations 201
space 142, 144, 146, 151, 153, 155, 176–7, 193
sacred 134–5
spirit 103, 106, 175
of God, *see* Holy Spirit
spirituality 121–2, 193
aboriginal/indigenous 27, 107
creation 28
ecofeminist 101
ecological 169, 179
and ethics 121
Finnish 113, 117, 119–21
liturgical 175–6
Orthodox 179
state 5–6, 24–6, 29, 31, 42–4, 48, 58–60, 62, 64, 69, 79, 196–7, 203, 205–6
stewardship 28, 116, 204
subsidiarity 206–7
supernatural realm 6n. 12, 135
sustainability 3, 16, 18, 35, 73, 79, 82–6, 94, 148, 196, 207
symbols 127, 129, 168–73
religious 26, 28, 118, 121–1, 132, 136
syncretism 94, 96, 99–100, 106

Index of Subjects

technology 27, 156, 179, 203
teleology 65, 71–3
theocracy 59
theosis 177
third world 106–7
time 142–4, 146, 150–5, 157, 176, 193
totalitarianism 154
trade 2n. 2, 29, 33
traditions 60–1, 148, 154, 170
transcendence 25, 116, 121, 141n. 1
transformation
   religious 120, 122
   social 8, 168, 173, 204
trees 81, 120, 133–5, 143, 152
Trinity, Holy 176
trust 64, 69, 72, 93, 162,
   and climate change 10, 199–200
Tschechia 3
Turkey 61

UNFCCC, *see* United Nations Framework Convention on Climate Change
United Kingdom (UK) 2n. 3, 191
   budget report 58
United Nations (UN) 204–5
United Nations Conference on Environment and Development 102
United Nations Framework Convention on Climate Change (UNFCCC) 189–93, 197, 200, 206
United Nations Summit on Climate Change (COP 15) 3, 5, 58, 189–92, 194, 196, 201, 205
United States (US) 12, 83, 99, 141
unity, of the church 163, 167, 170, 176
uranium 10, 111–19, 121
urbanization 84

values 35, 47–8, 52, 120–1, 129, 175
   Christian 116, 163–5
Vatican 94, 105
Viliui Sakha people 195–6
violence 93, 106n. 28, 146, 179, 198

against nature 49, 51–2, 154–5
in nature 51
virtue 71, 189, 204–7
vocation 177
   of church 162–3
   of public theology 165

war 64, 69, 133
   Cold War 93
water 15–18, 101, 111–12, 133–4, 141–3, 161, 194–6
wealth 52, 71, 83, 197
   and nature 71–3, 80–1
welfare 16
   economic 78, 80, 83, 85
   social 42–3, 83
Western world 5, 8, 11, 42, 50, 59, 68, 96, 103–4, 106–7, 118–21, 130, 192–3, 195, 197–8, 200, 203, 207
wilderness 107n. 30, 150, 154, 156
wisdom 44, 51, 151
   nature 98–9, 126–7, 132–6
   practical 205–6
   theology of 116–17, 120–1
   see also Jesus as Sophia
women 46, 133–5, 202
   and climate change 198, 201
   and nature 98, 103–6
   romantic view of 103–4, 106–7
World Council of Churches (WCC) 2
World Economic Summit 47
World Forum for Liberation and Theology 96
World Social Forum 47, 96
World Wildlife Fund 44
work 67–8, 79, 84, 105, 132
   of Christ 10, 129, 132
   of Holy Spirit 177
   labour unions 92, 94
   of memory 143, 150–1, 153
worship 135, 167, 176n. 121

Yanomani people 195

Index of Names

Aigner, Ilse 40
Altner, Günther 50
Amery, Carl 49
Anderson, Pamela Sue 155
Aquinas 62, 206
Aristotle 42, 199, 205
Augé, Marc 150
Augustine 144n. 6

Bate, Stuart 129–30
Beck, Ulrich 5–7
Beckmann, Andreas 78
Bedford-Strohm, Heinrich 8, 143, 151n. 28, 153–4, 162
Benedict XVI 203–4
Bergmann, Sigurd 39, 151
Bevans, Stephen 128
Birch, Bruce 149
Bobbio, Noberto 63
Böckenförde, Ernst Wolfgang 48
Boff, Leonardo 9, 91, 97–8, 103–8
Bria, Ion 175–6
Bujo, Bénézet 130
Bulgakov, Sergii 133
Bush, George W. 194, 197

Carmody, John 131n. 32
Carson, Rachel 30
Casey, Edward 146
Cassirer, Ernst 168
Christopher, John 30
Cicero 60
Cobb, C. W. 84
Crate, Susan 195

da Silva, Lula 47
Daly, Herman 192n. 4
De Gruchy, John 164, 167
De Lange, Harry 87
De Tocqueville, Alexis 43
De Vries, Hent 59

Deane-Drummond, Celia 6, 11, 44, 131–3
D'Entrèves, A. P. 60, 62
Delich, Francisco 149
Dennett, Daniel 143–4

Eagleton, Terry 68–9
Eerola, Toni 118
El Serafy, Salah 85
Ely, John 62, 71, 73
Escobar, Arturo 98

Ferguson, Adam 42
Fetscher, Iring 78
Finnis, John 63, 66
Francis of Assisi 114

Gebara, Ivone 9, 91, 97–8, 101, 104–6, 108
Geertz, Clifford 169, 171, 173
Gilligan, Carol 105
Golding, William 65
Gore, Al 30
Goudzwaard, Bob 87
Grim, John 4, 12
Grotius 198
Gutiérrez, Gustavo 93

Habermas, Jürgen 43–4, 48
Heidegger, Martin 141
Higgs, Eric 156
Hobbes, Thomas 60, 62–9, 72
Hoekstra, Kinch 65
Huber, Wolfgang 162

Immler, Hans 78
Irarrazával, Diego 99

Jackson, Tim 192n. 4
Jenkins, Willis 147
Jenson, Robert 63, 70–1
John Paul II 93
Jordan, William 156

Kant, Immanuel 63
Keifert, Patrick R. 175
King, Martin Luther 45
Kopenawa, David 195–6
Kronlid, David 199–200, 206
Kuckartz, Udo 53

Lehmann, David 92–3
Lewis, C. S. 70
Liedke, Gerhard 50
Lima Silva, Silvia Regina 97
Locke, John 62
Lorentzen, Lois 107
Louv, Richard 150
Lovelock, James 26
Luhmann, Niklas 22–3

Manner, Pessi 114
Margalit, Avishai 155
Masson, Father Joseph 128
May, Lord Robert 5
McFague, Sallie 125n. 1, 147
Moltmann, Jürgen 50, 162
Murray, Robert 50

Nascimento, Amós 100
Neisser, Ulric 145n. 8
Nicholls, Vincent 191
Niebuhr, H. Richard 129–30, 164n. 13, 174nn. 105; 107
Northcott, Michael 192–3
Nussbaum, Martha 189, 192, 197–203, 205–7

Obama, Barack 58n. 4
Okure, Teresa 130
Orsi, Robert A. 99–100

Pershing, Jonathan 58n. 4
Petrella, Iván 107n. 32
Pui-Lan, Kwok 125, 127, 131–2

Radford Ruether, Rosemary 120, 125n. 1, 135
Rasmussen, Larry 49, 149

Rautavuori, Armi 115–16
Rawls, John 44–5, 48, 198, 198–9n. 20, 199nn. 22; 24, 200n. 28
Reich, Utz Peter 83
Ricoeur, Paul 145–6
Riekkinen, Bishop Wille 113–16, 118

Santmire, H. Paul 147
Sathler, Josué A. 100
Scott, Peter Manley 8–11, 151, 154
Sen, Amartya 198
Shepard, Bonnie 95
Shorter, Aylward 128, 130
Smit, Dirk 164, 167–8, 175
Smith, Adam 42
Sobrino, Jon 131
Söder, Markus 39–40
Stackhouse, Max 164–6
Stahmer, Carsten 83
Stinton, Diane 126n. 3
Storrar, William 164, 167
Sununu, John 194

Tamayo, Juan José 97
Tanner, Kathryn 72
Theobald, Adolf 83
Thiemann, Ronald 45n. 21, 47, 164–5, 175
Todorov, Tzvetan 145, 154
Tracy, David 164, 166
Tucker, Mary Evelyn 4, 12

Vanderheiden, Steve 193, 197, 199n. 24
Vester, Frederic 80
Volf, Miroslav 146

Wallace, Mark 147
Weber, Max 27
Weeramantry, Christopher 12
Wehner, Ursula 83
Westbury, Chris 143–4
Westermann, Claus 50
White, Lynn 26–7, 49
Wiesel, Elie 144
Williams, Rowan 59